THE MACARTHUR NEW TESTAMENT COMMENTARY

JOHN 12-21

John MacArthur

MOODY PUBLISHERS/CHICAGO

Library of Congress Cataloging-in-Publication Data

MacArthur, John, 1939-
     John 12-21 / John MacArthur.
        p. cm.– (The MacArthur New Testament commentary)
     Includes bibliographical references and index.
     ISBN-13: 978-0-8024-0824-2
     ISBN-10: 0-8024-0824-9
     1. Bible. N.T. John XII-XXI—Commentaries. I. Title.

BS2615.53.M34 2008
226.5'077—dc22

                                                      2007047180

We hope you enjoy this book from Moody Publishers. Our goal is to provide high-quality, thought-provoking books and products that connect truth to your real needs and challenges. For more information on other books and products written and produced from a biblical perspective, go to www.moodypublishers.com or write to:

Moody Publishers
820 N. LaSalle Boulevard
Chicago, IL 60610

1 3 5 7 9 10 8 6 4 2

Printed in the United States of America

To David and Mary Anne Wismer,
who share my love for the Truth, written and incarnate,
and whose abundant kindness and lasting friendship
have graced my life with encouragement and joy.

Contents

Preface

The message of John's gospel is simple. The apostle writes with straightforward clarity and in words that make the truth accessible to every reader. That fact is critical, because this is the saving gospel, written for unbelievers. John said so:

> Many other signs Jesus also performed in the presence of the disciples, which are not written in this book; but these have been written so that you may believe that Jesus is the Christ, the Son of God; and that believing you may have life in His name. (John 20:30–31)

I have tried in this commentary to keep verbiage out and say only what is directly helpful to the understanding of the text. There is little digression and no attempt to give embellishing content. This is a departure from the style of my other commentaries, where I often introduce an abundance of related theological and illustrative material. That is not to say there are not glorious themes throughout John that can and should be developed in the process of exposition, and by comparing Scripture with Scripture. But for the most part I have left that task to others this time, in favor of flow and concise adherence to the apostle John's own stated intent. At times I felt I should write more; sometimes less. But my deliberate goal throughout has been to serve the inspired message by restraint, minimizing interruptions, and letting the Word speak without adding anything more than essential explanations, without drifting from the text itself into parallel passages—thus keeping the simplicity and clarity of the Spirit's inspired truth uncluttered. I hope I have done that.

In this profound yet plain account of the coming of the Son of God to redeem sinners is the most needed message anyone will ever hear or understand. With just a little clarification and background, it proclaims to the mind of the willing and humble sinner the truth that transforms eternally.

JOHN MACARTHUR
February 2008

The Climax of Love and Hate (John 12:1–11)

Jesus, therefore, six days before the Passover, came to Bethany where Lazarus was, whom Jesus had raised from the dead. So they made Him a supper there, and Martha was serving; but Lazarus was one of those reclining at the table with Him. Mary then took a pound of very costly perfume of pure nard, and anointed the feet of Jesus and wiped His feet with her hair; and the house was filled with the fragrance of the perfume. But Judas Iscariot, one of His disciples, who was intending to betray Him, said, "Why was this perfume not sold for three hundred denarii and given to poor people?" Now he said this, not because he was concerned about the poor, but because he was a thief, and as he had the money box, he used to pilfer what was put into it. Therefore Jesus said, "Let her alone, so that she may keep it for the day of My burial. For you always have the poor with you, but you do not always have Me." The large crowd of the Jews then learned that He was there; and they came, not for Jesus' sake only, but that they might also see Lazarus, whom He raised from the dead. But the chief priests planned to put Lazarus to death also; because on account of him many of the Jews were going away and were believing in Jesus. (12:1–11)

The incarnation of the Lord Jesus Christ marks the zenith of history. His life not only divides the calendar (B.C. means "before Christ"; A.D. ["anno Domini"] means "in the year of the Lord"), but also human destiny. As Jesus Himself warned those who rejected Him, "Unless you believe that I am He, you will die in your sins" (John 8:24), and on another occasion, "Do you suppose that I came to grant peace on earth? I tell you, no, but rather division" (Luke 12:51; cf. Luke 2:34). Like no one else, Jesus Christ evokes the antithetical extremes of love and hate, devotion and rejection, worship and blasphemy, and faith and unbelief. How people respond to Him divides the sheep from the goats; the wheat from the tares; believers from unbelievers; the saved from the lost.

John wrote his gospel to present Jesus as the Son of God and the Messiah (20:31). In so doing, he also recorded how people reacted to Jesus' messianic claims and miraculous signs. The apostle accordingly cites numerous examples of those who believed in Jesus (1:35–51; 2:11; 4:28–29, 41–42, 53; 6:69; 9:35–38; 10:42; 11:27, 45; 12:11; 16:27, 30; 17:8; 19:38–39; 20:28–29), and those who rejected Him (1:10–11; 2:20; 3:32; 5:16–18, 38–47; 6:36, 41–43, 64, 66; 7:1, 5, 20, 26–27, 30–52; 8:13–59; 9:16, 29, 40–41; 10:20, 25–26; 11:46–57; 12:37–40).

In this passage, which relates the story of Mary's anointing of Jesus, the themes of belief and unbelief are particularly clear. The worshipful act of Mary epitomizes faith and love; the cold, calculated, cynical response of Judas epitomizes unbelief and hatred. The section also records other reactions to Jesus, including the devoted service of Martha, the indifference of the crowd, and the hostility of the religious leaders.

The Lord's raising of Lazarus had stirred up murderous opposition from the hostile Jewish leaders (11:46–53). They decided that they had to kill both Jesus and Lazarus. Since His hour to die had not yet come (7:30; 8:20; 12:23; 13:1), Jesus left the vicinity of Jerusalem and stayed in the village of Ephraim (11:54), about a dozen miles to the north on the edge of the wilderness. From there He made a brief visit to Samaria and Galilee (Luke 17:11–19:28) and then, **six days before the Passover, came** once more **to Bethany.** His arrival would have been on the Saturday before the Passover. (Because the distance people were permitted to travel on the Sabbath was limited [cf. Acts 1:12], the Lord may have arrived after sundown on Friday. That, according to Jewish reckoning, would have been after the Sabbath had begun.) John described **Bethany** as the village **where Lazarus** lived, and Lazarus as its now most famous resident, since **Jesus had raised** him **from the dead.**

From the account of the supper given there in His honor, five varied reactions to Jesus emerge: Martha responded with heartfelt service,

Mary with humble sacrifice, Judas with hypocritical self-interest, the people with hollow superficiality, and the religious leaders with hostile scheming.

THE HEARTFELT SERVICE OF MARTHA

So they made Him a supper there, and Martha was serving; but Lazarus was one of those reclining at the table with Him. (12:2)

The Sanhedrin had decreed that anyone who knew where Jesus was should report that information to them (11:57). But rather than turning Him in like some criminal, the Lord's friends in Bethany gave **a supper** in His honor. The purpose of the event was to express their love for Him, and especially their gratitude for His raising of Lazarus. Since *deipnon* (**supper**) refers to the main meal of the day, it would have been a lengthy one, designed with much time for leisurely conversation. The guests were surely **reclining,** leaning on one elbow with their heads toward a low, U-shaped table. How many people were there is not known, but at least Jesus, the Twelve, Mary, Martha, Lazarus, and probably Simon the leper were present.

Luke records a visit by Jesus to the home of Mary and Martha several months earlier, which provides insight into Martha's attachment to serving, even when it was not the priority:

> Now as they were traveling along, He entered a village; and a woman named Martha welcomed Him into her home. She had a sister called Mary, who was seated at the Lord's feet, listening to His word. But Martha was distracted with all her preparations; and she came up to Him and said, "Lord, do You not care that my sister has left me to do all the serving alone? Then tell her to help me." But the Lord answered and said to her, "Martha, Martha, you are worried and bothered about so many things; but only one thing is necessary, for Mary has chosen the good part, which shall not be taken away from her." (Luke 10:38–42)

Even after such a rebuke, here again being true to her interest, **Martha was** involved in **serving** the meal. (That John describes **Lazarus** as **one of** the guests **reclining at the table with** Jesus suggests that the feast was not in his and his sisters' home.) Matthew 26:6 and Mark 14:3 make more than a suggestion, stating specifically that the meal was held in the house of Simon the leper. Though the descriptive name stuck to him, he obviously had been healed from his disease, for people would never have gathered in the home of someone with an active case of leprosy. Not only would they have feared contagion, but also to socialize would have ceremonially defiled them, since lepers were unclean (Lev. 13:45). Nor is it likely that Simon would have owned a house and hosted a meal in it if he had still been sick, since lepers were social outcasts (Num. 5:2). Because cures for leprosy were beyond the limited medical knowledge of that time, it is reasonable to believe that Jesus had earlier healed him.

Though others were served also, Martha's service on this occasion was primarily directed at Jesus, and was commendable for two related reasons: it was motivated by loving gratitude to Him, and by a desire to generously honor Him in the way she best knew how. There was no rebuke as in the earlier incident. Like her, all Christians are to be engaged in selfless service (Rom. 12:11; cf. Gal. 5:13; Col. 3:24; Heb. 9:14). Jesus said, "The greatest among you shall be your servant" (Matt. 23:11) and declared of Himself, "I am among you as the one who serves" (Luke 22:27), and, "the Son of Man did not come to be served, but to serve" (Matt. 20:28). Paul repeatedly described himself as a bond servant of Jesus Christ (Rom. 1:1; 2 Cor. 4:5; Gal. 1:10; Phil. 1:1; Titus 1:1; cf. 1 Cor. 3:5; 4:1; 2 Cor. 3:6; 6:4; 11:23), as did James (James 1:1), Peter (2 Peter 1:1), Jude (Jude 1), and John (Rev. 1:1). In John 12:26 the Lord promised those who faithfully serve Him, "If anyone serves Me, he must follow Me; and where I am, there My servant will be also; if anyone serves Me, the Father will honor him." Although it tends to be overshadowed by Mary's dramatic act of worship, Martha's humble service on this occasion was no less commendable and pleasing to the Lord.

THE HUMBLE SACRIFICE OF MARY

Mary then took a pound of very costly perfume of pure nard, and anointed the feet of Jesus and wiped His feet with her hair; and the house was filled with the fragrance of the perfume. (12:3)

In keeping with her portrayal elsewhere in the Gospels (cf. 11:32–33; Luke 10:39), Mary once again appears as the more pensive, reflective, and emotional of the two sisters. In a startling, spontaneous outpouring of her love for Him, she **took a pound of very costly perfume of pure nard, and anointed the feet of Jesus. A pound** (a Roman measure, equivalent to about twelve ounces by today's standards) was a large amount of **perfume. Nard** was a fragrant oil extracted from the root and spike (hence the translation "spikenard" in some English versions) of a plant native to the mountains of northern India. Perfume made from **nard** was **very costly** because of the great distance from which it had to be imported. Mary's **nard** was **pure** in quality, making it even more valuable. Some were thinking it was worth "over three hundred denarii" (Mark 14:5), and Judas agreed with that valuation (John 12:5). As noted in the discussion of verse 5 below, such an amount would be equal to a year's wages. The expensive alabaster vial in which it was stored also added to its value (Matt. 26:7). She broke the vial (Mark 14:3), thus giving up the whole thing—both contents and container. The perfume likely made up a sizeable portion of Mary's net worth. But like David (2 Sam. 24:24), she refused to offer the Lord something that cost her nothing. She acted in unrestrained love.

Matthew's (26:7) and Mark's (14:3) parallel accounts note that Mary poured the perfume on Jesus' head, while John says that she **anointed** His **feet.** All three accounts are in perfect harmony. Since the Lord was reclining at a low table, with His feet extended away from it, Mary could have easily poured the perfume first on His head, then His body (Matt. 26:12), and finally on His feet. Then, in an act that shocked the onlookers even more than the pouring out of expensive perfume, she **wiped His feet with her hair.** The Jews considered washing the feet of another person to be degrading, a necessary task to be done only by the most menial slaves (cf. John 1:27). None of the Twelve at the coming Passover meal in the upper room were willing to serve the others by washing their feet, so in a supreme act and example of lowliness, Jesus did it (cf. 13:1–15). But even more shocking than her costly and lowly washing of Jesus' feet was the fact that Mary let down her hair. For a respectable Jewish woman to do that in public would have been considered indecent, perhaps even immoral. But Mary was not concerned with the shame she might face as a result. Instead, she was solely focused on pouring out her love and in honoring Christ, with no thought of any perceived shame that it might bring to her.

John's note that **the house was filled with the fragrance of the perfume** is the kind of vivid detail an eyewitness would recall. It also testifies to the extravagance of Mary's act of humble devotion. She was heedless of its cost, both financially and to her reputation. The measure of her love was her total abandonment to Jesus Christ. Consequently, Mary's noble act would, as the Lord declared, be spoken of as a memorial of her love wherever the gospel is preached (Mark 14:9).

It must be noted here that Luke records a very similar incident:

> Now one of the Pharisees was requesting Him to dine with him, and He entered the Pharisee's house and reclined at the table. And there was a woman in the city who was a sinner; and when she learned that He was reclining at the table in the Pharisee's house, she brought an alabaster vial of perfume, and standing behind Him at His feet, weeping, she began to wet His feet with her tears, and kept wiping them with the hair of her head, and kissing His feet and anointing them with the perfume. Now when the Pharisee who had invited Him saw this, he said to himself, "If

this man were a prophet He would know who and what sort of person
this woman is who is touching Him, that she is a sinner." (Luke 7:36–39)

That this is a completely different event is clear because it took place in
Galilee, not Bethany; it featured a woman who was a sinner (likely a
prostitute), not Mary; and occurred much earlier in our Lord's life, not
during Passion Week. It also was an event at the house of a Pharisee, not
Simon the leper.

THE HYPOCRITICAL SELF-INTEREST OF JUDAS

**But Judas Iscariot, one of His disciples, who was intending to
betray Him, said, "Why was this perfume not sold for three hundred denarii and given to poor people?" Now he said this, not
because he was concerned about the poor, but because he was a
thief, and as he had the money box, he used to pilfer what was
put into it. Therefore Jesus said, "Let her alone, so that she may
keep it for the day of My burial. For you always have the poor
with you, but you do not always have Me." (12:4–8)**

The stunned silence that must have followed Mary's startling and
unexpected act was suddenly broken by a voice raised in protest. The
conjunction *de* (**but**) introduces the stark contrast between Mary's self-
lessness and Judas's selfishness. As is always the case in the Gospels,
John's description of **Judas Iscariot** emphasizes two facts. First, he was
one of the Lord's **disciples** (Matt. 10:4; 26:14, 47; Mark 14:43; Luke 22:3,
47; John 6:71); second, he **was intending to betray Him** (Matt. 26:25;
27:3; Mark 3:19; 14:10; Luke 6:16; 22:4, 48; John 6:71; 13:2, 26–29; 18:2, 5; cf.
Acts 1:16). So shocking and singularly defining was Judas's betrayal that
the gospel writers could not think of him or refer to him apart from it.
That he was not merely a follower of Christ, but one of the Lord's inner
circle, makes his betrayal all the more heinous. It was the most despicable act in all of human history—and the one that merited the most
severe punishment. In the chilling words of the Lord Jesus Christ, "Woe to
that man by whom the Son of Man is betrayed! It would have been good
for that man if he had not been born" (Matt. 26:24).
    Wanting to appear philanthropic, Judas acted outraged over
such a profligate waste of money, exclaiming, **"Why was this perfume
not sold for three hundred denarii and given to poor people?"**
Chronologically, these are Judas's first recorded words in the New Testament. They expose the avarice, ambition, and selfishness that ruled his
heart. He had cast his lot with Jesus, expecting Him to usher in the politi-

cal, earthly messianic kingdom most Jewish people were looking for. As one of the inner circle, Judas had eagerly anticipated an exalted position in that kingdom. But now, for him, that dream had turned to ashes. Jesus had so antagonized the Jewish leaders that they intended to kill Him (John 7:1; 11:53). Not only that, the Lord Himself warned the disciples that His death was inevitable (e.g., Mark 8:31; 9:31; 10:33). And when the Galilean crowds sought to crown Jesus as the earthly king Judas thought He would be, the Lord refused to cooperate with them (John 6:14–15).

Disillusioned, Judas—facing the end of his ambitions—decided to at least get some financial compensation for the three years he had wasted on Jesus. John, not seeing it at that moment, but writing in retrospect many years later, makes the appropriate inspired comment on Judas's real motive: he **said this, not because he was concerned about the poor, but because he was a thief, and as he had the money box, he used to pilfer what was put into it.** As noted above, Mary's perfume was worth a lot of money; since a denarius was a day's wages for a common laborer (Matt. 20:2), **three hundred denarii** equaled a year's wages (allowing for Sabbaths and other holy days on which no work was done). Seeing that much money elude his grasp infuriated Judas, and he lashed out at Mary. "Judas' disapproval of Mary's action related not to loss of opportunity to do more for the poor but to his own loss of opportunity to steal from the common purse" (Colin Kruse, *The Gospel According to John*, The Tyndale New Testament Commentaries [Grand Rapids: Eerdmans, 2003], 263). So persuasive was his seemingly righteous indignation that others joined in his protest (Matt. 26:8–9; Mark 14:4–5).

Though some have tried to attribute noble motives to Judas (i.e., by arguing that he was a misguided patriot, trying to prod Christ into ushering in His kingdom), the New Testament portrays him as nothing but a greedy thief and a murderous traitor—even a Devil (John 6:70–71; cf. 13:2, 27). Judas is the greatest example of missed opportunity in history. He lived day in and day out with Jesus Christ, God incarnate, for three years. Yet in the end Judas rejected Him, betrayed Him, was overcome by guilt (but not genuine repentance), committed suicide, and went "to his own place" (Acts 1:25)—that is, hell (John 17:12) in its most potent form.

The Lord immediately defended Mary, sternly rebuking Judas (the verb translated **let alone** is in the second person singular, meaning "you") by commanding him, **"Let her alone, so that she may keep it for the day of My burial."** Jesus obviously did not mean that Mary would keep the perfume (or at least part of it) until His burial, since she had just poured it all out (cf. Mark 14:3). While commentators disagree on how to understand these words, the most satisfactory solution is to understand an ellipsis in the Lord's statement. Supplying the missing words, the sense would be, "Let her alone; she did not sell the perfume [as you wish she had], so that she could keep it for the day of my burial" (cf. D. A. Carson, *The Gospel According to John*, The Pillar New Testament Commentary (Grand Rapids: Eerdmans, 1991), 429–30; cf. Andreas J. Köstenberger, *John*, Baker Exegetical Commentary on the New Testament [Grand Rapids: Baker, 2004], 363–64).

Mary's act was a spontaneous outpouring of her love and devotion to Christ. Yet, like Caiaphas's unwitting prophecy (11:49–52), it had a deeper significance. In Matthew 26:12 Jesus said, "When she poured this perfume on My body, she did it to prepare Me for burial" (cf. Mark 14:8). The **burial** of which Jesus prophetically spoke was not the actual placing of His dead body in the tomb, but the anointing she had just done, which He saw as a symbol of His soon coming death and burial. Part of the lavish expenditures associated with many first-century funerals was the cost of perfumes to mask the odor of decay (cf. John 11:39). This act by Mary, as in the case of Caiaphas (11:49–52) revealed a far greater reality than she realized at the time. Her anointing prefigured the one Joseph of Arimathea and Nicodemus would later perform on His body after Jesus' death (John 19:38–40).

If Judas had really wanted to help the poor, he would not have lacked opportunity since, as Jesus reminded them all (the verb and pronoun in this phrase are plurals), **"You always have the poor with you"** (cf. Mark 14:7). The Lord was not disparaging the giving of charity to the poor (cf. Deut. 15:11), but rather was challenging the disciples to keep their priorities straight. The opportunity to do good to Him, as Mary had done, would not last long, because they would **not always have** Him physically present with them. Here again the Lord's words were a prediction of His coming death, now less than a week away.

Judas now stood at the crossroads. Unmasked as a hypocrite, pretending to care for the poor while in reality embezzling from the common purse, he faced the ultimate decision. He could fall at Jesus' feet in humble, penitent repentance, confess his sin, and seek forgiveness. Or he could pridefully harden his heart, refuse to repent, surrender to Satan's influence, and betray the Lord. Tragically and sinfully, he chose the latter course, with full and sole culpability for its consequences, though it fulfilled the purpose of God for the sacrifice of His Son (cf. 13:18–19). Immediately after this incident, "Judas Iscariot, who was one of the twelve, went off to the chief priests in order to betray Him to them. They were glad when they heard this, and promised to give him money. And he began seeking how to betray Him at an opportune time" (Mark 14:10–11).

THE HOLLOW SUPERFICIALITY OF THE PEOPLE

The large crowd of the Jews then learned that He was there; and they came, not for Jesus' sake only, but that they might also see Lazarus, whom He raised from the dead. (12:9)

After the Sabbath, a **large crowd of the Jews** who were in Jerusalem for Passover **learned that** Jesus **was** in Bethany. (The term **Jews** here does not refer to the religious leaders, but to the common people [cf. 11:55–56].) They **came** to Bethany **not for Jesus' sake only, but that they might also see Lazarus, whom He raised from the dead.** News of that sensational miracle had spread, and the curious crowd wanted to see both the miracle worker, and the one whom He had raised.

These people were not yet openly hostile to Jesus, like Judas and the religious leaders, but neither were they committed to Him, like Martha and Mary. They were the thrill seekers, following the latest sensation, superficially interested in Jesus, but spiritually indifferent and ultimately antagonistic to Him. Like the members of the Laodicean church, they were "lukewarm, and neither hot nor cold" (Rev. 3:16). At the triumphal entry they would hail Him, shouting "Hosanna! Blessed is He who comes in the name of the Lord, even the King of Israel" (John 12:13). But only a few days later they would scream, "Away with Him, away with Him, crucify Him!" (John 19:15), and some would come to mock Him as He was hanging on the cross (Matt. 27:39–40).

THE HOSTILE SCHEMING OF THE LEADERS

But the chief priests planned to put Lazarus to death also; because on account of him many of the Jews were going away and were believing in Jesus. (12:10–11)

By no means did the crowds that flocked to Bethany to see Jesus and Lazarus escape the notice of the Jewish authorities. The ruthless **chief priests** had already plotted to kill Jesus (11:53); now they expanded the plot and **planned to put Lazarus to death also.** As living proof of Jesus' miraculous power, the resurrected Lazarus presented a great threat to the Sadducees, because **on account of him many of the Jews were going away and were believing in Jesus** (cf. 11:48). He was an undeniable testimony to the Lord's messianic claims. Not only that, a resurrected man was also an embarrassment to the Sadducees in another way: they denied the resurrection of the dead (Matt. 22:23), and he was an undeniable refutation of that error. Unable to counter the incontrovertible testimony Lazarus provided by being alive, they sought to destroy the evidence by killing him. Their tangled web of deception was expanding, as Leon Morris notes: "It is interesting to reflect that Caiaphas had said, 'it is expedient for you that one man die for the people' (11:50). But one was not enough. Now it had to be two. Thus does evil grow" (*The Gospel According to John*, The New International Commentary on the New Testament [Grand Rapids: Eerdmans, 1979], 582).

No one is neutral regarding Jesus Christ; as He Himself warned, "He who is not with Me is against Me; and he who does not gather with Me, scatters" (Luke 11:23). Whether loving and serving Him, like Mary and Martha, being indifferent and vacillating toward Him, like the crowd, or hating and opposing Him, like Judas and the chief priests, everyone takes a stand somewhere. What that stand is determines each person's eternal destiny, since "there is salvation in no one else; for there is no other name under heaven that has been given among men by which we must be saved" (Acts 4:12).

The King Comes to Die (John 12:12–16)

2

On the next day the large crowd who had come to the feast, when they heard that Jesus was coming to Jerusalem, took the branches of the palm trees and went out to meet Him, and began to shout, "Hosanna! Blessed is He who comes in the name of the Lord, even the King of Israel." Jesus, finding a young donkey, sat on it; as it is written, "Fear not, daughter of Zion; behold, your king is coming, seated on a donkey's colt." These things His disciples did not understand at the first; but when Jesus was glorified, then they remembered that these things were written of Him, and that they had done these things to Him. (12:12–16)

The passing centuries have seen false messiahs, each claiming to be the one so eagerly anticipated by the Jewish people. Of these self-proclaimed deliverers, some were simply self-deceived, while others were purposefully exploitative; some sought personal prestige, others to rescue their people from oppression; some advocated violence, others prayer and fasting; some professed to be political deliverers, others to be religious reformers. But though their motives, methods, and claims varied, they all had one thing in common—they were satanic counterfeits of the true Messiah, Jesus of Nazareth.

About A.D. 44 Theudas (not the same individual mentioned in Acts 5:36) promised his followers that he would part the Jordan River. But before he was able to do so, Roman troops attacked and massacred many of his followers. The Egyptian for whom Paul was mistaken (Acts 21:38) had boasted that he would command the walls of Jerusalem to fall down. But, like Theudas, his plans were also foiled by Roman soldiers. Although the Egyptian managed to escape his attackers, several hundred of his followers were killed or captured (Josephus, *Antiquities* 20.8.6; *Wars of the Jews* 2.13.5). In the second century Simon Bar Cochba ("son of a star"; cf. Num. 24:17), who was identified as the messiah by the leading rabbi of the time, led a major Jewish uprising against Rome, conquering Jerusalem for three years, where he was called king and messiah. The Romans crushed the rebellion, retook Jerusalem, and massacred Bar Cochba and five to six hundred thousand of his followers. A fifth-century false messiah on the island of Crete promised to part the Mediterranean Sea so his followers could walk to Palestine on dry land. But the sea refused to part and some of his followers drowned. In the seventeenth century, Sabbethai Zebi proclaimed himself "king of the kings of the earth," and attracted a widespread following among the Jews of western Europe. Zebi later converted to Islam and was eventually executed. (For a further discussion of false messiahs throughout history, see J. E. Rosscup, "False Christs," in Merrill C. Tenney, ed., *The Zondervan Pictorial Encyclopedia of the Bible* [Grand Rapids: Zondervan, 1977], 2:495; James Orr, ed., *The International Standard Bible Encyclopedia,* 1st ed., s.v. "Christs, False.")

Jesus warned that as the second coming draws near, "many false prophets will arise and will mislead many," and many "false Christs ... will arise" (Matt. 24:11, 24). They will culminate in the ultimate deceiving false messiah, the Antichrist, the

> man of lawlessness ... the son of destruction, who opposes and exalts himself above every so-called god or object of worship, so that he takes his seat in the temple of God, displaying himself as being God.... [the] lawless one ... whom the Lord will slay with the breath of His mouth and bring to an end by the appearance of His coming; that is, the one whose coming is in accord with the activity of Satan, with all power and signs and false wonders, and with all the deception of wickedness for those who perish, because they did not receive the love of the truth so as to be saved. (2 Thess. 2:3–4, 8–10; cf. Rev. 13:1–18)

But the bogus claims of all such pretenders fall far short of the biblical qualifications for the Messiah. Jesus Christ alone possesses the credentials of the true Messiah; the words He spoke, the miracles He performed, and the prophecies He fulfilled prove that He was who He claimed to be (Matt. 26:63–64; John 4:25–26).

When John the Baptist sent his disciples to ask Him, "Are You the Expected One [the Messiah], or shall we look for someone else?" (Matt. 11:3), Jesus pointed to His miracles as proof that He was the Messiah: "Go and report to John what you hear and see," He told them. "The blind receive sight and the lame walk, the lepers are cleansed and the deaf hear, the dead are raised up" (vv. 4–5). Instead of extravagant stunts, like the one Satan challenged Him to perform (Matt. 4:5–6), the compassionate Savior chose to display His divine power by healing the sick (Matt. 4:23–24; 8:2–3, 5–13, 14–16; 9:2–7, 20–22, 27–30, 35; 12:9–13, 15; 14:14; 15:30; 19:2; 20:30–34; 21:14; Mark 6:5; 7:31–35; Luke 5:15; 6:17–19; 9:11; 14:1–4; 17:11–14; 22:51; John 4:46–53; 5:1–9; 6:2; 9:1–7), raising the dead (Matt. 9:23–25; Luke 7:11–15; John 11:43), and casting out demons (Matt. 4:24; 8:16, 28–33; 9:32–33; 12:22; 15:21–28; 17:14–18; Mark 1:39; Luke 11:14; 13:32).

It was because they had personally witnessed His incontestable miracles that the residents of Chorazin, Bethsaida, and Capernaum were under judgment and without excuse for not repenting and believing in Jesus as the Messiah and Lord (Matt. 11:20–24). Like them, all everywhere who saw His miraculous signs, but refused to believe in Him, were culpable (John 12:37–41). On the day of Pentecost, Peter boldly reminded the people of Israel, "Jesus the Nazarene, [was] a man attested to you by God with miracles and wonders and signs which God performed through Him in your midst, just as you yourselves know" (Acts 2:22). They could not plead ignorance.

Besides doing "the works which no one else did" (John 15:24), Jesus fulfilled the messianic prophecies found in the Old Testament. Those predictions included most notably His virgin birth (Isa. 7:14), sacrificial death (Isa. 52:13–53:12), and resurrection (Ps. 16:10; cf. Acts 13:35). (For a listing of more messianic prophecies fulfilled by Jesus, see John MacArthur, *The MacArthur Bible Commentary* [Nashville: Thomas Nelson, 2005], 78, 79, 145, 156, 667, 820, 828–29, 1084, 1236.)

In this section, which describes the event commonly known as the triumphal entry, Jesus officially presented Himself to Israel as the Messiah and Son of God. By so doing, He set in motion the chain of events that would quickly lead to His death at the exact time foreordained by God. As the King came to die, He did so at the proper moment, with the passionate multitude, in the predicted manner, and to the perplexity of His men. In keeping with the theme of his gospel (20:31), John highlighted Jesus' fulfillment of Old Testament prophecy throughout this account.

At the Proper Moment

On the next day (12:12*a*)

The next day was Monday morning, the day after the supper at Bethany (12:1–11). During the night, Judas had met with the chief priests and agreed to betray Jesus to them (Matt. 26:14–16). But Jesus was not at the mercy of His enemies' plots; He remained in absolute control of the circumstances. The divinely ordained time had come for Him to die (v. 23; cf. 13:1), but He would do so on His own terms. The Jewish leaders, fearful of how the large, volatile crowds in Jerusalem might react, wanted to put Jesus to death, but not during the Passover celebration (Matt. 26:3–5; cf. Luke 22:2). Their plan was to seize and execute Him after the feast was over and the people dispersed.

But regardless of His enemies' desires, the Lord would die at the precise time foreordained in God's eternal plan (cf. 10:17–18; 19:10–11; Acts 2:23; 4:27–28; Gal. 4:4–5); fittingly, the Lamb of God would be sacrificed on the same day that the Passover lambs were being sacrificed, because He is "Christ our Passover" sacrifice (1 Cor. 5:7). Therefore Jesus prepared to publicly enter Jerusalem to force the issue of His death. He knew that the accolades of the crowds would infuriate the Jewish leaders, and make them all the more desperate to kill Him. As always, God would use the foolishness and wickedness of evil men to accomplish His own purposes (cf. Gen. 50:20; Ps. 76:10; Acts 4:26–28).

Up to this point, the Lord did not allow His enemies to take His life. Hence He had avoided provoking unnecessary public confrontations with the hostile Jewish authorities. When "the Pharisees went out and conspired against Him, as to how they might destroy Him ... Jesus, aware of this, withdrew from there" (Matt. 12:14–15; cf. 8:4; 16:20; John 4:1–3; 7:1; 11:53–54). When confrontations did occur and His enemies sought to kill Him, He evaded them. The people of His hometown of Nazareth wanted to throw Him off a cliff, but Jesus "[passed] through their midst, [and] went His way" (Luke 4:30). On another occasion, enraged at His claim to be God (John 8:58), the hostile Jews "picked up stones to throw at Him, but Jesus hid Himself and went out of the temple" (v. 59; cf. 10:39). Jesus' commanding presence also prevented His enemies from seizing Him before the predetermined time (John 7:44–46).

The exact day that the Lord chose to enter Jerusalem fulfilled one of the most remarkable prophecies of the Old Testament, Daniel's prophecy of the seventy weeks (Dan. 9:24–26). Through Daniel, the Lord predicted that the time from Artaxerxes' decree ordering the rebuilding of the temple (in 445 B.C.) until the coming of the Messiah would be "seven weeks and sixty-two weeks" (Dan. 9:25; cf. Neh. 2:6), that is, 69 weeks total. The literal translation is "seven sevens and sixty-two sevens," seven being a common designation for a week. In the context of the passage, the idea is 69 weeks of years, or 69 times 7 years, which comes to a total of 483 Jewish years (which consisted of 360 days each, as was common in the ancient world). Several different systems of reckoning have endeavored to determine the chronology of the 483 years after Artaxerxes' decree, putting the date at either A.D. 30, 32, or 33, depending on the actual decree date and the complex calculations through those years. Of these explanations, the most detailed are Sir Robert Anderson's *The Coming Prince* and Harold Hoehner's *Chronological Aspects of the Life of Christ.* Based on all of the historical data, it is best to understand the triumphal entry as taking place on 9 Nisan, A.D. 30. But even the other dates offered by these authors (A.D. 32 or 33) leave one thing remaining undeniably clear: whatever may be the precise chronology, Jesus Christ is the only possible fulfillment of Daniel's prophetic timetable.

WITH THE PASSIONATE MULTITUDE

the large crowd who had come to the feast, when they heard that Jesus was coming to Jerusalem, took the branches of the palm trees and went out to meet Him, and began to shout, "Hosanna! Blessed is He who comes in the name of the Lord, even the King of Israel." (12:12b–13)

When the Lord left Bethany, He was accompanied by part of the "large crowd of the Jews" (v. 9) who had come there to see Him and Lazarus (v. 17). They would soon be joined by others of **the large crowd** of pilgrims **who had come to** Jerusalem for **the feast** (Passover). **When they heard that Jesus was coming to Jerusalem,** they came pouring out of the city to meet Him. The two great tides of people, fueled by the resurrection of Lazarus, flowed together to form a massive throng (some histories estimate that there may have been as many as one million people there for the Passover feast) that escorted Jesus into Jerusalem. (The accounts of the triumphal entry in the Synoptic Gospels also suggest that there were two crowds that converged around Jesus [Matt. 21:9; Mark 11:9].)

The excited people cut **branches** from **the** date **palm trees** that were plentiful in the vicinity of Jerusalem (and still grow there today). The Old Testament does not associate palm branches with Passover, but rather with the Feast of Tabernacles (Lev. 23:40). In the intertestamental period, however, palm branches became a general symbol of victory and celebration. When the Jews, led by Simon the Maccabee, recaptured Jerusalem from the Syrians, they "entered it with praise and palm branches" (1 Macc. 13:51; cf. 2 Macc. 10:7). Perhaps many in the crowd had that incident in mind as they waved their palm branches. Maybe, they hoped, Jesus would prove to be the great messianic King and military conqueror who would liberate them from the yoke of Rome and establish the promises to Abraham and David (Gen. 12:1–3; 2 Sam. 7:1–16).

Swept up in the emotional fervor of the moment, the crowd shouted, **"Hosanna! Blessed is He who comes in the name of the Lord, even the King of Israel." Hosanna,** a term of acclamation or praise, transliterates a Hebrew word that literally means, "Help, I pray," or "Save now, I pray" (cf. Ps. 118:25 NKJV). It was a term with which every Jew was familiar, since it came from the group of Psalms known as the Hallel (Pss. 113–18). The Hallel was sung each morning by the temple choir during the major Jewish festivals. The crowd also cried, **Blessed is He who comes in the name of the Lord,** quoting Psalm 118:26. By using that phrase, the people affirmed their hope that Jesus was the Messiah they were expecting. (The people of Israel, however, will truly be able to say those words to Jesus only at His second coming [Matt. 23:39].) That belief was further expressed by their hailing Him as **the King of Israel** (cf. v. 15; 1:49; 19:15, 19). Matthew records that the crowd also called Jesus the "Son of David" (Matt. 21:9, 15; 22:42), another messianic title.

In the past, the Lord had refused to be hailed as the king and military conqueror the people were sure the Messiah would be. In fact, He had dispersed the crowd that sought to make Him king (cf. John 6:14–15). But this time He accepted their acclamation, sending them into a frenzy of excitement. Finally, they thought, He was accepting the role they wanted Him to take, that of a political and military deliverer. But Jesus accepted their praise on His terms. As the one who came to save (Matt. 1:21), the one who came in the name of the Lord (John 5:43), and the rightful King of Israel (Matt. 27:11; John 1:49), He was entitled to the crowd's praise. Matthew records that when Jesus reached Jerusalem and entered the temple, "the chief priests and the scribes saw the wonderful things that He had done, and the children who were shouting in the temple, 'Hosanna to the Son of David,' [and] they became indignant and said to Him, 'Do You hear what these children are saying?'" (Matt. 21:15). The Lord replied by affirming His right to that praise: "Yes; have you never read, 'Out of the mouth of infants and nursing babies You have prepared praise for Yourself'?" (v. 16).

But far from being elated by the joyous cries of the giddy multitude, Jesus was grieved by the people's superficial attitude toward Him. He knew that many who were hailing Him as the Messiah that day would cry for His death the following Friday. Therefore

when He approached Jerusalem, He saw the city and wept ov
ing, "If you had known in this day, even you, the things which r
peace! But now they have been hidden from your eyes. For t
will come upon you when your enemies will throw up a bɛ
against you, and surround you and hem you in on every side, a
will level you to the ground and your children within you, and tɦ
not leave in you one stone upon another, because you did not
nize the time of your visitation." (Luke 19:41–44)

IN THE PREDICTED MANNER

**Jesus, finding a young donkey, sat on it; as it is written, "Fear
daughter of Zion; behold, your king is coming, seated on a (
key's colt."** (12:14–15)

The Synoptic Gospels describe how **Jesus** found the **you
donkey.** When the Lord and those with Him arrived on the outskirt
Jerusalem, He "sent two disciples, instruct them, 'Go into the villɛ
[probably Bethphage; cf. Matt. 21:1] opposite you, and immediately y
will find a donkey tied there and a colt with her; untie them and briɲ
them to Me. If anyone says anything to you, you shall say, "The Lord h,
need of them," and immediately he will send them'" (Matt. 21:1–3). Tɦ
disciples did as Jesus had commanded, and returned with a colt and iɩ
mother, which may have been brought along to help keep the colt docilɛ
(Matt. 21:6–7). Unsure of which animal the Lord intended to ride, they
laid their coats on both of them (Matt. 21:7). Then after Jesus indicated
that He would ride the colt, they helped Him to mount it (Luke 19:35). As
the procession continued, with Jesus now riding the young donkey, "most
of the crowd spread their coats in the road, and others were cutting
branches from the trees [only John's account specifies that they were
palm branches] and spreading them in the road" (Matt. 21:8). Spreading
garments in someone's path was a token of homage reserved for royalty
(cf. 2 Kings 9:13), and further expressed the crowd's belief that Jesus was
Israel's King (John 12:13; cf. Luke 19:38).

The Lord's choice of a mount was a purposeful, conscious fulfillment of Zechariah 9:9: **"Fear not,** (the words **fear not** were added from
Isa. 40:9) **daughter of Zion** (a reference to Jerusalem [cf. 2 Kings 19:21;
Isa. 10:32; Zech. 9:9] and by extension the whole nation); **behold, your
king is coming, seated on a donkey's colt."** If Jesus had been the
conquering warrior the people were hoping for, a war horse would have
been a more appropriate mount (cf. Rev. 19:11). By choosing to ride a
donkey, however, Jesus entered Jerusalem as the humble (Zech. 9:9; Matt.
21:5) Prince of Peace. Only when He returns the second time in judgment

will Jesus ride the white horse of the conqueror (Rev. 19:11).The symbolism of His humiliation was lost on the crowd, however, who continued to proclaim Jesus as the conquering King all the way into the city (cf. Matt. 21:15). As Leon Morris observes, "The meaning of the happenings of the life of Jesus are not open for every unregenerate man to see. They are revealed only by the Holy Spirit of God" (*The Gospel According to John,* The New International Commentary on the New Testament [Grand Rapids: Eerdmans, 1979], 587–88).

To the Perplexity of His Men

These things His disciples did not understand at the first; but when Jesus was glorified, then they remembered that these things were written of Him, and that they had done these things to Him. (12:16)

The people in the crowd were not the only ones who failed to grasp the significance of what was happening. John's parenthetical note (cf. 2:22) indicates that even the **disciples did not understand** the meaning of the triumphal entry at the time; they could not comprehend that at His first advent Jesus came not as conqueror but as Savior. Even after the resurrection, the disciples still asked hopefully, "Lord, is it at this time You are restoring the kingdom to Israel?" (Acts 1:6). It was not until the coming of the Holy Spirit after **Jesus was glorified** (cf. John 7:39) that the disciples **remembered that these things were written of Him, and that they had done these things to Him.** As Jesus had promised the Twelve, "The Helper, the Holy Spirit, whom the Father will send in My name, He will teach you all things, and bring to your remembrance all that I said to you" (John 14:26). "When He, the Spirit of truth, comes," the Lord added, "He will guide you into all the truth; for He will not speak on His own initiative, but whatever He hears, He will speak; and He will disclose to you what is to come" (16:13).

Jesus was a King like no other. Instead of the pomp and circumstance associated with earthly kings, He was meek and lowly (Matt. 11:29); instead of defeating His enemies by force, He conquered them by dying (Heb. 2:14; cf. Eph. 1:19–22; Col. 2:15). But though He was despised and rejected at His first advent (Isa. 53:3), Jesus Christ will one day return as the all-conquering King of Kings and Lord of Lords (Rev. 19:11–16), who will shatter His enemies and destroy them with a fierce and final judgment (Ps. 2:9; Rev. 19:15). Just as He perfectly fulfilled all of the Old Testament prophecies regarding His first coming, so He will also come again in exactly the manner foretold by the Scriptures.

The Gospel Reaches Out: A Preview of Gentile Salvation
(John 12:17–26)

3

So the people, who were with Him when He called Lazarus out of the tomb and raised him from the dead, continued to testify about Him. For this reason also the people went and met Him, because they heard that He had performed this sign. So the Pharisees said to one another, "You see that you are not doing any good; look, the world has gone after Him." Now there were some Greeks among those who were going up to worship at the feast; these then came to Philip, who was from Bethsaida of Galilee, and began to ask him, saying, "Sir, we wish to see Jesus." Philip came and told Andrew; Andrew and Philip came and told Jesus. And Jesus answered them, saying, "The hour has come for the Son of Man to be glorified. Truly, truly, I say to you, unless a grain of wheat falls into the earth and dies, it remains alone; but if it dies, it bears much fruit. He who loves his life loses it, and he who hates his life in this world will keep it to life eternal. If anyone serves Me, he must follow Me; and where I am, there My servant will be also; if anyone serves Me, the Father will honor him. (12:17–26)

Clearly, God commanded that the gospel be preached to all people, of every nation and ethnic background (Matt. 24:14; Mark 13:10; cf. Matt. 26:13; 28:19–20; Col. 1:23; Rev. 14:6).

Yet it was God's desire that the gospel be offered first to His chosen people, Israel (Amos 3:2; cf. Deut. 7:6–8; 10:15; 14:2; 1 Kings 3:8; 1 Chron. 16:13; Pss. 105:6; 135:4; Isa. 41:8–9; 44:1–2; Ezek. 20:5). Jesus told a Samaritan woman that "salvation is from the Jews" (John 4:22); that is, not only did it originate with them (since Jesus the Messiah was a Jew), but it also was offered to them first. When He sent the Twelve out on a preaching mission, the Lord charged them, "Do not go in the way of the Gentiles, and do not enter any city of the Samaritans; but rather go to the lost sheep of the house of Israel" (Matt. 10:5–6). And when a Gentile woman (Mark 7:26) begged Him to heal her demon-possessed daughter, Jesus tested her faith by telling her bluntly, "I was sent only to the lost sheep of the house of Israel" (Matt. 15:24). It was only after His death and resurrection, after Israel had officially rejected His ministry, that Jesus commanded the disciples that "repentance for forgiveness of sins ... be proclaimed in His name to all the nations, beginning from Jerusalem" (Luke 24:47). Paul and Barnabas declared to the hostile Jews in Pisidian Antioch, "It was necessary that the word of God be spoken to you first; since you repudiate it and judge yourselves unworthy of eternal life, behold, we are turning to the Gentiles" (Acts 13:46; cf. 18:5–6). The gospel, Paul wrote to the Romans, "is the power of God for salvation to everyone who believes, to the Jew first and also to the Greek" (Rom. 1:16).

In contrast to the privileges and blessings Israel enjoyed (cf. Rom. 9:4–5), the Gentiles were "separate from Christ, excluded from the commonwealth of Israel, and strangers to the covenants of promise, having no hope and without God in the world" (Eph. 2:12; cf. 1 Thess. 4:5). They were ignorant of God's revelation of Himself in Scripture (Rom. 2:14; cf. Ps. 147:19–20), and as a result were enslaved to idolatry (1 Cor. 12:2; cf. 10:20; 1 Chron. 16:26; Ps. 96:5; Jer. 2:11), with its resulting futility (Eph. 4:17–18) and corruption (Eph. 4:19; 1 Thess. 4:5; 1 Peter 4:3–4).

As the recipients of God's Old Testament covenant promises, the Jews considered themselves to be superior to the pagan Gentiles because of their God and had no interest in letting Gentiles in. For example, rather than proclaim God's message to the Gentile city of Nineveh as he had been called to do, Jonah fled in the opposite direction. He deeply resented the idea that Gentiles could know his God. After he (reluctantly) went and proclaimed God's impending judgment on the city, the people of Nineveh repented. Predictably, instead of bringing him joy,

> it greatly displeased Jonah and he became angry. He prayed to the Lord and said, "Please Lord, was not this what I said while I was still in my own country? Therefore in order to forestall this I fled to Tarshish, for I

knew that You are a gracious and compassionate God, slow to anger and abundant in lovingkindness, and one who relents concerning calamity." (Jonah 4:1–2)

So deeply ingrained was the Jews' prejudice against Gentiles that even the Jewish believers in Christ were slow to accept them as "fellow heirs and fellow members of the body, and fellow partakers of the promise in Christ Jesus through the gospel" (Eph. 3:6). Peter reminded the Gentiles gathered in Cornelius's house, "You yourselves know how unlawful it is for a man who is a Jew to associate with a foreigner or to visit him" (Acts 10:28). It took a vision from God (10:9–20, 34–35) to convince him to preach the gospel to the Gentiles. When Cornelius and the other Gentiles heard Peter's message, believed, and received the Holy Spirit, "all the circumcised believers who came with Peter were amazed, because the gift of the Holy Spirit had been poured out on the Gentiles also" (10:45). When Peter returned to Jerusalem, "those [believers] who were circumcised took issue with him, saying, 'You went to uncircumcised men and ate with them'" (Acts 11:3). In his defense, Peter related his vision and the salvation of the Gentiles (demonstrated by their receiving the Holy Spirit [vv. 15–17]) at Cornelius's house (vv. 4–17). It was only then that his accusers "quieted down and glorified God, saying, 'Well then, God has granted to the Gentiles also the repentance that leads to life'" (v. 18).

But the blessings of salvation were never meant to be limited exclusively to Israel. On the day the ark of the covenant was brought to Jerusalem, a song of thanksgiving was sung that included a reiteration of Israel's duty to declare the true God to the nations:

> Oh give thanks to the Lord, call upon His name; make known His deeds among the peoples. . . . Tell of His glory among the nations, His wonderful deeds among all the peoples. For great is the Lord, and greatly to be praised; He also is to be feared above all gods. For all the gods of the peoples are idols, but the Lord made the heavens. Splendor and majesty are before Him, strength and joy are in His place. Ascribe to the Lord, O families of the peoples, ascribe to the Lord glory and strength. Ascribe to the Lord the glory due His name; bring an offering, and come before Him; worship the Lord in holy array. Tremble before Him, all the earth; indeed, the world is firmly established, it will not be moved. (1 Chron. 16:8, 24–30)

The Jews' narrow, provincial, prejudicial attitude overlooked the Old Testament promises and their national mandate to proclaim the salvation of God to the Gentiles. In His covenant with Abraham, God promised him, "In you all the families of the earth will be blessed" (Gen.

12:3; cf. 22:18; 26:4; 28:14). Commenting on that promise, Paul wrote, "The Scripture, foreseeing that God would justify the Gentiles by faith, preached the gospel beforehand to Abraham, saying, 'All the nations will be blessed in you'" (Gal. 3:8). In Deuteronomy 32:21 God said of Israel, "They have made Me jealous with what is not God; they have provoked Me to anger with their idols. So I will make them jealous with those who are not a people; I will provoke them to anger with a foolish nation"; in Romans 10:19 the apostle Paul appealed to this passage as proof that the gospel would be extended to the Gentiles. In Psalm 22:27 David wrote, "All the ends of the earth will remember and turn to the Lord, and all the families of the nations will worship before You," while in Psalm 102:15 the psalmist added, "So the nations will fear the name of the Lord and all the kings of the earth Your glory." Isaiah predicted that God would "make [Messiah] a light of the nations so that [His] salvation may reach to the end of the earth" (Isa. 49:6; cf. 42:6). In Isaiah 45:22 God graciously calls to sinners, "Turn to Me and be saved, all the ends of the earth; for I am God, and there is no other."

In Romans 15:8–12, Paul emphasized that it has always been God's plan to bring Gentiles into His kingdom:

> For I say that Christ has become a servant to the circumcision on behalf of the truth of God to confirm the promises given to the fathers, and for the Gentiles to glorify God for His mercy; as it is written, "Therefore I will give praise to You among the Gentiles, and I will sing to Your name." Again he says, "Rejoice, O Gentiles, with His people." And again, "Praise the Lord all you Gentiles, and let all the peoples praise Him." Again Isaiah says, "There shall come the root of Jesse, and He who arises to rule over the Gentiles, in Him shall the Gentiles hope."

In that brief passage, Paul quoted from all three divisions of the Old Testament (cf. Luke 24:44), the Law (Deut. 32:43), the Prophets (Isa. 11:10), and the Psalms (18:49; 117:1), demonstrating to the Jews from their own Scriptures the truth of God's plan for Gentile salvation.

In this same vein, John 12:17–26 illustrates three perspectives on Jesus: that of the Pharisees, that of some Gentiles, and then that of the Lord Himself.

REJECTION BY THE PHARISEES

So the people, who were with Him when He called Lazarus out of the tomb and raised him from the dead, continued to testify about Him. For this reason also the people went and met Him, because they heard that He had performed this sign. So the Pharisees said

to one another, "You see that you are not doing any good; look, the world has gone after Him." (12:17–19)

As noted in the discussion of 12:12–13, some **people** accompanied Jesus from Bethany, while others came out from Jerusalem to meet Him. The two groups coalesced into a huge crowd that escorted Jesus into the city. On the way, those from Bethany **who were with Him when He called Lazarus out of the tomb and raised him from the dead, continued to testify about Him.** Their enthusiastic witness to **the people** who **went** out from Jerusalem **and met Him, because they heard that He had performed this sign,** amplified the powerful effect of the miracle to the masses coming for Passover (11:45; cf. 5:36; 10:38).

John's note that the **people** flocked to Jesus **because they heard that He had** raised Lazarus from the dead reveals the superficial nature of their faith. Their desire was that Jesus would accept the role of political ruler and military deliverer that they expected of the Messiah (cf. John 6:14–15; 12:13). They probably reasoned that since He had the power to raise to life one who had been dead for four days, He could surely use that power to free them from the yoke of Roman oppression. As was the case with so many other crowds that followed Jesus (cf. 2:23–25; 6:2, 14–15, 26, 60, 66; 12:42–43), this one consisted chiefly of thrill seekers. By the end of the week, when it became obvious that Jesus was not going to be the political Messiah they expected, the people followed the lead of the Pharisees and other leaders in rejecting Him. Many of the same voices that shouted "Hosanna" at the triumphal entry must have screamed "Crucify Him" on Good Friday.

In contrast to the crowd's superficial, fleeting attachment to Jesus, which ended in rejection, His true disciples persevere in believing in Him. The Lord said to "those Jews who had believed Him, 'If you continue in My word, then you are truly disciples of Mine'" (John 8:31). The writer of Hebrews warned that true believers "are not ... those who shrink back to destruction, but ... those who have faith to the preserving of the soul" (Heb. 10:39). A professed faith that does not "bear fruit in keeping with repentance" (Matt. 3:8) is dead, nonsaving faith (James 2:14–26). "Anyone who goes too far and does not abide in the teaching of Christ," the apostle John noted, "does not have God; the one who abides in the teaching, he has both the Father and the Son" (2 John 9). It is impossible for a true believer in Jesus Christ to fall away from Him permanently and completely. Those who do so prove that their faith was never genuine. In 1 John 2:19 John wrote of such people, "They went out from us, but they were not really of us; for if they had been of us, they would have remained with us; but they went out, so that it would be shown that they all are not of us."

The **Pharisees,** meanwhile, looked on the tumultuous scene with increasing frustration and alarm. It seemed to them that events were spiraling dangerously out of control; if Jesus led this rabid crowd in an armed revolt against the Romans, all would be lost. (Unlike the Sadducees, the Pharisees refused to compromise with the Romans. But unlike the Zealots, they did not physically assault them.) Further, they had ordered that anyone knowing Jesus' whereabouts was to tell them so they could arrest Him (11:57). Ironically, there, in plain sight, was the very one they wanted desperately to seize, surrounded by thousands of people. But instead of turning Jesus over to the authorities, the crowds were loudly hailing Him as the Messiah. Afraid of the crowd's reaction if they arrested Jesus openly, the Pharisees could only look on in frustration and dismay. Not surprisingly, they lashed out at **one another,** saying, **"You see that you are not doing any good."** Confronted with Jesus' incredible popularity, in spite of their best efforts to silence Him, they began to blame each other. They would have been wiser, as the eminent rabbi Gamaliel would later advise the Sanhedrin, to not have been "found fighting against God" (Acts 5:39), who overrules the plans of men to accomplish His purposes (cf. Gen. 50:20; 1 Kings 12:15; Jer. 10:23; Dan. 4:25–35).

The Pharisees' exclamation, **"Look, the world has gone after Him,"** expresses the depth of their consternation. The statement is hyperbole; the term **world** refers to people in general, not everyone in particular (cf. v. 47; 1:29; 3:17; 4:42; 14:22; 17:9, 21; 18:20; 21:25; Acts 17:6; 19:27). As with Caiaphas's prophecy (11:49–52), John probably intended the Pharisees' statement to be understood as an unwitting prediction of the gospel's spread throughout the world (Matt. 24:14; 26:13; 28:19–20; Luke 24:47; Acts 1:8). Eventually they succeeded in turning the people against Jesus with such hostility as to demand His execution in an act of final rejection by the nation.

ATTENTION BY THE GENTILES

Now there were some Greeks among those who were going up to worship at the feast; these then came to Philip, who was from Bethsaida of Galilee, and began to ask him, saying, "Sir, we wish to see Jesus." Philip came and told Andrew; Andrew and Philip came and told Jesus. (12:20–22)

As if to illustrate in a small and symbolic way the truth of the gospel's spread to the world, John introduced **some Greeks,** who were **among those who were going up to worship at the feast.** They were most likely Gentile proselytes to Judaism (or at least God-fearers [Acts

10:22; 17:4, 17; cf. 8:27]; Gentiles who had abandoned their pagan religion and turned to worship the true God), who had come to Jerusalem to celebrate Passover. Their **wish to see** (i.e., have an audience with) **Jesus** stood in direct contrast to the open hostility of the Jewish religious leaders, as well as the superficial interest of the fickle crowd. Significantly, just days before Jesus' own people would verbalize their final rejection in the cry for His crucifixion, Gentiles sought to know more about Him. Israel's willful rejection would be sealed by divine judgment, as God set the nation aside and turned to the rest of the world (cf. 10:16; 11:52) with the gospel and the commission to be a witnessing people on His behalf.

Israel's rejection had been foreseen in the Old Testament. In Romans 9:25–27 Paul quoted from Hosea and Isaiah to show that Israel will ultimately be restored to God. That necessarily implies her alienation from Him. Later in that same epistle, Paul explicitly stated that Israel has been judicially hardened by God: "For I do not want you, brethren, to be uninformed of this mystery—so that you will not be wise in your own estimation—that a partial hardening has happened to Israel until the fullness of the Gentiles has come in" (Rom. 11:25). God has temporarily set aside the nation aside in favor of the church, which consists of Gentiles and the believing remnant of Israel (cf. Rom. 9:27; 11:5, 17). Thus God's setting aside of the nation as a whole does not preclude individual Jews from being saved (cf. Rom. 10:1). Nor is it a final abandonment of Israel. Paul is clear in affirming the future salvation and restoration of Israel:

> And so all Israel will be saved; just as it is written, "The deliverer will come from Zion, He will remove ungodliness from Jacob." "This is My covenant with them, when I take away their sins." From the standpoint of the gospel they are enemies for your sake, but from the standpoint of God's choice they are beloved for the sake of the fathers; for the gifts and the calling of God are irrevocable. (Rom. 11:26–29)

This is an absolute guarantee based upon God's sovereign election and faithfulness to His irrevocable, unilateral, and unconditional covenants with and messianic kingdom promises to Israel (the Abrahamic covenant, Gen. 12, 15, 17; the Davidic covenant, 2 Sam. 7; and the new covenant, Jer. 31).

The text does not state who these Greeks were, where they were from, why they wanted to see Jesus, or why they **came to Philip.** Perhaps Jesus was then in the part of the temple to which they were not permitted to go (Gentiles could go no farther than the Court of the Gentiles). In that case, they may have seen Philip passing through the Court of the Gentiles, recognized him as one of Jesus' disciples, and approached him. That Philip and Andrew are Greek names is not significant, since many Jews also had Greek names. But John's note that Philip **was from Bethsaida**

of Galilee may suggest that the Greeks singled him out for that reason. **Bethsaida** was near the Gentile region known as the Decapolis (Matt. 4:25; Mark 5:20; 7:31), and they may have been from that region. Further, as a native of Galilee, Philip likely spoke Greek.

Unsure of how to handle these Gentiles, **Philip came and told Andrew** about their request. Perhaps Philip hesitated to take them directly to Jesus because he remembered the Lord's admonition to the Twelve: "Do not go in the way of the Gentiles, and do not enter any city of the Samaritans" (Matt. 10:5), and His declaration that He "was sent only to the lost sheep of the house of Israel" (Matt. 15:24). The Lord was also undoubtedly hard to reach in the crowds, and Philip may have wondered if it was possible or appropriate to interrupt Him. Furthermore, with Jesus' enemies watching His every move, Philip may have surmised that it was dangerous for the Jews to see Him talking with Gentiles. It was natural for him to approach Andrew, since they were both from Bethsaida (John 1:44), and Andrew was more of an insider among the Twelve (along with Peter, James, and John). Together, **Andrew and Philip came and told Jesus** about the Greeks' request for an interview.

The question arises as to why such an open-ended incident is included. Since there is no record that Jesus ever spoke to them, the best that can be said is that they represent Gentile interest—the wave of the near future as the Lord called the church, a new people made of Jews and Gentiles, to be His witness in the world.

THE SAVIOR'S PROVISION FOR AN INVITATION TO ALL

And Jesus answered them, saying, "The hour has come for the Son of Man to be glorified. Truly, truly, I say to you, unless a grain of wheat falls into the earth and dies, it remains alone; but if it dies, it bears much fruit. He who loves his life loses it, and he who hates his life in this world will keep it to life eternal. If anyone serves Me, he must follow Me; and where I am, there My servant will be also; if anyone serves Me, the Father will honor him. (12:23–26)

Jesus' reply appears as a puzzling response to the apostles. It does not appear at first glance to address the Greeks' request for a meeting. In fact, John does not even mention them again (though they may have been in the crowd that heard Jesus speak [v. 29]). The Lord's response is directed neither to Jews or Gentiles, but to all who choose to follow Him. Yet the coming of these Gentiles triggered the Lord's declaration, **"The hour has come for the Son of Man to be glorified"** (cf.

13:31–32; 17:1, 5; Isa. 52:13). Significantly, this is the first time that Jesus spoke of His **hour** as being present; in all previous references in John's gospel, it had not yet arrived (2:4; 7:30; 8:20; cf. 7:6, 8). From this point on the Lord referred to it as imminent (v. 27; 13:1; 16:32; 17:1).

In the context of the triumphal entry, the crowds no doubt interpreted Jesus' words to mean that He was about to overthrow the Romans and set up His earthly kingdom. They would have remembered the prophecy of Daniel 7:13–14 concerning the **Son of Man** (unmistakably a title signifying messiahship to those who knew the prophecy) and the establishing of His kingdom:

> I kept looking in the night visions,
> And behold, with the clouds of heaven
> One like a Son of Man was coming,
> And He came up to the Ancient of Days
> And was presented before Him.
> And to Him was given dominion,
> Glory and a kingdom,
> That all the peoples, nations and men of every language
> Might serve Him.
> His dominion is an everlasting dominion
> Which will not pass away;
> And His kingdom is one
> Which will not be destroyed.

Jesus' next statement, however, shattered any illusions the two men had, turning their dreams of conquest into a vision of death. The Lord introduced it with the solemn phrase **truly, truly, I say to you** (cf. 1:51; 3:3, 5, 11; 5:19, 24, 25; 6:26, 32, 47, 53; 8:51, 58; 10:1, 7; 13:16, 20, 21, 38; 14:12; 16:20, 23; 21:18), underscoring its significance. The Son of Man would be glorified, not by conquering the Romans and immediately establishing His kingdom as they so eagerly anticipated but by dying. Using an agricultural illustration that would have been familiar to His audience (cf. 4:35–38; Mark 4:1–32; Luke 17:6), Jesus told them: **Unless a grain of wheat falls into the earth and dies, it remains alone; but if it dies, it bears much fruit.** The Lord's point was that He would be glorified, but through death and resurrection. There could never be the establishing of His glorious kingdom with all its features promised in the Scriptures without the cross. Anyone who thinks that Jesus came to offer the kingdom to Israel without the cross, and thinks the cross was only a reaction because of Israel's unbelief, is a fool. That is the very word Jesus used to describe that assumption. He said to the disciples on the road to Emmaus,

"O foolish men and slow of heart to believe in all that the prophets have spoken! Was it not necessary for the Christ to suffer these things and to enter into His glory?" Then beginning with Moses and with all the prophets, He explained to them the things concerning Himself in all the Scriptures. (Luke 24:25–27)

Jesus knew that after the cross the gospel would spread far beyond the borders of Israel to all the nations of the world. Thus, He responded to the Greeks' interview request by pointing to His impending death. The Greeks wanted to see Him. But Jesus knew that the only way they could truly enjoy fellowship with Him was through His atoning sacrifice. Just as **a grain of wheat falls into the earth and dies** to produce a rich harvest, so also Christ's death would bear **much fruit** by providing salvation for many, of every tribe and language (Matt. 20:28; 26:28; Heb. 9:28; Rev. 5:9). That fruit would include countless Gentiles like these Greeks who desired to meet with Him.

Regardless of race, every person who through faith in Christ receives eternal life is part of the spiritual harvest that resulted from His death. Jesus' obedience "to the point of death, even death on a cross" (Phil. 2:8) was also the ultimate manifestation of His submission to the Father (John 4:34; 5:19, 30; 6:38) and refusal to seek His own glory (John 5:41; 7:18; 8:50).

Jesus then applied that truth with a general invitation illustrating the heart attitude required of one who receives His gift of salvation. The one who **loves his life** in this world (cf. 1 John 2:15–17), by preferring it over the interests of God's kingdom, ultimately **loses it.** On the other hand, the one **who hates his life in this world** by making Christ, not self, his first priority **will keep it to life eternal.** Hating one's life is a Semitic expression that has the connotation of giving preference to one thing over another (cf. Gen. 29:31; Deut. 21:15 [the word translated "unloved" by the NASB in those verses literally means, "hated"]; Luke 16:13; Rom. 9:13). In this context it refers to preferring Christ over one's family, possessions, goals, plans, desires—even one's own life (Luke 14:27). This call to sell all to buy the pearl, to purchase the treasure (Matt. 13:44–46), is the constant, unmistakable demand of the Gospels.

Jesus repeatedly cautioned those who would follow Him to consider the extreme cost that could entail:

He who loves father or mother more than Me is not worthy of Me; and he who loves son or daughter more than Me is not worthy of Me. And he who does not take his cross and follow after Me is not worthy of Me. He who has found his life will lose it, and he who has lost his life for My sake will find it. (Matt. 10:37–39)

> If anyone comes to Me, and does not hate his own father and mother and wife and children and brothers and sisters, yes, and even his own life, he cannot be My disciple. Whoever does not carry his own cross and come after Me cannot be My disciple. For which one of you, when he wants to build a tower, does not first sit down and calculate the cost to see if he has enough to complete it? Otherwise, when he has laid a foundation and is not able to finish, all who observe it begin to ridicule him, saying, "This man began to build and was not able to finish." Or what king, when he sets out to meet another king in battle, will not first sit down and consider whether he is strong enough with ten thousand men to encounter the one coming against him with twenty thousand? Or else, while the other is still far away, he sends a delegation and asks for terms of peace. So then, none of you can be My disciple who does not give up all his own possessions. (Luke 14:26–33)

In Luke 9:23–24 "He was saying to them all, 'If anyone wishes to come after Me, he must deny himself, and take up his cross daily and follow Me. For whoever wishes to save his life will lose it, but whoever loses his life for My sake, he is the one who will save it'" (cf. 17:33). Therefore "whoever exalts himself shall be humbled; and whoever humbles himself shall be exalted" (Matt. 23:12; cf. Luke 14:11; 18:14). In Luke 9:26 Jesus warned, "Whoever is ashamed of Me and My words, the Son of Man will be ashamed of him when He comes in His glory, and the glory of the Father and of the holy angels." Though it may not be required, being willing to give up everything to follow Christ is what separates true disciples from false professors. Jesus does not identify true saving faith by its perfection but by its affection. Those who truly come to Christ love Him above all else—all sin, all self-righteousness, all relationships, and all self-will.

The one who **serves** Jesus **must follow** Him; "the one who says he abides in Him ought himself to walk in the same manner as He walked" (1 John 2:6; cf. 1:7; 3:24; 4:15; 1 Cor. 11:1; Eph. 5:1; 1 Thess. 1:6). So true salvation is not only affection but also direction. To those who follow, Jesus made two ultimate and glorious promises. First, **where** He is, **there** His **servants will be also.** That is nothing less than a promise of eternal heaven. In John 14:3 Jesus told His disciples, "If I go and prepare a place for you, I will come again and receive you to Myself, that where I am, there you may be also" (cf. 17:24). In contrast, His enemies did not know where He was going (John 8:14; 9:29) and could not go there (John 7:34; 8:21).

The second blessed promise to the one who **serves** Jesus is that **the Father will honor him.** All human honors pale into insignificance compared to the eternal honor God will bestow on those who love and serve His Son. Those who "obtain the salvation which is in Christ Jesus [gain] with it eternal glory" (2 Tim. 2:10). Through the death of Jesus

Christ, God was "bringing many sons to glory" (Heb. 2:10). Though the world may hate those who serve the Lord Jesus Christ (John 15:18–19; 16:2; 17:14; 1 John 3:13; cf. Matt. 10:22; 24:9; Luke 6:22; 21:17), God's promise still holds true:"Those who honor Me I will honor" (1 Sam. 2:30). That promise, originally given to the Jews of the Old Testament, now extends through the cross to all people who truly believe.

Less than a week after Jesus spoke these words, He would die as God's once-for-all perfect and complete sacrifice for the sins of God's chosen. Through that sacrifice, He would abolish the social and cultural barriers that had previously separated Jews from Gentiles. In Ephesians 2:14–16 Paul wrote,

> For He Himself is our peace, who made both groups into one and broke down the barrier of the dividing wall, by abolishing in His flesh the enmity, which is the Law of commandments contained in ordinances, so that in Himself He might make the two into one new man, thus establishing peace, and might reconcile them both in one body to God through the cross, by it having put to death the enmity.

As a result,"the Gentiles are fellow heirs and fellow members of the body, and fellow partakers of the promise in Christ Jesus through the gospel" (Eph. 3:6), and "there is no distinction between Greek and Jew, circumcised and uncircumcised, barbarian, Scythian, slave and freeman, but Christ is all, and in all" (Col. 3:11; cf. Rom. 3:29; 4:11–12; 9:24; 10:11–13; 1 Cor. 12:13; Gal. 3:28).

Out of the tragedy of Israel's rejection of her Messiah came good, in keeping with God's eternal plan."By their [the Jews'] transgression," Paul explained,"salvation has come to the Gentiles" (Rom. 11:11). Israel's loss was the Gentiles' gain, as the blessings of salvation reached out to embrace to them. And, in the future, the salvation of the Gentiles will, in God's perfect time, provoke the Jews to jealousy and to salvation. Paul spells it out:

> I say then, they did not stumble so as to fall, did they? May it never be! But by their transgression salvation has come to the Gentiles, to make them jealous. Now if their transgression is riches for the world and their failure is riches for the Gentiles, how much more will their fulfillment be! But I am speaking to you who are Gentiles. Inasmuch then as I am an apostle of Gentiles, I magnify my ministry, if somehow I might move to jealousy my fellow countrymen and save some of them. For if their rejection is the reconciliation of the world, what will their acceptance be but life from the dead? (Rom. 11:11–15)

This will occur when in God's purpose He acts on the Jews, as described in Zechariah:

> I will pour out on the house of David and on the inhabitants of Jerusalem, the Spirit of grace and of supplication, so that they will look on Me whom they have pierced; and they will mourn for Him, as one mourns for an only son, and they will weep bitterly over Him like the bitter weeping over a firstborn....In that day a fountain will be opened for the house of David and for the inhabitants of Jerusalem, for sin and for impurity. (Zech. 12:10; 13:1)

Facing the Cross
(John 12:27–34)

4

"Now My soul has become troubled; and what shall I say, 'Father, save Me from this hour'? But for this purpose I came to this hour. Father, glorify Your name." Then a voice came out of heaven: "I have both glorified it, and will glorify it again." So the crowd of people who stood by and heard it were saying that it had thundered; others were saying, "An angel has spoken to Him." Jesus answered and said, "This voice has not come for My sake, but for your sakes. Now judgment is upon this world; now the ruler of this world will be cast out. And I, if I am lifted up from the earth, will draw all men to Myself." But He was saying this to indicate the kind of death by which He was to die. The crowd then answered Him, "We have heard out of the Law that the Christ is to remain forever; and how can You say, 'The Son of Man must be lifted up'? Who is this Son of Man?" (12:27–34)

Of all the truths in the Christian faith, the death of Jesus Christ, accompanied by His resurrection, is the most precious. Had He not died, there would be no substitute for sin. Were there no substitute, there would be no offer of salvation. Were there no salvation, there would be no hope. And were there no hope, there would be no future but hell.

It is no wonder, then, that the Christian faith centers on the death, burial, and resurrection of the Lord Jesus Christ. The glorious truth that the Son of God came to earth to die as a sacrifice for sin is the heart of God's redemptive plan. The Bible teaches that His death was predetermined by God in eternity past. Christ is "the Lamb slain from the foundation of the world" (Rev. 13:8 NKJV); His sacrificial death "was foreordained before the foundation of the world" (1 Peter 1:20 NKJV). From start to finish, the Scriptures emphasize the crucial significance of Christ's sacrifice as an offering for the sins of all who would ever believe—a substitutionary offering that satisfied or propitiated the wrath of God on behalf of all the elect (cf. Isa. 53:4–6; 2 Cor. 5:21; 1 Peter 2:24).

First, His death fulfilled prophecy. Though Israel failed to grasp it (1 Cor. 1:23; cf. Luke 24:25–27), the Old Testament clearly taught that the Messiah was to come and to die. According to Daniel's prophecy of the seventy weeks of years, after sixty-nine weeks (seven plus sixty-two), "the Messiah will be cut off" (Dan. 9:25–26). In Zechariah 12:10 God said,

> I will pour out on the house of David and on the inhabitants of Jerusalem, the Spirit of grace and of supplication, so that they will look on Me whom they have pierced; and they will mourn for Him, as one mourns for an only son, and they will weep bitterly over Him like the bitter weeping over a firstborn.

As a result of Messiah's death, "A fountain will be opened for the house of David and for the inhabitants of Jerusalem, for sin and for impurity" (Zech. 13:1).

The most detailed Old Testament prophecy of Messiah's death is in Isaiah 52:13–53:12, which predicts that Messiah would be "pierced through for our transgressions" and "crushed for our iniquities" (53:5); that "by oppression and judgment He [would be] taken away ... cut off out of the land of the living" (53:8); that "His grave [would be] assigned with wicked men, yet He [would be] with a rich man in His death" (53:9); that "the Lord [would be] pleased to crush Him, putting Him to grief," that "He would render Himself as a guilt offering" (53:10); and that God would bless Him "because He poured out Himself to death" (53:12).

The Old Testament also gave specific details concerning Messiah's death—every one of which was fulfilled in the death of Jesus Christ. Psalm 41:9 predicted that He would be betrayed by someone close to Him (cf. John 13:18); Zechariah 11:12–13 gave the exact amount of money His betrayer would receive (cf. Matt. 26:15). Isaiah 50:6 foretold the physical abuse that Christ would suffer at His trial (cf. Matt. 26:67; 27:26; Mark 15:16–19). Psalm 22 graphically depicted Christ's death by crucifixion, a form of execution foreign to the Jews:

> But I am a worm and not a man, a reproach of men and despised by the people. All who see me sneer at me; they separate with the lip, they wag the head, saying, "Commit yourself to the Lord; let Him deliver him; let Him rescue him, because He delights in him." (vv. 6–8; cf. Matt. 27:39–43)

> I am poured out like water, and all my bones are out of joint; my heart is like wax; it is melted within me. My strength is dried up like a potsherd, and my tongue cleaves to my jaws; and You lay me in the dust of death. For dogs have surrounded me; a band of evildoers has encompassed me; they pierced my hands and my feet. I can count all my bones. They look, they stare at me; they divide my garments among them, and for my clothing they cast lots. (vv. 14–18; cf. John 19:23–24, 37)

Psalm 69:21 predicted another detail of Christ's crucifixion: "They also gave me gall for my food and for my thirst they gave me vinegar to drink" (cf. Matt. 27:34, 48). Psalm 31:5 gave the words Christ would speak as He yielded up His life: "Into Your hand I commit my spirit" (cf. Luke 23:46), while Psalm 34:20 accurately depicted the fact that none of His bones would be broken (cf. John 19:32–36).

The Old Testament sacrifices all pointed forward to the final sacrifice made by Jesus Christ. The burnt offering (Lev. 1:3–17; 6:8–13) symbolized His atonement; the sin offering (Lev. 4:1–5, 13; 6:24–30) His propitiation; and the trespass offering (Lev. 5:14–6:7; 7:1–10) the redemption His death provides. That Christ was the fulfillment of the Old Testament sacrifices is also an important theme of the book of Hebrews (cf. 9:11–10:18).

Our Lord prophesied accurately the fulfillment of these predictions and gave even further details about His death before any of it had occurred at the hands of rejecting Jews and ignorant Romans:

> Then He took the twelve aside and said to them, "Behold, we are going up to Jerusalem, and all things which are written through the prophets about the Son of Man will be accomplished. For He will be handed over to the Gentiles, and will be mocked and mistreated and spit upon, and after they have scourged Him, they will kill Him; and the third day He will rise again." But the disciples understood none of these things, and the meaning of this statement was hidden from them, and they did not comprehend the things that were said. (Luke 18:31–34; cf. Matt. 20:17–19; Mark 10:32–34)

Second, the death of Christ is the subject of the New Testament. Roughly one-fifth of the material in the gospel accounts is devoted to the events of the last few days of His life. The death and resurrection of the

Lord Christ is the climactic point to which all previous material concerning His life leads, and from which the Acts and all the Epistles flow.

Third, Christ's death was the chief purpose of the incarnation. "For even the Son of Man did not come to be served, but to serve," Jesus declared, "and to give His life a ransom for many" (Mark 10:45). The writer of Hebrews noted that same truth when he wrote:

> Therefore, since the children share in flesh and blood, He Himself likewise also partook of the same, that through death He might render powerless him who had the power of death, that is, the devil, and might free those who through fear of death were subject to slavery all their lives. (Heb. 2:14–15)

The apostle John said of Jesus, "You know that He appeared in order to take away sins; and in Him there is no sin....The Son of God appeared for this purpose, to destroy the works of the devil" (1 John 3:5, 8). Summarizing the importance of Christ's death in connection with the incarnation, Henry C. Thiessen wrote,

> Christ did not come primarily to set us an example, or to teach us doctrine, but to die for us. His death was not an afterthought or an accident, but the accomplishment of a definite purpose in connection with the incarnation. The incarnation is not an end in itself; it is but a means to an end, and that end is the redemption of the lost through the Lord's death on the Cross. (*Lectures in Systematic Theology* [Grand Rapids: Eerdmans, 1949], 314)

Fourth, Jesus' death was the constant theme of His own teaching. Immediately after Peter's confession that He was "the Christ, the Son of the living God" (Matt. 16:16), "Jesus began to show His disciples that He must go to Jerusalem, and suffer many things from the elders and chief priests and scribes, and be killed, and be raised up on the third day" (v. 21; cf. 17:22–23; 20:17–19; 26:2). To Nicodemus, Jesus declared, "As Moses lifted up the serpent in the wilderness, even so must the Son of Man be lifted up" (John 3:14; cf. 8:28; 18:32); while in John 6:51 He said of Himself, "The bread also which I will give for the life of the world is My flesh." After His resurrection, Jesus chided two of His disciples for failing to grasp the necessity of His death: "O foolish men and slow of heart to believe in all that the prophets have spoken! Was it not necessary for the Christ to suffer these things and to enter into His glory?" (Luke 24:25–26). Shortly afterward He reminded the eleven apostles, "Thus it is written, that the Christ would suffer and rise again from the dead the third day" (v. 46). In Revelation 1:18 the glorified Christ proclaimed, "I was dead, and behold, I am alive forevermore."

Fifth, the death of Jesus Christ was the central theme of apostolic preaching. Paul wrote to the Corinthians, "For I delivered to you as of first importance what I also received, that Christ died for our sins according to the Scriptures" (1 Cor. 15:3). In the first Christian sermon ever preached, Peter declared to Israel, "[Jesus], delivered over by the predetermined plan and foreknowledge of God, you nailed to a cross by the hands of godless men and put Him to death. But God raised Him up again, putting an end to the agony of death, since it was impossible for Him to be held in its power" (Acts 2:23–24). He and his fellow preachers would repeat that theme throughout the early years of the church (Acts 3:13–15, 18; 4:10; 5:30; 7:52; 10:39; 13:27–29; 17:3; 26:23).

Sixth, the New Testament Epistles also instruct in the theology of Christ's death. In Romans 5:8–10 Paul noted that the cross demonstrates God's love for repentant sinners, justifies them, and reconciles them to God:

> But God demonstrates His own love toward us, in that while we were yet sinners, Christ died for us. Much more then, having now been justified by His blood, we shall be saved from the wrath of God through Him. For if while we were enemies we were reconciled to God through the death of His Son, much more, having been reconciled, we shall be saved by His life. (cf. 6:9–10; 8:34; 14:9; 2 Cor. 5:14; Gal. 2:21; Phil. 2:8; Col. 1:22)

Peter declared that "Christ also died for sins once for all, the just for the unjust, so that He might bring us to God, having been put to death in the flesh, but made alive in the spirit" (1 Peter 3:18), while the writer of Hebrews added that "Jesus, because of the suffering of death [was] crowned with glory and honor, so that by the grace of God He might taste death for everyone" (Heb. 2:9; cf. v. 14).

Seventh, the death of Christ is of supreme interest in heaven. At the transfiguration Moses and Elijah, "appearing in glory, were speaking of His departure which He was about to accomplish at Jerusalem" (Luke 9:31). The "sufferings of Christ" are something "into which angels long to look" (1 Peter 1:11–12). At the empty tomb after the resurrection, the two angels said to the women, "[Jesus] is not here, but He has risen. Remember how He spoke to you while He was still in Galilee, saying that the Son of Man must be delivered into the hands of sinful men, and be crucified, and the third day rise again" (Luke 24:6–7). In the apostle John's inspired vision of worship in heaven, "the four living creatures and the twenty-four elders fell down before the Lamb ... And they sang a new song, saying, 'Worthy are You to take the book and to break its seals; for You were slain, and purchased for God with Your blood men from every tribe and tongue and people and nation'" (Rev. 5:8–9). Uncounted thousands of angels echoed that mighty chorus, "saying with a loud voice, 'Worthy is the Lamb that was slain to receive power and riches and wisdom and might and honor and glory and blessing'" (v. 12).

Finally, the death of Christ is the heart of the church's ordinances. Baptism pictures the believer's union with Christ in His death (Rom. 6:1–4; Col. 2:12), and in the Lord's Supper believers remember and "proclaim the Lord's death until He comes" (1 Cor. 11:26; cf. Luke 22:19–20).

In the previous passage (vv. 23–26; cf. the exposition of those verses in chapter 3 of this volume), Jesus spoke of His impending death. In verses 27–34 we see the God-man grappling with the implications of that death. The passage reveals the anguish of Jesus, the answer of the Father, the anticipation of victory, and the abandonment by the people.

THE ANGUISH OF JESUS

"Now My soul has become troubled; and what shall I say, 'Father, save Me from this hour'? But for this purpose I came to this hour. Father, glorify Your name." (12:27–28*a*)

Knowing that His death was central to God's redemptive plan, Jesus "for the joy set before Him endured the cross" (Heb. 12:2). But there was another side to the cross, which the writer of Hebrews alluded to when he spoke in that same verse of the Lord "despising [its] shame." The anticipation of bearing the shame of sin, experiencing God's wrath, and being separated from the Father caused Christ's **soul** to **become troubled. Troubled** translates a form of the verb *tarassō*, which literally means, "to shake," or "to stir up" (cf. John 5:7, where it describes the stirring up of the pool of Bethesda). It is a strong word, used figuratively to speak of severe mental or spiritual agitation; of being disturbed, upset, unsettled, or horrified (cf. Matt. 2:3; 14:26; Luke 1:12; 24:38; John 11:33; 13:21; 14:1, 27; Acts 15:24). The perfect tense of the verb suggests that this was an ongoing struggle for the sinless Savior, as He recoiled in revulsion from the implications of bearing divine judgment for sin (2 Cor. 5:21; 1 Peter 2:24).

Christ did not go to the cross detached, indifferent, without feeling. "The Johannine Jesus is no docetic actor in a drama, about to play a part which he can contemplate dispassionately because it does not really involve himself" (F. F. Bruce, *The Gospel of John* [Grand Rapids: Eerdmans, 1983], 265). In His humanness, Jesus felt all the pain associated with bearing the curse for sin (Gal. 3:13). Because of that pain, "He offered up both prayers and supplications with loud crying and tears to the One able to save Him from death, and He was heard because of His piety" (Heb. 5:7).

Some commentators disconnect the two phrases **what shall I say** and **Father, save Me from this hour,** ending the former with a question mark and making the latter a petition to the Father. It seems better, however, to adopt the NASB punctuation and view the two phrases as expressing one hypothetical thought (cf. Andreas J. Köstenberger, *John*, Baker Exegetical Commentary on the New Testament [Grand Rapids: Baker, 2004], 381). Here, as in Gethsemane, Jesus in His humanity agonized over the unjust, cruel, shameful death that awaited Him.

The Lord voluntarily gave His life, as He declared in John 10:17–18:

> For this reason the Father loves Me, because I lay down My life so that I may take it again. No one has taken it away from Me, but I lay it down on My own initiative. I have authority to lay it down, and I have authority to take it up again.

Rebuking Peter for attacking one of those who came to arrest Him, Jesus said, "Do you think that I cannot appeal to My Father, and He will at once put at My disposal more than twelve legions of angels?" (Matt. 26:53). In other words, Jesus was no victim; He could have called on the Father to rescue Him at any time.

But Christ would not deviate from God's eternal plan of redemption, which called for Him to die as a sacrifice for sin (1 John 2:2; 4:10). Therefore He immediately answered His own hypothetical question in the negative: **But for this purpose I came to this hour.** Jesus would, in view of His own eternal joy, complete the mission the Father had assigned Him (cf. John 4:34; 5:30; 6:38; 18:37; Heb. 10:7).

In keeping with that resolve, Jesus prayed, **"Father, glorify Your name"** (cf. Matt. 6:9; Luke 11:2), essentially the same prayer that He would soon pray in Gethsemane: "Not My will, but Yours be done" (Luke 22:42). Our Lord's request indicates that as He had done perfectly throughout His life (John 7:18; 8:29, 50; 17:4; cf. Luke 2:49), He would **glorify** the **name** of the Father in His death. God receives glory when His attributes are manifested (cf. Ex. 33:18–19; 34:5–8), and nowhere was His magnanimous love for helpless sinners (Rom. 5:8), His holy wrath against sin (Rom. 5:9), His perfect justice (Rom. 3:26), His redeeming grace (Heb. 2:9), His forgiving mercy (Col. 2:13–14), or His infinite wisdom (1 Cor. 1:22–24) more clearly seen than in the substitutionary, propitiatory death of His Son.

THE ANSWER OF THE FATHER

Then a voice came out of heaven: "I have both glorified it, and will glorify it again." So the crowd of people who stood by and

heard it were saying that it had thundered; others were saying, "An angel has spoken to Him." Jesus answered and said, "This voice has not come for My sake, but for your sakes. (12:28b–30)

For the third time in Christ's earthly ministry, the Father's **voice came** audibly **out of heaven.** On the other occasions, at Jesus' baptism (Matt. 3:17) and the transfiguration (Matt. 17:5), the Father's voice affirmed that He was pleased with His Son. Now, as the cross approached, the Father again authenticated Him, thus reassuring the disciples that Christ's impending death in no way signified His disapproval. On the contrary, just as He had already **glorified** His name through Jesus' life and ministry, He would **glorify it again** through His death. Christ's sacrifice on the cross and His resurrection would mark not only the successful completion of the mission the Father had given Him to "seek and to save that which was lost" (Luke 19:10) and to "give His life a ransom for many" (Mark 10:45), but also His return to His full glory in the Father's presence. It was for the latter that Jesus prayed in His High Priestly prayer:

> Father, the hour has come; glorify Your Son, that the Son may glorify You, even as You gave Him authority over all flesh, that to all whom You have given Him, He may give eternal life. This is eternal life, that they may know You, the only true God, and Jesus Christ whom You have sent. I glorified You on the earth, having accomplished the work which You have given Me to do. Now, Father, glorify Me together with Yourself, with the glory which I had with You before the world was. (John 17:1–5)

The Father's audible voice confirming that He had heard and answered Jesus' prayer was obvious to all, though the bewildered **crowd of people who stood by and heard it** were unable to grasp its true significance. Some, seeking to explain the powerful voice as a natural phenomenon, **were saying that it had thundered.** Thunder was often associated in the Old Testament with the voice of God (e.g., Ex. 19:16, 19; 2 Sam. 22:14; Job 37:2–5; 40:9; Pss. 18:13; 29:3), while in Revelation it emanates from heaven (Rev. 4:5; 11:19; 14:2). Others, though they did not understand the words, at least recognized the sound as a voice. They speculated that **an angel** had **spoken to** Jesus (angels frequently spoke to people in the Old Testament; e.g., Gen. 19:1–22; 1 Kings 13:18; 19:5; Dan. 4:13–17; 10:4ff.; Zech. 1:9, 14ff.; 2:3; 3:1; 4:1). Both theories were incorrect —the sound was neither thunder nor angelic speech. Like those who accompanied Paul on the road to Damascus, the crowd heard the sound of the voice, but did not understand the meaning of the words (Acts 9:7; 22:9).

The crowd's inability to understand God's voice illustrates the hard-heartedness that was typical of the people, who had likewise failed to hear the voice of God's word (Mark 4:15) and His Son (John 8:43). The issue is not that God is silent, but that fallen, sinful people are deaf. This reality is the result of sinful fallenness and divine sovereign judgment (cf. Isa. 6:9–10; Matt. 13:14–15; John 12:40; Acts 28:26–27). Therefore "while hearing they do not hear, nor do they understand" (Matt. 13:13). Unbelievers, being dead in sin (Eph. 2:1), members of Satan's kingdom (Col. 1:13), and blinded by him to the truth of the gospel (2 Cor. 4:4) have no capacity for understanding God's Word. As Paul wrote to the Corinthians, "a natural man does not accept the things of the Spirit of God, for they are foolishness to him; and he cannot understand them, because they are spiritually appraised" (1 Cor. 2:14).

The heavenly **voice,** Jesus told the crowd, **has not come for My sake, but for your sakes.** At first glance the Lord's statement seems puzzling. Since the voice came in response to His prayer, "Father, glorify Your name," how could Jesus say that it was not for His sake? In keeping with Semitic idiom (cf. R. V. G. Tasker, *The Gospel According to St. John*, The Tyndale New Testament Commentaries [Grand Rapids: Eerdmans, 1975], 152–53), the meaning appears to be that the voice did not come exclusively for Jesus' sake (since He did not need to hear the Father's audible voice to know that His prayer was answered [cf. 11:42]). The voice came to strengthen the faith of those standing nearby (cf. similar expressions in v. 44; 4:21). In particular,

> this miraculous reply was for the disciples, that they might hear directly and with their own ears both that the Father had, indeed, answered Jesus and what that answer was. It was another attestation of the Father, of the clearest and the strongest kind, that Jesus was his well-beloved Son. (R. C. H. Lenski, *The Interpretation of St. John's Gospel* [repr.; Peabody, Mass.: Hendrickson, 1998], 873)

Even though the bystanders did not understand the words, the Father's audible answer to Jesus' prayer still conveyed to them divine affirmation of the Son.

THE ANTICIPATION OF VICTORY

Now judgment is upon this world; now the ruler of this world will be cast out. And I, if I am lifted up from the earth, will draw all men to Myself." But He was saying this to indicate the kind of death by which He was to die. (12:31–33)

As He anticipated the triumph of the cross, Jesus rejoiced in three significant victories it would accomplish. First, His death would bring **judgment . . . upon this world.** As it does frequently in John's writings, the term **world** designates the evil, satanic system and all who are in it, who are in rebellion against God (cf. John 7:7; 8:23, 44; 14:17; 15:18–19; 17:9, 14–16; 1 John 2:15–17; 3:13; 4:4–5; 5:4–5, 19). The world's apparent victory over Christ at the cross was in reality its own death knell; the doom of the unbelieving **world** was sealed by its rejection of Jesus Christ (cf. Acts 17:31). Though Jesus came to save, not to judge (v. 47; 3:17; cf. Luke 19:10), those who reject Him through all of history since then condemn themselves to the eternal judgment of hell (3:18, 36; 9:39; 12:48).

Not only would Christ's death bring judgment on the evil world system, but also at the same time on its wicked **ruler,** Satan (cf. 14:30; 16:11; Luke 4:5–6; 2 Cor. 4:4; Eph. 2:2; 1 John 5:19). Scripture reveals several times when Satan **will be cast out.** Here he is cast out in the sense that he loses his authority and influence. If his domain (the world) is judged and destroyed, he will have nothing left to rule. During the tribulation Satan will be permanently cast out of heaven, to which he has had access to accuse believers (Rev. 12:10). At the end of the tribulation, Satan will be cast into the bottomless pit for the duration of the millennial kingdom (Rev. 20:1–3). Finally, at the end of the millennium, Satan will be cast into the lake of fire, where he will be punished for eternity (Rev. 20:10). As was the case with the world, Satan's apparent victory at the cross in reality marked his utter defeat. In the words of the writer of Hebrews, "through [His] death [Jesus would] render powerless him who had the power of death, that is, the devil" (Heb. 2:14; cf. 1 Cor. 15:25–26; Rev. 12:11).

In contrast to the first two, the final victory accomplished at the cross is couched in positive terms. When He is **lifted up from the earth** (a reference to His crucifixion, which everyone understood as John's footnote in verse 33, **But He was saying this to indicate the kind of death by which He was to die,** indicates [cf. John 3:14; 8:28]), Jesus declared that He **will,** by means of that sacrifice for sin, **draw all men to** Himself. That does not, of course, mean that **all** humanity will be redeemed, as some universalists think. The phrase **all men** refers specifically to those (the "much fruit" of 12:24; cf. 6:44) who will come. The **all men** are those who will be drawn to salvation from all types and classes of people. The phrase also stresses that all who are saved are saved by believing in the work of Christ on the cross. There is no access to God apart from the cross, because only through Christ's death is sin satisfactorily atoned for (Matt. 20:28; Rom. 3:24–25; Heb. 9:12; 10:4–12; 1 Peter 1:18–19; 2:24; 3:18; 1 John 2:2; 4:10; Rev. 5:9) and divine forgiveness granted (Matt. 26:28; Eph. 1:7; Col. 1:13–14).

The Abandonment by the People

The crowd then answered Him, "We have heard out of the Law that the Christ is to remain forever; and how can You say, 'The Son of Man must be lifted up'? Who is this Son of Man?" (12:34)

Unable to accept the truth that the Messiah was to die, **the crowd then answered** Jesus, **"We have heard out of the Law** (a reference to the entire Old Testament, not just the Pentateuch) **that the Christ is to remain forever; and how can You say, 'The Son of Man must be lifted up'?"** Based on such passages as Isaiah 9:7, Ezekiel 37:25, and especially Daniel 7:13 where Messiah is called the "Son of Man" (cf. Dan. 2:44), they assumed that He would come to defeat all God's enemies and establish an everlasting kingdom of peace and righteousness. That, of course, is exactly what the Lord Jesus Christ will do at His second coming. The crowd, however, overlooked the clear teaching of the Old Testament that at His first advent Messiah would come to die as a sacrifice for sins (see the discussion of this point earlier in this chapter). In light of that misunderstanding, the crowd's mocking question, **"Who is this Son of Man?"** (i.e., "What kind of a Son of Man are you talking about?") can only signal their belief that Jesus was not him. They could not reconcile Jesus' prediction of His death (12:23–26) with their belief that the Messiah was to be a triumphant conqueror (cf. John 6:14–15).

Resisting all temptation to turn aside (especially in Gethsemane) from the agony of the cross, Jesus completed the mission for which He had come into the world—to die for God (cf. Heb. 10:5–9). He did so in several ways. First, Christ's death was a sacrifice to God, paying the price for sinners' violation of His holy law (Isa. 53:10; Heb. 7:27; 9:26, 28; 10:10, 19). Second, Christ's death was an act of submission to God (Rom. 5:19; Phil. 2:8; Heb. 5:8; 10:5–10). Third, Christ's death was a substitution offered to God on behalf of sinners (Isa. 53:4–6, 11–12; 2 Cor. 5:14, 21; Heb. 9:28; 1 Peter 2:24). Fourth, Christ's death was a satisfaction to end God's wrath against sin on behalf of the elect (Rom. 3:25; Heb. 2:17; 1 John 2:2; 4:10). As a result, there is no longer any condemnation for believers (Rom. 8:1; cf. John 5:24). Finally, Christ's death redeemed believers to God (Matt. 20:28; Acts 20:28; Rom. 3:24; 1 Cor. 1:30; Gal. 3:13; Eph. 1:7; Col. 1:14; 1 Tim. 2:6; Titus 2:14; Heb. 9:12; 1 Peter 1:18–19) and reconciled them to God (Rom. 5:10–11; 2 Cor. 5:18–20; Eph. 2:16; Col. 1:20–22) as His sons (Matt. 5:9, 45; John 12:36; Rom. 8:14–15, 19; 2 Cor. 6:18; Gal. 3:26; 4:5–6; Eph. 1:5; Heb. 12:5–8).

Thus, as the writer of Hebrews declares, "It was fitting for Him, for whom are all things, and through whom are all things, in bringing many sons to glory, to perfect the author of their salvation through sufferings" (Heb. 2:10). Because Jesus Christ endured the death that God required for sin, believers will enjoy the everlasting glory of eternal life.

The Day the Light Went Out
(John 12:35–50)

5

So Jesus said to them, "For a little while longer the Light is among you. Walk while you have the Light, so that darkness will not overtake you; he who walks in the darkness does not know where he goes. While you have the Light, believe in the Light, so that you may become sons of Light." These things Jesus spoke, and He went away and hid Himself from them. But though He had performed so many signs before them, yet they were not believing in Him. This was to fulfill the word of Isaiah the prophet which he spoke: "Lord, who has believed our report? And to whom has the arm of the Lord been revealed?" For this reason they could not believe, for Isaiah said again, "He has blinded their eyes and He hardened their heart, so that they would not see with their eyes and perceive with their heart, and be converted and I heal them." These things Isaiah said because he saw His glory, and he spoke of Him. Nevertheless many even of the rulers believed in Him, but because of the Pharisees they were not confessing Him, for fear that they would be put out of the synagogue; for they loved the approval of men rather than the approval of God. And Jesus cried out and said, "He who believes in Me, does not believe in Me but in Him who sent Me.

He who sees Me sees the One who sent Me. I have come as Light into the world, so that everyone who believes in Me will not remain in darkness. If anyone hears My sayings and does not keep them, I do not judge him; for I did not come to judge the world, but to save the world. He who rejects Me and does not receive My sayings, has one who judges him; the word I spoke is what will judge him at the last day. For I did not speak on My own initiative, but the Father Himself who sent Me has given Me a commandment as to what to say and what to speak. I know that His commandment is eternal life; therefore the things I speak, I speak just as the Father has told Me." (12:35–50)

Though human beings often lose control of their emotions, God never does. This is most clearly seen in His patience toward the wicked who continually offend His holiness. God could rightfully destroy all sinners at the very first moment they transgress His law and at all subsequent transgressions. Instead, He patiently bears with them, extending to them the hope of salvation. Even when He has been wronged, His patience is infinitely perfect. The godly Puritan preacher Stephen Charnock described God's forbearance with these words:

> Men that are great in the world are quick in passions, and are not so ready to forgive an injury, or bear with an offender, as one of a meaner rank. It is a want [lack] of a power over a man's self that makes him do unbecoming things upon a provocation. A prince that can bridle his passion, is a king over himself, as well as over his subjects. God is slow to anger, *because* [He is] great in power: he hath no less power over himself than over his creatures. (*The Existence and Attributes of God* [repr.; Grand Rapids: Baker, 1979], 2:474. Emphasis added.)

Because God is "compassionate and gracious" (Ps. 103:8; cf. 111:4; 112:4; 116:5; Ex. 34:6; 2 Chron. 30:9; Neh. 9:17, 31; Joel 2:13; Jonah 4:2), He is "slow to anger" (Ps. 103:8; cf. 86:15; 145:8; Ex. 34:6; Num. 14:18; Neh. 9:17; Joel 2:13; Jonah 4:2; Nah. 1:3). God's slowness to anger, or patience, manifests itself primarily in His delaying judgment on sin; He is "patient . . . not wishing for any to perish but for all to come to repentance" (2 Peter 3:9), because "the patience of our Lord [is] salvation" (v. 15). God's continued patience has caused godly saints throughout the centuries to marvel at His long-suffering. In the words of Arthur W. Pink:

> How wondrous is God's patience with the world today. On every side people are sinning with a high hand. The Divine law is trampled under foot and God Himself openly despised. It is truly amazing that He does not instantly strike dead those who so brazenly defy Him. Why does He not suddenly cut off the haughty infidel and blatant blasphemer, as He

did Ananias and Sapphira? Why does He not cause the earth to open its mouth and devour the persecutors of His people, so that, like Dathan and Abiram, they shall go down alive into the Pit? And what of apostate Christendom, where every possible form of sin is now tolerated and practiced under cover of the holy name of Christ? Why does not the righteous wrath of Heaven make an end of such abominations? Only one answer is possible: because God bears with "much longsuffering the vessels of wrath fitted to destruction." (Arthur W. Pink, *The Attributes of God* [Grand Rapids: Baker, 1975], 64)

God initially manifested His patience in the garden of Eden. When Adam and Even first sinned, He could have ended the human race by immediately judging those two. Instead, He spared them, even allowing Adam to live for 930 years (Gen. 5:5). This established His long pattern with sinners.

Before His judgment on all humanity by the flood, "the Lord saw that the wickedness of man was great on the earth, and that every intent of the thoughts of his heart was only evil continually" (Gen. 6:5). The human race had become so evil that "the Lord was sorry that He had made man on the earth, and He was grieved in His heart" (6:6) and said, "I will blot out man whom I have created from the face of the land, from man to animals to creeping things and to birds of the sky; for I am sorry that I have made them" (v. 6:7). Yet even in the face of that extreme provocation, God still delayed His judgment. He declared, "My Spirit shall not strive with man forever, because he also is flesh; nevertheless his days shall be one hundred and twenty years" (6:3). That was the period "when the patience of God kept waiting in the days of Noah" (1 Peter 3:20), while Noah continually preached of God's righteousness, calling people to recognize their sin and repent in trust and submission to God (2 Peter 2:5).

Throughout human history, God has shown remarkable tolerance with entire nations of people who rejected Him. In Genesis 15:16 He told Abraham that there would be a lengthy delay in His judgment of the Canaanites because "the iniquity of the Amorite is not yet complete." Similarly, God delayed the judgment on Assyria prophesied by Nahum for a generation or more. "In the generations gone by," Paul told the pagans at Lystra, "[God] permitted all the nations to go their own ways; and yet He did not leave Himself without witness, in that He did good and gave you rains from heaven and fruitful seasons, satisfying your hearts with food and gladness" (Acts 14:16–17). The apostle declared to the Greek philosophers in Athens that God had "overlooked the times of ignorance" (Acts 17:30); that is, He had withheld the full measure of His judgment for a certain period of time (cf. Rom. 3:25).

More than any other nation, Israel experienced God's patience. Throughout their history, the people of Israel were, as Stephen characterized the Sanhedrin, "stiff-necked and uncircumcised in heart and ears [and] always resisting the Holy Spirit" (Acts 7:51; cf. Deut. 10:16; 2 Kings 17:14; 2 Chron. 30:8; Neh. 9:29; Jer. 7:26; 17:23; 19:15). In Jeremiah God offered this rebuke of Israel: "This has been your practice from your youth, that you have not obeyed My voice.... Indeed the sons of Israel and the sons of Judah have been doing only evil in My sight from their youth; for the sons of Israel have been only provoking Me to anger by the work of their hands" (Jer. 22:21; 32:30). Yet despite Israel's continual provocation, God, "being compassionate, forgave their iniquity and did not destroy them; and often He restrained His anger and did not arouse all His wrath" (Ps. 78:38). "For the sake of My name I delay My wrath," God told wayward Israel, "and for My praise I restrain it for you, in order not to cut you off" (Isa. 48:9; cf. 57:11). In Luke 13:6–9 Jesus told a parable illustrating God's patience toward His people:

> A man had a fig tree which had been planted in his vineyard; and he came looking for fruit on it and did not find any. And he said to the vineyard-keeper, "Behold, for three years I have come looking for fruit on this fig tree without finding any. Cut it down! Why does it even use up the ground?" And he answered and said to him, "Let it alone, sir, for this year too, until I dig around it and put in fertilizer; and if it bears fruit next year, fine; but if not, cut it down."

God also is patient with individual sinners. In Romans 2:4 Paul asked, "Do you think lightly of the riches of His kindness and tolerance and patience, not knowing that the kindness of God leads you to repentance?" Later in that same epistle, he wrote, "God, although willing to demonstrate His wrath and to make His power known, endured with much patience vessels of wrath prepared for destruction" (Rom. 9:22). The apostle's words to Timothy sum up his spiritual autobiography: "Yet for this reason I found mercy, so that in me as the foremost, Jesus Christ might demonstrate His perfect patience as an example for those who would believe in Him for eternal life" (1 Tim. 1:16). Peter reminded his readers that God is "patient toward [lost sinners], not wishing for any to perish but for all to come to repentance" (2 Peter 3:9; cf. Ezek. 18:23).

It is because of His patience that He has not yet returned in final judgment. As the renowned preacher Charles Spurgeon stated in a sermon on God's long-suffering:

> We have waited for [our Lord's] footfall at the dead of night, and looked out for him through the gates of the morning, and expected him in the heat of the day, and reckoned that he might come ere yet another sun went down; but he is not here! He waits. He waits very, very long. Will he not come?

Longsuffering is that which keeps him from coming. He is bearing with men. Not yet the thunderbolt! Not yet the riven heavens and the reeling earth! Not yet the great white throne, and the day of judgment; for he is very pitiful, and beareth long with men! Even to the cries of his own elect, who cry day and night unto him—he is not in haste to answer,—for he is very patient, slow to anger, and plenteous in mercy. ("God's Longsuffering: An Appeal to Conscience," in *The Metropolitan Tabernacle Pulpit* [Pasadena, Tex.: Pilgrim Publications, 1985], 33:678)

Nonetheless, the fact that God is slow to anger does not mean that He is incapable of anger, even if sinners may think otherwise. "Because the sentence against an evil deed is not executed quickly," wrote Solomon, "therefore the hearts of the sons of men among them are given fully to do evil" (Eccl. 8:11). Second Chronicles 36:15 describes God's patience with rebellious Israel: "The Lord, the God of their fathers, sent word to them again and again by His messengers, because He had compassion on His people and on His dwelling place." But eventually God's patience ended. When Israel "continually mocked the messengers of God, despised His words and scoffed at His prophets . . . the wrath of the Lord arose against His people, until there was no remedy" (v. 16; cf. Neh. 9:30; Jer. 44:22). God's patience with sinners will eventually run out, which serves as a sobering warning for those who would abuse it.

The time of [God's] patience will have an end. . . . Though he be patient with most, yet he is not in the same degree with all; every sinner hath his time of sinning, beyond which he shall proceed no further . . . and for particular persons, the time of life, whether shorter or longer, is the only time of long-suffering . . . the time of patience ends with the first moment of the soul's departure from the body. This [present] time only is the "day of salvation." (Charnock, *The Existence and Attributes of God,* 2:509, 510, 511)

Verses 35–50, which record Christ's final appeal to Israel, are a summary of His entire public ministry. For more than three years, Jesus had presented Himself to the people of Israel as the Messiah and proclaimed the gospel of the kingdom. He had substantiated His claims by teaching with power and authority unrivaled by anyone before Him (Matt. 7:28–29; Mark 1:22; Luke 4:32; John 7:46). He had also performed miraculous works that no one else had ever done (John 15:24). Even so, throughout His ministry Jesus had faced unbelief, hatred, hostility, and rejection, particularly from Israel's religious leaders. That unbelief and rejection would soon reach its zenith at the cross.

This poignant passage records the Lord's final call to belief, uncovers the fatal causes of unbelief, and lays out the fateful consequences of both belief and unbelief.

THE FINAL CALL TO BELIEF

So Jesus said to them, "For a little while longer the Light is among you. Walk while you have the Light, so that darkness will not overtake you; he who walks in the darkness does not know where he goes. While you have the Light, believe in the Light, so that you may become sons of Light." These things Jesus spoke, and He went away and hid Himself from them. (12:35–36)

At the triumphal entry, the momentarily frenzied crowds had hailed Jesus as the Messiah and King. But they viewed the Messiah as an earthly king, a powerful military leader who would overthrow the Romans (cf. chapters. 2 and 3 of this volume). Jesus, however, rebuffed their attempts to force Him into the role of political and military deliverer (John 6:14–15). And when He began to speak of dying (John 12:24), the people abandoned Him altogether; they were unable to grasp the concept of a murdered Messiah (which even His disciples were slow to accept; cf. Matt. 16:21–23). Their hopes were shattered and they rendered their final verdict on Jesus: that He was an impostor and not the real Son of Man (cf. the exposition of 12:34 in the previous chapter of this volume).

But despite their rejection, in His persistent and intense love for them, Jesus extended to them one final invitation to acknowledge Him as Lord and Savior. That invitation not only expressed the compassionate cry of His heart for Israel's salvation (cf. Matt. 23:37; Luke 13:34; 19:41), but it also delivered a warning (cf. Matt. 23:38–39; Luke 13:35; 19:42–44). Speaking of His impending death, Jesus cautioned His hearers that it would be only **for a little while longer** that **the Light,** a reference to Himself as the Light of the World (cf. v. 46; 1:4–9; 3:19–21; 8:12; 9:5), would be **among** them. Paul described Christ as "the Light of the knowledge of the glory of God" shining in the darkness (2 Cor. 4:6). Soon He would be gone, and the people to whom He came would be plunged back into darkness (cf. 2 Cor. 3:14–16).

Jesus repeatedly used the phrase **a little while** to emphasize the brevity of His remaining time on earth. Earlier He had said to the unbelieving Jews, "For a little while longer I am with you, then I go to Him who sent Me" (7:33). Jesus told the disciples in the upper room the night before His death, "Little children, I am with you a little while longer. You will seek Me; and as I said to the Jews, now I also say to you, 'Where I am going, you cannot come'" (13:33), and, "A little while, and you will no longer see Me; and again a little while, and you will see Me" (16:16). The Lord knew that only a short time remained for people to hear and respond to Him. The "day of salvation" (2 Cor. 6:2) was waning and the darkness was fast approaching. Those who failed to appropriate the light would lose it.

Therefore Jesus exhorted His hearers to **walk while** they still had **the Light** with them **so that darkness** would **not overtake** them, because **he who walks in the darkness does not know where he goes** (cf. 1 John 2:11). In an era before electric lights, people traveled only during the daylight hours, when they could see clearly and walk safely. The Lord likened those who failed to heed His warning to travelers caught out after nightfall, lost in the pitch blackness of a starless, moonless night. The only way for them to avoid being lost in spiritual darkness was, **while** they still had **the Light,** to **believe in the Light.** The glorious promise to those who do is **that** they will **become sons of Light** (cf. 1 Thess. 5:5; 1 John 1:5–7), and radiate the light of God's glory in Christ into a dark world (Matt. 5:14–16; Eph. 5:8; Phil. 2:15).

The sobering truth is that when sinners persistently reject Him, God may ultimately remove His grace and judge them. Nehemiah records God's extraordinary patience with Israel: "You bore with them for many years, and admonished them by Your Spirit through Your prophets" (9:30*a*). But when "they would not give ear … [God] gave them into the hand of the peoples of the lands" (9:30*b;* cf. Judg. 10:13; 2 Kings 17:13–18; 2 Chron. 15:2; 24:20). In Psalm 81:11–12 God lamented, "My people did not listen to My voice, and Israel did not obey Me. So I gave them over to the stubbornness of their heart, to walk in their own devices." Hosea records God's shocking statement, "Ephraim (a symbolic name for the northern kingdom [Israel]) is joined to idols; let him alone" (Hos. 4:17). Because of Israel's hard-hearted rejection of Him, God abandoned the people to the consequences of their sin. When Israel "rebelled and grieved His Holy Spirit," God eventually "turned Himself to become their enemy, He fought against them" (Isa. 63:10). Three times in Romans 1:18–32, Paul spoke of God's wrathful judgment in abandoning sinners to the consequences of their sin (vv. 24, 26, 28). Hebrews 10:26–27 warns that for those who "go on sinning willfully [refusing to repent] after receiving the knowledge of the truth, there no longer remains a sacrifice for sins, but a terrifying expectation of judgment and the fury of a fire which will consume the adversaries."

Those who reject Jesus Christ, never embracing Him in saving faith, will inevitably face God's vengeance, wrath, and judgment in eternal punishment.

John's statement, **these things Jesus spoke, and He went away and hid Himself from them,** marks the tragic climax of the Lord's public ministry to Israel. The sun of opportunity had set, God's patience was at an end, and Jesus' solemn warnings, "I go away, and you will seek Me, and will die in your sin; where I am going, you cannot come" (John 8:21) and, "You will not see Me until you say, 'Blessed is He who comes in the name of the Lord!'" (Matt. 23:39) were about to be realized. Unlike earlier incidents (5:13; 8:59; 10:39; 11:54; Luke 4:30), this time "by his withdrawal, his self-conscious hiding from the people, [Jesus] is acting out the judicial warning he has just pronounced" (D. A. Carson, *The Gospel According to John,* The Pillar New Testament Commentary (Grand Rapids: Eerdmans, 1991), 447).

Despite massive and incontrovertible evidence, the Jewish people had concluded that Jesus was not the Messiah and should be executed as an impostor. In the next section, John gives the biblical explanation for Israel's shocking rejection of Jesus Christ, showing how it could be that "those who were His own did not receive Him" (1:11).

The Fatal Causes of Unbelief

But though He had performed so many signs before them, yet they were not believing in Him. This was to fulfill the word of Isaiah the prophet which he spoke: "Lord, who has believed our report? And to whom has the arm of the Lord been revealed?" For this reason they could not believe, for Isaiah said again, "He has blinded their eyes and He hardened their heart, so that they would not see with their eyes and perceive with their heart, and be converted and I heal them." These things Isaiah said because he saw His glory, and he spoke of Him. Nevertheless many even of the rulers believed in Him, but because of the Pharisees they were not confessing Him, for fear that they would be put out of the synagogue; for they loved the approval of men rather than the approval of God. (12:37–43)

Skeptics sometimes argue that Israel's rejection of Jesus Christ casts doubt on the truth of His claims. It seems incredible to them that most of the Jewish people, especially the religious leaders who were steeped in the text of the Old Testament, could have missed the obvious implications of His miracles. Such a shortsighted view, however, ignores the power of sin (John 3:19–20) and Satan (John 8:44; 2 Cor. 4:4) to blind people to the truth. Thus, as John reminds his readers, **though** Jesus **had performed so many signs before** the Jewish people, **yet they were not believing in Him.** Jesus' miracles were unmistakably legitimate, and left no excuse for Israel's unbelief; the people had hardened their hearts against the truth. Far from calling into question the veracity of the evidence, such unbelief revealed the depth of their depravity (1 Cor. 2:14). Significantly, though they attributed His miracles to satanic power (Matt. 12:24), Jesus' opponents—unlike modern skeptics—never denied their reality (cf. John 11:47). The fact of unbelief in the face of such irrefutable and powerful evidence makes clear the limitations of apologetics. While evidences can be given for gospel truth, the response of the sinner is not limited to the mind and human reason—salvation requires a regenerated heart, the work of the Holy Spirit (see the discussion of John 3:1ff. in *John 1–11*, The MacArthur New Testament Commentary [Chicago: Moody, 2006], chaps. 8–9).

John lists two causes for Israel's unbelief, one divine and the other human. Taken together, they illustrate the interface between divine sovereignty and human responsibility.

Israel's unbelief and rejection of Jesus Christ was not, of course, outside of God's plan. On the contrary, it **was to fulfill the word of Isaiah the prophet** as the purpose clause (introduced by the Greek conjunction *hina*) that begins verse 38. Predicting Israel's unbelief, Isaiah wrote in Isaiah 53:1 (NKJV), **Lord, who has believed our report?** The answer is, very few (cf. Matt. 7:13–14; Luke 13:23–24). Incredibly, that was true even though **the arm of the Lord** was **revealed** to the people of Israel through the miracles Christ performed. The **reason they could not believe,** as **Isaiah said again** (Isa. 6:10), was that God had **blinded their eyes and . . . hardened their heart, so that they would not see with their eyes and perceive with their heart, and be converted and** [have God] **heal them** (cf. Rom. 9:18). Israel's rejection of Christ was not merely foreseen, it was by God's sovereign design (cf. Rom. 9–11); it was a judgment act on His part.

In His sovereign grace, God has brought good out of that rejection. As Paul wrote in Romans 11:11, it was "by [Israel's] transgression [that] salvation has come to the Gentiles." God's plans cannot be thwarted by anything sinful people can do (Gen. 50:20 [cf. 45:5]; Ps. 76:10).

Before turning to the second cause of Israel's unbelief, John inserted the important footnote, **These things Isaiah said because he saw His glory, and he spoke of Him.** It reveals several important truths. First, Isaiah 6:10, which John had just quoted, referred to Isaiah's vision of God (cf. Isa. 6:5). That the apostle applied it to Jesus Christ clearly testifies to His deity. John's statement also shows that Israel's prophesied unbelief was specifically unbelief in Christ. Further, it reveals that Jesus, in keeping with His role as judge (cf. John 5:22, 27, 30; 9:39), is the one who judicially hardened Israel. Finally John, inspired by the Holy Spirit, attributed both quotes (6:10; 53:1) to Isaiah. That makes it clear that he was the author of the entire book (as opposed to modern critical scholarship, which attributes Isaiah to multiple authors).

Israel's rejection of Jesus Christ was the culmination of years of rebellion, misused privileges, and forsaking of divine truth. The terrible result was that when the truth came in the person of Jesus Christ, many could not believe. Thinking they could see, they were in reality spiritually blind (cf. Matt. 15:14; 23:16, 17, 19, 24, 26; John 9:40–41).

But God's sovereign, judicial hardening of Israel did not negate the culpability of those who refused to believe in Christ. As Leon Morris notes, "When John quotes 'he hath blinded their eyes . . .' he does not mean that the blinding takes place without the will, or against the will of these people....These men chose evil. It was their own deliberate choice, their own fault. Make no mistake about that" (*The Gospel According to John*, The New International Commentary on the New Testament [Grand Rapids: Eerdmans, 1979], 604). D. A. Carson adds, "God's judicial hardening is not presented as the capricious manipulation of an arbitrary potentate cursing morally neutral or even morally pure beings, but as a holy condemnation of a guilty people who are condemned to do and be what they themselves have chosen" (*John*, 448–49).

It is a sobering reality that those who persistently harden their hearts against God may find themselves hardened by Him. The historical record of God's dealings with Pharaoh illustrates that principle, noting ten times that he hardened his own heart (Ex. 7:13, 14, 22; 8:15, 19, 32; 9:7, 34, 35; 13:15) and ten times that God hardened his heart (Ex. 4:21; 7:3; 9:12; 10:1, 20, 27; 11:10; 14:4, 8, 17). Isaiah, in one of the clearest evangelistic texts in the Old Testament, cried out, "Seek the Lord *while He may be found*; call upon Him *while He is near*" (Isa. 55:6; emphasis added.). God hardened the hearts of those who refused to believe in Jesus (v. 40) so that they could not believe (v. 39).

The personal choice involved in rejecting Jesus Christ is illustrated by **the rulers** who **believed in Him.** Their faith was inadequate, irresolute, and spurious, as John's note that **because of the Pharisees they were not confessing Him** (cf. Matt. 10:33), **for fear that they would be put out of the synagogue,** indicates. The religious authorities had already decreed that dreaded punishment, which cut a person off from Jewish religious and social life, for anyone who confessed Jesus as the Messiah (9:22; cf. 7:13). That **they loved the approval of men rather than the approval of God** gives further evidence that these **rulers** possessed no more than a superficial religion. "How can you believe," Jesus scathingly asked the religious leaders, "when you receive glory from one another and you do not seek the glory that is from the one and only God?" (5:44). Tragically, they loved their self-exalting religion and their prestigious position in the synagogue and the Sanhedrin so much that they refused Christ. Such love for the world showed that they did not love God (James 4:4; 1 John 2:15). "For what will it profit a man if he gains the whole world and forfeits his soul?" Jesus asked, "Or what will a man give in exchange for his soul?" (Matt. 16:26). In contrast, Jesus promised true believers, "If anyone serves Me, he must follow Me; and where I am, there My servant will be also; if anyone serves Me, the Father will honor him" (John 12:26). The parable of the Pharisee and the tax collector shows how far the self-righteous were from God and true righteousness (cf. Luke 18:9–14).

THE FATEFUL CONSEQUENCES OF BELIEF AND UNBELIEF

And Jesus cried out and said, "He who believes in Me, does not believe in Me but in Him who sent Me. He who sees Me sees the One who sent Me. I have come as Light into the world, so that everyone who believes in Me will not remain in darkness. If anyone hears My sayings and does not keep them, I do not judge him; for I did not come to judge the world, but to save the world. He who rejects Me and does not receive My sayings, has one who judges him; the word I spoke is what will judge him at the last day. For I did not speak on My own initiative, but the Father Himself who sent Me has given Me a commandment as to what to say and what to speak. I know that His commandment is eternal life; therefore the things I speak, I speak just as the Father has told Me." (12:44–50)

Since Jesus had already withdrawn (v. 36), the words recorded in verses 44–50 were not spoken on this occasion. John included them here to summarize Christ's public ministry to Israel, which had ended. The truths they contain emphasize the importance of the Savior's ministry and the fatal error of refusing to believe in Him. They also reveal several consequences of both belief and unbelief.

Jesus' statement, **He who believes in Me, does not believe in Me but in Him who sent Me,** is reminiscent of similar statements in 5:24; 8:19; and 10:38 (cf. 13:20; 14:6). It emphasizes the impossibility of believing in the Father apart from believing in Jesus Christ. In the upper room Discourse, Jesus reiterated the declaration, **He who sees Me sees the One who sent Me** in the familiar words, "He who has seen Me has seen the Father" (John 14:9; cf. 15:24; Col. 1:15; Heb. 1:3). These first two sayings reveal that those who believe in Christ enjoy a personal knowledge of both the Father and the Son (cf. John 14:23).

Jesus taught the truth that He came **as Light into the world, so that everyone who believes in** Him **will not remain in darkness** in such passages as John 8:12; 9:5; and 12:35–36. Those who believe in Him are "rescued … from the domain of darkness, and transferred … to the kingdom of His beloved Son" (Col. 1:13). As noted in the discussion of verses 35 and 36 above, they become "sons of Light."

The Lord's words **If anyone hears My sayings and does not keep them** shift the focus from the blessings of belief to the dire consequences of unbelief. Failure to obey Jesus Christ characterizes unbelievers (3:36; cf. Rom. 2:8; 11:30–32; 15:31; 2 Thess. 1:8; Titus 1:16; 3:3; 1 Peter 4:17); thus Paul describes them as "sons of disobedience" (Eph. 2:2; 5:6; Col. 3:6). At His first coming, Jesus did **not judge** such people, since He **did not come to judge the world, but to save the world** (cf. 3:17; Luke 9:56; 19:10; 1 Tim. 1:16; 1 John 4:14). Yet Jesus will judge unrepentant sinners in the future (Acts 17:31; Rom. 2:16; cf. Heb. 9:27; Rev. 20:11–15). The Lord's point here is that the one **who rejects** Him **and does not receive** His **sayings, has one who judges him; the word** Jesus **spoke is what will judge him at the last day.** Those who reject the truth Jesus taught condemn themselves (cf. 8:37, 43, 47; 14:24; Matt. 7:24–27; 13:19–22); those who refuse His salvation will receive His judgment. As the writer of Hebrews warned, "See to it that you do not refuse Him who is speaking. For if those did not escape when they refused him who warned them on earth, much less will we escape who turn away from Him who warns from heaven" (Heb. 12:25).

Jesus' words determine people's eternal destinies, not only because of who He is but also because He speaks for His Father (cf. 4:34; 5:30; 6:38). Therefore, no one can reject His words with impunity. **For I did not speak on My own initiative,** He said, **but the Father Himself who sent Me has given Me a commandment as to what to say and what to speak. I know that His commandment is eternal life** (cf. 5:24; 6:63, 68; 20:31); **therefore the things I speak, I speak just as the Father has told Me.** Though fully equal in nature to the Father (Phil. 2:6; Col. 1:15; 2:9), Jesus assumed a submissive role during the incarnation (Phil. 2:7; Heb. 5:8). He spoke only the words the Father gave Him (cf. 3:34; 7:16; 8:26–28, 40; 14:10, 24; 17:8, 14), which are unchangeable and absolute (Matt. 5:18; 24:35; 1 Peter 1:25).

As God's chosen nation (Amos 3:2), Israel had received many blessings, some of which Paul enumerated in Romans 9:4–5: "the adoption as sons, and the glory and the covenants and the giving of the Law and the temple service and the promises, whose are the fathers." But above all, it was from the Jewish people that the Messiah came (v. 5). Tragically, when He came, they rejected Him. They refused to accept His call to believe in Him, and ignored His warnings of the consequences of unbelief. Finally, God hardened them, and those who were unwilling to believe became unable to believe. Having been entrusted with such great privileges, Israel was accountable for much (cf. Luke 12:48). Therefore Jesus pronounced the nation's judgment in His chilling words, "Behold, your house is left to you desolate; and I say to you, you will not see Me until the time comes when you say, 'Blessed is He who comes in the name of the Lord!'" (Luke 13:35). A generation later, Israel's doom would fall at the hands of the Romans. Jerusalem and the temple would be destroyed, and the people would be scattered and troubled under divine discipline even to the present. But the story does not end there. Because of His great love for His people, God will one day redeem the remnant of His chosen people, "and so all Israel will be saved" (Rom. 11:26).

The Humility of Love
(John 13:1–17)

6

Now before the Feast of the Passover, Jesus knowing that His hour had come that He would depart out of this world to the Father, having loved His own who were in the world, He loved them to the end. During supper, the devil having already put into the heart of Judas Iscariot, the son of Simon, to betray Him, Jesus, knowing that the Father had given all things into His hands, and that He had come forth from God and was going back to God, got up from supper, and laid aside His garments; and taking a towel, He girded Himself. Then He poured water into the basin, and began to wash the disciples' feet and to wipe them with the towel with which He was girded. So He came to Simon Peter. He said to Him, "Lord, do You wash my feet?" Jesus answered and said to him, "What I do you do not realize now, but you will understand hereafter." Peter said to Him, "Never shall You wash my feet!" Jesus answered him, "If I do not wash you, you have no part with Me." Simon Peter said to Him, "Lord, then wash not only my feet, but also my hands and my head." Jesus said to him, "He who has bathed needs only to wash his feet, but is completely clean; and you are clean, but not all of you." For He knew the one who was betraying Him; for this reason He said,

"Not all of you are clean." So when He had washed their feet, and taken His garments and reclined at the table again, He said to them, "Do you know what I have done to you? You call Me Teacher and Lord; and you are right, for so I am. If I then, the Lord and the Teacher, washed your feet, you also ought to wash one another's feet. For I gave you an example that you also should do as I did to you. Truly, truly, I say to you, a slave is not greater than his master, nor is one who is sent greater than the one who sent him. If you know these things, you are blessed if you do them. (13:1–17)

Contemporary society is obsessed with love. From romantic movies to popular songs to cheap paperback novels, romance is a primary theme in both entertainment and in everyday conversations. It is also big business, as newspaper columnists, talk show hosts, and Internet websites offer pertinent advice to the lovelorn. But despite all the world's talk about love, very few people actually understand the real thing.

The modern world's version of love is unabashedly narcissistic, totally self-focused, and shamelessly manipulative. It sees others merely as a means of self-gratification. Not surprisingly, relationships between selfish people usually do not last. If a current partner fails to live up to expectations (or they find someone more exciting), they move on. People are takers, not givers; humility is considered a weakness; selfishness a virtue.

In sharp contrast to that self-centered kind of love, the Bible teaches that the essence of love is self-sacrifice. Instead of tearing others down, biblical love seeks to build them up (1 Cor. 8:1); instead of first pursuing its own good, it pursues the good and interests of other people (1 Cor. 10:24); instead of seeking to have its needs met, it seeks to meet the needs of another (Gal. 5:13; Heb. 6:10).

The Bible's teaching about love reaches its pinnacle in 1 Corinthians 13:4–8, the most magnificent description of love ever penned:

> Love is patient, love is kind and is not jealous; love does not brag and is not arrogant, does not act unbecomingly; it does not seek its own, is not provoked, does not take into account a wrong suffered, does not rejoice in unrighteousness, but rejoices with the truth; bears all things, believes all things, hopes all things, endures all things. Love never fails.

To love like that requires above all else humility, for only humble people can put the interests of others ahead of their own (Phil. 2:3–4). Thus Paul exhorted the Ephesians to act "with all humility and gentleness, with patience, showing tolerance for one another in love" (Eph. 4:2). Jesus taught that those who humbly love others will be exalted, not those who promote themselves (Luke 14:11; 18:14;); humility, not pride, is the mark of true greatness (Matt. 18:4; 20:26; 23:11) and brings God's blessing (Ps. 25:9; Prov. 3:34 [NKJV]; 22:4; Isa. 57:15; 66:2; 1 Peter 5:5).

While 1 Corinthians 13 is the supreme description of love, the Lord Jesus Christ is the supreme example of love. The most significant way that He showed His love was, of course, by dying as a sacrifice for sinners when "He humbled Himself by becoming obedient to the point of death, even death on a cross" (Phil. 2:8). As the Lord Himself said, "Greater love has no one than this, that one lay down his life for his friends" (John 15:13). Paul reminded the Ephesians, "Christ ... loved you and gave Himself up for us, an offering and a sacrifice to God as a fragrant aroma ... Christ also loved the church and gave Himself up for her" (Eph. 5:2, 25). "We know love by this," John wrote, "that He laid down His life for us" (1 John 3:16).

Because He is by nature "gentle and humble in heart" (Matt. 11:29; cf. Zech. 9:9; 2 Cor. 10:1), Christ exhibited humble love throughout His entire earthly ministry. That love is notably exemplified in the incident described in this passage, the washing of the disciples' feet. It is a fitting introduction to a new section of John's gospel—one that features Christ's sacrificial death.

In the prologue to his gospel, John had informed his readers that there would be two reactions to the Lord Jesus Christ. Many of His people (Israel) would not accept Him; though "He came to His own ... those who were His own did not receive Him" (1:11). In the first twelve chapters, John recorded the tragic story of Israel's rejection of her Messiah. But though the nation as a whole rejected Christ, some individuals did receive Him (1:12). It is to that "little flock" (Luke 12:32) that Jesus here turned in the final hours of His earthly ministry.

As chapter 13 opens, Jesus' public ministry to Israel has ended. After issuing a final invitation to believe in Him, Jesus "went away and hid Himself from them" (12:36; cf. the exposition of this verse in the previous chapter of this volume). In chapters 13 through 17, Jesus turned from public ministry to those who rejected Him to private ministry to those who received Him. He gave a practical demonstration of His continuing love for the disciples (13:1–17), assured them of the hope of heaven (14:1–3), guaranteed them power for ministry (14:12) and provision for their needs (14:13–14), and promised them the Holy Spirit (14:16–17; 15:26; 16:7), divine truth in the Word of God (14:26; 16:13), peace (14:27), and joy (15:11; 16:22). The common theme that runs throughout these five chapters is Christ's love for His own. As His earthly ministry drew to a close on the night before His crucifixion, Jesus sought to reassure them of that enduring love He had for them.

The account of the first expression of His love, the washing of the disciples' feet, may be discussed under four headings. We see the sublime riches of Christ's love, the satanic rejection of His love, the shocking revelation of His love, and the suitable response to His love.

THE SUBLIME RICHES OF CHRIST'S LOVE

Now before the Feast of the Passover, Jesus knowing that His hour had come that He would depart out of this world to the Father, having loved His own who were in the world, He loved them to the end. (13:1)

The **Feast of the Passover** was the annual Jewish festival commemorating God's deliverance of Israel from bondage in Egypt. The name derived from the angel of death's passing over the houses of the Hebrews when he killed the firstborn of the Egyptians (Ex. 12:7, 12–13). This Passover would be the last divinely authorized one. From this point on there would be a new memorial—not one recalling the lambs' blood on the doorposts but the blood of the Lamb of God (1:29, 36; Rev. 5:6; 6:9; 7:10, 17; 14:4, 10; 15:3; 19:9; 22:1, 3) "poured out for many for forgiveness of sins" (Matt. 26:28). The Last Supper celebrated by the Lord with His disciples gave Him opportunity to use the elements of the Passover meal to form a transition from the old covenant Passover to the new covenant Lord's Supper (1 Cor. 11:23–26).

An apparent discrepancy exists at this point between John's chronology and that of the Synoptic Gospels. The latter clearly state that the Last Supper was a Passover meal (Matt. 26:17–19; Mark 14:12–16; Luke 22:7–15). John 18:28, however, records that the Jewish leaders "led Jesus from Caiaphas into the Praetorium, and it was early [Friday morning; the day of the crucifixion]; and they themselves did not enter into the Praetorium so that they would not be defiled, but might eat the Passover." Further, according to John 19:14 Jesus' trial and crucifixion took place on "the day of preparation for the Passover," not the day after the eating of the Passover meal. Thus the Lord was crucified at the same time that the Passover lambs were being killed (cf. 19:36; Ex. 12:46; Num. 9:12). The challenge, then, is to explain how Jesus and the disciples could have eaten the Passover meal on Thursday evening if the Jewish leaders had not yet eaten it on Friday morning.

The answer lies in understanding that the Jews had two different methods of reckoning days. Ancient Jewish sources suggest that Jews from the northern part of Israel (including Galilee, where Jesus and most of the Twelve were from) counted days from sunrise to sunrise. Most of the Pharisees apparently also used that method. On the other hand, the

Jews in the southern region of Israel counted days from sunset to sunset. That would include the Sadducees (who of necessity lived in the vicinity of Jerusalem because of their connection with the temple). Though no doubt confusing at times, that dual method of reckoning days would have had practical benefits at Passover, allowing the feast to be celebrated on two consecutive days. That would have eased the crowded conditions in Jerusalem, especially in the temple, where all the lambs would not have had to be killed on the same day.

Thus, there is no contradiction between John and the Synoptics. Being Galileans, Jesus and the Twelve would have viewed Passover day as running from sunrise on Thursday to sunrise on Friday. They would have eaten their Passover meal on Thursday evening. The Jewish leaders (the Sadducees), however, would have viewed it as beginning at sunset on Thursday and ending at sunset on Friday. They would have eaten their Passover meal on Friday evening. (For a further discussion of this issue, see Harold W. Hoehner, *Chronological Aspects of the Life of Christ* [Grand Rapids: Zondervan, 1977], 74–90; Robert L. Thomas and Stanley N. Gundry, *A Harmony of the Gospels* [Chicago: Moody, 1979], 321–22).

John repeated Jesus' declaration that His **hour had come** (12:23); no longer was it future as in 2:4; 7:30; and 8:20 (cf. 7:6, 8). The Lord knew that the time had come for Him to **depart out of this world to the Father.** He was in full control of everything that was happening, and was never a victim of circumstances, or of men's evil schemes.

Though He yearned to return to His full glory in the Father's presence (cf. 17:5), Jesus never wavered in His focus on loving **His own** (cf. 10:29) **who were in the world.** The Lord **loved them to the end.** *Telos* (**end**) means "perfection," or "completeness," and signifies that Jesus loves His own with the fullest measure of love. There is a general sense in which God loves the world (John 3:16) of lost sinners (Matt. 5:44–45; Titus 3:4), but He loves His own with a perfect, eternal, redeeming love—a love "which surpasses knowledge" (Eph. 3:19). The words of the hymn writer capture the Lord's marvelous love for believers:

> Loved with everlasting love,
> Led by grace that love to know;
> Gracious Spirit from above,
> Thou hast taught me it is so!
> O, this full and perfect peace!
> O, this transport all divine!
> In a love which cannot cease,
> I am His, and He is mine.

In Romans 8:35–39 Paul exulted,

> Who will separate us from the love of Christ? Will tribulation, or distress, or persecution, or famine, or nakedness, or peril, or sword? Just as it is written, "For Your sake we are being put to death all day long; we were considered as sheep to be slaughtered." But in all these things we over-whelmingly conquer through Him who loved us. For I am convinced that neither death, nor life, nor angels, nor principalities, nor things present, nor things to come, nor powers, nor height, nor depth, nor any other created thing, will be able to separate us from the love of God, which is in Christ Jesus our Lord.

Even the imminent arrival of His own death could not separate His disciples from His love. That reality becomes even more wonderfully clear in His prayer in the seventeenth chapter.

THE SATANIC REJECTION OF CHRIST'S LOVE

During supper, the devil having already put into the heart of Judas Iscariot, the son of Simon, to betray Him, (13:2)

The attention abruptly shifts from the brilliant light of Christ's love to the satanic darkness of Judas's heart. Even before this final **supper** began, **the devil** had **already put into the heart of Judas Iscariot, the son of Simon, to betray Him.** The contrast between Christ's love and Judas's hatred is stark; the latter provides the black backdrop against which the former appears all the more glorious.

By humbly washing Judas's feet, which He would shortly do, Jesus met the greatest injury and insult imaginable with humble love. Consistent with His command to show love to one's enemies (Matt. 5:44), He did just that. But tragically, Judas was unmoved by the Lord's manifestation of love for him; the same act that drew the other disciples to Christ repelled him.

Judas's greed and ambition had long since opened the door to the Devil's influence (cf. 12:4–6). Although Satan inspired his betrayal of Jesus Christ, Judas was fully responsible for his heinous act. His own evil heart desired the same thing Satan did—Jesus' death. Satan and Judas were in complete accord; they were coconspirators in the plot to kill Jesus Christ. Soon, Judas would be under Satan's complete control (v. 27) and would carry out his plan to betray the Son of God (v. 30; cf. Matt. 26:24). (For more information on Judas, see chapter 7 of this volume.)

THE SHOCKING REVELATION OF CHRIST'S LOVE

Jesus, knowing that the Father had given all things into His hands, and that He had come forth from God and was going back to God, got up from supper, and laid aside His garments; and taking a towel, He girded Himself. Then He poured water into the basin, and began to wash the disciples' feet and to wipe them with the towel with which He was girded. So He came to Simon Peter. He said to Him, "Lord, do You wash my feet?" Jesus answered and said to him, "What I do you do not realize now, but you will understand hereafter." Peter said to Him, "Never shall You wash my feet!" Jesus answered him, "If I do not wash you, you have no part with Me." Simon Peter said to Him, "Lord, then wash not only my feet, but also my hands and my head." Jesus said to him, "He who has bathed needs only to wash his feet, but is completely clean; and you are clean, but not all of you." For He knew the one who was betraying Him; for this reason He said, "Not all of you are clean." (13:3–11)

John's declaration that Jesus knew **that the Father had given all things into His hands** (cf. 3:35; 17:2; Matt. 11:27; 28:18), **and that He had come forth from God** (cf. 3:13; 5:37; 6:46, 57; 7:29; 8:18, 42; 12:49; 16:27–28; 17:8) **and was going back to God** (cf. 6:62; 7:33; 14:12, 28; 16:5, 10, 17, 28; 17:11, 13) reiterates and amplifies the apostle's earlier statement that Jesus was about to return to the Father (v. 1). By stressing Jesus' exaltation, John revealed the depth of His humility. Incredibly, incomprehensibly, the glorious Creator and Ruler of the universe was about to humbly wash the disciples' dirty feet—a menial task reserved for the lowest of slaves (even Jewish slaves were not required to perform it, only Gentiles). "With such power and status at his disposal, we might have expected him to defeat the devil in an immediate and flashy confrontation, and to devastate Judas with an unstoppable blast of divine wrath. Instead, he washes his disciples' feet, including the feet of the betrayer" (D. A. Carson, *The Gospel According to John,* The Pillar New Testament Commentary (Grand Rapids: Eerdmans, 1991), 462).

Having walked through the dirt streets of Jerusalem to the upper room, the disciples' feet, protected only by sandals, would naturally have been dirty, and while they were reclining for a long meal, offensive. Since there was no servant there to do it, one of the Twelve should have volunteered to wash the feet of the others. But the Lord's admonition, "The greatest among you shall be your servant" (Matt. 23:11) had fallen on deaf ears. Instead of humbling themselves, the disciples were continuing their ongoing debate over which of them was the greatest (Luke 22:24; cf.

Mark 9:34), and angling for the prominent positions in the kingdom (Matt. 20:20–24). That being the case, the last thing any of them did was to perform the task of the lowest slave (though they no doubt would have been happy to wash the Lord's feet).

And so supper began with everyone's feet still unwashed, as each of the Twelve waited for someone else to take action. Finally, in a stunning display of humility that was also a pointed rebuke of the disciples' prideful ambition, the incarnate Son of God **got up from supper, and laid aside His garments; and taking a towel, He girded Himself. Then He poured water into the basin, and began to wash the disciples' feet and to wipe them with the towel with which He was girded.** The rebuked, embarrassed, and chastened disciples watched in awkward, painful silence as the Lord, clad as a slave, knelt before each of them in turn and washed their soiled feet.

Not surprisingly **Simon Peter,** never at a loss for words, was the first to protest. When Jesus **came to** him, Peter, displaying the embarrassment of them all, asked incredulously, **"Lord, do You wash my feet?"** The disciples were still fervently expecting the inauguration of the kingdom (cf. Acts 1:6), and Peter was appalled at this act of self-abasement on the part of the divine King. For a superior to wash the feet of an inferior was unheard of in either Jewish or Roman culture. But Peter's outburst reflected his ignorance, as the Lord's reply, **"What I do you do not realize now, but you will understand hereafter,"** indicates. Only later, after Christ's death, resurrection, and ascension, would Peter (and the rest of the disciples) finally realize that in the incarnation "the Son of Man did not come to be served, but to serve, and to give His life a ransom for many" (Matt. 20:28). Many years later Peter would write,

> You were not redeemed with perishable things like silver or gold from your futile way of life inherited from your forefathers, but with precious blood, as of a lamb unblemished and spotless, the blood of Christ. (1 Peter 1:18–19)

> He Himself bore our sins in His body on the cross, so that we might die to sin and live to righteousness; for by His wounds you were healed. (1 Peter 2:24)

> For Christ also died for sins once for all, the just for the unjust, so that He might bring us to God, having been put to death in the flesh, but made alive in the spirit. (1 Peter 3:18)

As he had done once before (Matt. 16:22), Peter rashly presumed to tell the Lord what to do, declaring emphatically (there is a double negative in the Greek text), **"Never shall You wash my feet!"** Though

Peter's modesty may appear praiseworthy, the Lord desires obedience above all else (cf. 1 Sam. 15:22). Once again the Lord patiently **answered him, "If I do not wash you, you have no part with Me."** Jesus' reply served two purposes. First, it corrected Peter's (and the rest of the Twelve's) misunderstanding of His messianic mission. In His first advent, Jesus did not come as the conquering King but as the selfless sacrifice for the sins of His people (Isa. 53:4–6, 10–12; Eph. 5:2; Heb. 9:26; 10:12); to humble "Himself by becoming obedient to the point of death, even death on a cross" (Phil. 2:8). Peter needed to accept the reality of the Lord's humiliation.

But the Lord's words also mean that only those cleansed by Him have a relationship to Him. Washing is a common biblical metaphor for spiritual cleansing (cf. Num. 19:17–19; Ps. 51:2; Isa. 4:4; Ezek. 36:24–27; Zech. 13:1; Acts 22:16; 1 Cor. 6:11; Eph. 5:26; Titus 3:5; Heb. 10:22), and only those who place their faith in Jesus Christ as Lord and confess their sins are cleansed by Him (John 15:3; 1 John 1:7–9) and are united to Him in eternal life.

In keeping with his impulsive nature, Peter immediately jumped to the opposite extreme (cf. Matt. 14:28 with 14:30; 16:16 with 16:22; 26:33, 35 with 26:69–75), exclaiming, **"Lord, then wash not only my feet, but also my hands and my head."** Though he may have missed the Lord's point and thought He was referring to a physical washing, whatever Jesus was offering, Peter wanted all of it. Continuing His spiritual application of the principle of washing, **Jesus said to** Peter, **"He who has bathed needs only to wash his feet."** In physical terms, those who have already **bathed** do not need to take another bath every time their feet get dirty. They need **only to wash** their **feet** because they are **completely clean.** Similarly the complete cleansing of the redeemed at salvation never needs to be repeated. God has graciously justified and imputed Christ's righteousness to believers (2 Cor. 5:21; Phil. 3:8–9), and His atoning death provides complete forgiveness of all their sins (Col. 2:13; Titus 2:14; 1 John 1:7, 9). But they still need the daily cleansing for sanctification from the defilement of the sin that remains in them (Phil. 2:12; 3:12–14).

Jesus then assured the disciples, **"You are clean,"** since they had experienced the cleansing of redemption. **But** that was **not** true of **all of** them—there was one notable exception. Since the Lord **knew the one who was betraying Him** (though the disciples did not at this point; cf. 13:21–22), **for this reason He said, "Not all of you are clean."** The one who was not clean was, of course, Judas Iscariot, **the one who was betraying Him.** The Lord's words were also a last appeal and warning to Judas who was on the brink of executing his wicked scheme. But Judas would not be deterred.

Jesus was not taken by surprise by Judas's treachery. Long before that night He had said regarding him, "Did I Myself not choose you, the twelve, and yet one of you is a devil?" (John 6:70). All aspects of Christ's death—including Judas's betrayal—were part of God's predetermined plan (Acts 2:23). As noted earlier, however, that does not excuse Judas of personal responsibility for his wicked act (Matt. 26:24).

THE SUITABLE RESPONSE TO CHRIST'S LOVE

So when He had washed their feet, and taken His garments and reclined at the table again, He said to them, "Do you know what I have done to you? You call Me Teacher and Lord; and you are right, for so I am. If I then, the Lord and the Teacher, washed your feet, you also ought to wash one another's feet. For I gave you an example that you also should do as I did to you. Truly, truly, I say to you, a slave is not greater than his master, nor is one who is sent greater than the one who sent him. If you know these things, you are blessed if you do them. (13:12–17)

Having **washed** the disciples' feet, **and taken His garments and reclined at the table again,** Jesus taught them the lesson He wanted them to learn. The theological truths pictured in verses 7–11 (Jesus' humiliation at His first coming and the once-for-all cleansing of justification versus the daily cleansing of sanctification), though of great importance, are not the main truths the Lord sought to communicate. The primary principle Jesus wanted the disciples to learn was the importance of humble, loving service. That becomes clear because **He said to them, "Do you know what I have done to you? You call Me Teacher and Lord; and you are right, for so I am. If I then, the Lord and the Teacher, washed your feet, you also ought to wash one another's feet."** This was a crucial lesson for the disciples, constantly bickering over who was the greatest, to learn. If the Lord of Glory was willing to humble Himself and take on the role of the lowest of slaves, how could the disciples do any less? Jesus had once asked, "Why do you call Me, 'Lord, Lord,' and do not do what I say?" (Luke 6:46); here He was in effect saying, "Why do you call Me 'Lord, Lord,' and do not follow My example?"

Some argue from this passage that foot washing is an ordinance for the church, along with baptism and the Lord's Supper (Communion). But Jesus said, **"I gave you an example that you also should do *as* I did to you,"** not, "what I did to you." Further, "Wise theologians and expositors have always been reluctant to raise to the level of universal rite something that appears only once in Scripture" (Carson, *John*, 468). (The only other reference to foot washing, 1 Tim. 5:10, is not in the context of a church rite, but of good deeds performed by individuals.)

To elevate the outward act of foot washing to the status of an ordinance is to minimize the important lesson Jesus was teaching. The Lord gave an example of humility, not of foot washing; His concern was for the inner attitude, not the outward rite. The latter is meaningless apart from the former.

To refuse to follow Jesus' example of humble service is to pridefully elevate oneself above Him, since **a slave is not greater than his master, nor is one who is sent greater than the one who sent him** (cf. similar sayings in 15:20; Matt. 10:24; Luke 6:40; 22:27). No servant dares to regard any task as beneath him if his master has performed it.

The Lord's concluding thought, **"If you know these things, you are blessed if you do them,"** reflects the biblical truth that blessing flows from obedience. The opening words of the Psalms emphasize that truth:

> How blessed is the man who does not walk in the counsel of the wicked,
> Nor stand in the path of sinners,
> Nor sit in the seat of scoffers!
> But his delight is in the law of the Lord,
> And in His law he meditates day and night.
> He will be like a tree firmly planted by streams of water,
> Which yields its fruit in its season
> And its leaf does not wither;
> And in whatever he does, he prospers. (Ps. 1:1–3)

Psalm 119:1 declares, "How blessed are those whose way is blameless, who walk in the law of the Lord" (cf. Ps. 128:1). In Proverbs 16:20 Solomon declared, "He who gives attention to the word will find good, and blessed is he who trusts in the Lord." "My mother and My brothers," Jesus declared, "are these who hear the word of God and do it" (Luke 8:21). Later in Luke's gospel, He affirmed, "Blessed are those who hear the word of God and observe it" (Luke 11:28).

This passage reveals one essential way that believers can obey God and receive His blessing: by following the example of His Son. "The one who says he abides in Him," John wrote in his first epistle, "ought himself to walk in the same manner as He walked" (1 John 2:6). Serving others in the humility of love is imitating Jesus Christ (cf. Phil. 2:5).

Unmasking the Betrayer (John 13:18–30)

7

"I do not speak of all of you. I know the ones I have chosen; but it is that the Scripture may be fulfilled, 'He who eats My bread has lifted up his heel against Me.' From now on I am telling you before it comes to pass, so that when it does occur, you may believe that I am He. Truly, truly, I say to you, he who receives whomever I send receives Me; and he who receives Me receives Him who sent Me." When Jesus had said this, He became troubled in spirit, and testified and said, "Truly, truly, I say to you, that one of you will betray Me." The disciples began looking at one another, at a loss to know of which one He was speaking. There was reclining on Jesus' bosom one of His disciples, whom Jesus loved. So Simon Peter gestured to him, and said to him, "Tell us who it is of whom He is speaking." He, leaning back thus on Jesus' bosom, said to Him, "Lord, who is it?" Jesus then answered, "That is the one for whom I shall dip the morsel and give it to him." So when He had dipped the morsel, He took and gave it to Judas, the son of Simon Iscariot. After the morsel, Satan then entered into him. Therefore Jesus said to him, "What you do, do quickly." Now no one of those reclining at the table knew for what purpose He had said this to him. For some were supposing,

because Judas had the money box, that Jesus was saying to him, "Buy the things we have need of for the feast"; or else, that he should give something to the poor. So after receiving the morsel he went out immediately; and it was night. (13:18–30)

The word "traitor" is an ugly word in any language. There are few people more despised than those who betray their country, cause, or trust. Nations have generally reserved the severest punishment—often the death penalty—for those who commit acts of treason.

History has known many notorious traitors. During the Peloponnesian War, the Athenian general Alcibiades, nephew of the famous Greek statesman Pericles and a boyhood friend of Socrates, betrayed Athens's plans to the city's bitter rival, Sparta. As a result, the Athenians were defeated in battle by the Spartans. The Athenian soldier and historian Xenophon, a disciple of Socrates, also turned traitor and fought for Sparta against his native city. King Leonidas of Sparta and his vastly outnumbered force held the pass of Thermopylae against the Persians until a traitor showed the Persians a way to outflank them. Attacked from the rear, Leonidas and his men bravely fought to the last man in one of history's most famous last stands.

During the American Revolution, Simon Girty, a deserter from the Continental Army, led raiding parties of Native Americans against the colonists. Girty was much feared for his brutality, so much so that he was dubbed the "Great Renegade." But the most infamous traitor of the Revolutionary War (and indeed in all of American history) was Benedict Arnold. Annoyed at being passed over for promotion and seeking money to fund his extravagant lifestyle, Arnold offered to surrender the key fort at West Point to the British. When British Major John André, the liaison between Arnold and British General Sir Henry Clinton, was captured carrying incriminating papers, Arnold's plot was exposed. He deserted to the British, and fought against his own countrymen. He died in exile in England, scorned by Americans and British alike.

The French general Henri Pétain was hailed as the savior of Verdun in World War I. But after France fell to the Germans in World War II, he became the head of the Vichy government, which collaborated with the Nazis. Vidkun Quisling, whose name has become a synonym for "traitor," headed the puppet regime established by the Nazis in Norway. The English traitor William Joyce ("Lord Haw Haw"), and the American traitors Iva Ikuko Toguri D'Aquino ("Tokyo Rose") and Mildred Elizabeth Gillars ("Axis Sally") lent their voices to Nazi and Japanese propaganda broadcasts.

The Bible also records its share of traitors, including Absalom, who sought to usurp the throne of his father, David (2 Sam. 15:10–13);

Ahithophel, David's erstwhile counselor who joined Absalom's rebellion (2 Sam. 15:31); Sheba, who led a revolt of the northern tribes soon after Absalom's revolt was crushed (2 Sam. 20:1–2); Jeroboam, whose rebellion against Solomon resulted in the division of Israel into two kingdoms, Israel and Judah (1 Kings 11:26ff.); Baasha, who murdered Jeroboam's son Nadab and reigned in his place (1 Kings 15:25–28); Zimri, who killed Baasha's son Elah and took his place (1 Kings 16:8–20); Athaliah, Israel's only queen, who seized power after the death of her son, King Ahaziah (2 Kings 11:1–16); the servants of Joash, who conspired against him and killed him (2 Kings 12:20–21); the unnamed conspirators who assassinated King Amaziah (2 Kings 14:18–20); Shallum, whose conspiracy ended the brief reign of King Zechariah (2 Kings 15:8–10); Menahem, who similarly murdered and replaced Shallum (2 Kings 15:14); Pekah, who overthrew and murdered Menahem's son Pekahiah (2 Kings 15:23–25); Hoshea, who killed Pekah and became the last king of the northern kingdom (2 Kings 15:30); Amon's servants, who conspired against him and murdered him (2 Kings 21:23); and Bigthan and Teresh, whose plot against King Ahasuerus was uncovered by Mordecai (Est. 2:21–23).

But the most notorious traitor—both in the Bible and in all of human history—was Judas Iscariot. Judas had the incredible privilege of being one of the twelve closest followers of the Lord Jesus Christ during His earthly ministry. Yet inconceivably, after more than three years of living constantly with the incomparably perfect Jesus, observing the miracles He performed, and hearing His teaching, Judas betrayed Him to His death. The dark, tragic story of Judas reveals the depths of evil to which the human heart is capable of sinking, even in the very best of circumstances.

The early church universally detested and scorned Judas. For instance, his name appears last in every New Testament list of the apostles, except for the one in Acts 1—where it does not appear at all. In addition, whenever the gospel writers mention Judas, they always identify him as the traitor who betrayed Jesus (cf. Matt. 10:4; 26:25, 48; 27:3; Mark 3:19; 14:44; Luke 6:16; John 6:71; 12:4; 18:2).

Little is known of Judas's life before he became an apostle. His father was Simon Iscariot (John 6:71; 13:2, 26). Their surname derives from two Hebrew words meaning "man of Kerioth." That suggests that Judas was from the village of Kerioth, either the one in Moab (Jer. 48:24, 41), or more likely the one in Judea, south of Hebron (Josh. 15:25). Thus Judas would have been the only one of the Twelve who was not a Galilean, though there is no evidence that the other apostles excluded or looked down on him as a result. Nevertheless, being an outsider no doubt made it easier for Judas to justify his treachery in his own mind. It also made it easier for him to hide his hypocrisy, since the other eleven would have known little about him or his background. Nevertheless, the other disciples trusted Judas implicitly, even making him their treasurer (John 12:6; 13:29). None of them even suspected Judas when Jesus announced in the upper room, "Truly, truly, I say to you, that one of you will betray Me" (John 13:21).

The Bible does not reveal when and where Judas first met Jesus. He may have been among the Judeans who flocked to hear John the Baptist (Matt. 3:1–5) bear witness to Christ. Or he may first have met the Lord at the beginning of His ministry when "Jesus and His disciples came into the land of Judea, and there He was spending time with them and baptizing" (John 3:22). When the Lord first called Judas to follow Him is likewise not recorded in Scripture. With the other eleven, he was named an apostle by Jesus after the Lord had spent a night in prayer (Luke 6:12–16). At that point (if he had not already done so), Judas left his former occupation and became a full-time follower of Christ. He even stayed with Him when many other false disciples abandoned Him (John 6:66–71). But though Judas closely accompanied Jesus, he never gave Him his soul.

Since Judas was obviously not attracted to Christ on a spiritual level, why did he follow Him? On the one hand Judas, like many of his fellow Jews, fervently hoped that Jesus would overthrow the Romans and restore Israel's political sovereignty. But Judas was also motivated by greed, the desire for power, and worldly ambition. As one of the inner circle of Jesus' followers, he no doubt hoped for an important position in the restored kingdom (as did the other disciples at first; cf. Matt. 20:20–24). Judas was not interested in the kingdom for salvation's sake, but for what he hoped to get out of it; namely, wealth, power, and prestige.

As time went on, Judas became increasingly disillusioned. Jesus showed no signs of becoming the conquering political and military messiah he fervently hoped for. In fact, Christ had rebuffed the people's attempt to make Him king (John 6:14–15). The Lord stressed the spiritual dimension of the kingdom, while Judas eagerly anticipated an earthly, political, and economic one. But he hid his growing disenchantment behind a façade of hypocrisy.

Just a few days before the Last Supper, however, an incident occurred that apparently was the last straw for Judas. At a dinner in Bethany, given in Jesus' honor, Mary the sister of Martha and Lazarus anointed Jesus with a large amount of expensive perfume. Shocked and outraged, Judas protested indignantly, "Why was this perfume not sold for three hundred denarii and given to poor people?" (John 12:5). Judas, of course, cared nothing for the poor; he "said this, not because he was concerned about the poor, but because he was a thief, and as he had the money box, he used to pilfer what was put into it" (v. 6). Losing out on the opportunity to embezzle from that vast sum of money (three hundred denarii amounted to a full year's wages for an average laborer) infuriated Judas. But so convincing was his outward display of pious hypocrisy that the rest of the disciples joined in his protest (Matt. 26:8–9).

Judas's simmering discontent then boiling over, he immediately after this incident "went to the chief priests and said, 'What are you willing to give me to betray Him to you?' And they weighed out thirty pieces of silver to him. From then on he began looking for a good opportunity to betray Jesus" (Matt. 26:14–16). That came down to telling the leaders where He would be at night away from the crowds. Judas could no longer contain his bitterness and disillusionment, which spilled forth in secret treachery.

But Judas's treachery would not remain hidden for long, because Jesus would expose it. The setting the Lord chose for unmasking His betrayer was His last meal with the disciples on the night before His death. Jesus had taught them the importance of humble service through His example of washing their feet (John 13:1–17). Then He concluded the lesson by proclaiming, "If you know these things, you are blessed if you do them" (v. 17). Now, in verses 18 to 30, the dialogue turns to the betrayer. Jesus contrasts the eleven eternally blessed loyal disciples with the eternally miserable traitor, Judas. The passage may be divided into four sections: the treachery anticipated (by the Old Testament), the treason announced (by Christ), the Twelve astonished (by the news), and the traitor addressed (by the Lord).

THE TREACHERY ANTICIPATED

"I do not speak of all of you. I know the ones I have chosen; but it is that the Scripture may be fulfilled, 'He who eats My bread has lifted up his heel against Me.'" (13:18)

Jesus wanted to make sure that the rest of the disciples understood when the betrayal and arrest took place that He was not a surprise victim of Judas's treachery. They might wonder why He chose Judas, and how He could have so completely misjudged his character. Therefore the Lord clarified His earlier declaration that the disciples were spiritually clean (13:10). However He did **not speak of all of** them; in His omniscience (cf. 2:24–25) "He knew the one who was betraying Him; for this reason He said, 'Not all of you are clean'" (v. 11)—only **the ones** whom He had **chosen** (cf. 15:16).

Jesus was not caught off guard; "He was not the deceived and helpless Victim of unsuspected treachery, but One sent by God to effect

God's purpose going forward calmly and unafraid, to do what God had planned for Him to do" (Leon Morris, *The Gospel According to John*, The New International Commentary on the New Testament [Grand Rapids: Eerdmans, 1979], 623). The Lord deliberately chose Judas so **that the Scripture may be fulfilled** (cf. 17:12). The **Scripture** the Lord specifically cited as being **fulfilled** in Judas's betrayal, **"He who eats My bread has lifted up his heel against Me"** (or in modern vernacular, "kicked Me when I was down") is Psalm 41:9. David lamented his betrayal by a close, trusted companion (one who had shared a meal with him; a symbol of intimate fellowship), possibly Ahithophel (2 Sam. 15:31), as rabbinic sources suggest. Another psalm that may refer to David's betrayal during the dark days of Absalom's revolt is Psalm 55. In verses 12–14 David wrote,

> For it is not an enemy who reproaches me,
> Then I could bear it;
> Nor is it one who hates me who has exalted himself against me,
> Then I could hide myself from him.
> But it is you, a man my equal,
> My companion and my familiar friend;
> We who had sweet fellowship together
> Walked in the house of God in the throng.

In both psalms David's experience points forward to Messiah's betrayal. Zechariah 11:12–13 also predicts Judas's betrayal—even giving the exact amount of money he would receive and what he would do with it afterward (cf. Matt. 27:3–10):

> I said to them, "If it is good in your sight, give me my wages; but if not, never mind!" So they weighed out thirty shekels of silver as my wages. Then the Lord said to me, "Throw it to the potter, that magnificent price at which I was valued by them." So I took the thirty shekels of silver and threw them to the potter in the house of the Lord.

Thus long before Judas was born, his duplicity was foreseen and designed into God's eternal plan.

But Judas's role in the divine plan was not something apart from his own desire; he was no robot, programmed to betray Jesus against his will. Judas freely chose to do what he did, and was fully accountable for his actions. The same tension between divine sovereignty and human choice is evident in Judas's becoming a disciple. He chose to follow Christ, yet he became a follower of Christ only because Christ chose him (cf. John 15:16)—though not, of course, to salvation. Judas's betrayal was predetermined, but that in no way contradicts the truth that he acted of his own volition. Jesus affirmed both truths when He said in Luke 22:22,

"For indeed, the Son of Man is going as it has been determined [God's sovereignty]; but woe to that man by whom He is betrayed [Judas's responsibility]!" The sovereign God, "who works all things after the counsel of His will" (Eph. 1:11), used the evil plans of Judas's wicked heart to bring about the good of redemption (cf. Gen. 50:20; Ps. 76:10).

Judas had every opportunity to turn from his sin. Much of Christ's teaching applied directly to him, such as the parables of the unjust steward (Luke 16:1–13) and the wedding garment (Matt. 22:11–14); and Jesus' preaching against the love of money (Matt. 6:19–34), greed (Luke 16:13), and pride (Matt. 23:1–12). Judas also heard the Lord's candid declaration to the Twelve, "Did I Myself not choose you, the twelve, and yet one of you is a devil?" (John 6:70), and His warning of the fearful judgment that awaited His betrayer: "Woe to that man by whom the Son of Man is betrayed! It would have been good for that man if he had not been born" (Matt. 26:24). And he had just heard Jesus declare that not all the disciples were spiritually cleansed (v. 10). But all of that left Judas unmoved. He resolutely hardened his heart and refused to repent.

THE TREASON ANNOUNCED

"From now on I am telling you before it comes to pass, so that when it does occur, you may believe that I am He. Truly, truly, I say to you, he who receives whomever I send receives Me; and he who receives Me receives Him who sent Me." When Jesus had said this, He became troubled in spirit, and testified and said, "Truly, truly, I say to you, that one of you will betray Me." (13:19–21)

As noted in the previous point, Jesus wanted to make sure that Judas's betrayal would not shake the other disciples' faith in Him. By telling them about it **before it** came **to pass,** He assured that in the future they could look back and know that He knew everything that was going to happen. Thus **when** the betrayal did **occur,** the disciples, though scattered and fearful, would recognize His omniscient foreknowledge (cf. 2:25) and believe in His deity. As He had done before in John's gospel (e.g., 8:24, 28, 58), Jesus took for Himself the divine name of God from Exodus 3:13–14, **I am** (the word **He** does not appear in the Greek text).

At first glance, Jesus' statement, **Truly, truly, I say to you, he who receives whomever I send receives Me; and he who receives Me receives Him who sent Me** (cf. Matt. 10:40; Mark 9:37; Luke 10:16) appears to be disconnected from the context. Yet upon further reflection the connection becomes evident. The disciples (the eleven) would be shocked by Jesus' prediction that one of them would betray Him. They might think that having a traitor in their midst would destroy their credibility as a group and end their mission. Further, if the Lord was betrayed to His death, their hope for the immediate establishment of the earthly messianic kingdom would die with Him.

But the Lord, dropping this statement into the middle of references to Judas, reassured the eleven apostles that Judas's treachery would not nullify their commission; He was still going to **send** them as His representatives in the world. The very title that Christ gave them (Luke 6:13) emphasizes that truth; the Greek word translated "apostle" (*apostolos*) refers to one sent out having the full authority of the person who sent him, much like an ambassador today. But though the apostles had a unique, nontransferable authority (cf. Eph. 2:20), all believers represent Jesus Christ in the world. As Paul reminded the Corinthians, "We are ambassadors for Christ, as though God were making an appeal through us"; begging sinners "on behalf of Christ [to] be reconciled to God" (2 Cor. 5:20; cf. Eph. 6:20). As citizens of heaven (Phil. 3:20), believers represent their King to a world of lost sinners, among whom they live "as aliens and strangers" (1 Peter 2:11).

Having prepared the disciples by reassuring them that they would continue to be His representatives, Jesus **became troubled in spirit, and testified and said, "Truly, truly, I say to you, that one of you will betray Me." Troubled** translates a form of the verb *tarassō*, a strong word used figuratively to speak of severe mental or spiritual turmoil. It describes the disciples' terror at seeing the Lord walking on the water (Matt. 14:26), Zacharias's fear when the angel Gabriel appeared to him in the temple (Luke 1:12), the disciples' fear when Jesus appeared to them after the resurrection (Luke 24:38), the deep anguish of Jesus' soul at Lazarus's tomb (John 11:33), and His distress at the prospect of facing the cross (John 12:27).

Several things **troubled** the Lord; His unrequited love for Judas, Judas's ingratitude for all the kindness He had shown him, the malevolent presence of Satan, who would shortly possess Judas (v. 27), the fearful fate that awaited Judas in hell, and the knowledge that the betrayal would lead Him to the cross, with its sin-bearing (2 Cor. 5:21) and separation from the Father (Matt. 27:46). "In the present passage, Jesus' emotions are shown to be in a state of turmoil, his whole inner self convulsing at the thought of one of his closest followers betraying him to his enemies" (Andreas J. Köstenberger, *John*, Baker Exegetical Commentary on the New Testament [Grand Rapids: Baker, 2004], 413). Such would be the terrible consequences of the betrayal Jesus now openly declared.

THE TWELVE ASTONISHED

The disciples began looking at one another, at a loss to know of which one He was speaking. There was reclining on Jesus' bosom one of His disciples, whom Jesus loved. So Simon Peter gestured to him, and said to him, "Tell us who it is of whom He is speaking." He, leaning back thus on Jesus' bosom, said to Him, "Lord, who is it?" (13:22–25)

Stunned by Jesus announcement, the disciples (with the exception of Judas, of course) were thrown into confusion, as D. A. Carson suggests:

> The Twelve were already somewhat disoriented by Jesus' allusions to his suffering and death, categories they still could not square with their conviction that he was the promised Messiah. Doubtless references to betrayal and treachery seemed similarly obscure. Perhaps some wondered if Jesus were referring to disciples just outside the ring of the Twelve; others might have wondered if betrayal would be inadvertent. Perhaps the notion of betrayal did not seem very threatening to them, since their Master could calm storms, raise the dead, feed the hungry, heal the sick. What possible disaster could befall him that he could not rectify? (*The Gospel According to John*, The Pillar New Testament Commentary (Grand Rapids: Eerdmans, 1991), 472)

Obviously, since they were alone in the room with Jesus (cf. Matt. 26:20; Mark 14:17–20; Luke 22:11, 14–15), they knew that one of their number—one of those with whom they had lived and ministered for more than three years, one of those whose feet Jesus had washed, one of those chosen to be His ambassadors—would do the unthinkable and betray Him. But which one? It is a tribute to the effectiveness of Judas's hypocrisy (and to Jesus kindly treating him no differently from the other eleven disciples) that no one suspected him. Instead of immediately accusing Judas, **the disciples began looking at one another, at a loss to know of which one He was speaking.** Mark records that "they began to be grieved and to say to Him one by one, 'Surely not I?'" (Mark 14:19)—even "Judas, who was betraying Him, said, "Surely it is not I, Rabbi?" (Matt. 26:25), thus maintaining his deceitful hypocrisy to the end. Luke adds that "they began to discuss among themselves which one of them it might be who was going to do this thing" (Luke 22:23). One can only wonder what Judas said.

Since the disciples had no clue as to who the betrayer might be, demonstrating the competence of Judas's hypocrisy, Peter at length took the initiative to find out. But rather than ask the Lord directly, he turned to the disciple who **was reclining on Jesus' bosom** (lying next to Him at the supper table) **whom Jesus loved.** That beloved disciple was John, who never names himself in his gospel. His deep love for Jesus stands in stark contrast to Judas's intense hatred. (For evidence that the beloved disciple was the apostle John, see *John 1–11*, The MacArthur New Testament Commentary [Chicago: Moody, 2006], 6–7.) Assuming John knew who the betrayer was, **Simon Peter gestured to** him to attract his attention **and said to him, "Tell us who it is of whom He is speaking."** But John did not know either, so he leaned **back thus on Jesus' bosom** and whispered **to Him, "Lord, who is it?"**

The Traitor Addressed

Jesus then answered, "That is the one for whom I shall dip the morsel and give it to him." So when He had dipped the morsel, He took and gave it to Judas, the son of Simon Iscariot. After the morsel, Satan then entered into him. Therefore Jesus said to him, "What you do, do quickly." Now no one of those reclining at the table knew for what purpose He had said this to him. For some were supposing, because Judas had the money box, that Jesus was saying to him, "Buy the things we have need of for the feast"; or else, that he should give something to the poor. So after receiving the morsel he went out immediately; and it was night. (13:26–30)

Evidently **Jesus** spoke so softly that only John heard when He **answered, "That is the one for whom I shall dip the morsel and give it to him"** (see the discussion of vv. 28–29 below). The **morsel** was a piece of unleavened bread, which was dipped into a mixture of bitter herbs, vinegar, water, salt, crushed dates, figs, and raisins. To be given the **morsel** by the host was to be singled out for special honor. Jesus thus made a gesture of honor toward Judas, showing kindness right up to the bitter end (cf. Rom. 2:4). But he was so far gone into his apostasy that even after the Lord **dipped the morsel . . . and gave it to Judas** the wretched traitor's heart remained implacably hardened. Judas spurned Christ's final gesture of love to him, just as he had all the previous ones for three years.

At that moment the day of salvation (cf. 2 Cor. 6:2) ended for Judas; hell arrived as **Satan then entered into** him. (The Devil evidently gained direct control over Judas on two occasions: just before the betrayal was arranged [Luke 22:3], and now as it was about to be carried out.) Divine mercy gave way to divine judgment and Judas was in essence handed over to Satan (cf. 1 Cor. 5:5; 1 Tim. 1:20). He had spurned Christ's love for the last time, and his eternal doom was sealed. F. F. Bruce writes,

> Jesus' action, in singling Judas out for a mark of special favour, may have been intended as a final appeal to him to abandon his treacherous plan and play the part of a true disciple. Up to that moment, the die had not been irrevocably cast. If Judas wavered for a second, it was only to steel himself to carry out his fatal resolution, to become the willing instrument of Satan whereas he might have been the free follower and messenger of his Master. Satan could not have entered into him had he not granted him admission. Had he been willing to say "No" to the adversary, all of his Master's intercessory power was available to him there and then to strengthen him. But when a disciple's will turns traitor, when the spiritual aid of Christ is refused, that person's condition is desperate indeed. (*The Gospel of John* [Grand Rapids: Eerdmans, 1983], 290)

Once Judas had irrevocably crossed that line, Jesus dismissed him, telling him, **"What you do, do quickly"** (cf. Matt. 26:50). Jesus controlled every detail of His death, proving the truth of His declaration, "No one has taken it away from Me, but I lay it down on My own initiative. I have authority to lay it down, and I have authority to take it up again. This commandment I received from My Father" (John 10:18). Christ was about to institute the Lord's Supper and He was not going to have it marred by Judas's (and Satan's) presence. As noted above, evidently only John heard Jesus say how He would point out His betrayer (and even he might not have realized that the betrayal was imminent). Hence **no one of those reclining at the table knew for what purpose He had said this to** Judas. They could only speculate that **because Judas had the money box, that Jesus was saying to him, "Buy the things we have need of for the feast"; or else, that he should give something to the poor** (which was traditionally done at Passover).

After receiving the morsel and hearing Jesus' words of dismissal, Judas **went out immediately.** Now that he had been exposed as the betrayer, he knew that he had to act quickly before the whole plot collapsed. He evidently went straight to the Sanhedrin and told them that the "opportune time" (Mark 14:11) when they could arrest Jesus "apart from the crowd" (Luke 22:6) had finally come. Judas knew that after the meal Jesus, "as was His custom" (Luke 22:39), would head for the Mount of Olives. He knew the exact location of Gethsemane, "for Jesus had often met there with His disciples" (John 18:2). John's footnote that **it was night** is more than the reminiscence of an eyewitness; it has a deeper significance. Not only had darkness descended over Jerusalem but also over Judas's heart. He was now completely under the sway of the power of darkness (cf. Luke 22:53; Acts 26:18; 2 Cor. 6:14–15; Eph. 6:12; Col. 1:13). The next time Judas appears in the narrative is at the head (Luke 22:47) of those coming to arrest Jesus (John 18:3–5).

Several lessons emerge from the tragic story of Judas's betrayal. First, Judas is history's greatest example of lost opportunity and wasted privilege. He heard Jesus teach day in and day out. Further, he had the opportunity to personally interact with Him. He witnessed firsthand the miracles Jesus performed that proved He was God in human flesh. Yet Judas refused Christ's invitation to exchange the oppressive burden of sin for the easy yoke of submission to Him (Matt. 11:28–30).

Second, Judas is the foremost illustration of the danger of loving money (1 Tim. 6:10). Money meant more to him than eternal salvation.

Third, Judas typifies the vileness of spiritual betrayal. In every age there have been Judases, who professed to follow Christ but turned against Him. Judas's life is also a sobering reminder of the need for self-examination (2 Cor. 13:5).

Fourth, Judas was living proof of Christ's patience, mercy, and loving-kindness. Even when he arrived with the mob to arrest Him, Jesus still addressed Judas as "friend" (Matt. 26:50).

Fifth, the example of Judas shows that the Devil will always be at work among God's people. Jesus illustrated that truth in the parable of the wheat and the tares (Matt. 13:24–30, 36–43).

Sixth, Judas proves the deadliness of hypocrisy. He was a fruitless branch, cast into the eternal fire of hell (John 15:6).

Finally, Judas demonstrated that there is nothing sinful men can do to thwart the sovereign will of God. Out of the seeming tragedy of the cross came the triumph of redemption; Satan's apparent victory was in reality his ultimate defeat (Heb. 2:14; 1 John 3:8; cf. Gen. 3:15). God used Judas's treachery for His own glory (cf. Gen. 50:20).

When Judas sold Jesus to His enemies he was in effect selling his own soul to the Devil. In the words of the poet,

> Still as of old
> Men by themselves are priced—
> For thirty pieces Judas sold
> Himself, not Christ

The Supreme Standard of Sacrificial Love
(John 13:31–38)

8

Therefore when he had gone out, Jesus said, "Now is the Son of Man glorified, and God is glorified in Him; if God is glorified in Him, God will also glorify Him in Himself, and will glorify Him immediately. Little children, I am with you a little while longer. You will seek Me; and as I said to the Jews, now I also say to you, 'Where I am going, you cannot come.' A new commandment I give to you, that you love one another, even as I have loved you, that you also love one another. By this all men will know that you are My disciples, if you have love for one another." Simon Peter said to Him, "Lord, where are You going?" Jesus answered, "Where I go, you cannot follow Me now; but you will follow later." Peter said to Him, "Lord, why can I not follow You right now? I will lay down my life for You." Jesus answered, "Will you lay down your life for Me? Truly, truly, I say to you, a rooster will not crow until you deny Me three times." (13:31–38)

Throughout history people have identified themselves as followers of Jesus Christ by various external marks, such as special clothes or even distinctive haircuts. In more recent times some have worn lapel pins, crosses or other jewelry, donned clothing with a Christian theme, affixed Christian bumper stickers to their cars, or sipped their coffee out of mugs emblazoned with a Christian logo.

These external displays of loyalty to Christ are not necessarily wrong, and at times can be helpful in drawing attention to one's Christian testimony. But it is not such superficial, outward symbols that ultimately mark a true follower of Jesus Christ; it is the internal attitudes of the heart (Matt. 5:8; Luke 8:15; Acts 15:9; 16:14; Rom. 2:29; 10:9–10; 2 Cor. 4:6; 2 Tim. 2:22; Heb. 10:22). Only those whose hearts have been transformed by the redeeming grace of God are His children (John 3:3–8; 2 Cor. 5:17; Titus 3:5; 1 Peter 1:3, 23).

That inner transformation results in a changed life, the external fruit of which is seen in a believer's behavior, including both attitudes and actions. Such fruit is detailed in such passages as Galatians 5:22–23; Ephesians 5:9; and Colossians 3:12–15 (cf. Luke 6:43–45), but at its most basic level, this fruit can be summed up in one word: *love*. Because Christians have been regenerated by the power of the Spirit (Titus 3:5–7), they are those who truly love God and love others (cf. Rom. 12:9–21; 1 Cor. 13:3–8; 1 Peter 1:22–25; 1 John 4:7–11). They are those who are enabled to obey the greatest commandments—"'You shall love the Lord your God with all your heart, and with all your soul, and with all your mind, and with all your strength.' The second is this, 'You shall love your neighbor as yourself'" (Mark 12:30–31). Unlike the unredeemed, who hate God and love themselves (cf. Eph. 2:1–3), Christians love the Lord (cf. John 8:42) and also love others (cf. Phil. 2:1–5).

Love for our triune God is most clearly demonstrated not through lip service, but through obedience. Jesus Himself explained to His disciples, "If you love Me, you will keep My commandments" (John 14:15), and later told them, "You are My friends if you do what I command you" (John 15:14). To a crowd of Jews who had purportedly believed in Him, Jesus said, "If you continue in My word, then you are truly disciples of Mine; and you will know the truth, and the truth will make you free." Obedience is the visible demonstration of genuine love for Christ. Thus, as John wrote in his first epistle,

> By this we know that we have come to know Him, if we keep His commandments. The one who says, "I have come to know Him," and does not keep His commandments, is a liar, and the truth is not in him, but whoever keeps His word, in him the love of God has truly been perfected. By this we know that we are in Him: the one who says he abides in Him ought himself to walk in the same manner as He walked. (1 John 2:3–6)

The Bible repeatedly warns of those who claim to be Christ's disciples, but are not (cf. John 2:23–24; 6:60–66; 12:25–26).

Jesus depicted false disciples as seed that fell by the roadside, on rocky soil, or among thorns (Matt. 13:3–7), tares growing alongside wheat (Matt. 13:24–30), bad fish that are thrown away (Matt. 13:47–48), goats condemned to eternal punishment (Matt. 25:33, 41), foolish virgins shut out of the wedding feast (Matt. 25:1–12), worthless slaves who bury their master's talent in the ground (Matt. 25:24–30; cf. Luke 19:11–27), and those left standing outside when the head of the house shuts the door (Luke 13:25–27). The writer of Hebrews referred to them as those who manifest an evil, unbelieving heart by falling away from God (Heb. 3:12), who continue to sin willfully after receiving the knowledge of the truth (Heb. 10:26), and who fall away from the truth to eternal damnation (Heb. 10:39). In his first epistle John described them as apostates who leave the fellowship of believers (1 John 2:19). Like Demas, they profess to love Christ, but in reality they love this present world (2 Tim. 4:10; cf. 1 John 2:16–17).

What makes false disciples so difficult to detect is that they often have the outward trappings of genuine disciples, such as visible morality, an intellectual knowledge of the Bible, and even a level of involvement in the outward life of the church.

But such things are neutral; they neither prove nor disprove the genuineness of a person's faith. The rich young ruler was outwardly moral (Matt. 19:16–21), but went away from his encounter with Christ grieving and unsaved (v. 22). Jesus denounced the Pharisees as "whitewashed tombs which on the outside appear beautiful, but inside they are full of dead men's bones and all uncleanness" (Matt. 23:27). "So you, too," He continued, "outwardly appear righteous to men, but inwardly you are full of hypocrisy and lawlessness" (v. 28). Paul pointed out that both Gentiles (Rom. 1:21) and Jews (Rom. 2:17ff.) can have an intellectual knowledge of God's truth and yet be unsaved. Nor is active involvement in ministry a reliable indicator of saving faith. In Matthew 7:22–23 Jesus warned, "Many will say to Me on that day, 'Lord, Lord, did we not prophesy in Your name, and in Your name cast out demons, and in Your name perform many miracles?' And then I will declare to them, 'I never knew you; depart from Me, you who practice lawlessness.'" Both Judas (Matt. 27:3) and Felix (Acts 24:25) experienced conviction of sin, but remained unsaved. Making a decision to follow Christ is not necessarily a mark of genuine, saving faith either. The rocky soil in the parable of the soils pictures "those who, when they hear, receive the word with joy; and these have no firm root; they believe for a while, and in time of temptation fall away" (Luke 8:13). Similarly, "the seed which fell among the thorns, these are the ones who have heard, and as they go on their way they are choked with worries and riches and pleasures of this life, and bring no fruit to maturity" (v. 14).

John the Baptist challenged his hearers to "bear fruit in keeping with repentance" (Matt. 3:8) and Paul preached that people should perform "deeds appropriate to repentance" (Acts 26:20)—demonstrating a love for God (Luke 10:27; Rom. 8:28) that evidences itself in turning from sin (Prov. 28:13; 2 Cor. 7:10), portraying genuine humility (Ps. 51:17; Matt. 5:3), being committed to prayer (Luke 18:1; 1 Thess. 5:17), exhibiting self-lessness (1 John 2:9–10; 3:14–18), separating oneself from the world (James 4:4; 1 John 2:15–17), growing spiritually (Luke 8:15; John 15:1–2), being obedient (Matt. 7:21; 1 John 2:3–5), and cultivating a desire for God's Word (1 Peter 2:1–3).

Beginning in 13:31 and running through the end of chapter 16, Jesus gave a farewell address to the eleven apostles (Judas having been dismissed [13:27, 30]). The Lord's final charge to the men who would carry on His work included instruction, promises, warnings, and commandments. In this opening section of that address, the Lord highlights the premier mark of those who are His true disciples—namely, sincere, selfless love.

This passage emphasizes the supreme standard of that love by focusing on the person and work of Christ Himself. The profound expression, preeminent example, and powerful extent of Christ's sacrificial love are each displayed in these verses. They illustrate the quality of love that is to characterize those who call themselves His disciples.

THE PROFOUND EXPRESSION OF CHRIST'S LOVE

Therefore when he had gone out, Jesus said, "Now is the Son of Man glorified, and God is glorified in Him; if God is glorified in Him, God will also glorify Him in Himself, and will glorify Him immediately. Little children, I am with you a little while longer. You will seek Me; and as I said to the Jews, now I also say to you, 'Where I am going, you cannot come.'" (13:31–33)

Love's highest expression is self-sacrifice. As the Lord would later say to His disciples, "Greater love has no one than this, that one lay down his life for his friends" (John 15:13; cf. 10:11). Along these same lines, the apostle John wrote in his first epistle, "We know love by this, that He laid down His life for us; and we ought to lay down our lives for the brethren" (1 John 3:16). Jesus, therefore, pointed to His imminent crucifixion in order to underscore what He was about to teach the disciples concerning love.

In this passage, Jesus viewed His death in terms of the glorification that would result from it. Though the crucifixion was the point of His greatest humiliation (Phil. 2:8), it was also the event by which He is most glorified (cf. John 17:4–5; Phil. 2:9–11). His entire ministry pointed to the cross (Mark 10:45), making it the glorious climax of the life He lived perfectly in keeping with His Father's will.

With Judas irrevocably committed to betraying Him, Jesus dismissed him (v. 30). Only then, **when he had gone out,** did the Lord begin His farewell address to the eleven remaining apostles. With the cross only hours away, Jesus' thoughts turned to the fullness of glory that awaited Him in the Father's presence (John 17:5). He made three statements regarding that glory, which He would soon reassume.

The first statement, **"Now is the Son of Man glorified"** (cf. Dan. 7:13–14), refers to His death on the cross the next day. The cross appeared to be a shameful, disastrous defeat for Jesus. Yet it was through the cross, where He gave His life for sinners, that Christ's glory was displayed most clearly. In Acts 3:13 Peter declared to the very people who had crucified Jesus, "The God of Abraham, Isaac and Jacob, the God of our fathers, has glorified His servant Jesus, the one whom you delivered and disowned in the presence of Pilate, when he had decided to release Him."

Jesus was glorified through the cross in several ways. First, His death purchased salvation by satisfying the demands of God's justice for all who would believe in Him. Paul wrote to the Colossians that God, "having canceled out the certificate of debt consisting of decrees against us, which was hostile to us ... has taken it out of the way, having nailed it to the cross" (Col. 2:14; cf. 1:19–22; Rom. 3:25; 5:8–9; Eph. 2:16; Heb. 2:17; 1 John 2:2; 4:10). The death of Jesus Christ also destroyed the power of sin; by "sending His own Son in the likeness of sinful flesh and as an offering for sin, [God] condemned sin in the flesh" (Rom. 8:3; cf. 6:6). Finally, His death destroyed the power of Satan, ending the reign of terror of "him who had the power of death" (Heb. 2:14; cf. Isa. 25:8; Hos. 13:14; 1 Cor. 15:54–57; 2 Tim. 1:10; 1 John 3:8).

Not only was Jesus glorified through His death, **God** also was **glorified in Him.** Through the cross, God's glorious nature was supremely put on display.

First, Christ's death displayed God's power. The fiendish hatred of Satan and the desperate wickedness of the world tried with all their might to destroy Jesus Christ, but failed. God manifested His power by raising Him from the dead (Acts 3:15; 4:10; 13:30; Rom. 10:9; Gal. 1:1; Col. 2:12; 1 Peter 1:21), thus destroying the power of Satan, sin, and death.

Second, Christ's death declared God's justice. The penalty for sinners' violation of His holy law had to be paid, and since "the wages of sin is death" (Rom. 6:23), someone had to die. Therefore "the Lord has caused the iniquity of us all to fall on [Christ]" (Isa. 53:6; cf. v. 11; Heb. 9:28;

1 Peter 2:24). It was only through the sacrifice of His Son that God could "be just and the justifier of the one who has faith in Jesus" (Rom. 3:26).

Third, Christ's death revealed God's holiness. Never did God so clearly manifest His holy hatred for sin than in the suffering and death of His Son. The Father loves the Son with an infinite love. Yet when Jesus became a curse for believers on the cross (Gal. 3:13), the Father, whose "eyes are too pure to approve evil, and . . . can not look on wickedness with favor" (Hab. 1:13), turned away from Him. That caused Jesus to cry out in agony, "My God, My God, why have You forsaken Me?" (Matt. 27:46).

Fourth, Christ's death expressed God's faithfulness. From the moment Adam's and Eve's disobedience plunged the human race into sin, God promised a redeemer (Gen. 3:15; cf. Isa. 52:13–53:12; Matt. 1:21). Even though it cost Him His only Son, He kept that promise.

Finally, in keeping with the overall theme of this passage, Christ's death was the most powerful demonstration of God's love in all of history. To the Romans Paul wrote, "God demonstrates His own love toward us, in that while we were yet sinners, Christ died for us" (Rom. 5:8). "In this is love," John added, "not that we loved God, but that He loved us and sent His Son to be the propitiation for our sins" (1 John 4:10; cf. vv. 9, 14; Gal. 4:4–5).

The last statement Christ made regarding His glorification, **if God is glorified in Him, God will also glorify Him in Himself,** looks beyond the cross to His exaltation to the Father's right hand (Matt. 26:64; Acts 2:33; 5:31; 7:55–56; Rom. 8:34; Eph. 1:20; Col. 3:1; Heb. 1:3, 13; 8:1; 10:12; 12:2; 1 Peter 3:22). Paul had this aspect of Christ's glory in mind when he wrote to the Philippians, "For this reason also, God highly exalted Him, and bestowed on Him the name which is above every name" (Phil. 2:9; cf. Acts 2:33; 7:55; Rom. 8:34; Col. 3:1; Heb. 1:3; 10:12). It was to this glory that Jesus longed to return (John 17:5). The Lord could say that the Father would **glorify Him immediately** because His resurrection and ascension would shortly follow the cross. This was "the joy set before Him" for which He willingly "endured the cross, despising the shame"; His coronation when He "sat down at the right hand of the throne of God" (Heb. 12:2).

But Jesus' glorification meant that He would have to leave the disciples—a truth they found difficult to understand and accept (cf. 14:1; 16:16–18; Matt. 16:21–22; Acts 1:9–11). A few days earlier they had heard Him warn the Jews, "For a little while longer the Light is among you. Walk while you have the Light, so that darkness will not overtake you; he who walks in the darkness does not know where he goes. While you have the Light, believe in the Light, so that you may become sons of Light" (12:35–36). Now gently, using the affectionate term *teknia* (**little children**), the Lord reminded the disciples of that reality, telling them, **"I am**

with you a little while longer." After He was gone, they would long for His visible presence, but **as** He had **said to the Jews** (cf. 7:34; 8:21), He **now . . . also** said **to** them, **"Where I am going, you cannot come."** Not only was the Lord leaving the disciples, He was also going where they would be unable to immediately follow Him. Unlike the unbelieving Jews (7:34), however, the disciples would one day see Jesus again (v. 36; 16:16).

The disciples loved Christ deeply and depended on Him totally. Knowing that He soon would be leaving them was both painful and frightening. His imminent death was certainly not what they would have chosen. And yet, it was both the most necessary and the most loving act Christ could perform on their behalf. As the Lord had taught them earlier, "I am the good shepherd; the good shepherd lays down His life for the sheep" (John 10:11). He had come to die for them, and for all who would believe in Him.

At the cross, the love of God through Christ was put on display in an unsurpassable and eternally unique way (cf. John 3:16). Earlier in this chapter, the Lord had illustrated His humble, sacrificial love by washing the disciples' feet (13:5–15). Now He pointed to the far greater demonstration of His sacrificial love—the cross. It is this infinite expression of love that undergirds the Lord's subsequent command.

The Preeminent Example of Christ's Love

"A new commandment I give to you, that you love one another, even as I have loved you, that you also love one another. By this all men will know that you are My disciples, if you have love for one another." (13:34–35)

The Lord's charge to the eleven apostles in one sense was not new. The Old Testament prescribed love for God (Deut. 6:5) and people (Lev. 19:18), as Jesus Himself affirmed (Matt. 22:34–40). But it was a **new commandment** (cf. 1 John 2:7–8; 3:11; 2 John 5) in the sense that it presented a higher standard of love—one based on the example of the Lord Jesus Christ Himself. Believers face the daunting challenge of loving **one another even as** Jesus **loved** them (cf. 15:12–13, 17). Of course, to love like that is impossible apart from the transforming power of the new covenant (Jer. 31:31–34). It is only "because the love of God has been poured out within our hearts through the Holy Spirit who was given to us" (Rom. 5:5; cf. Gal. 5:22) that believers can love as Jesus commanded.

Christ's example of selfless, sacrificial love sets the supreme standard for believers to follow. D. A. Carson writes,

> The *new command* is simple enough for a toddler to memorize and appreciate, profound enough that the most mature believers are repeatedly embarrassed at how poorly they comprehend it and put it into practice…The more we recognize the depth of our own sin, the more we recognize the love of the Saviour; the more we appreciate the love of the Saviour, the higher his standard appears; the higher his standard appears, the more we recognize in our selfishness, our innate self-centredness, the depth of our own sin. With a standard like this, no thoughtful believer can ever say, this side of the parousia, "I am perfectly keeping the basic stipulation of the new covenant." (*The Gospel According to John*, The Pillar New Testament Commentary [Grand Rapids: Eerdmans, 1991], 484. Italics in original.)

In Ephesians 5:2 Paul exhorted, "Walk in love, just as Christ also loved you and gave Himself up for us." Such love is "patient, … is kind and is not jealous; … does not brag and is not arrogant, does not act unbecomingly; it does not seek its own, is not provoked, does not take into account a wrong suffered, does not rejoice in unrighteousness, but rejoices with the truth; bears all things, believes all things, hopes all things, endures all things" (1 Cor. 13:4–7). If the church ever consistently loved like that, it would have a powerful impact on the world.

In his book *The Mark of the Christian*, Francis Schaeffer listed two practical ways Christians can manifest love for each other. They can do so first by being willing to apologize and seek forgiveness from those they have wronged. What causes the sharpest, most bitter disputes in the body of Christ are not doctrinal differences, but the unloving manner in which those differences are handled. Being willing to apologize to those whom we have offended is crucial to preserving the unity of the body of Christ. In the Sermon on the Mount, Jesus taught that reconciliation with other people is a prerequisite to worshiping God: "Therefore if you are presenting your offering at the altar, and there remember that your brother has something against you, leave your offering there before the altar and go; first be reconciled to your brother, and then come and present your offering" (Matt. 5:23–24).

A second practical way to demonstrate love is to grant forgiveness. In light of the eternal forgiveness that comes through the cross, Christians should be eager to forgive the temporal offenses committed against them (Matt. 18:21–35; cf. 6:12, 14–15). Because God's love has transformed believers' hearts, they are able to extend that love to others in forgiveness. "In this is love," wrote John in his first epistle, "not that we loved God, but that He loved us and sent His Son to be the propitiation for our sins. Beloved, if God so loved us, we also ought to love one another" (1 John 4:10–11). In Luke 17:3–4 Jesus commanded, "Be on your guard! If your brother sins, rebuke him; and if he repents, forgive him. And if he sins against you seven times a day, and returns to you seven times, saying, 'I repent,' forgive him." In Ephesians 4:32 Paul wrote, "Be kind to one another, tender-hearted, forgiving each other, just as God in Christ also has forgiven you" (cf. Col. 3:13).

The Lord's command to love extends beyond the church to embrace all people. Paul's prayer for the Thessalonians was that they would "increase and abound in love for one another, and for all people" (1 Thess. 3:12). He exhorted the Galatians to "do good to all people, and especially to those who are of the household of the faith" (Gal. 6:10). The writer of Hebrews charged his readers, "Do not neglect to show hospitality to strangers, for by this some have entertained angels without knowing it" (Heb. 13:2).

The Lord's statement, **"By this all men will know that you are My disciples"** reveals the effect of believers' having **love for one another:** the world will know that we belong to Him. The church may be orthodox in its doctrine and vigorous in its proclamation of the truth, but that will not persuade unbelievers unless believers love each other. In fact, Jesus gave the world the right to judge whether or not someone is a Christian based on whether or not that person sincerely loves other Christians. Francis Schaeffer writes,

> The church is to be a loving church in a dying culture. . . . In the midst of the world, in the midst of our present dying culture, Jesus is giving a right to the world. Upon his authority he gives the world the right to judge whether you and I are born-again Christians on the basis of our observable love toward all Christians.
>
> That's pretty frightening. Jesus turns to the world and says, "I've something to say to you. On the basis of my authority, I give you a right: you may judge whether or not an individual is a Christian on the basis of the love he shows to all Christians." In other words, if people come up to us and cast into our teeth the judgment that we are not Christians because we have not shown love toward other Christians, we must understand that they are only exercising a prerogative which Jesus gave them. (*The Mark of the Christian* [Downers Grove, Ill.: InterVarsity, 1970], 12–13)

One's love for other believers also assures that believer that his faith is genuine. As John wrote, "We know that we have passed out of death into life, because we love the brethren" (1 John 3:14; cf. 2:10; 4:12).

THE POWERFUL EXTENT OF CHRIST'S LOVE

Simon Peter said to Him, "Lord, where are You going?" Jesus answered, "Where I go, you cannot follow Me now; but you will follow later." Peter said to Him, "Lord, why can I not follow You right now? I will lay down my life for You." Jesus answered, "Will you lay down your life for Me? Truly, truly, I say to you, a rooster will not crow until you deny Me three times." (13:36–38)

Jesus' dialogue with Peter doubly illustrates the extent of Christ's love, made possible through His sacrifice on the cross. On the one hand, their conversation demonstrated the eternal significance of Christ's love —because He guaranteed the eternal life of His disciples. On the other hand, it also evidenced the power of Christ's love, since it would prove greater than the disloyal cowardice of Peter (and the other disciples).

Disturbed by the Lord's declaration that He was leaving them (cf. the discussion of v. 33 above), Peter asked, **"Lord, where are You going?"** His anxious question reflects the disciples' continual inability and unwillingness to accept that Jesus was to leave them. Not long after his magnificent confession that Jesus is "the Christ, the Son of the living God" (Matt. 16:16), Peter rashly "took Him aside and began to rebuke Him, saying, 'God forbid it, Lord! This [His death; v. 21] shall never happen to You'" (v. 22). The disciples were unable to harmonize Jesus' repeated statements that He was going to die (e.g., Matt. 16:21; 17:22–23; 20:17–19; Mark 9:31–32; Luke 18:31–34; 24:6–7, 26) with their preconceived concept of the establishment of the kingdom and the fulfillment of the Old Testament covenants and promises by the Messiah.

Jesus had told the unbelieving Jews, "I go away, and you will seek Me, and will die in your sin; where I am going, you cannot come" (8:21; cf. 7:34). In contrast, His reply to Peter, **"Where I go, you cannot follow Me now; but you will follow later,"** offered the disciples hope. It was not yet the time in God's eternal plan for Peter (and, by implication, the rest of the eleven) to **follow** Jesus to heaven; that would come **later** (cf. 21:18–19).

Though Peter was not satisfied with the Lord's answer (as his hasty reply indicates), the power of Christ's love is displayed in Jesus' response. Because He had set His love upon them, choosing them as His disciples (cf. John 15:16) and loving them enough to die for them (cf. John 13:1), they would one day join Him in His heavenly glory (cf. John 14:2). Nothing, not their coming defection and denial nor even their own future deaths, would be able to separate them from the love of their Lord. As Paul explained in Romans 8:38–39: "For I am convinced that neither death, nor life, nor angels, nor principalities, nor things present, nor things to come, nor powers, nor height, nor depth, nor any other created thing, will be able to separate us from the love of God, which is in Christ Jesus our Lord."

Unwilling to let the issue go, Peter impulsively demanded, **"Lord, why can I not follow You right now?"** Then, vastly overestimating his strength, he added, **"I will lay down my life for You."** The parallel accounts in the Synoptic Gospels reveal just how vehement Peter's boast really was: "But Peter said to Him, 'Even though all may fall away because of You, I will never fall away'" (Matt. 26:33); "But Peter kept saying insistently, 'Even if I have to die with You, I will not deny You!'" (Mark 14:31); "But he said to Him, 'Lord, with You I am ready to go both to prison and to death!'" (Luke 22:33). Following Peter's lead, the rest of the disciples "all were saying the same thing also" (Mark 14:31). Events would prove them all to be drastically overestimating themselves (Matt. 26:56, 69–75); tragically, Jesus' solemn prediction, **"Will you lay down your life for Me** (an ironic statement; it was the Lord who would lay down His life for Peter)**? Truly, truly, I say to you, a rooster will not crow until you deny Me three times,"** would be fulfilled. "Sadly, good intentions in a secure room after good food are far less attractive in a darkened garden with a hostile mob. At this point in his pilgrimage, Peter's intentions and self-assessment vastly outstrip his strength" (Carson, *John*, 486). Evidently Christ's words subdued Peter, who remained uncharacteristically silent through the rest of the Lord's farewell discourse (Peter does not reappear in the narrative until 18:10).

Peter's foolish, though well-intentioned boast was the first thing that led to his failing the test of loyalty to Christ. Another contributing factor was his failure to "keep watching and praying that [he might] not enter into temptation" (Matt. 26:41). Those two manifestations of his pride and overconfidence plunged Peter into the depths of cowardice and remorseful despair (Luke 22:61–62).

But that was not the end of the story for Peter. Christ's love for him would not let Peter slip away (cf. John 6:37, 39; 10:28–29). After being restored by Jesus (John 21:15–17—note the emphasis on love in Christ's restoration of Peter) and filled with the Spirit (Acts 2:1–4), Peter became the leader of the early church. He fearlessly preached the gospel (Acts 2:14–36; 3:12–26), and wrote two epistles in which he distilled some of the painful lessons he had learned (cf. 1 Peter 4:7; 5:5).

Before the end of his life, Peter had come to understand the supreme standard that Christ's love set for him personally and for all those who love the Lord. He willingly died for his Lord (21:18–19). Having been profoundly impacted by Christ's example and been the direct beneficiary of Christ's sacrifice, Peter instructed his readers to "love one another from the heart" (1 Peter 1:22), since they had been redeemed "with precious blood, as of a lamb unblemished and spotless, the blood of Christ" (1:19). They were those who had "tasted the kindness of the Lord" (2:3), and who had Christ as "an example for [them] to follow in His steps" (2:21). Thus, they were to "above all, keep fervent in [their] love for one another, because love covers a multitude of sins" (4:8).

Through His death on the cross, Christ not only exemplified perfect love, He also made it possible for those who were once sinners to be made right before God. Only those who have been regenerated and given the Holy Spirit can love like He loved (cf. 1 Peter 1:22–23; 1 John 2:7–9; 4:7–11). For those who are believers, the sacrificial love of Christ is the supreme standard of what genuine love looks like. It marks His true disciples, and it guarantees both their future salvation and present sanctification. The love of Christ is indeed a glorious truth. As the hymn writer appropriately wrote:

> O the deep, deep love of Jesus, vast, unmeasured, boundless, free!
> Rolling as a mighty ocean in its fullness over me!
> Underneath me, all around me, is the current of Thy love
> Leading onward, leading homeward to Thy glorious rest above!
>
> O the deep, deep love of Jesus, spread His praise from shore to shore!
> How He loveth, ever loveth, changeth never, nevermore!
> How He watches o'er His loved ones, died to call them all His own;
> How for them He intercedeth, watcheth o'er them from the throne!
>
> O the deep, deep love of Jesus, love of every love the best!
> 'Tis an ocean full of blessing, 'tis a haven giving rest!
> O the deep, deep love of Jesus, 'tis a heaven of heavens to me;
> And it lifts me up to glory, for it lifts me up to Thee!

Comfort for Troubled Hearts
(John 14:1–14)

9

"Do not let your heart be troubled; believe in God, believe also in Me. In My Father's house are many dwelling places; if it were not so, I would have told you; for I go to prepare a place for you. If I go and prepare a place for you, I will come again and receive you to Myself, that where I am, there you may be also. And you know the way where I am going." Thomas said to Him, "Lord, we do not know where You are going, how do we know the way?" Jesus said to him, "I am the way, and the truth, and the life; no one comes to the Father but through Me. If you had known Me, you would have known My Father also; from now on you know Him, and have seen Him." Philip said to Him, "Lord, show us the Father, and it is enough for us." Jesus said to him, "Have I been so long with you, and yet you have not come to know Me, Philip? He who has seen Me has seen the Father; how can you say, 'Show us the Father'? Do you not believe that I am in the Father, and the Father is in Me? The words that I say to you I do not speak on My own initiative, but the Father abiding in Me does His works. Believe Me that I am in the Father and the Father is in Me; otherwise believe because of the works themselves. Truly, truly, I say to you, he who believes in Me, the works that I do, he will do also;

and greater works than these he will do; because I go to the Father. Whatever you ask in My name, that will I do, so that the Father may be glorified in the Son. If you ask Me anything in My name, I will do it." (14:1–14)

Life in this fallen, sin-cursed world is packed with trouble and trials. Instead of pretending they do not exist, Scripture faces the hardships of life directly. Job, no stranger to suffering, declared, "Man, who is born of woman, is short-lived and full of turmoil" (Job 14:1). Eliphaz, one of Job's would-be counselors, noted that "man is born for trouble, as sparks fly upward" (Job 5:7). In Jeremiah 20:18 the prophet lamented, "Why did I ever come forth from the womb to look on trouble and sorrow, so that my days have been spent in shame?" Knowing that His followers would face trouble in this life, the Lord Jesus Christ commanded them, "Do not worry about tomorrow; for tomorrow will care for itself. Each day has enough trouble of its own" (Matt. 6:34). In John 16:33 He reiterated the reality, saying, "In the world you have tribulation." Paul and Barnabas reminded believers in Asia Minor that "through many tribulations we must enter the kingdom of God" (Acts 14:22).

But the blessed promise of Scripture is that God, "the Father of mercies and God of all comfort" (2 Cor. 1:3; cf. Isa. 51:12), will comfort His children. As Paul went on to write, He "comforts us in all our affliction so that we will be able to comfort those who are in any affliction with the comfort with which we ourselves are comforted by God. For just as the sufferings of Christ are ours in abundance, so also our comfort is abundant through Christ" (vv. 4–5). God comforts because He is "compassionate and gracious" (Ex. 34:6; cf. Deut. 4:31; 2 Chron. 30:9; Neh. 9:17, 31; Pss. 78:38; 103:8; 111:4; 116:5; Lam. 3:22; Dan. 9:9; Joel 2:13; Jonah 4:2; James 5:11).

God initially comforts His people by granting them forgiveness, salvation, and the Holy Spirit, who is the Comforter (14:16, 26). Jesus promised that "those who mourn" over their sin, "shall be comforted" (Matt. 5:4; cf. Isa. 12:1–2; 40:1–2; 51:11–12; 52:9). That eternally decreed comfort (2 Thess. 2:16) will culminate in the perfect peace and eternal bliss of heaven (Isa. 25:8; Rev. 7:17; 21:4).

God not only promises comfort to believers in the future, but also in the trials and difficulties of this present life. In the most beloved of the Psalms, David wrote confidently, "Even though I walk through the valley of the shadow of death, I fear no evil, for You are with me; Your rod and Your staff, they comfort me" (Ps. 23:4). In Psalm 86:17 he exulted, "You, O Lord, have helped me and comforted me." Speaking from his own experience, Paul wrote that "God ... comforts the depressed" (2 Cor. 7:6). The apostle reminded the Thessalonians that God would "comfort and strengthen [their] hearts in every good work and word" (2 Thess. 2:17).

God comforts His people when they cry out to Him in prayer. The psalmist prayed, "O may Your lovingkindness comfort me ... My eyes fail with longing for Your word, while I say, 'When will You comfort me?'" (Ps. 119:76, 82). The Word also is a source of comfort: "This is my comfort in my affliction, that Your word has revived me.... I have remembered Your ordinances from of old, O Lord, and comfort myself" (Ps. 119:50, 52). The Holy Spirit, the divine Comforter (NASB, "Helper"; John 14:16, 26; 15:26; 16:7), also comforts Christians: "So the church throughout all Judea and Galilee and Samaria enjoyed peace, being built up; and going on in the fear of the Lord and in the comfort of the Holy Spirit, it continued to increase" (Acts 9:31).

On the night before His death, the Lord Jesus Christ addressed the eleven remaining disciples (minus Judas) in the upper room. Though the cross, with its sin-bearing (2 Cor. 15:21) and separation from the Father (Matt. 27:46), was imminent, Jesus' focus was not on His own ordeal. Instead, He was concerned for the disciples, whose world was about to be shattered. They were already hurting, confused, and anxious because of the impending loss of their beloved Master. Soon He would be gone, and they would "weep and lament" (16:20). Because of His perfect and complete love for the disciples (cf. the discussion of 13:1 in chapter 6 of this volume), Jesus sought to comfort them in the face of His departure. The first fourteen verses of chapter 14 lay the foundation for that comfort—not only for the disciples gathered in the upper room but also for all believers. Comfort comes from trusting Jesus Christ's presence, preparation, proclamation, person, power, and promise.

COMFORT COMES FROM
TRUSTING CHRIST'S PRESENCE

"Do not let your heart be troubled; believe in God, believe also in Me. (14:1)

The last few days had been an emotional roller coaster for the disciples. Their fervent messianic hopes had reached an apex during the dizzying excitement of the triumphal entry—only to be dashed when Jesus publicly announced His impending death: "Truly, truly, I say to you, unless a grain of wheat falls into the earth and dies, it remains alone; but if it dies, it bears much fruit" (John 12:24), and then repeated that prediction privately to them: "Little children, I am with you a little while longer. You will seek Me; and as I said to the Jews, now I also say to you, 'Where I am going, you cannot come'" (13:33).

Like their fellow Jews, the disciples saw the Messiah as a conquering king. He would, they passionately believed, free Israel from bondage to Rome, restore her sovereignty and glory, and extend it over the world. The concept of a dying Messiah had no place in their theology (cf. Luke 24:21). On a more personal note, the disciples had forsaken everything to follow Jesus (Matt. 19:27); now He apparently was forsaking them.

Other events of that evening in the upper room had added to the emotional turmoil that the disciples felt. They had been shamed by their prideful refusal to wash each other's feet, which prompted Jesus to humbly do what they refused to do (13:3–5). They were dumbfounded to hear Jesus predict that one of them would betray Him (13:21–22) and appalled at the news that their stalwart leader Peter, seemingly the strongest and boldest of them all, would cravenly deny Christ (13:38). They were also no doubt unsettled because they sensed that the Lord Himself was troubled (13:21).

Thus when Jesus told them, **Do not let your heart be troubled** (cf. Gen. 15:1; 26:24; 46:3; Ex. 14:13; Num. 21:34; Deut. 1:21, 29; 20:1; 31:6; Josh. 1:9; 11:6; 1 Chron. 22:13; 28:20; Prov. 3:25; Isa. 37:6; 41:10, 13, 14; 43:1, 5; 44:2, 8; 51:7; Jer. 1:8; 42:11; 46:27–28; Lam. 3:57; Joel 2:21; Hag. 2:5; Zech. 8:13, 15; Matt. 10:31; Acts 18:9; 27:24; 1 Peter 3:14; Rev. 2:10), He was not telling them not to start being troubled. They were already troubled, and He was telling them to stop. **Troubled** translates a form of the verb *tarassō* ("to shake," or "to stir up"). It is used to describe the literal stirring up of the pool of Bethesda (5:7) and, figuratively, of severe mental or spiritual agitation (Matt. 2:3; 14:26; Luke 1:12; 24:38; John 11:33; 13:21; Acts 15:24). As always, Jesus knew the disciples' hearts; He understood their confusion and concerns. Ever the compassionate Savior, He sympathized with their sorrow and grief (Isa. 53:3–4; Heb. 4:15). Even though the disciples were oblivious to His pain, He felt theirs and sought to comfort them.

The Lord then added a second command. Just as the disciples **believe in God,** they are to **believe also in** Him. Christ affirmed His deity, placing Himself on a par with the Father as an appropriate object of faith. In calling them to hope in God, Jesus was calling His disciples to put their hope in Him.

Despite occasional lapses into idolatry, Israel had a heritage of faith and trust in God. Abraham "believed in the Lord; and He reckoned it to him as righteousness" (Gen. 15:6). Moses' charge to the nation, "Hear, O Israel! The Lord is our God, the Lord is one!" (Deut. 6:4), captures the essence of Old Testament faith. David cried, "To You, O Lord, I lift up my soul. O my God, in You I trust" (Ps. 25:1–2; cf. 42:5, 11). In another psalm he wrote, "But as for me, I trust in You, O Lord, I say, 'You are my God'" (Ps.

31:14). In a passage especially appropriate for the disciples' situation, David declared confidently,"When I am afraid, I will put my trust in You" (Ps. 56:3; cf. vv. 4, 11). King Hezekiah was commended because "he trusted in the Lord, the God of Israel; so that after him there was none like him among all the kings of Judah, nor among those who were before him" (2 Kings 18:5). In short, all "those who know [God's] name will put their trust in [Him]" (Ps. 9:10; cf. 21:7; 22:4, 5, 9; 26:1; 28:7; 31:6, 14; 32:10; 33:21; 37:3, 5; 40:4; 52:8; 55:23; 62:8; 84:12; 86:2; 91:2; 112:7; 115:9–11; 125:1; 143:8; Prov. 3:5; 16:20; 22:19; 28:25; 29:25; Isa. 12:2; 26:3–4; 50:10; Jer. 17:7; Dan. 6:23).

Many in Israel believed in God despite never having seen Him. Even Moses "endured, as seeing Him who is unseen" (Heb. 11:27), since, as God Himself declared to him,"You cannot see My face, for no man can see Me and live!" (Ex. 33:20; cf. Deut. 4:12; John 1:18; 6:46; 1 Tim. 6:16). The disciples needed to have that same kind of faith in Jesus when He was no longer visibly present with them. The Lord was not calling the disciples to believe savingly in Him; they had already done so (13:10–11). The present tense form of the verb *pisteuō* (**believe**) refers instead to an ongoing trust in Him. Though they genuinely believed in Jesus, the disciples' faith was already beginning to waver. Soon, when He was taken from them and they faced the traumatic events of His betrayal, arrest, trial, and crucifixion, it would reach its lowest ebb.

But Christ did not need to be visibly present for the disciples to receive comfort and strength from Him. In fact, Jesus commended the faith of those who had not seen Him (John 20:29; cf. 1 Peter 1:8). Though He would no longer be visibly present with the disciples, Christ's promise, "I will never desert you, nor will I ever forsake you" (Heb. 13:5; cf. Gen. 28:15; Deut. 31:6, 8; Josh. 1:5; 1 Sam. 12:22; 1 Chron. 28:20; Ps. 37:25, 28; Isa. 41:10), would still hold true.

It is the post-Pentecost ministry of the Holy Spirit to make believers aware of Christ's comforting presence. Later in this chapter Jesus promised,

> I will ask the Father, and He will give you another Helper, that He may be with you forever; that is the Spirit of truth, whom the world cannot receive, because it does not see Him or know Him, but you know Him because He abides with you and will be in you. I will not leave you as orphans; I will come to you. (vv. 16–18)

In 15:26 He told the disciples,"When the Helper comes, whom I will send to you from the Father, that is the Spirit of truth who proceeds from the Father, He will testify about Me" (cf. 16:7, 13–14).

The presence of Christ is enough to calm the believing heart in whatever perplexing, troubling situation it finds itself. As the godly Puritan John Owen noted, "A sense of God's presence in love is sufficient to rebuke all anxiety and fears; and not only so, but to give, in the midst of them, solid consolation and joy" (*The Forgiveness of Sin* [repr.; Grand Rapids: Baker, 1977], 17).

COMFORT COMES FROM
TRUSTING CHRIST'S PREPARATION

In My Father's house are many dwelling places; if it were not so, I would have told you; for I go to prepare a place for you. If I go and prepare a place for you, I will come again and receive you to Myself, that where I am, there you may be also. (14:2–3)

Another offering to comfort the disciples was the revelation that their separation from Him would not be permanent. Jesus' words, **if it were not so, I would have told you,** assured the disciples that He was telling them the truth. He was going away in part to **prepare a place for** them where they would be reunited with Him in His heavenly glory (John 17:24).

The **Father's house** is another name for heaven, which is variously described as a country (Heb. 11:16), due to its vastness; a city (Heb. 12:22), emphasizing its large number of inhabitants; a kingdom (2 Tim. 4:18), because God is its King (Dan. 4:37; cf. Matt. 11:25; Acts 17:24); paradise (Luke 23:43; 2 Cor. 12:4; Rev. 2:7), because of its indescribable beauty; and a place of rest (cf. Heb. 4:1–11), where the redeemed are free from the wearying conflict with sin, Satan, and the evil world system that hates those who love Christ (John 15:19; 17:14).

The **dwelling places** of which the Lord spoke must not be pictured as separate buildings, as if heaven were a giant housing tract. The picture is rather of a father building additional rooms onto his house for his sons and their families, as was often done in Israel. In modern terms, the dwelling places might be pictured as rooms or apartments in the Father's spacious house. The emphasis is on heaven's intimacy, where "the tabernacle of God is among men, and He will dwell among them, and they shall be His people, and God Himself will be among them" (Rev. 21:3). That there will be **many** such dwelling places means there will be room for all whom God, in His infinite love and mercy, has chosen to redeem. According to Revelation 21:16, "The city [the New Jerusalem] is laid out as a square, and its length is as great as the width; and he measured the city with the rod, fifteen hundred miles; its length and width and height are equal." In terms of modern measurements, the base of the city alone is over two million square miles—more than half the size of the United States. Its height adds exponentially to its living space.

The place the Lord Jesus Christ is preparing for believers is a place of dazzling, inexpressible beauty:

> Then one of the seven angels who had the seven bowls full of the seven last plagues came and spoke with me, saying, "Come here, I will show you the bride, the wife of the Lamb." And he carried me away in the Spirit to a great and high mountain, and showed me the holy city, Jerusalem, coming down out of heaven from God, having the glory of God. Her brilliance was like a very costly stone, as a stone of crystal-clear jasper. It had a great and high wall, with twelve gates, and at the gates twelve angels; and names were written on them, which are the names of the twelve tribes of the sons of Israel. There were three gates on the east and three gates on the north and three gates on the south and three gates on the west. And the wall of the city had twelve foundation stones, and on them were the twelve names of the twelve apostles of the Lamb. The one who spoke with me had a gold measuring rod to measure the city, and its gates and its wall. The city is laid out as a square, and its length is as great as the width; and he measured the city with the rod, fifteen hundred miles; its length and width and height are equal. And he measured its wall, seventy-two yards, according to human measurements, which are also angelic measurements. The material of the wall was jasper; and the city was pure gold, like clear glass. The foundation stones of the city wall were adorned with every kind of precious stone. The first foundation stone was jasper; the second, sapphire; the third, chalcedony; the fourth, emerald; the fifth, sardonyx; the sixth, sardius; the seventh, chrysolite; the eighth, beryl; the ninth, topaz; the tenth, chrysoprase; the eleventh, jacinth; the twelfth, amethyst. And the twelve gates were twelve pearls; each one of the gates was a single pearl. And the street of the city was pure gold, like transparent glass. I saw no temple in it, for the Lord God the Almighty and the Lamb are its temple. And the city has no need of the sun or of the moon to shine on it, for the glory of God has illumined it, and its lamp is the Lamb. The nations will walk by its light, and the kings of the earth will bring their glory into it. In the daytime (for there will be no night there) its gates will never be closed; and they will bring the glory and the honor of the nations into it; and nothing unclean, and no one who practices abomination and lying, shall ever come into it, but only those whose names are written in the Lamb's book of life. (Rev. 21:9–27)

Jesus' promise, **I will come again and receive you to Myself, that where I am, there you may be also,** refers to the rapture of the church (1 Cor. 15:51–54; 1 Thess. 4:13–18; Rev. 3:10). The absence of any reference to judgment indicates that the Lord was not referring here to His second coming to earth to judge and establish His kingdom (Matt.

13:36–43, 47–50; 24:29–44; 25:31–46; Rev. 19:11–15), but rather to the catching up of the believers into heaven (cf. 1 Thess. 4:13–18; 1 Cor. 15:51–57). Further differences between the two events reinforce that truth. At the second coming angels gather the elect (Matt. 24:30–31), but here Jesus told the disciples He would personally come for them. At the second coming the saints will return with Christ (Rev. 19:8, 14) as He comes to set up His earthly kingdom (Rev. 19:11–20:6); here He promises to return for them. Between the rapture and the second coming, the church will celebrate the marriage supper of the Lamb (Rev. 19:7–10), and believers will receive their rewards (1 Cor. 3:10–15; 4:5; 2 Cor. 5:10). When He returns in judgment and kingdom glory, the saints will come with Him (Rev. 19:7, 11–14).

COMFORT COMES FROM
TRUSTING CHRIST'S PROCLAMATION

And you know the way where I am going." Thomas said to Him, "Lord, we do not know where You are going, how do we know the way?" Jesus said to him, "I am the way, and the truth, and the life; no one comes to the Father but through Me." (14:4–6)

Since He had already told them that He was returning to the Father (e.g., 7:33; 13:1, 3), Jesus expected the disciples to **know the way where** He was **going.** But by this time their minds were so rattled (cf. the discussion of v. 1 above) that they were not sure of anything. **Thomas** vocalized their perplexity when he **said to Him, "Lord, we do not know where You are going, how do we know the way?"** (cf. Peter's similar question in 13:36). By now they understood that Jesus was going to die. But their knowledge stopped at death; they had no firsthand experience of what lay beyond the grave. Furthermore, Jesus Himself had told them that at this time they could not go where He was going (13:33, 36). If they did not know where the Lord was going, how could they know the way to get there?

Jesus' reply, **"I am the way, and the truth, and the life; no one comes to the Father but through Me,"** is the sixth "I AM" statement in John's gospel (cf. 6:35; 8:12; 10:7, 9, 11, 14; 11:25; the seventh comes in 15:1, 5). Jesus alone is the **way** to God (10:7–9; Acts 4:12) because He alone is the **truth** (John 1:14, 17; 18:37; Rev. 3:7; 19:11) about God and He alone possesses the **life** of God (John 1:4; 5:26; 11:25; 1 John 1:1; 5:20). The purpose of this gospel is to make those things known, so they are repeated throughout the book so as to lead people to faith and salvation (20:31).

The Bible teaches that God may be approached exclusively through His only-begotten Son. Jesus alone is the "door of the sheep" (10:7); all others are "thieves and robbers" (v. 8), and it is only the one who "enters through [Him who] will be saved" (v. 9). The way of salvation is a narrow path entered through a small, narrow gate, and few find it (Matt. 7:13–14; cf. Luke 13:24). "There is salvation in no one else," Peter boldly affirmed, "for there is no other name under heaven that has been given among men by which we must be saved" (Acts 4:12). Thus, it is "he who believes in the Son [who] has eternal life; but he who does not obey the Son will not see life, but the wrath of God abides on him" (John 3:36), and "no man can lay a foundation other than the one which is laid, which is Jesus Christ" (1 Cor. 3:11), because "there is one God, and one mediator also between God and men, the man Christ Jesus" (1 Tim. 2:5).

The postmodern belief that there are many paths to religious truth is a satanic lie. F. F. Bruce writes,

> He [Jesus] is, in fact, the only way by which men and women may come to the Father; there is no other way. If this seems offensively exclusive, let it be borne in mind that the one who makes this claim is the incarnate Word, the revealer of the Father. If God has no avenue of communication with mankind apart from his Word . . . mankind has no avenue of approach to God apart from that same Word, who became flesh and dwelt among us in order to supply such an avenue of approach. (*The Gospel of John* [Grand Rapids: Eerdmans, 1983], 298)

Jesus alone reveals God (John 1:18; cf. 3:13; 10:30–38; 12:45; 14:9; Col. 1:15, 19; 2:9; Heb. 1:3), and no one who rejects His proclamation of the truth can legitimately claim to know God (John 5:23; 8:42–45; 15:23; Matt. 11:27; 1 John 2:23; 2 John 9). It was because the early Christians taught that Jesus Christ is the only way to salvation that Christianity became known as "The Way" (Acts 9:2; 19:9, 23; 22:4; 24:14, 22).

COMFORT COMES FROM
TRUSTING CHRIST'S PERSON

If you had known Me, you would have known My Father also; from now on you know Him, and have seen Him." Philip said to Him, "Lord, show us the Father, and it is enough for us." Jesus said to him, "Have I been so long with you, and yet you have not come to know Me, Philip? He who has seen Me has seen the Father; how can you say, 'Show us the Father'? Do you not believe that I am in the Father, and the Father is in Me? The words that I say to you I do not speak on My own initiative, but the Father

abiding in Me does His works. Believe Me that I am in the Father and the Father is in Me; otherwise believe because of the works themselves. (14:7–11)

To bolster the disciples' wavering faith, vocalized by Thomas (v. 5), Jesus pointed them back to the truth that He is God incarnate. **"If you had known Me,"** He chided them (the verbs in v. 7 are plurals, indicating that the Lord was no longer addressing Thomas alone as in v. 6, but all the disciples), **"you would have known My Father also."** If the disciples had fully grasped who Jesus was, they would have known the Father as well.

The Lord's statement was nothing less than a claim to full deity and equality with the Father. He is the way to God (v. 6) because He is God. He is not merely a manifestation of God; He is God manifested. That truth, a constant theme in John's gospel (e.g., 1:1–3, 14, 17, 18; 5:18; 8:58; 10:30–33; 19:7; 20:28–29), is the watershed that divides true from false views of Christ. Many throughout history and today have regarded Jesus as nothing more than a good man; an exemplary, virtuous moral or religious teacher. But that is impossible. No one who claimed to be God incarnate, if his claim were false, could be a good man. If he knew his claim was false, he would be an evil deceiver; if he sincerely believed it was true when it was not, he would be a raving lunatic. But the evidence conclusively shows that Christ was neither a liar nor insane. Rather He was God, exactly as He claimed to be. (For a further defense of this truth, see John MacArthur, *John 1–11,* The MacArthur New Testament Commentary [Chicago: Moody, 2006], chapters 7, 15, 24.) How each person reacts to Christ's claim determines his or her eternal destiny (John 8:24).

It is possible to interpret the phrase **from now on you know Him, and have seen Him** as referring to that very moment in the upper room. However Philip's question in verse 8, suggesting that the disciples still did not understand Jesus' point, argues against an immediate fulfillment of His words. It was only after Christ's death, resurrection, ascension, and the coming of the Spirit at Pentecost (John 14:17, 26; 15:26; 16:13) that the disciples would finally understand Jesus' deity and relationship to the Father (John 20:28; Acts 2:22ff.; 3:12ff.; 4:8–12; 5:29–32). Because that understanding would certainly come in the future, Jesus spoke of it as if it were a present reality.

Thomas was silenced by Jesus' reply to his question, but **Philip** was still not satisfied. Expressing the disciples' continuing lack of understanding, Philip **said to Him, "Lord, show us the Father."** He was not content with indirect knowledge of God, even that given by Jesus Himself. Instead, he wanted a visible manifestation of the Father's presence to sustain his faith. Perhaps he had in mind the experiences of Jacob (Gen.

32:30), Samson's parents (Judg. 13), Moses (Ex. 33:18–23; 34:6–7), the elders of Israel (Ex. 24:9–10), Isaiah (Isa. 6:1–4), and Ezekiel (Ezek. 1:1ff.). Such a theophany, Philip added, would be **enough** to reassure them (the plural pronoun **us** suggests that Philip spoke for the others as well).

The Lord's reply, **"Have I been so long with you, and yet you have not come to know Me, Philip?"** was a rebuke both to Philip for his faithless request and, by extension, the rest of the disciples for their wavering faith. (The first occurrence of **you** in the English translation reflects a plural pronoun in the Greek text.) Reiterating the truth of His deity and oneness with the Father (v. 7), Jesus told Philip and the others plainly, **"He who has seen Me has seen the Father; how can you say, 'Show us the Father'?"** (cf. v. 20; 1:18; 10:38; 12:45; 15:24; 17:11, 21–23).

Christ's words are tinged with sadness. Such ignorance on the part of unbelievers (cf. John 1:10; 8:19; 16:3) was deplorable, but expected. But the Lord had poured His life into these men. They had lived day in and day out with the "image of the invisible God" (Col. 1:15; cf. 2 Cor. 4:4); the one in whom "all the fullness of Deity dwells in bodily form" (Col. 2:9); the "radiance of [God's] glory and the exact representation of His nature" (Heb. 1:3). Yet despite being with Him for so long, the disciples still did not fully comprehend the truth about Jesus and His union with the Father. This confusion seems to be related to Jesus' failure to live up to their messianic expectations. They were still wondering after the resurrection (Acts 1:6). That was both inexcusable for them and disappointing to Jesus.

The Lord's further question in verse 10, **"Do you not believe that I am in the Father?"** and His command in verse 11, **"Believe Me that I am in the Father and the Father is in Me,"** suggest the cure for the disciples' confusion and turmoil. Faith is not only the means of appropriating salvation (Eph. 2:8; cf. Acts 15:9; 20:21; 26:18; Rom. 3:22, 25–28, 30; 4:5; 5:1; Gal. 2:16; 3:7–9, 24, 26; Phil. 3:9; 2 Thess. 2:13; 2 Tim. 3:15), it is also the very essence of sustaining the Christian life (Acts 6:5; 11:24; 2 Cor. 5:7; Gal. 2:20; Eph. 6:16; 1 Thess. 5:8; 1 Tim. 4:12; 6:11; 2 Tim. 2:22; Heb. 13:7).

But the Christian faith is neither a blind, irrational, "leap in the dark" nor a vague, mystical faith in faith itself. It rests on the solid ground of overwhelming evidence. Jesus shored up the disciples' sagging faith by reminding them first of His **words,** which He did **not speak on** His **own initiative,** but through the abiding power of the **Father.** John the Baptist testified of Christ, "For He whom God has sent speaks the words of God" (John 3:34). Jesus declared in John 7:16, "My teaching is not Mine, but His who sent Me." In 12:49 He added, "For I did not speak on My own initiative, but the Father Himself who sent Me has given Me a commandment as to what to say and what to speak." So powerful were the Lord's words that at the conclusion of the Sermon on the Mount, "when Jesus had finished these words, the crowds were amazed at His teaching; for He was teaching them as one having authority, and not as their scribes" (Matt. 7:28–29). Explaining to their superiors why they failed to seize Him, those sent to arrest Jesus said in awe, "Never has a man spoken the way this man speaks" (John 7:46). The powerful, divine words of Jesus Christ, which penetrate the heart and mind, are the answer to the cry of the redeemed, "Increase our faith!" (Luke 17:5; cf. 2 Cor. 10:15).

Not only is faith based on the words of Christ, but also on the unprecedented (John 15:24; cf. 9:32; Matt. 9:33; Mark 2:12), undeniable (John 3:2; 7:31; 11:47) miraculous works He performed. Therefore, He challenged the disciples, **"Believe Me that I am in the Father and the Father is in Me; otherwise believe because of the works themselves."** In John 5:36 Jesus declared, "The works which the Father has given Me to accomplish—the very works that I do—testify about Me, that the Father has sent Me," while in 10:25 He added, "The works that I do in My Father's name, these testify of Me" (cf. vv. 32, 37–38; Matt. 11:2–5; Acts 5:22–23). His claim to be equal with God (cf. John 5:18) was not only established by His own self-testimony (and the testimony of John the Baptist [5:31–34] and of the Old Testament Scriptures [5:39–46]), but confirmed by the mighty and extensive supernatural works that the Spirit enabled Him to accomplish in the will of the Father (John 5:36–37).

COMFORT COMES FROM
TRUSTING CHRIST'S POWER

Truly, truly, I say to you, he who believes in Me, the works that I do, he will do also; and greater works than these he will do; because I go to the Father. (14:12)

The astonishing promise to the one **who believes in** Christ is that **the works that** He does, **he will do also; and greater works than these he will do.** The **greater works** to which Jesus referred were not greater in power than those He performed, but greater in extent. The disciples would indeed perform miraculous **works,** as Jesus had (cf. Acts 5:12–16; Heb. 2:3–4). But those physical miracles were not primarily what Jesus had in mind, since the apostles did not do more powerful miracles than He had. When the Lord spoke of His followers performing **greater works,** He was referring to the extent of the spiritual miracle of salvation. Jesus never preached outside of Palestine, yet His followers would spread the gospel throughout the world. Jesus had only a limited outreach to Gentiles (cf. Mark 7:26ff.), but the disciples (particularly Peter and later Paul) would reach the Gentile world with the gospel. The number of believers in Christ would also grow far beyond the hundreds (Acts 1:15; 1 Cor. 15:6) that were numbered during His lifetime.

The power to perform those greater works would only be available **because** Jesus was going **to the Father.** It was only then that He would send the Holy Spirit (John 7:39; cf. 14:16–17, 26; 15:26; 16:13; Acts 1:5) to indwell believers (Rom. 8:9–11) and empower them for ministry (Acts 1:8; 1 Cor. 12:4–11; cf. Eph. 3:20).

Christ's promise to send the Holy Spirit offered further comfort to the disciples. Though Jesus would no longer be visibly present with them, the Spirit would provide them with all the power they needed to extend the work He had begun (cf. Acts 1:8).

COMFORT COMES FROM
TRUSTING CHRIST'S PROMISE

Whatever you ask in My name, that will I do, so that the Father may be glorified in the Son. If you ask Me anything in My name, I will do it. (14:13–14)

As if His pledge to send the Holy Spirit to empower them was not enough, the Lord gave the disciples another incredible pledge. During their time with Him, they had depended on Jesus to supply all their needs (cf. Luke 22:35). He had provided food for them (Luke 5:4–6; John 21:5–12), and on one occasion even paid Peter's taxes (Matt. 17:24–27). Now He was about to leave them, and they, having left everything to follow Him (Matt. 19:27), must have wondered where their resources would come from.

Anticipating their concern, Jesus promised that even after He was gone, He would continue to supply the disciples' needs from heaven. Repeating it twice for emphasis, the Lord reassured them, **Whatever you ask in My name, that will I do . . . If you ask Me anything in My name, I will do it.** Prayer would bridge the gap between their needs and His abundant, limitless, undepleted resources (cf. Phil. 4:19). The ultimate purpose for Christ's gracious provision, as is true of everything that God does, is **that the Father may be glorified in the Son.**

To **ask in** Jesus' **name** does not mean to frivolously tack the words "in Jesus' name" onto the end of a prayer. It is not a magic formula that obligates God to grant every selfish request that people make. To pray in Jesus' name has a far more profound and serious meaning.

First, it means to make requests consistent with God's will and the purposes of His kingdom. In His model prayer, Jesus taught His followers to pray, "Your kingdom come. Your will be done, on earth as it is in heaven" (Matt. 6:10).

Second, it is to acknowledge one's spiritual poverty, lack of self-sufficiency, and utter unworthiness to receive anything from God based on one's own merits (Matt. 5:3). It is to approach God based on the merits of Jesus Christ (cf. John 16:26-28) and to acknowledge one's complete dependence on Him to supply every need (Matt. 6:25–32; Phil. 4:19).

Finally, it is to express a sincere desire that God would be glorified in His answer. It is to align one's requests with the Father's supreme goal of glorifying the Son. When believers pray in this way, they pray in keeping with Jesus' **name**—His person, His purposes, and His preeminence.

So in readying the disciples for His departure, the Lord emphasized His continual care for them—concerning Himself with their comfort even in the face of His own imminent suffering. Out of His profound love for them and for all who would follow them in faith, He gave them tangible and reliable reasons to hope.

Christ's message of comfort and hope is as applicable today as it was in the upper room two millennia ago. This world is full of false hopes. But apart from the Spirit-given assurance of Christ's continuing presence, the confidence that He is preparing a place in heaven, the conviction that He is the only way to God, the realization that He is God incarnate, the recognition of His sustaining power, and the certain expectation that He will perfectly fulfill His promises with heavenly supply and regularity, all other sources of comfort and hope are nothing more than "broken cisterns that can hold no water" (Jer. 2:13). They will ultimately disappoint, whereas Jesus never fails.

The Legacy of Jesus
(John 14:15–26)

10

"If you love Me, you will keep My commandments. I will ask the Father, and He will give you another Helper, that He may be with you forever; that is the Spirit of truth, whom the world cannot receive, because it does not see Him or know Him, but you know Him because He abides with you and will be in you. I will not leave you as orphans; I will come to you. After a little while the world will no longer see Me, but you will see Me; because I live, you will live also. In that day you will know that I am in My Father, and you in Me, and I in you. He who has My commandments and keeps them is the one who loves Me; and he who loves Me will be loved by My Father, and I will love him and will disclose Myself to him." Judas (not Iscariot) said to Him, "Lord, what then has happened that You are going to disclose Yourself to us and not to the world?" Jesus answered and said to him, "If anyone loves Me, he will keep My word; and My Father will love him, and We will come to him and make Our abode with him. He who does not love Me does not keep My words; and the word which you hear is not Mine, but the Father's who sent Me. These things I have spoken to you while abiding with you. But the Helper, the Holy Spirit, whom the Father will send in My name, He will teach

you all things, and bring to your remembrance all that I said to you." (John 14:15–26)

As people grow older, they naturally spend more and more time thinking about the legacy they will leave behind. They begin to consider how they will be remembered, and what they will hand down to those coming after them. Like never before, they reflect on the heritage they have built over their lifetime.

On the financial front, many plan for the distribution of the wealth they have accumulated, wanting to make sure it goes to their heirs of choice, and not to the government or an unacceptable third party. Not surprisingly, addressing such concerns has become big business. There are innumerable estate planners, investment counselors, and attorneys offering means to accomplish people's differing objectives. Television commercials tout life insurance and exhort seniors not to burden their families with expensive funeral costs. Local bookstores are fully stocked with self-help books and computer programs dealing with estate planning. Special seminars are frequently offered on how to handle wills and trusts. All of this is predicated on people's desire to preserve their wealth and pass it on to the next generation.

Such concerns are valid. The Bible speaks of the importance of wise stewardship (cf. Prov. 27:23–27; Matt. 25:14–30; Luke 16:11), and assumes that people will leave an inheritance to those who come after them (Prov. 13:22; 17:2; 19:14; 20:21; Matt. 21:38; Luke 12:13; 15:11–12). But of far greater importance than the corruptible, earthly inheritance they leave others is the incorruptible heavenly inheritance God has for every child of His. That inheritance is "imperishable and undefiled and will not fade away, reserved in heaven for [them]" (1 Peter 1:4; cf. Eph. 1:11). It is far beyond human understanding, prompting Paul to write, "I pray that the eyes of your heart may be enlightened, so that you will know what is the hope of His calling, what are the riches of the glory of His inheritance in the saints" (Eph. 1:18).

No human merit can qualify lost sinners to receive the riches of heaven; only those who "turn from darkness to light and from the dominion of Satan to God [and] receive forgiveness of sins [will receive] an inheritance among those who have been sanctified by faith in [Christ]" (Acts 26:18; cf. 20:32). They, "being justified by His grace, [are] made heirs according to the hope of eternal life" (Titus 3:7; cf. Heb. 9:15). Believers receive their inheritance from all three members of the Trinity. The Father "has qualified us to share in the inheritance of the saints in Light" (Col. 1:12); we are "fellow heirs with Christ" (Rom. 8:17; cf. Col. 3:24); and "the Holy Spirit ... is given as a pledge of our inheritance" (Eph. 1:13–14).

But that inheritance is not merely after death. God provides rich blessings for His children in this life that are a foretaste of the full riches that await them in heaven. On the night before His death, the Lord Jesus Christ revealed those blessings to His disciples, who were at that time in desperate need of great comfort and encouragement. As noted in the previous chapter of this volume, the disciples were distraught over the impending loss of the Master they loved and on whom they depended. Concerned about their anxieties, even in the face of His own death, Jesus selflessly sought to relieve their fears with stunning and gracious promises that would provide everything they needed.

And those promises the Lord made are not restricted to the apostles and their associates. They are for all true believers—those who prove the genuineness of their love for Christ by keeping His **commandments** (vv. 21–24; 15:10, 14; cf. 8:31; 12:48). Those **commandments** include more than the ones He gave in the immediate context (vv. 21–24; 13:34–35). They encompass His entire revelation of the Father's will (John 3:11–13, 32–34; 7:16; 8:26, 28, 38, 40; 12:49; 14:10; 15:15; 17:8, 14).

Obedience is a hallmark of genuine saving faith and love for God. Those who are truly saved, by grace alone, will invariably respond with a life of submission and service. With their hearts regenerated (John 3:5; Titus 2:4–7; cf. Eph. 2:4–10) and their minds renewed (cf. Rom. 12:2; Eph. 4:23), genuine Christians cannot help but outwardly reflect who they are on the inside—new creatures in Christ (2 Cor. 5:17).

Throughout His ministry, Jesus repeatedly emphasized the obedience that characterizes all who savingly believe. "Why do you call Me, 'Lord, Lord,'" Jesus demanded, "and do not do what I say?" (Luke 6:46). The one who "does not obey the Son will not see life, but the wrath of God abides on him" (John 3:36). Those "who are selfishly ambitious and do not obey the truth, but obey unrighteousness, [will face God's] wrath and indignation" (Rom. 2:8). It was Paul's privilege through God's grace "to bring about the obedience of faith among all the Gentiles for His name's sake" (Rom. 1:5; cf. 15:18; 16:26; Acts 6:7). At His second coming Jesus will "[deal] out retribution to those who do not know God and to those who do not obey the gospel of our Lord Jesus" (2 Thess. 1:8). To "all those who obey Him [Jesus is] the source of eternal salvation" (Heb. 5:9). The elect were chosen "to obey Jesus Christ" (1 Peter 1:2), while the unregenerate are those who "do not obey the gospel of God" (1 Peter 4:17).

John emphasized the inseparable link between love and obedience in his first epistle:

> By this we know that we have come to know Him, if we keep His commandments. The one who says, "I have come to know Him," and does not keep His commandments, is a liar, and the truth is not in him; but whoever keeps His word, in him the love of God has truly been perfected. (1 John 2:3–5)

The one who keeps His commandments abides in Him, and He in him. (1 John 3:24)

By this we know that we love the children of God, when we love God and observe His commandments. For this is the love of God, that we keep His commandments; and His commandments are not burdensome. (1 John 5:2–3)

Thus it is to the eleven disciples, and by extension all the faithful, that the Lord speaks these words of promise and provision. Although He would no longer be visibly present with His disciples, they would not be left alone. Jesus promised them (and all subsequent believers) four permanent sources of power and comfort: the presence of the Spirit, the presence of the Son, the presence of the Father, and the presence of the truth.

THE PRESENCE OF THE SPIRIT

I will ask the Father, and He will give you another Helper, that He may be with you forever; that is the Spirit of truth, whom the world cannot receive, because it does not see Him or know Him, but you know Him because He abides with you and will be in you. (14:16–17)

In verse 15 Jesus had spoken of the disciples' love for Him; here He revealed His love for them. In keeping with His intercessory work as their Great High Priest, Jesus promised to **ask the Father** to send His people **another Helper**—the Holy Spirit. *Paraklētos* (**Helper**) is a term the meaning of which cannot be exhausted by any one word. It literally means "one called alongside to help" and has the connotation of a helper, comforter, counselor, exhorter, intercessor, encourager, and advocate (defense attorney).

Allos (**another**) refers specifically to another of the same kind. For example in Matthew 13:24, 31, and 33, each succeeding parable is called "another" (*allos*) in the same category (they are all parables about the nature of the kingdom). In Mark 4:36 *allos* describes "other" boats of a similar style; in Mark 12:4 "another" slave of the same vineyard owner; in John 12:29 "others" in the same crowd; and in John 18:15–16 (cf. 20:2, 3, 4, 8) "another" disciple (the apostle John), who was of the same group as Peter.

While in English there is only one word for "another," there is a second Greek word used often in the New Testament. It is, in contrast to *allos*, the word *heteros*, which describes another thing of a completely different nature (cf. the English word *heterodoxy*). In Acts 7:18 Stephen spoke of "another [*heteros*] king over Egypt who knew nothing about Joseph." That pharaoh was not only from a different dynasty, but also had a radically different attitude toward the children of Israel. In Romans 7 Paul used *heteros* to distinguish the "law of sin" (v. 23) from the absolutely opposite "law of God" (v. 22). Perhaps the most striking illustration of the difference between *allos* and *heteros* is in Galatians 1:6–7. There Paul rebuked those who were following a "different (*heteros*) gospel" than the one they had received. That false gospel was "not another (*allos*)" of the same kind as the true gospel, since there is only one true gospel.

Summarizing the distinction between *allos* and *heteros*, the noted Greek scholar Richard C. Trench wrote,

> *Allos* … is the numerically distinct. But *heteros* … superadds the notion of qualitative difference. One is "divers," the other is "diverse." There are not a few passages in the N. T. whose right interpretation, or at any rate their full understanding, will depend on an accurate seizing of the distinction between these words. (*Synonyms of the New Testament* [repr.; Grand Rapids: Eerdmans, 1983], 357)

Hence, Jesus' promise was that He would send **another** (*allos*) **Helper** exactly like Himself, a person who could adequately take His place and empower His work. The Holy Spirit is the perfect substitute for the Lord Jesus Christ—the original **Helper** (cf. 1 John 2:1, where "Advocate" translates *paraklētos*). Like Jesus, the Holy Spirit would teach (John 14:26), strengthen (Eph. 3:16), and intercede for the disciples (Rom. 8:26). Though His departure was imminent, the Lord promised **that** the Holy Spirit would **be with** them **forever.**

Contrary to the false teaching of cults such as the Jehovah's Witnesses and the assumption of many professed Christians, the Holy Spirit is not an impersonal force or power. The Bible clearly teaches that He is a person, and that is true because He is God.

Scripture reveals that the Holy Spirit possesses the attributes of personhood: intellect (He knows the thoughts of God [1 Cor. 2:11] and has a mind [Rom. 8:27]); emotion (He can be grieved [Eph. 4:30; cf. Isa. 63:10]); and will (He distributes spiritual gifts in the church according to His will [1 Cor. 12:11]). He also does things that only a person can do, such as teach (Luke 12:12; John 14:26); testify (John 15:26; Rom. 8:16), lead and direct (Matt. 4:1; Acts 13:4; 16:6–7; Rom. 8:14), give guidance (Mark 13:11; Acts 15:28), convict (John 16:7–8), speak (Acts 8:29; 10:19; 13:2; 20:23; 21:11; 1 Tim. 4:1; Rev. 22:17), intercede (Rom. 8:26), and reveal (Mark 12:36; Luke 2:26; 1 Cor. 2:10; Acts 1:16; 4:25; 28:25; Heb. 3:7; 10:15–17; 2 Peter 1:21; cf. 2 Sam. 23:2; Ezek. 11:5). Nor can an impersonal force be lied to (Acts 5:3), blasphemed (Matt. 12:31), or insulted (Heb. 10:29). Further, the New Testament refers to the Holy Spirit using masculine pronouns, even though the Greek noun *pneuma* (spirit) is neuter.

The Bible also teaches the deity of the Holy Spirit. As the third person of the Trinity, He is associated with God the Father and God the Son. He is called the Spirit of God (Ezek. 11:24; Matt. 3:16) and the Spirit of Jesus (Acts 16:7; Gal. 4:6; Phil. 1:19; 1 Peter 1:11). He is mentioned with them in the Trinitarian baptism formula in Matthew 28:19 (cf. Isa. 48:16; 2 Cor. 13:14). The Holy Spirit possesses divine attributes, including eternity (Heb. 9:14), omniscience (1 Cor. 2:10–11), omnipresence (Ps. 139:7), omnipotence (as demonstrated by His power to create; Gen. 1:2; Job 33:4), veracity (truthfulness; 1 John 5:6), and the power to give life (He is called the "Spirit of life" in Rom. 8:2).

The Holy Spirit does the works that only God can do, including creating the universe (cf. Gen. 1:2 with Ps. 33:6–9), inspiring Scripture (cf. 2 Peter 1:21 with 2 Tim. 3:16), regenerating lost sinners (John 3:6; Titus 3:5), and sanctifying believers (2 Thess. 2:13; 1 Peter 1:2).

Finally, Scripture unequivocally states that the Holy Spirit is God. Acts 5:3 says that Ananias lied to the Holy Spirit, while verse 4 says he lied to God. Paul's declaration in 2 Corinthians 3:17, "Now the Lord is the Spirit," also unmistakably affirms the deity of the Holy Spirit.

Jesus called the Holy Spirit **the Spirit of truth** (cf. 15:26; 16:13) to emphasize His work of revealing spiritual truth to believers. In particular, the Holy Spirit was to reveal to the apostles the inspired truth of the New Testament (John 14:26; 16:13), as He had revealed the Old Testament (2 Peter 1:19–21). (For a further discussion of this point, see the exposition of v. 26 below.) **The world,** on the other hand, **cannot receive** the Holy Spirit **because it does not see Him or know Him.** Just as the world failed to recognize Jesus Christ (John 1:10; Acts 13:27), so also would it fail to recognize the Holy Spirit.

Unregenerate people cannot comprehend spiritual truth. "A natural man does not accept the things of the Spirit of God," wrote Paul, "for they are foolishness to him; and he cannot understand them, because they are spiritually appraised" (1 Cor. 2:14; cf. vv. 7–13; 1 John 2:20, 27). Not surprisingly, on the day of Pentecost some of the bystanders derisively accused the Spirit-filled believers of being drunk (Acts 2:13). Jesus cautioned the disciples in advance that despite the Spirit's work in and through them, they would still face hostility and rejection from the unbelieving world (cf. 15:19; 16:33).

Though the world would not recognize the Spirit, the disciples would **know Him because,** Jesus told them, **He abides with you and will be in you.** The Lord's promise that the Spirit would indwell the disciples in the future does not mean the Holy Spirit was not present or active before Pentecost (cf. Gen. 6:3; 1 Chron. 12:18; Pss. 51:11; 139:7–12;

143:10; Ezek. 36:27). No one in any era of redemptive history could be saved, sanctified, empowered for service and witness, or guided in understanding Scripture and praying in the will of God apart from the Spirit's internal soul work. That He was already present with the disciples, before the cross, is clear from the present tense of the verb translated **abides.** One author explains the Holy Spirit's ministry prior to the church age with these words:

> Old Testament saints had to be regenerated by the Spirit to experience their spiritual blessings. The Spirit effected this regeneration when the person placed his or her faith in Jehovah God and became a genuine part of the covenant community. Regeneration essentially involved a "circumcised heart," which demonstrated itself in heartfelt participation in the sacrificial system, plus a life of obedience to God's revelation. . . . Theologically, it would seem that some ministry of the Spirit had to be constantly applied to the old covenant believer. To distinguish it from the intimacy of new covenant indwelling, perhaps this ministry is best designated "abiding." In the words of the prophet Haggai, "As for the promise which I made you when you came out of Egypt, My Spirit is abiding in your midst; do not fear!" (Hag. 2:5 NASB). The Spirit dwelt "with" the Old Testament saints through the community but would not be "in" them individually and intimately (John 14:17) [since] the Old Testament saints could not have enjoyed the benefits of the new covenant before it had been inaugurated. (Larry Pettegrew, *The New Covenant Ministry of the Holy Spirit* [Grand Rapids: Kregel, 2001], 27–28)

Under the old covenant, the Spirit was present with believers in a general sense. But soon, as Christ promised His disciples, the Comforter would in an unprecedented way personally and permanently indwell those who believed. There was to come for believers a giving of the Spirit by which unique power would be provided for ministry and evangelism. That happened on the day of Pentecost, when the Spirit was given to believers in a new fullness that became normative for all believers since (Rom. 8:9; 1 Cor. 12:13).

THE PRESENCE OF THE SON

I will not leave you as orphans; I will come to you. After a little while the world will no longer see Me, but you will see Me; because I live, you will live also. In that day you will know that I am in My Father, and you in Me, and I in you. (14:18–20)

Like a dying father concerned about his children (cf. 13:33; 21:5; Mark 10:24), Jesus promised the disciples that He would not **leave** them **as orphans.** The reference to His leaving is a veiled reference to His death, and graphically expresses the sense of loss the disciples would experience. As foreboding as that loss seemed, it would only be temporary, as the Lord's promise **I will come to you** indicates. The primary reference is to His resurrection, after which they would see Him again (cf. John 20:19–29; Acts 1:3; 1 Cor. 15:3–8). But because of His union with the Holy Spirit in the Godhead, Jesus would also abide with them through His Spirit, who would be poured out at Pentecost (cf. 16:16; Matt. 28:20; Rom. 8:9; Phil. 1:19; 1 Peter 1:11; 1 John 4:13).

After a little while—only a few hours remained until the crucifixion—Jesus would be dead, and the unbelieving **world** would **no longer see** Him. They would not see Him physically after His resurrection (since He apparently appeared only to His disciples [cf. 1 Cor. 15:1–11]) nor would they have any capacity to know Christ's presence through the indwelling Holy Spirit (since they are spiritually dead [Eph. 2:1] and "devoid of the Spirit" [Jude 19]). In contrast to the unbelieving world, the Lord promised His disciples, **you will see Me; because I live** (cf. 1:4; 6:48, 57; 14:6) **you will live also** (cf. 3:15, 16; 3:36; 4:14; 5:24, 39–40; 6:27, 58; 11:25). As witnesses to the resurrected Savior, the disciples would be given visible proof that they too would one day be raised (1 Cor. 15:20–21, 35–58). Moreover, being spiritually alive because of Christ's resurrection and the indwelling of the Spirit, believers are able to perceive Jesus' presence in this life (cf. Heb. 13:5–6).

The Son is not only in union with the Spirit but also with the **Father. In that day** (after the resurrection and the coming of the Spirit), He said, **you will know that I am in My Father.** Though no human mind can fully understand that union, being hidden in the mysterious depths of the Trinity (cf. Job 11:7; Rom. 11:33), the disciples and all believers have recognized its reality. They would soon come to understand the truth that baffled them at the present (cf. 14:8–9).

Then Jesus made a profound promise. Not only would the disciples **know** that He is **in** the **Father,** but also, as He went on to tell them, **you** will understand that you are **in Me, and I in you.** Through the indwelling of the Spirit, believers are united with Jesus. (That union, of course, is not one of essence; believers do not become part of the Godhead.) Several New Testament metaphors depict the nature of that union. Jesus is the vine and believers are the branches (John 15:5); they are the body of which He is the head (1 Cor. 12:27; Eph. 1:22–23; 4:15–16; 5:23; Col. 1:18; 2:19); they are stones in the spiritual house of which He is the cornerstone (Eph. 2:20–22; 1 Peter 2:4–6); they are the bride and He is the groom (2 Cor. 11:2; Eph. 5:22–24; Rev. 19:7).

Further expressing that union, the Bible teaches that believers are "in Christ." In Romans 8:1 Paul declared, "Therefore there is now no condemnation for those who are in Christ Jesus." To the Corinthians he wrote, "But by His doing you are in Christ Jesus, who became to us wisdom from God, and righteousness and sanctification, and redemption" (1 Cor. 1:30), and, "Therefore if anyone is in Christ, he is a new creature; the old things passed away; behold, new things have come" (2 Cor. 5:17; cf. Rom. 16:7; Phil. 4:21; Col. 1:2, 28; 2 Tim. 3:12; 1 Peter 3:16; 5:14).

Not only are believers in Christ; He also abides in them (cf. John 6:5; 14:20, 23; 15:4–5; 17:23, 26). "If Christ is in you," Paul wrote, "though the body is dead because of sin, yet the spirit is alive because of righteousness" (Rom. 8:10). "Test yourselves to see if you are in the faith," the apostle challenged the Corinthians, "examine yourselves! Or do you not recognize this about yourselves, that Jesus Christ is in you—unless indeed you fail the test?" (2 Cor. 13:5). In Galatians 2:20 he noted, "I have been crucified with Christ; and it is no longer I who live, but Christ lives in me; and the life which I now live in the flesh I live by faith in the Son of God, who loved me and gave Himself up for me." Paul prayed for the Ephesians that "Christ [might] dwell in [their] hearts through faith" (Eph. 3:17) and reminded the Colossians of "the riches of the glory of this mystery ... which is Christ in you, the hope of glory" (Col. 1:27).

Jesus thus reassured His worried disciples that His death would not end their relationship with Him. Their union with Him was indissoluble, as is true for all believers. Nothing can separate His own from His presence or His love (Rom. 8:38–39).

THE PRESENCE OF THE FATHER

"He who has My commandments and keeps them is the one who loves Me; and he who loves Me will be loved by My Father, and I will love him and will disclose Myself to him." Judas (not Iscariot) said to Him, "Lord, what then has happened that You are going to disclose Yourself to us and not to the world?" Jesus answered and said to him, "If anyone loves Me, he will keep My word; and My Father will love him, and We will come to him and make Our abode with him. He who does not love Me does not keep My words; and the word which you hear is not Mine, but the Father's who sent Me." (14:21–24)

Only those who obey His **commandments** (cf. the discussion of v. 15 above) enter into union with Christ. Their obedience is not the cause of their salvation, "because by the works of the Law no flesh will be justified in [God's] sight" (Rom. 3:20; cf. v. 28; 4:13; 5:1; Gal. 2:16; 3:11; Eph. 2:8–9; Titus 3:5), but rather the inevitable result of it. Obedience, flowing from a heart transformed by the regenerating power of the Holy Spirit (cf. James 2:14–26), marks the one who truly **loves** Jesus Christ. Such obedient love is the outworking of the love the Holy Spirit pours into the redeemed heart at salvation (Rom. 5:5; Gal. 5:22).

It is only the one **who loves** Christ who **will be loved by** the **Father** (cf. 16:27; 17:23). Jesus said, "He who does not honor the Son does not honor the Father who sent Him" (John 5:23) and "He who hates Me hates My Father also" (John 15:23). No one who rejects the Lord Jesus Christ can truly know, love, or honor God, because "the Father loves the Son" (John 3:35; 5:20), "and no one knows the Son except the Father; nor does anyone know the Father except the Son, and anyone to whom the Son wills to reveal Him" (Matt. 11:27). Along with the Father, Jesus will love those who love Him (cf. John 13:1, 34; 15:9; Eph. 5:25; Rev. 1:5), and **will disclose** Himself **to** them.

Expressing the bewilderment that the others no doubt felt, **Judas (not Iscariot) said to** Jesus, **"Lord, what then has happened that You are going to disclose Yourself to us and not to the world?"** As John's parenthetical note indicates, this was **not** Judas **Iscariot,** but Judas the son of James (Luke 6:16). In Matthew 10:3, he is also called Thaddeus (some Greek manuscripts add a third name, Lebbaeus). Judas assumed that Jesus was speaking of returning physically to establish His earthly kingdom (cf. Acts 1:6). He could not understand how, that being the case, Jesus would **disclose** Himself to the disciples, **and not to the world.** After all, Jesus was the Savior of the world (John 4:42); the rightful heir of the earth (Heb. 1:2); the King of Kings and Lord of Lords (Rev. 19:16). The good news of the forgiveness and salvation that He brought was to be proclaimed throughout the whole world (Matt. 28:19). Why then, Judas wondered, was Jesus not going to make Himself known to everyone?

Jesus' reply, **If anyone loves Me, he will keep My word** (cf. 17:6), explained that He will not reveal Himself to those who refuse to love and obey Him. This is the third time in this section (cf. vv. 15, 21) that Christ linked obedience with genuine love for Him (cf. 8:31). Not only will He love those who love Him (cf. 1 Peter 1:1–2), the **Father** also **will love** them. Further, both the Father and the Son **will come to** them **and make** their **abode with** them. The Lord's declaration, **"He who does not love Me does not keep My words,"** emphasized yet again, this time negatively, the inseparable connection between love for Him and obedience to Him. Jesus will not make Himself known to those who reject Him (cf. John 7:17; 8:47). Such people also do not know the Father, since Jesus' message was not His, **but the Father's who sent** Him (cf.

v. 10; 3:34; 7:16; 8:28, 38, 40; 12:49; 17:8). Therefore to reject Jesus is also to reject the Father (cf. 5:23; 15:23). To have Jesus is to have the Father.

THE PRESENCE OF THE TRUTH

"These things I have spoken to you while abiding with you. But the Helper, the Holy Spirit, whom the Father will send in My name, He will teach you all things, and bring to your remembrance all that I said to you." (14:25–26)

Throughout His ministry, Jesus had been the source of truth for the disciples (cf. v. 6). **"These things** (the Father's word; v. 24)," He reminded them, **"I have spoken to you while abiding with you."** But just as He would not leave them without a source of comfort, so also He would not leave the disciples without a source of truth. He would send the Holy Spirit, the "Spirit of truth" (v. 17), to guide and teach them. Apart from His revelation, there is no way to know spiritual truth. Since "the world through its wisdom did not come to know God" (1 Cor. 1:21), fallen mankind is "always learning and never able to come to the knowledge of the truth" (2 Tim. 3:7). It is only when people are "saved [that they] come to the knowledge of the truth" (1 Tim. 2:4).

Even the disciples, before Pentecost, found it difficult to understand all that Jesus taught them. According to John 2:22, it was not until after the resurrection that they understood His teaching in verse 19. Nor did they grasp the full significance of the triumphal entry until after Jesus had been glorified (John 12:16). Because of their obtuseness, Jesus told them, "I have many more things to say to you, but you cannot bear them now" (16:12). They needed instruction, so Jesus promised them, **The Holy Spirit, whom the Father will send in My name** (cf. Acts 2:33) **He will teach you all things, and bring to your remembrance all that I said to you** (cf. 16:13). The phrase, **in My name,** means "on My behalf," as it also does in verse 13. Just as Jesus came in the Father's name (5:43), so also will the Spirit come in Jesus' name. As another Comforter like Jesus, the Spirit will always act in perfect harmony with Christ's desires, purposes, and will. "He will glorify Me," Jesus would later tell the disciples, "for He will take of Mine and will disclose it to you" (16:14). In the divine plan, the Spirit's ministry is to testify about Christ (15:26), not draw attention to Himself (cf. 16:13).

The Spirit is the believer's resident truth teacher (1 John 2:20, 27); by illuminating God's Word to their understanding, He thus grants Christians the knowledge of God that leads them to spiritual maturity.

But Christ's promise that the Spirit would **bring to** their

remembrance all that He had **said to** them was primarily a promise to the apostles of divine inspiration. The Holy Spirit's supernatural guidance granted them an inerrant understanding of Jesus Christ's person and teaching. The apostles (and their close associates) recorded that divinely inspired truth in the Gospels and the rest of the New Testament.

Peter described the process of inspiration in 2 Peter 1:20–21: "But know this first of all, that no prophecy of Scripture is a matter of one's own interpretation, for no prophecy was ever made by an act of human will, but men moved by the Holy Spirit spoke from God." The apostle Paul declared, "All Scripture is inspired by God" (lit., "God-breathed," 2 Tim. 3:13). The Holy Spirit inspired the very words of Scripture, not merely the thoughts of the writers (1 Cor. 2:13). The Bible is therefore inerrant and authoritative, and thus the only infallible rule of faith and practice. It alone contains "the sacred writings which are able to give [one] the wisdom that leads to salvation through faith which is in Christ Jesus" (2 Tim. 3:15). For the redeemed, the Bible is "the sword of the Spirit" (Eph. 6:17) and is "profitable for teaching, for reproof, for correction, for training in righteousness; so that the man of God may be adequate, equipped for every good work" (2 Tim. 3:16–17).

Armed with the truth and accompanied by the presence of God, the disciples and their contemporaries would soon be those who "turned the world upside down" (Acts 17:6 KJV). But in this moment of distress, just hours before the cross, the situation looked desperately hopeless. Aware of the disciples' distress, Jesus pointed them to the ultimate and only sure source of hope—the triune God. In the same way that the promise of God's presence heartened them two millennia ago, it should still bring confidence and courage to believers today, since it provides comfort both now (2 Cor. 1:3–4; cf. Pss. 23:4; 86:17; Matt. 5:4; Acts 9:31), and forever (Isa. 25:8; 2 Thess. 2:16; Rev. 7:17; 21:4).

Supernatural Peace

(John 14:27)

11

"Peace I leave with you; My peace I give to you; not as the world gives do I give to you. Do not let your heart be troubled, nor let it be fearful." (14:27)

Turmoil, both public and personal, is a reality that marks this fallen world. Such unrest is perhaps most clearly seen on the international level, as nations clash against each other in war. Many years ago, historians calculated that in the previous 3,500 years, the world had seen less than 300 years of peace (cf. Will and Ariel Durant, *The Lessons of History* [New York: Simon and Schuster, 1968], 81). It has also been estimated that in the last five and a half millennia, more than 8,000 peace treaties have been broken, and more than 14,000 wars fought with a combined total of about four billion casualties. Even though there have always been illusions of global peace, this world continues to be unsuccessful in the effort to pursue that elusive goal.

The concept of peace is, of course, much broader than just the realm of international social harmony. People want peace in their personal lives, relief from the relentless pressures and problems that each day brings. The language of peace fills conversation. People seek "peace and quiet" to be refreshed from the din of life; they are told to "make peace" with their past; they expect local law enforcement to "keep the peace" and stop those who disturb them. Even when this life ends, the concept of "resting in peace" is so commonplace it has become a synonym for death itself.

Sadly, though people pursue it their entire lives, left to themselves they have no idea how to find true peace. Those who look for it in temporal things like social change, economic stability, or some recreational experience are always disappointed. Only God's Word can authoritatively point to the relationship that produces lasting peace.

Both the Old and New Testaments underscore the divine source and character of true peace. One of the most important theological terms in the Old Testament is the word *shalom* ("peace"). The word, which occurs approximately 250 times, was sometimes used as a greeting (Judg. 19:20; 1 Sam. 25:6, 35), as it is in modern Hebrew. *Shalom* can also refer to the absence of strife between people (Gen. 26:29), nations (1 Kings 4:24), and between God and man (Ps. 85:8). In this latter sense, it will be the hallmark of the future messianic kingdom (Ps. 29:11; Isa. 2:4; 9:6–7; 52:7; 54:13; 57:19; 66:12; Ezek. 37:26; Hag. 2:9). But *shalom* also speaks of personal peace—not merely in the negative sense of absence of trouble or conflict, but positively of completeness, wholeness, contentment, welfare, health, prosperity, harmony, and fulfillment. Peace is one of the blessings that flow from a right relationship to God.

True biblical peace does not depend on the circumstances of life, but lives above them. One Greek lexicon defines the New Testament word for peace (*eirēnē*) as "the tranquil state of a soul assured of its salvation through Christ, and so fearing nothing from God and content with its earthly lot, of whatsoever sort that is." It was this type of peace that characterized the apostle Paul, who wrote: "I have learned to be content in whatever circumstances I am. I know how to get along with humble means, and I also know how to live in prosperity; in any and every circumstance I have learned the secret of being filled and going hungry, both of having abundance and suffering need" (Phil. 4:11–12). Paul remained calm and at peace in the midst of the most trying circumstances, such as being thrown into prison (Acts 16:23–25), savagely attacked by an unruly mob (Acts 21:30–39), or caught in a raging storm at sea (Acts 27:21–25).

Humanity defines peace primarily in negative terms. For example, in some languages the word for peace means, "to be without trouble," "to have no worries," or "to sit down in one's heart." Peace to most people means the absence of war, strife, quarrels, disagreements, hostility, or unrest. They see it as deliverance from or the absence of any external conflict and every inner turmoil, resulting in an undisturbed and tranquil state of mind. But this understanding of peace is incomplete, because true peace is much more than just the absence of conflict. Armed with an inadequate definition, unbelievers are incapable of finding peace. They do not understand what they are looking for, and therefore fail to look in the right place.

There is only one source of true peace, as this simple yet profound verse (27a–b) reveals. The setting in which this magnificent promise was given is the upper room on the night before Christ's death. The Lord, knowing His disciples were brokenhearted because He was leaving them, gave the eleven a farewell message of comfort and hope. As noted in the previous chapter of this volume, Jesus promised them that through the indwelling of the Holy Spirit He would continue to be with them, as would the Father and the truth. That marvelous legacy would turn the disciples' temporary sorrow over His death into eternal joy. It also served as the basis for the supernatural peace that He now promised to them.

This one brief statement reflects four features of divine peace: its nature, source, contrast, and result.

THE NATURE OF PEACE

Peace I leave with you; (14:27a)

Objectively, **peace** in the New Testament has to do with a person's standing before God; subjectively, with the believer's resulting experience of peace in everyday living. Peace with God, of course, is the bedrock on which all other peace is based. If there is no peace with God, then there cannot be any real peace in this life. Thus, objective peace is a necessary prerequisite for subjective peace, neither of which are possible for the unsaved person to enjoy.

Since the rebellion of Adam and Eve (cf. Gen. 3), the human race has been at war with God. All violate His holy law and deny Him glory, and therefore are His enemies. The Bible calls this rebellion sin, and declares every human being (with the exception of Jesus Christ) to be a sinner (Rom. 3:23). From birth, every man and woman opposes God— both by heritage (Rom. 5:18; cf. Pss. 51:5; 58:3) and by personal choice (cf. Rom. 3:10–18). No one is neutral because, as Jesus said in Luke 11:23, "He who is not with Me is against Me; and he who does not gather with Me, scatters." In Genesis 8:21 God's own commentary on His fallen creation was that "the intent of man's heart is evil from his youth" (cf. Job 15:14). Thus, having set themselves against God's law, all people inevitably face His wrath and the penalty of eternal punishment.

Humanity hates God (cf. John 15:18–19; 1 John 2:16–17), and all who are part of the world system cannot be at peace with Him: "You adulteresses, do you not know that friendship with the world is hostility toward God? Therefore whoever wishes to be a friend of the world makes himself an enemy of God" (James 4:4).

The good news, however, is that enemies of God can be reconciled to enjoy eternal peace with Him through faith in the Lord Jesus Christ; for it is through Him that God has chosen "to reconcile all things to Himself, having made peace through the blood of His cross" (Col. 1:20; cf. Acts 10:36; Eph. 2:14–17). In Romans 5:1 Paul wrote, "Therefore, having been justified by faith, we have peace with God through our Lord Jesus Christ." Because Christ paid sin's penalty on the cross, those who trust in Him are "reconciled to God through the death of His Son" (Rom. 5:10; cf. v. 11; 2 Cor. 5:18–21; Col. 1:22). At the moment of justification, the rebellion ends, all sins are forgiven, and enemies become sons of God (cf. Rom. 8:12–17).

As a result, those who formerly had a "mind set on the flesh [resulting in] death" now have a "mind set on the Spirit [resulting in] life and peace" (Rom. 8:6). Thus Paul called the gospel the "gospel of peace" (Eph. 6:15), because it is the good news of how sinful rebels can be at peace with God through Christ.

The sacrifice of Jesus Christ to satisfy God's holiness was necessary so there could be peace between sinful men and holy God, since righteousness and peace are inseparably linked (cf. Ps. 85:10). Because God is holy and just, He requires that a penalty be paid when sinners violate His law. It is only because Christ's sacrifice fully satisfied the demands of divine justice that God can "be just and the justifier of the one who has faith in Jesus" (Rom. 3:26). Though perfectly righteous, Christ was punished in the place of all who believe as though He were a sinner, so that they through faith in Him could be treated as though they were perfectly righteous. Thus, through Christ's substitutionary atonement and the imputation of His righteousness to sinful men (2 Cor. 5:21), the enemies of God can become His friends (James 2:23).

That objective peace of justification results in experiential peace. This is not peace with God but "the peace of God, which surpasses all comprehension," meaning that it transcends human insight, analysis, and understanding. This peace "will guard [believers'] hearts and [their] minds in Christ Jesus" (Phil. 4:7). The Greek word translated "guard" is a military term meaning, "to keep watch over." The peace of God protects believers from anxiety, doubt, fear, and distress. Thus, it is not passive but active; far from being affected by circumstances, it triumphs over them, turning sorrow into joy, fear into boldness, and doubt into confidence. This is the peace that Jesus promised to His followers.

Experiential peace is an essential part of the Christian life. "The kingdom of God," wrote Paul, "is not eating and drinking, but righteousness and peace and joy in the Holy Spirit" (Rom. 14:17). Later in Romans the apostle added this benediction:"Now may the God of hope fill you with all joy and peace in believing, so that you will abound in hope by the power of the Holy Spirit" (15:13). Paul gave a similar benediction at the end of 2 Thessalonians:"Now may the Lord of peace Himself continually grant you peace in every circumstance" (2 Thess. 3:16). Peace is one of the fruit of the Spirit (Gal. 5:22)—given by the Helper whom Christ sent to indwell His people (cf. the discussion of John 14:16–17 in the previous chapter of this volume). Such peace not only manifests itself in private tranquility, but also in harmony with other believers (Mark 9:50; Rom. 14:19; 2 Cor. 13:11; Eph. 4:3; 1 Thess. 5:13; 1 Tim. 3:3; Titus 3:2).

THE SOURCE OF PEACE

My peace I give to you; (14:27b)

Because He is the "God of peace" (Rom. 15:33; 16:20; Phil. 4:9; 1 Thess. 5:23; Heb. 13:20; cf. Judg. 6:24; Isa. 9:6; 1 Cor. 14:33; 2 Cor. 13:11; 2 Thess. 3:16), God is the one source of all true peace; hence Jesus said, **My peace I give.** As with every blessing in the Christian life, peace comes from all three persons of the Trinity. The oft-repeated salutation in the New Testament Epistles, "Grace to you and peace from God our Father and the Lord Jesus Christ" (Rom. 1:7; 1 Cor. 1:3; 2 Cor. 1:2; Gal. 1:3; Eph. 1:2; Phil. 1:2; Col. 1:2; 2 Thess. 1:2; cf. Eph., 6:23; 1 Tim. 1:2; 2 Tim. 1:2; Titus 1:4; Philem. 3; 2 John 3) indicates that God the Father and Jesus Christ are the source of peace. It is the ministry of the Holy Spirit to impart that peace to believers (Gal. 5:22). Like the rest of the legacy Jesus left the disciples, the **peace** He promised to **give** them would come in fullness on the day of Pentecost.

Christ called that peace, **My peace.** It is the same peace that kept Him calm in the face of mockery, scorn, hostility, hatred, betrayal, and death (cf. 1 Peter 2:23). Christ's peace provides believers with a serenity and freedom from worry and anxiety that is unaffected by and triumphs over even the most difficult of circumstances. In the midst of the trials and temptations of life, believers do well to fix their "eyes on Jesus, the author and perfecter of faith, who for the joy set before Him endured the cross, despising the shame, and has sat down at the right hand of the throne of God" (Heb. 12:2). It is only in looking to Christ that anyone can find peace and settled confidence in the midst of any hardship.

THE CONTRAST TO PEACE

not as the world gives do I give to you. (14:27*c*)

In the truest sense, no real peace is to be found in the **world.** Godless people in a godless world are by nature enemies of God and in a state of resultant turmoil. The **world** only offers an experience of a momentary, fleeting tranquility through self-indulgence, materialism, love, romance, substance abuse, false religion, psychotherapy, or a host of other placebos. But the world's pseudopeace is in reality the bliss of ignorance. If unbelievers understood the wrath of God, and the agonizing, unrelieved, eternal torment awaiting them in hell, they would never enjoy a moment's peace in this life.

The Bible repeatedly emphasizes that the world's peace is inadequate. "'There is no peace for the wicked,' says the Lord" in Isaiah 48:22. In Isaiah 57:21 the prophet echoed the Lord's words: "'There is no peace,' says my God, 'for the wicked.'" In Jeremiah 6:14 God excoriated the false prophets who had "healed the brokenness of [His] people superficially, saying, 'Peace, peace,' but there is no peace" (cf. 8:11; Ezek. 13:10, 16). "If you had known in this day, even you, the things which make for peace!" Jesus lamented over Jerusalem, "But now they have been hidden from your eyes" (Luke 19:42). The apostle Paul wrote of unbelievers that "the path of peace they have not known" (Rom. 3:17). In the end times, "while [unbelievers] are saying, 'Peace and safety!' then destruction will come upon them suddenly like labor pains upon a woman with child, and they will not escape" (1 Thess. 5:3). Like wayward Israel finally admitted, "We waited for peace, but no good came; for a time of healing, but behold, terror!" (Jer. 8:15). The world's peace is only an illusion. A peace based on temporarily positive circumstances or ignorant escapism is not genuine peace at all. The reason people lack peace is not emotional, psychological, or circumstantial, but theological. As noted earlier in this chapter, only those who know Jesus Christ can have peace with God and, subsequently, experience true peace in this life.

THE PURSUIT OF PEACE

"Do not let your heart be troubled, nor let it be fearful." (14:27*d*)

After promising to give His disciples peace, Jesus repeated His command that they **not let** their **heart be troubled, nor let it be fearful** (see the exposition of v. 1 in chapter 9 of this volume). There is no inconsistency between Christ's promise and His command, however. The

Bible teaches that Christians are responsible to appropriate God's promises. The Holy Spirit indwells and empowers believers, but they in turn are to be filled with (Eph. 5:18) and walk in the Spirit (Gal. 5:16, 25). Christians have been given eternal life; in response they are to "consider [themselves] to be dead to sin, but alive to God in Christ Jesus" (Rom. 6:11) and "present [themselves] to God as those alive from the dead" (v. 13). The Holy Spirit is their supernatural teacher (1 John 2:20, 27), yet that does not negate believers' responsibility to study the Scriptures diligently (2 Tim. 2:15). The same apostle Paul who wrote "I have been crucified with Christ; and it is no longer I who live, but Christ lives in me" (Gal. 2:20) also wrote "Therefore I run in such a way, as not without aim; I box in such a way, as not beating the air; but I discipline my body and make it my slave, so that, after I have preached to others, I myself will not be disqualified" (1 Cor. 9:26–27).

As is the case with all of God's promises, then, believers are responsible to appropriate Christ's promise of peace. Psalm 34:14 commands God's people to "seek peace and pursue it" (cf. 1 Peter 3:11), while Psalm 119:165 declares that "those who love Your law have great peace, and nothing causes them to stumble." Similarly, Isaiah 26:3 reveals that it is those who steadfastly trust Him that God keeps in perfect peace, and Isaiah 32:17 links experiencing peace with living a righteous life. Paul instructed Timothy to pursue peace (2 Tim. 2:22), and Peter exhorted his readers, "Therefore, beloved, since you look for these things, be diligent to be found by Him in peace, spotless and blameless" (2 Peter 3:14). James also connected peace with godly living when he wrote, "But the wisdom from above is first pure, then peaceable ... And the seed whose fruit is righteousness is sown in peace by those who make peace" (James 3:17–18). In fact, one way God produces peace in our lives is by chastening us: "All discipline for the moment seems not to be joyful, but sorrowful; yet to those who have been trained by it, afterwards it yields the peaceful fruit of righteousness" (Heb. 12:11).

When we trust in His goodness, faithfulness, and provision, God fills us "with all joy and peace in believing" (Rom. 15:13). To live in anguish over the past, anxiety concerning the present, or apprehension about the future is to fail to appropriate that peace. As noted earlier, believers are to be "anxious for nothing, but in everything by prayer and supplication with thanksgiving let [their] requests be made known to God. And the peace of God, which surpasses all comprehension, will guard [their] hearts and [their] minds in Christ Jesus" (Phil. 4:6–7).

In the Sermon on the Mount, Jesus pointed out the sinful folly of allowing fear and worry to corrode the believer's experience of divine peace:

For this reason I say to you, do not be worried about your life, as to what you will eat or what you will drink; nor for your body, as to what you will put on. Is not life more than food, and the body more than clothing? Look at the birds of the air, that they do not sow, nor reap nor gather into barns, and yet your heavenly Father feeds them. Are you not worth much more than they? And who of you by being worried can add a single hour to his life? And why are you worried about clothing? Observe how the lilies of the field grow; they do not toil nor do they spin, yet I say to you that not even Solomon in all his glory clothed himself like one of these. But if God so clothes the grass of the field, which is alive today and tomorrow is thrown into the furnace, will He not much more clothe you? You of little faith! Do not worry then, saying, "What will we eat?" or "What will we drink?" or "What will we wear for clothing?" For the Gentiles eagerly seek all these things; for your heavenly Father knows that you need all these things. But seek first His kingdom and His righteousness, and all these things will be added to you. So do not worry about tomorrow; for tomorrow will care for itself. Each day has enough trouble of its own. (Matt. 6:25–34)

God has forgiven the past, provided for the present, and guaranteed the future, leaving nothing to legitimately disrupt the believer's peace. Applying that principle to his most difficult circumstances, the apostle Paul wrote to the Corinthians,

We are afflicted in every way, but not crushed; perplexed, but not despairing; persecuted, but not forsaken; struck down, but not destroyed ... For momentary, light affliction is producing for us an eternal weight of glory far beyond all comparison, while we look not at the things which are seen, but at the things which are not seen; for the things which are seen are temporal, but the things which are not seen are eternal. (2 Cor. 4:8–9, 17–18)

The good news of the gospel is that the war between the sinner and God can end, since the treaty ending that war was purchased by the blood of the Lord Jesus Christ. The resulting experiential peace becomes a guiding and controlling principle in every believer's life. In Colossians 3:15 Paul exhorted Christians, "Let the peace of Christ rule in your hearts, to which indeed you were called in one body; and be thankful." *Brabeuō* ("rule") was used to describe the work of an umpire in deciding the outcome of an athletic event. Believers can allow Christ's peace to referee the choices they make by asking two crucial questions. First, they should ask whether what they are considering is consistent with the reality that they are now at peace with Christ and thus part of His kingdom (cf. Col. 1:13). Anything that would disrupt the oneness and harmony they enjoy with Him must be rejected. Paul illustrated that principle in 1 Corinthians 6:17–18 when he wrote, "The one who joins himself to the Lord is one spirit with Him. Flee immorality." Their union with Christ compels Christians to purity.

A second consideration concerns how the choice will affect the peace of mind that comes with a clear conscience (cf. Rom. 14:22–23; 1 Cor. 8:12). Thoughts, words, and deeds consistent with the peace of Christ will result in a clear, good, and blameless conscience (Acts 23:1; 24:16; 2 Cor. 1:12; 1 Tim. 1:5, 19; 3:9; 2 Tim. 1:3; Heb. 13:18; 1 Peter 3:16); those that are not will result in a troubled, accusing conscience (1 Sam. 24:5). Christians who live in unrepentant sin forfeit the experience of peace and assurance that is Christ's legacy to His people. Remembering his sin with Bathseba, David declared to God:

> When I kept silent about my sin, my body wasted away
> Through my groaning all day long;
> For day and night Your hand was heavy upon me;
> My vitality was drained away as with the fever heat of summer.
> I acknowledged my sin to You,
> And my iniquity I did not hide ∙
> I said, "I will confess my transgressions to the Lord";
> And You forgave the guilt of my sin. (Ps. 32:3–5)

The unsettled, guilt-ridden conscience is made whole when the believer confesses his sin to God and repents (cf. 2 Cor. 7:10; 1 John 1:9). Knowing that his sin has been forgiven (through the cross) and that his relational fellowship with God has been restored (through confession and repentance), the believer can once again experience the profound peace that God offers to all of His children.

On the night before His death, the Lord promised supernatural peace to His troubled disciples. By pointing to Himself as the giver of peace, rather than to the fearful circumstances they faced in His absence, Jesus offered His followers a peace that is unmoved by the events of this world and that lasts forever. It was this peace that characterized Him throughout His sufferings. And it would also mark His followers through the many persecutions they would face on His behalf.

Charles Wesley, the famous hymn writer, summed up the God-focused nature of the Christian's peace with these fitting words:

> I rest beneath the Almighty's shade,
> My griefs expire, my troubles cease;
> Thou, Lord, on whom my soul is stayed,
> Wilt keep me still in perfect peace.

What Jesus' Death Meant to Him (John 14:28–31)

12

"You heard that I said to you, 'I go away, and I will come to you.' If you loved Me, you would have rejoiced because I go to the Father, for the Father is greater than I. Now I have told you before it happens, so that when it happens, you may believe. I will not speak much more with you, for the ruler of the world is coming, and he has nothing in Me; but so that the world may know that I love the Father, I do exactly as the Father commanded Me. Get up, let us go from here." (14:28–31)

The death and resurrection of the Lord Jesus Christ are the central truths of the Christian faith. As J. C. Ryle declared more than 150 years ago, Christ's death is "the *grand peculiarity of the Christian religion.* Other religions have laws and moral precepts,—forms and ceremonies,—rewards and punishments. But other religions cannot tell us of a dying Saviour. They cannot show us the cross. This is the crown and glory of the Gospel" (J. C. Ryle, *The Cross: A Call to the Fundamentals of Religion* [repr.; Pensacola, Fla.: Chapel Library, 1998], 18; emphasis in original). The cross is at the very heart of all that believers hold dear. In the words of John F. Walvoord:

No event of time or eternity compares with the transcending significance of the death of Christ on the cross. Other important undertakings of God such as the creation of the world, the incarnation of Christ, His resurrection, the second coming, and the creation of the new heavens and the new earth become meaningless if Christ did not die....

In the study of Christ in His sufferings and death, one is in a holy of holies, a mercy seat sprinkled with blood, to which only the Spirit-taught mind has access. In His death Christ supremely revealed the holiness and righteousness of God as well as the love of God which prompted the sacrifice. In a similar way the infinite wisdom of God is revealed as no human mind would ever have devised such a way of salvation, and only an infinite God would be willing to sacrifice His Son. (*Jesus Christ Our Lord* [Chicago: Moody, 1974], 153)

Christ's sacrificial death was the ultimate goal of the incarnation. The reason He came (John 12:27) was "to give His life a ransom for many" (Mark 10:45) so that through His death He might reconcile sinners to God (2 Cor. 5:18–21). The cross was neither a disruption of the divine plan, nor an accident, but was exactly what God had designed from before time began (2 Tim. 1:9). That is evident from the Lord's repeated predictions regarding His death at the hands of wicked men (Matt. 12:40; 16:4, 21; 17:12, 22–23; 20:17–19, 28; 26:2, 28, 31; Mark 9:9; Luke 17:25; 22:15; 24:6–7, 25–26; John 2:19–21; 3:14; 8:28; 10:11, 17–18; 12:27, 32–33; 15:13; 18:11, 32). His suffering was also foretold by the Old Testament prophets (cf. Ps. 22:1, 16, 18; Isa. 52:13–53:12; Dan. 9:26; Zech. 12:10), John the Baptist (John 1:29, 36), and Moses and Elijah at the transfiguration (Luke 9:30–31).

Christ's once-for-all sacrifice is, of course, central to the life of His true church. Baptism pictures believers' union with Him in His death (cf. Rom. 6:3); in celebrating Communion they "proclaim the Lord's death until He comes" (1 Cor. 11:26); in preaching the gospel they "preach Christ crucified" (1 Cor. 1:23).

Christ's death brings to life all the rich blessings of salvation. Through His death believers are justified—a legal term meaning "to declare righteous." Paul wrote that those who place their faith in Jesus Christ are "justified by His blood ... justified as a gift by His grace through the redemption which is in Christ Jesus . . . who was delivered over because of our transgressions, and was raised because of our justification" (Rom. 5:9; 3:24; 4:25). God declares repentant sinners righteous because Christ's death paid the penalty for their sins and His righteousness is imputed to them (Rom. 5:19; 1 Cor. 1:30; 2 Cor. 5:21; Phil. 3:9).

Christ's death also redeems His people from slavery to sin. "In Him [Christ]," Paul declared, "we have redemption through His blood, the forgiveness of our trespasses, according to the riches of His grace" (Eph.

1:7; cf. Rom. 3:24; Gal. 3:13). It was "not through the blood of goats and calves, but through His own blood, [that Christ] entered the holy place once for all, having obtained eternal redemption" (Heb. 9:12). "The Son of Man," Jesus said, "did not come to be served, but to serve, and to give His life a ransom for many" (Matt. 20:28; cf. 1 Tim. 2:6; Titus 2:14; 1 Peter 1:18; 2:24; Rev. 1:5; 5:9).

Christ was able to ransom the elect because His death propitiated (appeased, satisfied) God's holy wrath against sin. Paul wrote in Romans 3:25 that "God displayed [Jesus] publicly as a propitiation in His blood through faith." Christ was able "to make propitiation for the sins of the people" (Heb. 2:17) because "He Himself is the propitiation for our sins" (1 John 2:2; cf. 4:10).

Since God determined that "without shedding of blood there is no forgiveness" of sin (Heb. 9:22), it was essential for Christ to die to obtain that forgiveness for believers. On the night before His death, Jesus said, "This is My blood of the covenant, which is poured out for many for forgiveness of sins" (Matt. 26:28). It is through the sacrifice of God's "beloved Son" that "we have redemption, the forgiveness of sins" (Col. 1:13–14). Later in that same epistle Paul wrote,

> When you were dead in your transgressions and the uncircumcision of your flesh, He made you alive together with Him, having forgiven us all our transgressions, having canceled out the certificate of debt consisting of decrees against us, which was hostile to us; and He has taken it out of the way, having nailed it to the cross. (Col. 2:13–14)

John reminded his readers that "if we walk in the Light as He Himself is in the Light, we have fellowship with one another, and the blood of Jesus His Son cleanses us from all sin" (1 John 1:7; cf. Rev. 7:14).

The death of Christ reconciles all believing sinners to God. To the Romans Paul wrote, "For if while we were enemies we were reconciled to God through the death of His Son, much more, having been reconciled, we shall be saved by His life. And not only this, but we also exult in God through our Lord Jesus Christ, through whom we have now received the reconciliation" (Rom. 5:10–11). In 2 Corinthians 5:19 he noted that "God was in Christ reconciling the world to Himself, not counting their trespasses against them." He told the Colossians that it pleased the Father "through [Christ] to reconcile all things to Himself, having made peace through the blood of His cross ... He has now reconciled you in His fleshly body through death, in order to present you before Him holy and blameless and beyond reproach" (Col. 1:20, 22).

Leon Morris summarized what Christ's death means for believers in the following list. By His death

1. We are redeemed, Ephesians 1:7; 1 Peter 1:19
2. We are made nigh to God, Ephesians 2:13
3. We are reconciled to God, Colossians 1:20, 21; Romans 5:10
4. Jew and Gentile are now made one, Ephesians 2:16
5. We are cleansed, Hebrews 9:14; 1 John 1:7
6. We are justified, Romans 5:9
7. We are sanctified, Hebrews 10:10; 13:12
8. We are perfected forever, Hebrews 10:14
9. We have been purchased unto God, Revelation 5:9
10. The bond that was against us has been nailed to the cross, Colossians 2:14
11. We have boldness to enter into the holy place, Hebrews 10:19
12. We are loosed from our sins, Revelation 1:5
13. We may overcome by the blood of the Lamb, Revelation 12:11
14. By His cross peace with God has been secured, Colossians 1:20
15. His blood establishes a new covenant, 1 Corinthians 11:25
16. His death was to redeem us from all iniquity, Titus 2:14

(*The Cross in the New Testament* [Grand Rapids: Eerdmans, 1965], 425–26)

As he contemplated all that Christ's death means to believers, Paul could only exclaim, "May it never be that I would boast, except in the cross of our Lord Jesus Christ, through which the world has been crucified to me, and I to the world" (Gal. 6:14), and "I determined to know nothing among you except Jesus Christ, and Him crucified" (1 Cor. 2:2). Because of its supreme significance, it is not surprising that countless words have been written expounding the vast, rich meaning of Christ's death for believers.

What is not so often considered is what the Lord's death meant to Him. Even Christ's eleven closest followers, on the eve of the crucifixion, did not grasp the significance of Jesus' death from the divine perspective. All the hopes, dreams, and ambitions of the apostles centered on their Master. They had forsaken everything to follow Jesus, rightly believing that He was Israel's long-awaited Messiah. The disciples expected Him to overthrow the Romans, restore Israel's sovereignty and glory, and grant them important positions in the restored kingdom (Matt. 19:27; 20:20–21). But they were slowly beginning to understand that when He had predicted His death (see the references above), Jesus had meant exactly what He said.

The Lord had supplied all the disciples' physical, emotional, and spiritual needs. As a result, they loved Him deeply and could not imagine life without their beloved Teacher. They reacted to Jesus' impending death with shock and fear in the face of such an incomparable loss. Knowing what they were thinking, the Lord spent much of His last night with the disciples comforting and encouraging them. He reassured them that although He would no longer be visibly present with them, He would still take care of them. The Holy Spirit, the Helper whom Christ would send, would come to indwell them, empower them, and guide them.

But despite the Lord's promises to them, including the guarantee of His resurrection, the disciples were still severely disturbed, prompting His command to them in 14:27, "Do not let your heart be troubled, nor let it be fearful." The disciples were troubled in part because their faith was weak (cf. Matt. 6:30; 8:26; 14:31; 16:8; 17:20). But beyond that, their anxiety stemmed from selfish shortsightedness. They saw the Lord's death only in terms of what would be loss to them, not what would be gain to Him.

The disciples' selfishness prompted the Lord's rebuke, **"You heard that I said to you, 'I go away** (cf. 7:33; 8:21; 13:33, 36; 14:2–4, 12; 16:7, 10)**, and I will come to you'** (14:3, 18, 23; 16:22). **If you loved Me, you would have rejoiced."** Since the noblest love does "not seek its own" (1 Cor. 13:5), but rather what is best for its object, Jesus exposed the weakness of the disciples' love, and called them to view the cross from His perspective.

This passage reveals four facets of what Jesus' death meant to Him, each of which reflects an important aspect of His work. Through His death His ministry would be vindicated, His message would be verified, His mission would be victorious, and His motivation would be validated.

His Ministry Would Be Vindicated

because I go to the Father, for the Father is greater than I. (14:28*b*)

After His humiliation in the incarnation, Jesus longed to **go to the Father.** The reference is to His restoration and exaltation to the Father's right hand (Matt. 26:64; Acts 2:33; 5:31; 7:55, 56; Rom. 8:34; Eph. 1:20; Col. 3:1; Heb. 1:3; 8:1; 10:12; 12:2; 1 Peter 3:22). The Son of God left the indescribable glories of heaven, where He experienced perfect fellowship with the Father (John 1:1; cf. 3:35; 10:17; Matt. 3:17; 17:5; Eph. 1:6; Col. 1:13), and became a man (cf. Rom. 8:3–4; Phil. 2:5–8; 1 John 4:2–3). Though He was sinless, He had experienced human weaknesses, such as fatigue (Matt. 8:24), hunger (Matt. 4:2), and thirst (John 4:7). Now He was returning to the fullness of the glory He had experienced from all eternity in the Father's presence. Jesus expressed His yearning for that glory when He prayed, "Father, the hour has come; glorify Your Son, that the Son may glorify You ... Now, Father, glorify Me together with Yourself, with the glory which I had with You before the world was" (John 17:1, 5; cf. v. 24).

In being exalted to the Father's right hand (Ps. 110:1; Luke 22:69;

Acts 7:55ff; Rom. 8:34; Eph. 1:20; Col. 3:1; Heb. 1:3; 8:1; 10:12; 12:2; 1 Peter 3:22), Christ's ministry would be eternally vindicated by God—His exaltation being the culmination of the Father's approval of His earthly life and death. Because Christ had accomplished the Father's will perfectly, He eagerly looked forward to His Father's heavenly presence, where He would return to full glory. Though the cross would be excruciating, Jesus knew that the Father "[would raise] Him from the dead and [would seat] Him at His right hand in the heavenly places, far above all rule and authority and power and dominion, and every name that is named, not only in this age but also in the one to come" (Eph. 1:20–21; cf. Isa. 53:10). As one scholar writes:

> When Jesus' self-humbling reached the absolute depths in His shameful death, God the Father decisively intervened. In vindication and approval of the Son's self-humbling, the Father magnificently exalted Him to the highest place in the universe. The Father clearly rewarded His Son for His perfectly obedient life and death.... In exalting Jesus Christ, God the Father vindicated Him. (David J. MacLeod, "The Exaltation of Christ: An Exposition of Philippians 2:9–11," *Bibliotheca Sacra* 158/632 [October 2001]: 439, 41)

Jesus' affirmation, **the Father is greater than I,** has been twisted by heretical groups into an incorrect assertion of His inferiority to the Father. After repeatedly asserting His deity and full equality with the Father (e.g., John 5:17–18; 8:58; 10:30; 14:9), Jesus would not have reversed Himself and denied that equality. Thus, the Lord was not speaking here of His essential nature as God, but of His submissive role during His ministry on earth. In essence and being, the Father and the Son are eternally coequal; but in role and function, the Son submitted Himself to the Father's will at the incarnation. Christ's statement reflected the perspective of a humble servant, the role He had assumed during His earthly ministry. "Truly, truly, I say to you," He had said earlier in John's gospel, "the Son can do nothing of Himself, unless it is something He sees the Father doing; for whatever the Father does, these things the Son also does in like manner" (5:19; cf. v. 30; 4:34; 6:38; 8:29, 42; 12:49; 14:10).

In the incarnation

> Christ Jesus ... although He existed in the form of God, did not regard equality with God a thing to be grasped, but emptied Himself, taking the form of a bond-servant, and being made in the likeness of men. Being found in appearance as a man, He humbled Himself by becoming obedient to the point of death, even death on a cross. (Phil. 2:5–8)

He "was made for a little while lower than the angels," but now, "because of the suffering of death [He would be] crowned with glory and honor"

(Heb. 2:9; cf. Phil. 2:9–11). Having submitted Himself to the Father in death, He has been gloriously vindicated by the Father ever since.

D. A. Carson captures the essence of what it meant to Jesus to return to the Father when he writes,

> If Jesus' disciples truly loved him, they would be glad that he is returning to his Father, *for* he is returning to the sphere where he belongs, to the glory he had with the Father before the world began (17:5), to the place where the Father is undiminished in glory, unquestionably greater than the Son in his incarnate state. To this point the disciples have responded emotionally entirely according to their perception of *their own* gain or loss. If they had loved Jesus, they would have perceived that his departure to his own "home" was *his* gain and rejoiced with him at the prospect. As it is, their grief is an index of their self-centredness. (*The Gospel According to John*, The Pillar New Testament Commentary [Grand Rapids: Eerdmans, 1991], 508. Italics in original.)

HIS MESSAGE WOULD BE VERIFIED

Now I have told you before it happens, so that when it happens, you may believe. I will not speak much more with you, (14:29–30*a*)

As noted earlier, the disciples believed that Jesus was the Messiah and the Son of God. In fact, on at least two occasions they had emphatically affirmed that belief. In response to the Lord's query, "But who do you say that I am?" (Matt. 16:15), Peter, as usual the spokesman for the rest, replied, "You are the Christ, the Son of the living God" (v. 16). After many superficial disciples

> withdrew and were not walking with Him anymore.... Jesus said to the twelve, "You do not want to go away also, do you?" Simon Peter answered Him, "Lord, to whom shall we go? You have words of eternal life. We have believed and have come to know that You are the Holy One of God." (John 6:66–69; cf. 1:41, 45–49; Matt. 14:33)

But despite their confident testimonies, they still struggled with doubt. That prompted Jesus to rebuke them repeatedly for their lack of faith, and caused them to cry out to Him, "Increase our faith!" (Luke 17:5).

As He had done a short while earlier (13:19), Jesus strengthened that wavering faith by reminding them, **I have told you before it happens, so that when it happens, you may believe.** The disciples understood from the Old Testament that only God can predict the future. In Isaiah 42:9 God said, "Behold, the former things have come to pass, now I declare new things; before they spring forth I proclaim them to you." In 46:9–10 He added, "I am God, and there is no one like Me, declaring the end from the beginning, and from ancient times things which have not been done, saying, 'My purpose will be established, and I will accomplish all My good pleasure.'" Later in Isaiah God reminded idolatrous Israel, "I declared the former things long ago and they went forth from My mouth, and I proclaimed them. . . . Therefore I declared them to you long ago, before they took place I proclaimed them to you," and then explained that He had done so "that [they] would not say, 'My idol has done them, and my graven image and my molten image have commanded them' " (48:3, 5).

In contrast, Israel's idols were exposed as false gods by their inability to foretell the future; they were unable to answer God's challenge to "announce to us what is coming; declare the things that are going to come afterward, that we may know that you are gods" (Isa. 41:22–23). Since the false gods, being lifeless and useless, could not predict the future, God said disdainfully to them, "Behold, you are of no account, and your work amounts to nothing; he who chooses you is an abomination" (v. 24).

Therefore when the predictions Jesus made came to pass, the disciples' faith in Him increased greatly. For example, John 2:19–21 records Jesus' prediction of His death and resurrection. Verse 22 then notes that "when He was raised from the dead, His disciples remembered that He said this; and they believed the Scripture and the word which Jesus had spoken." In 16:1–3 Jesus predicted that the disciples would face persecution. Then in verse 4 He told them, "But these things I have spoken to you, so that when their hour comes, you may remember that I told you of them." But despite the Lord's many predictions of His resurrection, the disciples did not fully believe until after it actually happened. John records that it was only when he and Peter found the tomb empty that "he saw and believed. For as yet they did not understand the Scripture, that He must rise again from the dead" (20:8–9). The fulfillment of His predictions helped convince the disciples of Jesus' deity, just as He had intended (cf. 13:19 where "He" does not appear in the Greek text, indicating that Jesus was taking for Himself the name of God [Ex. 3:14; cf. John 8:24, 28, 58; 18:5–6]).

The Lord's words, **I will not speak much more with you,** do not signal the end of His discourse, which actually continues through the end of chapter 16. Rather, they are a reminder to the disciples that His time with them on earth was drawing to its close. Jesus was fully aware of all that was to happen to Him; He was never taken by surprise. He knew exactly how much time He had left with the eleven before the servants of the Enemy arrived to seize Him.

HIS MISSION WOULD BE VICTORIOUS

for the ruler of the world is coming, and he has nothing in Me; (14:30b)

This is the second of three references in John's gospel to Satan as **the ruler of the world** (12:31; 16:11; cf. Luke 4:5–6; 2 Cor. 4:4; Eph. 2:2; 1 John 5:19). The Devil, of course, is not the legitimate ruler of the world, but a divinely permitted usurper. He is the **ruler** of the evil **world** system that is in rebellion against God (cf. 7:7; 8:23; 14:17; 15:18–19; 17:14–16; 1 John 2:15–17; 3:1, 13; 4:4–5; 5:4–5, 19). Jesus saw Satan **coming** in the persons of Judas, the Jewish leaders, and the Roman soldiers, who would shortly arrest Him in Gethsemane.

Jesus had been in conflict with Satan throughout His life. When He was an infant, Satan prompted Herod to try to kill Him, along with the other male children in the vicinity of Bethlehem (Matt. 2:16). At the outset of His ministry, Jesus "was in the wilderness forty days being tempted by Satan" (Mark 1:13). Nor were Satan's temptations limited to that initial encounter; they persisted throughout the Lord's earthly ministry (Luke 4:13; Heb. 4:15), and culminated in Gethsemane (Luke 22:39–46). Satan repeatedly attempted to kill Jesus before the cross by inciting evil men against Him (e.g., Mark 14:1; Luke 4:28–30; John 5:18; 7:1; 8:59; 10:39; 11:53–54; cf. Matt. 21:38).

Finally, in a few short hours, Jesus' lifelong conflict with the Devil would reach its triumphant climax. Satan would finally succeed in having Him killed, but in so doing would bring about his own destruction. Far from being Satan's victim, "the Son of God appeared for this purpose, to destroy the works of the devil" (1 John 3:8) "... that through death He might render powerless him who had the power of death, that is, the devil" (Heb. 2:14). The cross marked Satan's ultimate defeat, though the final sentence against him will not be carried out until the end of the millennium. At that point his final assault against God's people will be thwarted, and he will be cast into the lake of fire, where he will be punished for eternity (Rev. 20:10).

Jesus' emphatic declaration (there is a double negative in the Greek text) "Satan **has nothing in Me**" explains why the Devil could not hold Him in death. The phrase is a Hebrew idiom meaning that the Devil could make no legal claim against Jesus. "How could he?" asks D. A. Carson, "Jesus is not of this world (8:23), and he has never sinned (8:46). The devil could have a hold on Jesus only if there were a justifiable charge against Jesus. Jesus' death would then be his due, and the devil's triumph" (*The Gospel According to John*, 509).

HIS MOTIVATION WOULD BE VALIDATED

but so that the world may know that I love the Father, I do exactly as the Father commanded Me. Get up, let us go from here." (14:31)

Far from marking His defeat at the hands of Satan, Christ's death was the ultimate proof to **the world** of His **love** for **the Father.** Jesus had just emphasized that the essential test of love is obedience (vv. 15, 21, 23). He would demonstrate His love for the Father by doing **exactly as the Father commanded** Him.

The phrase **get up, let us go from here** signals an obvious transition in the narrative. At this point Jesus and the disciples evidently left the upper room and began walking through Jerusalem, headed for Gethsemane. While they walked, Jesus continued His teaching. (John 18:1 does not describe the Lord and the disciples leaving the upper room, as some think. It refers to their leaving the city of Jerusalem and crossing the Kidron valley, east of the city. Gethsemane lay across the valley on the slopes of the Mount of Olives.)

The sum of all that Jesus' death meant to Him was joy; it was "for the joy set before Him [that He] endured the cross, despising the shame, and has sat down at the right hand of the throne of God" (Heb. 12:2). The path to that eternal joy led through suffering. John Piper writes, "First the agony of the cross, then the ecstasy of heaven. There was no other way.... The passion of Christ did not merely precede the crown; it was the price, and the crown was the prize. He died to have it" (*Fifty Reasons Why Jesus Came to Die* [Wheaton: Crossway, 2006], 114, 116–17).

Having triumphed over death, Jesus has returned to the glory that He had from all eternity in heaven (Luke 24:26; John 13:31–32; 17:1, 5; Phil. 2:8–9; Heb. 2:9) at the Father's right hand (Rom. 8:34; Eph. 1:20; Col. 3:1; Heb. 1:3; 8:1; 1 Peter 3:22). There He receives forever the unceasing and undiminishing praise of the "living creatures and the elders" (Rev. 5:11), who cry out "saying with a loud voice, 'Worthy is the Lamb that was slain to receive power and riches and wisdom and might and honor and glory and blessing'" (v. 12).

The Vine and the Branches
(John 15:1–11)

13

"I am the true vine, and My Father is the vinedresser. Every branch in Me that does not bear fruit, He takes away; and every branch that bears fruit, He prunes it so that it may bear more fruit. You are already clean because of the word which I have spoken to you. Abide in Me, and I in you. As the branch cannot bear fruit of itself unless it abides in the vine, so neither can you unless you abide in Me. I am the vine, you are the branches; he who abides in Me and I in him, he bears much fruit, for apart from Me you can do nothing. If anyone does not abide in Me, he is thrown away as a branch and dries up; and they gather them, and cast them into the fire and they are burned. If you abide in Me, and My words abide in you, ask whatever you wish, and it will be done for you. My Father is glorified by this, that you bear much fruit, and so prove to be My disciples. Just as the Father has loved Me, I have also loved you; abide in My love. If you keep My commandments, you will abide in My love; just as I have kept My Father's commandments and abide in His love. These things I have spoken to you so that My joy may be in you, and that your joy may be made full." (15:1–11)

The Bible uses many analogies to depict God's relationship to His people. He is their Father (Matt. 6:9; Rom. 1:7), they are His children (John 1:12; Rom. 8:16–17, 21; Phil. 2:15; 1 John 3:1–2; cf. Rom. 8:14, 19; Gal. 3:26; 4:6; Heb. 12:7) and the members of His household (Eph. 2:19; 1 Tim. 3:15; 1 Peter 4:17); He is their King, they are His subjects (Matt. 25:34); He is the Creator, they are His creatures (Pss. 24:1; 95:6; 100:3; 119:73; 139:13; Eccl. 12:1; Eph. 2:10); He is the Shepherd, they are His sheep (Pss. 23:1; 28:9; 79:13; 95:7; 100:3; Isa. 40:11; John 10:11, 14, 26; Heb. 13:20; 1 Peter 2:27; 5:4); He is the builder, they are the building (Eph. 2:20–22; Heb. 3:4); He is the master, they are His slaves (Matt. 10:24–25; Rom. 14:4; Eph. 6:9; Col. 4:1; 2 Tim. 2:21; Jude 4); Christ is their husband, they are His bride (2 Cor. 11:2; Rev. 19:7; 21:9; cf. Isa. 54:5; Jer. 31:32); He is the head, they are His body (Eph. 1:22–23; 4:15; Col. 1:18; 2:19) .

Believers' vital relationship with Jesus Christ is depicted in this passage in another familiar analogy. Just as a branch depends entirely on the vine for life, sustenance, growth, and fruit, so believers depend completely on the divine Lord as the source of their spiritual life and effect. And just as a branch cannot bear fruit unless it is connected to the vine, so believers cannot bear spiritual fruit apart from their life-giving union with Christ. As He said in verse 5, "Apart from Me you can do nothing."

Jesus presented this analogy to His disciples in the upper room on the night before His death. It was a time of intense drama. One of the twelve men closest to Him, Judas Iscariot, had revealed himself to be a traitor. By this time, Judas had already left to sell out the Lord to the Jewish authorities and set in motion the events leading to Jesus' arrest and murder (13:26–30). The Lord and the remaining eleven disciples were about to leave the upper room for Gethsemane, where Christ would agonize in prayer to the Father, and then be taken prisoner.

The central truth the Lord wanted to communicate in this symbol is the importance of abiding in Him (vv. 4, 5, 6, 7, 9, 10). In the most basic sense, whether or not a person abides in Christ reveals whether they are saved (vv. 2, 6). It must be noted that this simple and, I think, obvious premise rescues the text from many unnecessary misinterpretations. And it is only to the degree the redeemed abide in Christ that they can bear spiritual fruit. Those principles will be more fully developed in the exposition that follows.

Menō ("abide") describes something that remains where it is, continues in a fixed state, or endures. In this context the word refers to maintaining an unbroken communion with Jesus Christ. The Lord's command "Abide in Me" (v. 4) is primarily a plea to false disciples of Christ to repent and express true faith in Him. It also serves to encourage genuine believers to abide in Him in the fullest, deepest, most complete sense.

Always the master storyteller, Jesus wove all the key figures of that night's events into His analogy: He is the vine, the Father the vinedresser, the abiding branches illustrate the eleven and all other true disciples, and the nonabiding branches picture Judas and all other false disciples like him. One last time before His death, Jesus warned against following the pattern of Judas. He challenged all who claim to believe in Him to demonstrate the genuineness of their faith by enduring faith in Him.

THE VINE

I am the true vine . . . I am the vine (1a, 5a)

Spoken just hours before His death, this is the last of the seven "I AM" statements in John's gospel, all of which affirm Christ's deity (6:35; 8:12; 10:7, 9, 11, 14; 11:25; 14:6; cf. 8:24, 28, 58; 13:19; 18:5–6). As God in human flesh, Jesus rightly pointed to Himself as the source of spiritual life, vitality, growth, and productivity.

The imagery is ancient, as the Old Testament portrays Israel as God's **vine.** In Psalm 80:8 the psalmist wrote, "You removed a vine from Egypt; You drove out the nations and planted it." Through the prophet Jeremiah, God said to Israel, "I planted you a choice vine, a completely faithful seed" (Jer. 2:21). Israel was the channel through which God's covenant blessings flowed to the world.

But Israel proved to be a fruitless, unfaithful vine. The Old Testament laments Israel's failure to produce good fruit and warns of God's impending judgment. In Jeremiah 2:21 God demanded of the nation, "How then have you turned yourself before Me into the degenerate shoots of a foreign vine?" In Hosea He lamented, "Israel is a luxuriant vine; he produces fruit for himself. The more his fruit, the more altars he made; the richer his land, the better he made the sacred pillars" (Hos. 10:1; cf. Isa. 27:2–6; Jer. 12:10–13; Ezek. 15:1–8; 19:10–14).

Nowhere in the Old Testament is Israel's faithless rejection of God's gracious, tender care more poignantly depicted than in Isaiah 5:1–7:

> Let me sing now for my well-beloved a song of my beloved concerning His vineyard. My well-beloved had a vineyard on a fertile hill. He dug it all around, removed its stones, and planted it with the choicest vine. And He built a tower in the middle of it and also hewed out a wine vat in it; then He expected it to produce good grapes, but it produced only worthless ones. "And now, O inhabitants of Jerusalem and men of Judah, judge between Me and My vineyard. What more was there to do for My vineyard that I have not done in it? Why, when I expected it to produce good grapes did it produce worthless ones? So now let Me tell

you what I am going to do to My vineyard: I will remove its hedge and it will be consumed; I will break down its wall and it will become trampled ground. I will lay it waste; it will not be pruned or hoed, but briars and thorns will come up. I will also charge the clouds to rain no rain on it." For the vineyard of the Lord of hosts is the house of Israel and the men of Judah His delightful plant. Thus He looked for justice, but behold, bloodshed; for righteousness, but behold, a cry of distress.

In Matthew 21:33–43 Jesus told a similar parable, illustrating Israel's rejection of God's messengers, which would culminate in their murder of Him:

> "Listen to another parable. There was a landowner who planted a vineyard and put a wall around it and dug a wine press in it, and built a tower, and rented it out to vine-growers and went on a journey. When the harvest time approached, he sent his slaves to the vine-growers to receive his produce. The vine-growers took his slaves and beat one, and killed another, and stoned a third. Again he sent another group of slaves larger than the first; and they did the same thing to them. But afterward he sent his son to them, saying, 'They will respect my son.' But when the vine-growers saw the son, they said among themselves, 'This is the heir; come, let us kill him and seize his inheritance.' They took him, and threw him out of the vineyard and killed him. Therefore when the owner of the vineyard comes, what will he do to those vine-growers?" They said to Him, "He will bring those wretches to a wretched end, and will rent out the vineyard to other vine-growers who will pay him the proceeds at the proper seasons." Jesus said to them, "Did you never read in the Scriptures, 'The stone which the builders rejected, this became the chief cornerstone; this came about from the Lord, and it is marvelous in our eyes'? Therefore I say to you, the kingdom of God will be taken away from you and given to a people producing the fruit of it."

Israel's apostasy made it an empty vine, and for a long time disqualified as the channel for God's blessings. Those blessings now come only from union with Jesus Christ, the **true vine.** "Theologically, John's point is that Jesus displaces Israel as the focus of God's plan of salvation, with the implication that faith in Jesus becomes the decisive characteristic for membership among God's people" (Andreas J. Köstenberger, *John,* Baker Exegetical Commentary on the New Testament [Grand Rapids: Baker, 2004], 448).

Alēthinos (**true**) refers to what is real as distinct from a type (cf. Heb. 8:2; 9:24), perfect as distinct from the imperfect, or genuine rather than what is counterfeit (cf. 1 Thess. 1:9; 1 John 5:20; Rev. 3:7, 14; 6:10; 19:11). Jesus is the true vine in the same sense that He is the true light (John 1:9), the final and complete revelation of spiritual truth, and the true bread out of heaven (John 6:32), the final and only source of spiritual sustenance.

THE VINEDRESSER

My Father is the vinedresser. (1*b*)

That Jesus designates the **Father** as **the vinedresser** while assigning Himself the role of the vine is in no way a denial of His deity and full equality with the Father. During His incarnation, without diminishing His deity one iota, Jesus willingly assumed a subordinate role to the Father (see the discussion of 14:28 in chapter 12 of this volume). Moreover, the point of the analogy is not to define the relationship of the Father to the Son, but to emphasize the Father's care for the vine and the branches.

Geōrgos (**vinedresser**) refers to one who tills the soil; hence a farmer (2 Tim. 2:6; James 5:7), or a vine-grower (Matt. 21:33, 34, 35, 38, 40, 41; Mark 12:1, 2, 7, 9). It is in the latter sense that Jesus used it here. Apart from planting, fertilizing, and watering the vine, the vinedresser had two primary responsibilities in caring for it. First, he removed the branches that did not bear fruit. Second, he pruned the ones that did bear fruit, thus enabling them to bear more fruit. It is with those two types of branches that the rest of Christ's analogy is primarily concerned.

THE VINE BRANCHES

Every branch in Me that does not bear fruit, He takes away; and every branch that bears fruit, He prunes it so that it may bear more fruit. You are already clean because of the word which I have spoken to you. Abide in Me, and I in you. As the branch cannot bear fruit of itself unless it abides in the vine, so neither can you unless you abide in Me. I am the vine, you are the branches; he who abides in Me and I in him, he bears much fruit, for apart from Me you can do nothing. If anyone does not abide in Me, he is thrown away as a branch and dries up; and they gather them, and cast them into the fire and they are burned. If you abide in Me, and My words abide in you, ask whatever you wish, and it will be done for you. My Father is glorified by this, that you bear much fruit, and so prove to be My disciples. Just as the Father has loved Me, I have also loved you; abide in My love. If you keep My commandments, you will abide in My love; just as I have kept My Father's commandments and abide in His love. These things I have spoken to you so that My joy may be in you, and that your joy may be made full." (15:2–11)

As noted above, the two types of branches represent the two types of disciples outwardly professing attachment to Jesus: the genuine branches that abide in Him, and the false branches that do not.

THE BLESSINGS OF ABIDING BRANCHES

every branch that bears fruit, He prunes it so that it may bear more fruit. You are already clean because of the word which I have spoken to you. Abide in Me, and I in you. As the branch cannot bear fruit of itself unless it abides in the vine, so neither can you unless you abide in Me. I am the vine, you are the branches; he who abides in Me and I in him, he bears much fruit, for apart from Me you can do nothing. . . . If you abide in Me, and My words abide in you, ask whatever you wish, and it will be done for you. My Father is glorified by this, that you bear much fruit, and so prove to be My disciples. Just as the Father has loved Me, I have also loved you; abide in My love. If you keep My commandments, you will abide in My love; just as I have kept My Father's commandments and abide in His love. These things I have spoken to you so that My joy may be in you, and that your joy may be made full." (15:2*b*–5, 7–11)

Three distinguishing marks of the true branches stand out in this analogy. First, they bear **fruit** (vv. 2, 4, 5, 8). That characteristic most clearly sets them apart from the false branches (cf. vv. 2, 8). Second, they also **abide** (remain; continue) **in** Christ's **love** (v. 9). Finally, they operate in full cooperation with the source of life, keeping His commandments by following the perfect example of the Lord Jesus Christ, who always obeyed the Father (v. 10). As Jesus had earlier told those who professed faith in Him, "If you continue in My word, then you are truly disciples of Mine" (John 8:31). Obedience proves that a person's love for Christ is genuine (John 14:15, 21, 23), a point John makes clear in his first epistle: believers confess their sins (1:9), unbelievers deny them (1:8, 10); believers obey God's commandments (2:3), unbelievers do not (2:4); believers demonstrate love for others (2:10), unbelievers do not (2:9, 11); believers live in patterns of righteous (3:6), unbelievers do not (3:9).

But that does not mean that those who love Christ will always obey perfectly; there are times when we lapse into disobedience and fail to abide fully in Christ. Paul admonished the Corinthians,

> I, brethren, could not speak to you as to spiritual men, but as to men of flesh, as to infants in Christ. I gave you milk to drink, not solid food; for you were not yet able to receive it. Indeed, even now you are not yet

able, for you are still fleshly. For since there is jealousy and strife among you, are you not fleshly, and are you not walking like mere men? (1 Cor. 3:1–3)

Jesus rebuked the Ephesian church for its diminished devotion to Him: "I have this against you, that you have left your first love" (Rev. 2:4). John, after making the absolute statement "My little children, I am writing these things to you so that you may not sin," immediately added "If anyone sins, we have an Advocate with the Father, Jesus Christ the righteous; and He Himself is the propitiation for our sins; and not for ours only, but also for those of the whole world" (1 John 2:1–2). Therefore the Lord's exhortation to abide in Him is appropriate not only for unbelievers, but also to remind and warn believers who are not abiding in Him in the fullest sense.

Because He wants them to be spiritually productive, the Father takes **every branch that bears fruit** and **prunes it so that it may bear more fruit.** Pruning

> was . . . an essential part of first-century viticultural practice, as it is today. The first pruning occurred in spring when vines were in flowering stage. This involved four operations: (1) the removal of the growing tips of vigorous shoots so that they would not grow too rapidly; (2) cutting off one or two feet from the end of growing shoots to prevent entire shoots being snapped off by the wind; (3) the removal of some flower or grape clusters so that those left could produce more and better-quality fruit; and (4) the removal of suckers that arose from below the ground or from the trunk and main branches so that the strength of the vine was not tapped by the suckers. (Colin Kruse, *The Gospel According to John*, The Tyndale New Testament Commentaries [Grand Rapids: Eerdmans, 2003], 315)

The Father prunes the true branches by removing anything that would sap their spiritual energy and hinder them from fruitful results. His pruning involves cutting away anything that limits righteousness, including the discipline that comes from trials, suffering, and persecution. The knowledge that the Father uses the pain that Christians endure for their ultimate good should eliminate all fear, self-pity, and complaining. The classic text in Hebrews reminds those undergoing God's painful, pruning chastening,

> It is for discipline that you endure; God deals with you as with sons; for what son is there whom his father does not discipline? But if you are without discipline, of which all have become partakers, then you are illegitimate children and not sons. Furthermore, we had earthly fathers to discipline us, and we respected them; shall we not much rather be

subject to the Father of spirits, and live? For they disciplined us for a short time as seemed best to them, but He disciplines us for our good, so that we may share His holiness. All discipline for the moment seems not to be joyful, but sorrowful; yet to those who have been trained by it, afterwards it yields the peaceful fruit of righteousness. (Heb. 12:7–11; cf. 1 Cor. 11:32)

In the Father's infinite wisdom and absolute, sovereign control of all of life's circumstances, He "causes all things to work together for good to those who love God, to those who are called according to His purpose" (Rom. 8:28; cf. 5:3–5; Gen. 50:20; Deut. 8:16; 2 Cor. 4:16–18; James 1:2–4).

But suffering is merely the handle of the Father's knife; the blade is the Word of God. **You are already clean,** Jesus told the eleven true disciples, **because of the word which I have spoken to you.** Because they had embraced the gospel through Christ's teaching, the eleven had been regenerated by the Holy Spirit (cf. John 3:3–8; Titus 3:4–7). That same gospel is found today in the Scriptures, the "word of Christ" (Col. 3:16). The Word is instrumental in believers' initial cleansing at salvation (cf. Rom. 1:16), and it also continually purges, prunes, and cleanses them.

God uses His Word as the pruning knife, because it "is living and active and sharper than any two-edged sword, and piercing as far as the division of soul and spirit, of both joints and marrow, and able to judge the thoughts and intentions of the heart" (Heb. 4:12), but He uses affliction to prepare His people for the Word's pruning. The psalmist affirmed the connection between affliction and the Word's work in his life when he wrote, "Before I was afflicted I went astray, but now I keep Your word.... It is good for me that I was afflicted, that I may learn Your statutes" (Ps. 119:67, 71). Psalm 94:12 also makes that connection: "Blessed is the man whom You chasten, O Lord, and whom You teach out of Your law."

The Lord's words emphasize two important truths regarding spiritual conduct: **Abide in Me, and I in you. As the branch cannot bear fruit of itself unless it abides in the vine, so neither can you unless you abide in Me. I am the vine, you are the branches; he who abides in Me and I in him, he bears much fruit, for apart from Me you can do nothing.** First, since all true believers, those who **abide** in Christ and He in them, will bear spiritual fruit, there is no such thing as a fruitless Christian. John the Baptist challenged his hearers to "bear fruit in keeping with repentance" (Matt. 3:8), and warned that "every tree that does not bear good fruit is cut down and thrown into the fire" (v. 10). Contrasting true and false teachers, Jesus said, "Every good tree bears good fruit, but the bad tree bears bad fruit. A good tree cannot produce bad fruit, nor can a bad tree produce good fruit. Every tree that does not bear good fruit is cut down and thrown into the fire. So then, you will know them by their fruits" (Matt. 7:17–20). In Luke 6:43 He added, "There is no good tree which produces bad fruit, nor, on the other hand, a bad tree which produces good fruit."

Second, believers cannot bear fruit on their own, because as He plainly stated, **As the branch cannot bear fruit of itself unless it abides in the vine, so neither can you unless you abide in Me. I am the vine, you are the branches; he who abides in Me and I in him, he bears much fruit, for apart from Me you can do nothing** (cf. Hos. 14:8). There may be times when believers have lapses, when they fail to be faithful to their life in Christ. But true branches, through whom the life of the vine flows, cannot ultimately fail to produce fruit (cf. Pss. 1:1–3; 92:12–14; Prov. 11:30; 12:12; Jer. 17:7–8; Matt. 13:23; Rom. 7:4; Gal. 5:22–23; Eph. 5:9; Phil 1:11; Col. 1:10; James 3:17).

A popular misconception equates fruit with outward success. By that common standard, external religion, superficial righteousness, having a large church, a popular ministry, or a successful program are considered fruitful. But the Bible nowhere equates fruit with superficial, external behavior or results, which deceivers and hypocrites, as well as non-Christian cults and religions can duplicate. Instead, Scripture defines fruit in terms of spiritual qualities. "The fruit of the Spirit," Paul reminded the Galatians, "is love, joy, peace, patience, kindness, goodness, faithfulness, gentleness, self-control" (Gal. 5:22–23). Those Christlike traits mark those through whom His life flows.

Praise offered to God is also fruit. The writer of Hebrews exhorts his readers, "Through Him then, let us continually offer up a sacrifice of praise to God, that is, the fruit of lips that give thanks to His name" (Heb. 13:15; cf. Isa. 57:19; Hos. 14:2).

The Bible also identifies sacrificial love in meeting the needs of others as fruit. Referring to the monetary gift he was collecting for the needy believers at Jerusalem, Paul wrote to the Romans, "Therefore, when I have finished this, and have put my seal on this fruit of theirs, I will go on by way of you to Spain" (Rom. 15:28). Acknowledging the Philippians' financial support of his ministry, Paul told them, "Not that I seek the gift, but I seek the fruit that abounds to your account" (Phil. 4:17 NKJV). Supporting others who are in need is a tangible expression of love, which is one of the fruit of the Spirit (Gal. 5:22).

Fruit may also be defined as holy, righteous, God-honoring behavior in general. Such conduct is "fruit in keeping with repentance" (Matt. 3:8); the fruit produced by the good soil (Matt. 13:23) of a transformed life; the "fruit of the Light [that] consists in all goodness and righteousness and truth" (Eph. 5:9); the "fruit of righteousness which comes through Jesus Christ, to the glory and praise of God" (Phil. 1:11); the "peaceful fruit of righteousness" (Heb. 12:11). Paul prayed that the Colossians would be continually "bearing fruit in every good work" (Col. 1:10), because Christians were "created in Christ Jesus for good works, which God prepared beforehand so that we would walk in them" (Eph. 2:10).

Finally, the Bible defines fruit as converts to the gospel—not the artificial fruit of superficial "believers," but genuine disciples who abide in the true vine. Referring to the Samaritans who were coming out to Him from the village of Sychar, many of whom would believe savingly in Him (John 4:39, 41), Jesus said, "Already he who reaps is receiving wages and is gathering fruit for life eternal; so that he who sows and he who reaps may rejoice together" (v. 36). He declared of His sacrificial death, "Truly, truly, I say to you, unless a grain of wheat falls into the earth and dies, it remains alone; but if it dies, it bears much fruit" (John 12:24). Paul expressed his desire to the Christians in Rome to win converts in the imperial capital: "I do not want you to be unaware, brethren, that often I have planned to come to you (and have been prevented so far) so that I may obtain some fruit among you also, even as among the rest of the Gentiles" (Rom. 1:13). At the close of his letter, Paul greeted "Epaenetus, who is the firstfruits of Achaia to Christ" (16:5 NKJV). In 1 Corinthians 16:15 the apostle referred to "the household of Stephanas," as "the first fruits of Achaia," while in Colossians 1:6 he rejoiced that "in all the world also it [the gospel; v. 5] is constantly bearing fruit and increasing." John wrote of the 144,000 evangelists, who will be redeemed during the tribulation, "These have been purchased from among men as first fruits to God and to the Lamb" (Rev. 14:4).

Another blessing comes in Jesus' promise **If you abide in Me, and My words abide in you, ask whatever you wish, and it will be done for you.** That sweeping, all-encompassing promise presupposes that three conditions are met. First, the prayer Jesus promises to answer must be offered in His name; that is, consistent with His person and will, and so that He might display His glory in answering it (cf. the exposition of 14:13–14 in chapter 9 of this volume).

Second, the promise is only to those who **abide** in (have a permanent union with) Jesus Christ. God does not obligate Himself to answer the prayers of unbelievers, though He may choose to do so if it suits His sovereign purposes.

The final condition is that Christ's **words abide in** the person making the request. **Words** translates the plural form of the noun *rhēma,* and refers to the individual utterances of Christ. The promise of answered prayer comes only to those whose lives are controlled by the specific commands of God's Word (cf. Ps. 37:4). On the other hand, both Psalm 66:18 and James 4:3 warn that those controlled by sinful, selfish desires will not have their prayers answered.

The true branches also have the privilege of living lives that glorify God. **My Father is glorified by this,** Jesus told the disciples, **that you**

bear much fruit, and so prove to be My disciples. The greatest theme in the universe is the glory of God, and to live a life that brings God glory is the believer's highest privilege and duty. Only those who are in union with Christ can glorify God. Paul wrote, "I will not presume to speak of anything except what Christ has accomplished through me" (Rom. 15:18; cf. 1 Cor. 15:10; Gal. 2:20; Col. 1:29).

Jesus further promised that those who abide in Him will experience His love. **Just as the Father has loved Me,** He said, **I have also loved you; abide in My love.** The way to do that is to **keep** His **commandments, just as** He **kept** His **Father's commandments and abides in His love.** Righteous obedience is the key to experiencing God's blessing.

The crowning blessing, to which all the rest contribute, is full and complete joy. The Lord promised to impart to believers His **joy**—the joy that He shares in intimate fellowship with the Father. **These things I have spoken to you,** Jesus said to the eleven, **so that My joy may be in you, and that your joy may be made full.** The Lord promised that His own joy will permeate and control the lives of those who walk in communion with Him. Just a short time later, Jesus reiterated this promise in His High Priestly Prayer to the Father: "But now I come to You; and these things I speak in the world so that they may have My joy made full in themselves" (John 17:13). Such joy comes only to the obedient, as David learned to his sorrow. After his terrible sin with Bathsheba, he cried out, "Restore to me the joy of Your salvation" (Ps. 51:12). But the obedient receive "joy inexpressible and full of glory" (1 Peter 1:8).

THE BURNING OF NON-ABIDING BRANCHES

Every branch in Me that does not bear fruit, He takes away; . . . If anyone does not abide in Me, he is thrown away as a branch and dries up; and they gather them, and cast them into the fire and they are burned. (2*a*, 6)

A very different fate awaits the branches that do **not bear fruit.** Because they are detrimental to the health of the vine, the vinedresser would cut off the dry, lifeless, withered branches. In the Lord's analogy, the vinedresser (the Father) **takes** the unregenerate false branches **away** from their superficial attachment to the vine, and they are **thrown away.**

The reference here is not, as some imagine, to true Christians losing their salvation, nor are these fruitless but genuine Christians (an impossibility, as we have seen). That these branches bear no fruit marks them as unbelieving, false disciples since, as noted previously, all true

Christians bear fruit. Further, Jesus promised that He will not cast out any true disciples: "All that the Father gives Me will come to Me, and the one who comes to Me I will certainly not cast out" (John 6:37).

The phrase **in Me** in this case cannot have the Pauline connotation of believers' union with Christ; it merely describes those who outwardly attach themselves to Him (cf. Matt. 13:20–22; Rom. 9:6–8; 11:16–24; 1 John 2:19). Such people will always be present with the true church. The New Testament describes them as tares among the wheat (Matt. 13:25–30); bad fish that are thrown away (Matt. 13:48); goats condemned to eternal punishment (Matt. 25:33, 41); those left standing outside when the head of the house shuts the door (Luke 13:25–27); foolish virgins shut out of the wedding feast (Matt. 25:1–12); useless slaves who bury their master's talent in the ground (Matt. 25:24–30); apostates who eventually leave the fellowship of believers (1 John 2:19), manifest an evil, unbelieving heart by abandoning the living God (Heb. 3:12), continue to sin willfully after receiving the knowledge of the truth (Heb. 10:26), and fall away from the truth to everlasting destruction (Heb. 10:39). Although they imagine that they are on their way to heaven, they are actually on the broad path leading to hell (Matt. 7:13–14).

Right in their presence was the quintessential example of a false branch—Judas Iscariot. Outwardly, he was indistinguishable from the other eleven apostles—so much so that when Jesus announced earlier that night, "Truly, truly, I say to you, that one of you will betray Me" (John 13:21), the other "disciples began looking at one another, at a loss to know of which one He was speaking" (v. 22). They finally had to ask Him to point out His betrayer (vv. 23–26). But Judas had never been saved. In John 6:70–71 Jesus said to the apostles, "'Did I Myself not choose you, the twelve, and yet one of you is a devil?' Now He meant Judas the son of Simon Iscariot, for he, one of the twelve, was going to betray Him."

The ultimate fate that awaits the false branches is to be **cast . . . into the fire and . . . burned.** In Matthew 13:49–50 Jesus warned that "at the end of the age the angels will come forth and take out the wicked from among the righteous, and will throw them into the furnace of fire; in that place there will be weeping and gnashing of teeth" (cf. Matt. 3:10–12; 7:19; 25:41; Mark 9:43–48; Luke 3:17). Their anguished protest, "Lord, Lord, did we not prophesy in Your name, and in Your name cast out demons, and in Your name perform many miracles?" (Matt. 7:22) will evoke the chilling reply from the Lord, "I never knew you; depart from Me, you who practice lawlessness" (v. 23).

The choice that faces every person is clear. To abide in Christ as a genuine disciple will produce righteous behavior and result in eternal joy and blessing. But those whose profession of faith is false, like Judas, will be fruitless and ultimately cast into eternal torment in hell. The

Lord's sobering pronouncement concerning Judas, "Woe to that man by whom the Son of Man is betrayed! It would have been good for that man if he had not been born" (Matt. 26:24), applies to all pseudodisciples. In the words of Peter,

> If, after they have escaped the defilements of the world by the knowledge of the Lord and Savior Jesus Christ, they are again entangled in them and are overcome, the last state has become worse for them than the first. For it would be better for them not to have known the way of righteousness, than having known it, to turn away from the holy commandment handed on to them (2 Peter 2:20–21).

The Friends of Jesus (John 15:12–16)

14

"This is My commandment, that you love one another, just as I have loved you. Greater love has no one than this, that one lay down his life for his friends. You are My friends if you do what I command you. No longer do I call you slaves, for the slave does not know what his master is doing; but I have called you friends, for all things that I have heard from My Father I have made known to you. You did not choose Me but I chose you, and appointed you that you would go and bear fruit, and that your fruit would remain, so that whatever you ask of the Father in My name He may give to you." (15:12–16)

In a world awash in relativism, the Bible is unique in both its clarity and authority. Where many people see gray, God's Word speaks in terms that are black and white. The Bible is absolute, definitive, and provocative, unconcerned with political correctness and therefore unafraid to confront people with the reality of their condition. As a result, Scripture makes stark contrasts between those who are saved and those who are lost (Luke 19:10); those who are with Jesus and those who are against Him (Luke 11:23); those in the world and those not in the world (John 15:19; 17:14, 16; cf. 1 John 2:15–17); those who are children of God and those who are children of the Devil (1 John 3:10); those in the kingdom of God's beloved Son, and those in the satanic kingdom of darkness (Col. 1:13).

In this passage, Jesus introduces another aspect of this contrast—between those who are His friends, and those who are friends of the world. Friendship with Jesus Christ results in an intimate relationship with God and brings "joy inexpressible and full of glory" (1 Peter 1:8). On the other hand, "friendship with the world is hostility toward God. Therefore whoever wishes to be a friend of the world makes himself an enemy of God" (James 4:4) and is subject to His wrath (Nah. 1:2).

The Bible calls those who know and love the Lord Jesus Christ by many names and titles. Those titles include believers (Acts 5:14; 1 Thess. 1:7; 2:10); beloved of God (Rom. 1:7); beloved brethren (1 Cor. 15:58; Phil. 4:1; James 1:16); the called (Rom. 1:6); children of God (John 1:12; 11:52; Phil. 2:15; 1 John 3:1–2); children of promise (Gal. 4:28); children of light (Eph. 5:8; cf. 1 Thess. 5:5); sons of the resurrection (Luke 20:36); Christians (Acts 11:26; 1 Peter 4:16); disciples (Acts 6:1–2; 11:26); the elect (Matt. 24:22, 24, 31; Luke 18:7; Rom. 8:33); the godly (2 Peter 2:9); heirs of God (Rom. 8:17; Gal. 4:7; cf. James 2:5; 1 Peter 3:7); heirs of promise (Gal. 3:29; Heb. 6:17); heirs of salvation (Heb. 1:14 KJV); the righteous (Hab. 2:4; Matt. 13:43; 25:46; Luke 14:14; Rom. 1:17; Heb. 12:23); lights in the world (Phil. 2:15; cf. Matt. 5:14); living stones (1 Peter 2:5); members of the body of Christ (Eph. 5:30); people of God (Heb. 11:25; 1 Peter 2:10); a chosen race, a royal priesthood, a holy nation, a people for God's own possession (1 Peter 2:9); the salt of the earth (Matt. 5:13); slaves of Christ (1 Cor. 7:22; Eph. 6:6); slaves of righteousness (Rom. 6:18); vessels for honor (2 Tim. 2:21); vessels of mercy (Rom. 9:23); and saints (Acts 9:13; Rom. 1:7; 1 Cor. 1:2; Col. 1:12). But "friend" captures a unique aspect of communion with the Lord.

This brief passage reveals four characteristics of Jesus' friends: They are those who love each other, obey Him, know divine truth, and have been specially chosen by the Lord Himself.

THE FRIENDS OF JESUS LOVE EACH OTHER

This is My commandment, that you love one another, just as I have loved you. Greater love has no one than this, that one lay down his life for his friends. (15:12–13)

For the second time that evening in the upper room, Jesus gave the **commandment** that His followers are to **love one another** (cf. 13:34). Love is the fulfillment of the commandments Jesus had referred to in 15:10. Paul expressed that same principle to the Christians at Rome:

Owe nothing to anyone except to love one another; for he who loves his neighbor has fulfilled the law. For this, "You shall not commit adultery, you shall not murder, you shall not steal, you shall not covet," and if there is any other commandment, it is summed up in this saying, "You shall love your neighbor as yourself." Love does no wrong to a neighbor; therefore love is the fulfillment of the law. (Rom. 13:8–10)

Only those who abide in Him have the capacity to love divinely as Jesus loved. At the new birth, the "love of God [was] poured out within [their] hearts through the Holy Spirit who was given to [them]" (Rom. 5:5; cf. Gal. 5:22). What Paul wrote concerning the Thessalonians, "Now as to the love of the brethren, you have no need for anyone to write to you, for you yourselves are taught by God to love one another" (1 Thess. 4:9), is true of all Christians. Love for fellow believers characterizes the redeemed, as John repeatedly emphasized in his first epistle:

The one who says he is in the Light and yet hates his brother is in the darkness until now. The one who loves his brother abides in the Light and there is no cause for stumbling in him. But the one who hates his brother is in the darkness and walks in the darkness, and does not know where he is going because the darkness has blinded his eyes. (2:9–11)

By this the children of God and the children of the devil are obvious: anyone who does not practice righteousness is not of God, nor the one who does not love his brother. (3:10)

We know that we have passed out of death into life, because we love the brethren. He who does not love abides in death. Everyone who hates his brother is a murderer; and you know that no murderer has eternal life abiding in him. (3:14–15)

Beloved, let us love one another, for love is from God; and everyone who loves is born of God and knows God. The one who does not love does not know God, for God is love. (4:7–8)

If someone says, "I love God," and hates his brother, he is a liar; for the one who does not love his brother whom he has seen, cannot love God whom he has not seen. (4:20)

Whoever believes that Jesus is the Christ is born of God, and whoever loves the Father loves the child born of Him. (5:1)

The daunting standard for believers' love for each other is set forth in Jesus' words **just as I have loved you.** They are to love each other as the Lord Jesus Christ loves them. That does not mean, of course, that believers can love to the limitless extent or in the perfect manner that He does. But just as Jesus loved sacrificially, so also must they. "Walk in love," Paul wrote in Ephesians 5:2, "just as Christ also loved you and gave Himself up for us, an offering and a sacrifice to God as a fragrant aroma." The love believers have for each other is marked by a selfless devotion to meeting one another's needs; it is not mere sentiment, or superficial attachment. In fact, Christians' love for each other is the church's most powerful apologetic to the unbelieving world (John 13:35).

The Lord's death, at that point only a matter of hours away, was the supreme evidence of His love, as His statement **Greater love has no one than this, that one lay down his life for his friends** indicates. Jesus did not die for Himself, but so that others might live. In Romans 5:6–8 Paul wrote,

> For while we were still helpless, at the right time Christ died for the ungodly. For one will hardly die for a righteous man; though perhaps for the good man someone would dare even to die. But God demonstrates His own love toward us, in that while we were yet sinners, Christ died for us.

In a marvelously concise statement—only fifteen words in the Greek text—Paul summarized Christ's substitutionary atonement for believers: "He made Him who knew no sin to be sin on our behalf, so that we might become the righteousness of God in Him" (2 Cor. 5:21). Peter reminded his readers that "Christ also died for sins once for all, the just for the unjust, so that He might bring us to God" (1 Peter 3:18). Echoing the Lord's words in this passage, John wrote, "We know love by this, that He laid down His life for us; and we ought to lay down our lives for the brethren" (1 John 3:16). Then the apostle expressed the practical implications of that truth: "But whoever has the world's goods, and sees his brother in need and closes his heart against him, how does the love of God abide in him? Little children, let us not love with word or with tongue, but in deed and truth" (vv. 17–18). The friends of Jesus Christ show their love for one another by humbly meeting each other's needs.

THE FRIENDS OF JESUS OBEY HIM

You are My friends if you do what I command you. (15:14)

The essence of sin is rebellion against God's law. Samuel rebuked Saul for his failure to do what God had commanded him: "Has the Lord as much delight in burnt offerings and sacrifices as in obeying the voice of the Lord? Behold, to obey is better than sacrifice, and to heed than the fat of rams" (1 Sam. 15:22). Samuel then equated rebellion with sin:"For rebellion is as the sin of divination, and insubordination is as iniquity and idolatry" (v. 23). The New Testament also defines sin as rebellion. John wrote,"Everyone who practices sin also practices lawlessness; and sin is lawlessness" (1 John 3:4; cf. Matt. 7:23; 13:41; 23:28; 2 Cor. 6:14).

Because all sin is rebellion against God, turning from sin necessarily implies obedience to God. A person cannot submit to God while at the same time openly rebelling against Him; the same life cannot be characterized both by lawlessness and obedience (1 John 3:6; 5:18). Thus, obedience and faith are closely linked throughout Scripture. Conversion takes place when those who "were slaves of sin" become "obedient from the heart" (Rom. 6:17). Acts 6:7 describes the salvation of "a great many of the priests" as their "becoming obedient to the faith." Those who "will pay the penalty of eternal destruction, away from the presence of the Lord and from the glory of His power" (2 Thess. 1:9) are "those who do not obey the gospel of our Lord Jesus" (v. 8). Peter also defined unbelievers as "those who do not obey the gospel of God" (1 Peter 4:17). Paul declared that the goal of his apostolic ministry was "to bring about the obedience of faith among all the Gentiles" (Rom. 1:5; cf. 15:18; 16:26). The heroes of faith listed in Hebrews 11 demonstrated the reality of their faith by their obedience. So closely is obedience related to saving faith that Hebrews 5:9 uses it as a synonym for faith:"Having been made perfect, [Jesus] became to all those who obey Him the source of eternal salvation." Peter wrote that believers were "chosen ... to obey Jesus Christ" (1 Peter 1:1–2). John 3:36 also equates believing with obeying, noting that "he who believes in the Son has eternal life; but he who does not obey the Son will not see life, but the wrath of God abides on him." When informed that His mother and brothers were looking for Him, Jesus replied,"'Who are My mother and My brothers?' Looking about at those who were sitting around Him, He said,'Behold My mother and My brothers! For whoever does the will of God, he is My brother and sister and mother'" (Mark 3:33–35).

W. E. Vine points out another link between faith and obedience:

Peithō [to obey] and *pisteuō*,"to trust," are closely related etymologically; the difference in meaning is that the former implies the obedience that is produced by the latter, cp. Heb. 3:18, 19, where the disobedience of the Israelites is said to be the evidence of their unbelief.... When a man obeys God he gives the only possible evidence that in his heart he believes God. ... *Peithō* in N.T. suggests an actual and outward result of the inward persuasion and consequent faith. (*Vine's Expository Dictionary of Old and New Testament Words* [Old Tappan, N.J.: Revell, 1981], 3:124)

Obedience, of course, does not earn salvation. Salvation is solely "by grace ... through faith ... not as a result of works, so that no one may boast" (Eph. 2:8–9). God "saved us, not on the basis of deeds which we have done in righteousness, but according to His mercy, by the washing of regeneration and renewing by the Holy Spirit" (Titus 3:5). Paul, who so strongly emphasized the connection between saving faith and obedience, also wrote, "By the works of the Law no flesh will be justified in His sight ... For we maintain that a man is justified by faith apart from works of the Law" (Rom. 3:20, 28; cf. Gal. 2:16). He based his hope of salvation solely on being "found in Him, not having a righteousness of [his] own derived from the Law, but that which is through faith in Christ, the righteousness which comes from God on the basis of faith" (Phil. 3:9).

Obedience is not the means of salvation, but it is the inevitable result; it is the proof that a person has a saving relationship with Jesus Christ. The branches that abide in Christ, the true vine, will inevitably bear fruit (see the exposition of 15:1–11 in the previous chapter of this volume); His sheep hear His voice and follow Him (John 10:27); true disciples obey His Word (John 8:31). Good works save no one, but a faith devoid of them is dead and cannot save (James 2:14–26; cf. Eph. 2:10).

THE FRIENDS OF JESUS KNOW DIVINE TRUTH

No longer do I call you slaves, for the slave does not know what his master is doing; but I have called you friends, for all things that I have heard from My Father I have made known to you. (15:15)

The term **slaves** did not have many of the negative connotations in Jewish culture that it does today. In fact, some of the most noble figures in the Old Testament were described as slaves (Heb. `ebed) of God, including Moses (Num. 12:7), Caleb (Num. 14:24), Joshua (Josh. 24:29), Job (Job 1:8), David (2 Sam. 7:5), Isaiah (Isa. 20:3), and even the Messiah (Isa. 42:1). In the New Testament Paul (Rom. 1:1), James (James 1:1), Peter (2 Peter 1:1), Jude (Jude 1), and John (Rev. 1:1) similarly called themselves slaves (*doulos*) of Jesus Christ. The term reflected their utter submission to and dependence on their heavenly Master. This word, *doulos,* and the related verb *douleuō,* always and only refer to slavery. *Doulos* is the corresponding word to *kurios* (lord). Jesus is Lord, believers are His slaves. *Doulos* is, however, usually translated "servant," or "bond-servant." But their nearly 150 uses in the New Testament are to be understood as references to slavery. A slave was bought, owned, subjected to, provided for, and protected by his master (*kurios*). He lived in total submission to the will of his master.

Slaves did not usually have an intimate relationship with their earthly masters; **the slave** would normally **not know what his master** was **doing;** that is, he was not privy to his plans. Masters did not disclose their goals and purposes to their slaves; they merely instructed them as to what they wanted them to do.

While it is true that the followers of Jesus are also designated as slaves, that is not sufficient to fully convey our relationship to the Lord. Incredibly, we are also called His **friends**—a more exalted title even than "disciple." In the Old Testament only Abraham had the privilege of being named the friend of God (2 Chron. 20:7; Isa. 41:8; James 2:23). A custom from biblical times sheds light on the great honor believers have in being the friends of Jesus Christ. William Barclay writes,

> This phrase is lit up by a custom practised at the courts both of the Roman emperors and of kings in the middle east. At these courts, there was a very select group called *the friends of the king,* or *the friends of the emperor.* At all times, they had access to the king; they even had the right to come to his bedchamber at the beginning of the day. He talked to them before he talked to his generals, his rulers and his statesmen. The friends of the king were those who had the closest and the most intimate connection with him. (*The Gospel of John,* vol. 2, The New Daily Study Bible [Louisville: Westminster John Knox Press, 2001], 207–8. Italics in original.)

It is that kind of intimate access that Jesus graciously grants to His friends.

Because they are His friends, Jesus promised to share with believers **all things that** He had **heard from** the **Father.** They "will know the truth, and the truth will make [them] free" (John 8:32). In John 17:6–8 Jesus prayed to the Father,

> I have manifested Your name to the men whom You gave Me out of the world; they were Yours and You gave them to Me, and they have kept Your word. Now they have come to know that everything You have given Me is from You; for the words which You gave Me I have given to them; and they received them and truly understood that I came forth from You, and they believed that You sent Me.

When the disciples asked Him, "Why do You speak to them [the crowds] in parables?" (Matt. 13:10), Jesus replied, "To you it has been granted to know the mysteries of the kingdom of heaven, but to them it has not been granted" (v. 11). In Luke 10:23–24 He told them, "Blessed are the eyes which see the things you see, for I say to you, that many prophets and kings wished to see the things which you see, and did not see them, and to hear the things which you hear, and did not hear them."

The friends of Jesus have insight into "the mystery which has been kept secret for long ages past, but now is manifested, and by the Scriptures of the prophets, according to the commandment of the eternal God, has been made known to all the nations, leading to obedience of faith" (Rom. 16:25–26). The term "mystery" in the New Testament refers to things hidden in the past, but now revealed by Jesus to the apostles, and through them to all believers. The New Testament reveals the mysteries of the kingdom of heaven (Matt. 13:11), the mystery of Israel's hardening (Rom. 11:25), the mystery of the gospel (Eph. 6:19), the mystery of the rapture (1 Cor. 15:51), the mystery of God's will (Eph. 1:9), the mystery that Jews and Gentiles would be one body in Christ (Eph. 3:4–6), the mystery of the union of Christ and the church (Eph. 5:32), the mystery of Christ's indwelling of believers (Col. 1:26–27), the mystery that the Messiah would be God incarnate (Col. 2:2), the mystery of lawlessness, which will be fully revealed in the person of the Antichrist (2 Thess. 2:7), the mystery of the faith (1 Tim. 3:9), and the mystery of godliness (1 Tim. 3:16).

Their ability to understand the spiritual truths Jesus reveals to them sets His friends apart from the unredeemed, who have no such privileges:

> Now we have received, not the spirit of the world, but the Spirit who is from God, so that we may know the things freely given to us by God, which things we also speak, not in words taught by human wisdom, but in those taught by the Spirit, combining spiritual thoughts with spiritual words. But a natural man does not accept the things of the Spirit of God, for they are foolishness to him; and he cannot understand them, because they are spiritually appraised. But he who is spiritual appraises all things, yet he himself is appraised by no one. For who has known the mind of the Lord, that he will instruct him? But we have the mind of Christ. (1 Cor. 2:12–16)

THE FRIENDS OF JESUS HAVE BEEN SPECIALLY CHOSEN BY HIM

You did not choose Me but I chose you, and appointed you that you would go and bear fruit, and that your fruit would remain, so that whatever you ask of the Father in My name He may give to you. (15:16)

In a reversal of the customary Jewish practice (normally would-be disciples approached a rabbi they wanted to follow), the disciples did not **choose** Jesus **but** He **chose** them. The knowledge that Jesus **chose** them (and by extension all believers) to salvation apart from any merit of their own (v. 19; John 6:44, 65; Acts 13:48; Rom. 8:28–30; Gal. 1:15; Eph. 1:4; 2 Thess. 2:13; 2 Tim. 1:9; 2:10; 1 Peter 1:1–2) eliminates any pretense of spiritual pride that Christians might otherwise feel (cf. Rom. 3:27; 4:2; 1 Cor. 1:26–31; Gal. 6:14; Eph. 2:9).

Not only did Jesus choose the disciples for salvation, He also **appointed** them for service. The word translated **appointed** is a form of the verb *tithēmi,* which has here the connotation of being set apart or ordained for special service (cf. its similar usage in Acts 20:28; 1 Cor. 12:28; 1 Tim. 1:12; 2:7; 2 Tim. 1:11).

Having chosen and trained the disciples, Jesus commanded them to **go** into the world, proclaim the good news about Him, **and bear fruit.** The Christian life is not a spectator sport; Jesus did not choose believers to stand idly by while the world continues on its way to hell. On the contrary, His explicit command is, "Go therefore and make disciples of all the nations, baptizing them in the name of the Father and the Son and the Holy Spirit, teaching them to observe all that I commanded you; and lo, I am with you always, even to the end of the age" (Matt. 28:19–20; cf. Luke 14:23).

When believers proclaim the gospel, those who respond savingly to it become **fruit** that will **remain** forever (cf. 4:36; Luke 16:9). That the Lord repeated the promise of verse 7 (see the exposition of that verse in chapter 13 of this volume), **whatever you ask of the Father in My name He** will **give to you,** emphasizes the essential link between prayer and evangelism (cf. Luke 10:2; 2 Thess. 3:1).

The privileges that characterize the friends of Jesus Christ carry with them corresponding responsibilities. It is their nature to love one another, yet the Bible commands them to "fervently love one another from the heart" (1 Peter 1:22). They know divine truth, yet they must study it diligently (2 Tim. 2:15). Jesus called His friends out of the world, so they must be careful not to love it (1 John 2:15). Those who have been granted the privilege of bearing fruit must submit to the Father's pruning, so they can bear even more fruit (15:2). The Lord's promise of answered prayer demands that believers pray effectively (James 5:16) and unceasingly (1 Thess. 5:17). In short, those who have been granted the inestimable privilege of being the friends of Jesus Christ must "walk in a manner worthy of the calling with which [they] have been called" (Eph. 4:1).

Hated by the World (John 15:17–25)

15

"This I command you, that you love one another. If the world hates you, you know that it has hated Me before it hated you. If you were of the world, the world would love its own; but because you are not of the world, but I chose you out of the world, because of this the world hates you. Remember the word that I said to you, 'A slave is not greater than his master.' If they persecuted Me, they will also persecute you; if they kept My word, they will keep yours also. But all these things they will do to you for My name's sake, because they do not know the One who sent Me. If I had not come and spoken to them, they would not have sin, but now they have no excuse for their sin. He who hates Me hates My Father also. If I had not done among them the works which no one else did, they would not have sin; but now they have both seen and hated Me and My Father as well. But they have done this to fulfill the word that is written in their Law, 'They hated Me without a cause.'" (15:17–25)

From its inception on the day of Pentecost, the church of Jesus Christ has always faced opposition. After Peter and John dramatically healed a man crippled from birth (Acts 3:1–11) and Peter preached a powerful evangelistic message (3:12–26), "the priests and the captain of the temple guard and the Sadducees came up to them, being greatly disturbed because they were teaching the people and proclaiming in Jesus the resurrection from the dead. And they laid hands on them and put them in jail until the next day, for it was already evening" (4:1–3). Shortly afterward, stung by the phenomenal growth of the early church, "the high priest rose up, along with all his associates (that is the sect of the Sadducees), and they were filled with jealousy. They laid hands on the apostles and put them in a public jail" (5:17–18). Because of his bold, fearless preaching of the gospel, Stephen was falsely accused, arrested, put on trial before the Sanhedrin, and stoned to death (6:8–7:60). After his death, a general persecution broke out against the church, spearheaded by the zealous Pharisee Saul of Tarsus (8:1–4). The first of the apostles to be martyred was James, the brother of John, who was killed by the wicked king Herod (12:1–2). Herod also imprisoned Peter—only to see him miraculously freed by an angel (12:3–11). According to tradition the rest of the Twelve (except for John, who was exiled to Patmos [Rev. 1:9]) would also eventually face martyrdom.

After his dramatic conversion on the road to Damascus, Paul soon encountered fierce opposition. His bold, fearless preaching of the gospel astonished and enraged the Jewish population of Damascus, who then sought to kill him. The apostle had to flee for his life, being lowered from the city wall at night in a basket (Acts 9:20–25). That incident charted the course for the rest of Paul's life and ministry. In the book of Acts, Luke records that, in the course of his missionary journeys, Paul was forced to flee from Iconium (Acts 14:5–6); was pelted with stones and left for dead at Lystra (Acts 14:19–20); was beaten and thrown into jail at Philippi (Acts 16:16–40); was forced to leave Thessalonica after his preaching sparked a riot (Acts 17:5–10); was also forced to flee from Berea after hostile Jews from Thessalonica followed him there (Acts 17:13–14); was mocked and ridiculed by Greek philosophers at Athens (Acts 17:16–34); was brought before a Roman proconsul at Corinth by his Jewish adversaries (Acts 18:12–17); and faced hostility both from Jews (Acts 19:9; cf. 20:18–19) and Gentiles (Acts 19:21–41; cf. 1 Cor. 15:32) at Ephesus. As he was about to sail from Greece to Syria, a Jewish plot against his life forced him to change his travel plans (Acts 20:3). En route to Jerusalem, he met the elders of the Ephesian church at Miletus and declared to them, "Bound in spirit, I am on my way to Jerusalem, not knowing what will happen to me there, except that the Holy Spirit solemnly testifies to me in every city, saying that bonds and afflictions await me" (Acts 20:22–23). In Jerusalem, Paul was recognized in the temple by Jews from Asia Minor and savagely beaten by the frenzied mob they stirred up. He was saved from certain death only when Roman soldiers arrived on the scene and arrested him (Acts 21:27–36). While Paul was in custody at Jerusalem, the Jews formed yet another plot against his life, prompting the Roman commander to send him under heavy guard to the governor at Caesarea (Acts 23:12–35).

Eventually, after a harrowing sea voyage and shipwreck (Acts 27:1–28:14), Paul, still in Roman custody, arrived at Rome. There he encountered opposition from the local Jewish leaders (28:17–29). Though the Romans released him after at least two years of imprisonment (28:30), Paul was eventually rearrested and executed during Nero's persecution.

Like Paul had before his conversion (Acts 26:9; Gal. 1:13–14; Phil. 3:6; 1 Tim. 1:13), the Jews considered Christians to be heretics. Thus, they believed that by persecuting the church they were honoring God. As Jesus told the disciples, "They will make you outcasts from the synagogue, but an hour is coming for everyone who kills you to think that he is offering service to God" (John 16:2). Furthermore some of the Jews, especially among the leaders, feared that the Christians' loyalty to Jesus as a king above Caesar might provoke Rome's wrath against the nation (cf. John 11:47–48; 19:12, 15).

The Romans persecuted Christians for several reasons. At first, they viewed Christianity as merely another Jewish sect. Since Judaism was a legally tolerated religion (*religio licita*), the Romans left the Christians alone. Thus, when the Jews at Corinth accused Paul before the Roman proconsul Gallio, he refused to intervene, deeming the matter an internal dispute within Judaism (Acts 18:12–15).

Eventually the Jews' hostility toward the Christians and the influx of Gentiles into the church led the Romans to recognize Christianity as distinct from Judaism. Christianity then became an illegal religion, proscribed by the Roman government. In addition to Christianity's illegal status, several factors prompted Roman persecution. Politically, the Christians' allegiance to Christ above Caesar aroused suspicions that they were disloyal to the state. To maintain control over their vast empire, the Romans required that their subjects' ultimate loyalty be to the emperor as the embodiment of the Roman state. And since "there was a union of religion and state in ancient Rome ... refusal to worship the goddess Roma or the divine emperor constituted treason" (Howard F. Vos, *Exploring Church History* [Nashville: Thomas Nelson, 1994], 26). Because the Christians refused to make the required sacrifice offered in worship to the emperor, they were seen as traitors. They also proclaimed the kingdom of God, which caused the Romans to suspect them of plotting to overthrow the government. To avoid harassment by government officials, Christians often held their meetings in secret and at night. That heightened the Romans' suspicions that they were hatching an anti-government plot. That Christians generally refused to serve in the Roman army also caused them to be viewed as disloyal.

The Romans also persecuted Christians for religious reasons. They allowed their subjects to worship whatever gods they liked, as long as they also worshiped the Roman gods. But Christians preached an exclusive message that there is only one God and only one way of salvation. That, coupled with their evangelistic efforts to win converts from other religions, went against the prevailing atmosphere of religious pluralism. Christians were denounced as atheists because they rejected the Roman pantheon of gods, and because they worshiped an invisible God, not an idol. The secrecy of the Christians' meetings led to lurid, false rumors of gross immorality. Misunderstanding about what was meant by eating and drinking the elements during the Lord's Supper led to charges of cannibalism. The Christians' practice of greeting each other with a holy kiss (Rom. 16:16; 1 Cor. 16:20; 2 Cor. 13:12; 1 Thess. 5:26; cf. 1 Peter 5:14) gave rise to allegations of incest and other sexual perversions.

Socially, the leaders of Roman society feared the influence of the Christians on the lower classes, from whose ranks the church drew many of its members (cf. 1 Cor. 1:26). Haunted by the ever-present specter of slave revolts, the wealthy aristocrats felt especially threatened by the Christians' teaching that all people are equal (Gal. 3:28; Col. 3:11; cf. Paul's letter to Philemon), though the church did not openly oppose slavery. Christians also held themselves aloof from much of the public life of the time. For obvious reasons, they could not be involved in the idolatrous temple worship that was such an important part of social life. But even sporting and theatrical events involved sacrifices to pagan deities that Christians could not participate in. The purity of their lives rebuked the debauched lifestyles of rich and poor alike and provoked further hostility (cf. 1 Peter 4:3–4).

Economic factors played an often overlooked role in the persecution of the early believers. Paul's exorcism of a demon from a fortune-telling slave girl at Philippi caused her masters, incensed by the loss of the revenue she brought them, to stir up hostility against him (Acts 16:16–24). Economic factors also played a significant role in provoking the riot at Ephesus (Acts 19:23–27). Early in the second century Pliny, the Roman governor of Bithynia, lamented in a letter to Emperor Trajan that the spread of Christianity had caused the pagan temples to be deserted and sales of sacrificial animals to plummet. In that superstitious age people also attributed plague, famine, and natural disasters to the Christians' forsaking of the traditional gods, prompting the Christian apologist Tertullian to remark sarcastically, "If the Tiber reaches the walls, if the Nile does not rise to the fields, if the sky doesn't move or the earth does, if there is famine, if there is plague, the cry is at once, 'Christians to the lion!'"

What, all of them to one lion?" (*Apology* 40.2, as cited in M. A. Smith, *From Christ to Constantine* [Downers Grove, Ill.: InterVarsity, 1973], 86).

For these and other reasons, Christianity became a hated and despised religious sect in the Roman Empire. In his letter to Emperor Trajan, Pliny scorned Christianity as a "depraved and extravagant superstition." Pliny went on to complain that "the contagion of this superstition [Christianity] has spread not only in the cities, but in the villages and rural districts as well" (cited in Henry Bettenson, ed., *Documents of the Christian Church* [London: Oxford University Press, 1967], 4). The Roman historian Tacitus, a contemporary of Pliny, described Christians as "a class hated for their abominations" (cited in Bettenson, *Documents,* 2) while Suetonius, another contemporary of Pliny, dismissed them as "a set of men adhering to a novel and mischievous superstition" (cited in Bettenson, *Documents,* 2).

The first official persecution of Christians by the Roman government came during the reign of Emperor Nero. In July of A.D. 64 a fire ravaged Rome, destroying or damaging much of the city. Popular rumors pinned the blame for the fire on Nero. Though the rumors were probably not true, Nero sought for scapegoats to shift the suspicion away from himself. He therefore blamed the Christians, who were already despised by the populace (as the quotes in the preceding paragraph indicate), and began to savagely persecute them. Christians were arrested, cruelly tortured, thrown to wild animals, crucified, and burned as torches to light Nero's gardens at night. The official persecution apparently was confined to the vicinity of Rome. But attacks on Christians undoubtedly spread, unchecked by the authorities, to other parts of the empire. According to tradition, Peter and Paul were martyred during Nero's persecution.

Three decades later, during the reign of Emperor Domitian, another government-sponsored persecution of Christians broke out. Little is known of the details, but it extended to the province of Asia (modern Turkey). The apostle John was banished from Ephesus to the island of Patmos, and among those martyred was a man (probably a pastor) named Antipas (Rev. 2:13).

In the second century and the first half of the third century, official persecution of Christians was sporadic. During the reign of Emperor Trajan early in the second century, Pliny, in the letter mentioned earlier, asked Trajan how to deal with the Christians in his region. Trajan replied that they were not to be sought out, but if accused (Trajan instructed Pliny to ignore anonymous accusations), they were to be brought to trial. Those who refused to recant were to be punished. Though Trajan's policy did not result in widespread persecution, it did result in the martyrdom of some, most notably the famous church father Ignatius. Trajan's policy remained in force for several decades, until the reign of Marcus Aurelius.

Under his rule the state took a more active role in ferreting out Christians. During his reign the famous Christian apologist Justin Martyr was executed, and a savage persecution broke out against the Christians in Lyons and Vienne in Gaul (modern France).

The first empire-wide persecution of the church took place under Emperor Decius in A.D. 250. Rome at that time faced serious internal (an economic crisis and various natural disasters) and external (barbarian incursions) problems. Decius was convinced that those difficulties resulted from the neglect of Rome's ancient gods. He issued an edict requiring everyone to offer a sacrifice to the gods and to the emperor and to obtain a certificate attesting that they had done so. Those who refused faced arrest, imprisonment, torture, and execution. Thankfully for the church, Decius's persecution was cut short by his death in battle in July A.D. 251.

The final and most violent empire-wide persecution of the church began in A.D. 303, during the reign of Diocletian. This persecution was nothing less than an all-out attempt to exterminate the Christian faith. Diocletian issued a series of edicts ordering that churches be destroyed, all copies of the Bible be burned, and all Christians offer sacrifices to the Roman gods on pain of death. The persecution subsided when Constantine and his co-emperor Licinius issued the Edict of Milan (A.D. 313), granting freedom of worship to members of all religions. But Licinius reneged on the agreement and persecution continued in some parts of the empire. It was not until Constantine became sole emperor in A.D. 324 that Roman persecution of Christians ended permanently.

Under the Roman Catholic Church, which replaced Imperial Rome as the dominant power during the Middle Ages, persecution broke out anew. Ironically, this time the persecution against true believers came from those who called themselves "Christian." The horrors of the Inquisition, the St. Bartholomew's Day Massacre, and the martyrdoms of many believers epitomized the Roman Church's effort to suppress the true gospel of Jesus Christ. More recently, believers have been brutally repressed by Communist and Islamic regimes. In fact, it has been estimated by none other than a Roman Catholic source that, in all of church history, roughly 70 million Christians have been killed for their profession of faith, with two-thirds of those martyrdoms occurring after the start of the twentieth century (Antonio Socci, *I Nuovi Persequitati* [*The New Persecuted*] (Casale Montferrato: Edizioni Piemme, 2002). The actual number is likely much greater. The Catholic journalist cited in this news article estimates that an average of 100,000 Christians have been killed every year since 1990.

In this passage the Lord Jesus Christ continued His farewell discourse to the disciples on the night before His death. His message up to this point had been one of comfort and hope. He had reassured the disciples of His continued love for them (chap. 13) and made several magnificent promises to them (chap. 14). But the disciples would still have to face the hostile, rebellious, Christ-rejecting world. The world would hate and persecute them as it had hated and persecuted their Master; facing that hostility is the cost of being His disciple (Mark 13:9–13; Acts 14:22; 2 Tim. 3:12). This was exactly what He had told them the night before on the Mount of Olives would be true through the whole period between His first and second comings (cf. Matt. 24:9–14; Mark 13:9–13; Luke 21:12–19).

Jesus balanced the promises of comfort and blessing with a warning to the disciples of the hostility that awaited them. In the face of the world's hatred, the disciples would need each other desperately. The Lord therefore repeated His earlier instruction, **"This I command you, that you love one another"** (cf. v. 12; 13:34–35). That command forms a transition between the Lord's promises to the disciples and His warning of the world's hatred—a warning that should also motivate them to love each other.

This passage reveals three reasons why the world hates believers: because the world rejects those who are not part of it, because the world hated Jesus, and because the world does not know God.

The World Rejects Those Who Are Not Part of It

If the world hates you . . . If you were of the world, the world would love its own; but because you are not of the world, but I chose you out of the world, because of this the world hates you. (15:18a–19)

Kosmos (**world**) refers in this context to the evil, fallen world system comprised of unregenerate people and controlled by Satan (John 12:31; 14:30; 16:11; 1 John 5:19; cf. Eph. 2:1–3). Because Satan hates God he also hates the true people of God. They are targets for his wrath as he "prowls around like a roaring lion, seeking someone to devour" (1 Peter 5:8; cf. Eph. 6:11). Since its ruler hates believers, it is hardly surprising that the world also **hates** them, **because** they **are not of the world.** The world resents believers because their godly lives condemn its evil works; "he who is upright in the way is abominable to the wicked" (Prov. 29:27). In 1 John 3:12 John illustrated that principle with the story of the first murder in human history: "Cain . . . was of the evil one and slew his brother. And for what reason did he slay him? Because his deeds were evil, and his brother's were righteous." On the other hand, the world applauds those who practice evil (Rom. 1:32).

Though believers live in the world (cf. 1 Cor. 5:9–10), they are to stand apart from it as an indictment of it. Paul charged the Philippians, "Prove yourselves to be blameless and innocent, children of God above reproach in the midst of a crooked and perverse generation, among whom you appear as lights in the world" (Phil. 2:15). "Do not participate in the unfruitful deeds of darkness," he admonished the Ephesians, "but instead even expose them" (Eph. 5:11).

While worldly people hate those who follow Jesus Christ, they love each other. Unbelievers are comfortable with and supportive of other unbelievers. **If you were of the world,** Jesus said, **the world would love its own.** The conditional clause in verse 18 (**If the world hates you**) expresses a condition assumed to be true. This conditional clause, however, expresses a condition assumed to be false; the Lord's statement might be translated, "If you were of the world (and you are not)…." Had the disciples been part of the world, they would have experienced the imperfect love the world has for its own. **Love** is from *phileō,* which refers to "natural affection and passion, and not [*agapaō*], the high, intelligent, purposeful love of an ethical state" (R. C. H. Lenski, *The Interpretation of St. John's Gospel* [repr.; Peabody, Mass.: Hendrickson, 1998], 1055).

Christians are not part of the world because Jesus **chose** them **out of the world** (cf. Acts 26:18; Col. 1:13; 2 Tim. 2:26; Heb. 2:14–15). The emphatic use of the pronoun *egō* (**I**) and the reflexive sense of the middle voice verb translated **chose** shows that Jesus chose them for Himself. All credit for the disciples' salvation belongs to Him (cf. John 15:16).

The doctrine of election silences human pride. Paul reminded the Ephesians that God "chose us in Him before the foundation of the world, that we would be holy and blameless before Him…. to the praise of the glory of His grace, which He freely bestowed on us in the Beloved" (Eph. 1:4, 6). To the Romans he wrote, "Where then is boasting? It is excluded. By what kind of law? Of works? No, but by a law of faith. For we maintain that a man is justified by faith apart from works of the Law" (Rom. 3:27–28). In the next chapter he added, "If Abraham was justified by works, he has something to boast about, but not before God" (4:2).

THE WORLD HATES BELIEVERS
BECAUSE IT HATED JESUS CHRIST

you know that it has hated Me before it hated you. . . .Remember the word that I said to you, 'A slave is not greater than his master.' If they persecuted Me, they will also persecute you; if they kept My word, they will keep yours also. (15:18*b*, 20)

Christians should not be surprised at the world's hostility toward them, since it **hated** Jesus (cf. 7:7) **before it hated** them (cf. 17:14). That hatred has been manifested throughout John's gospel. In 5:16 "the Jews were persecuting Jesus, because He was doing these things on the Sabbath"; in verse 18 "the Jews were seeking all the more to kill Him, because He not only was breaking the Sabbath, but also was calling God His own Father, making Himself equal with God"; in 7:1 "the Jews were seeking to kill Him"; in verse 32 "the chief priests and the Pharisees sent officers to seize Him"; in 8:59 and 10:31 "they picked up stones to throw at Him"; in 11:47–53 they plotted to kill Him; eventually they arrested Him, beat Him, scourged Him, and crucified Him. No wonder, then, that the writer of Hebrews called on his readers to "consider Him who has endured such hostility by sinners against Himself" (Heb. 12:3).

Jesus' **word that** He had earlier **said to** the disciples, **A slave is not greater than his master,** refers to His statement in 13:16. There, however, the Lord was speaking of humblest service of a slave. He, "the Lord and the Teacher" (v. 14) had humbly washed their feet, and the disciples were to follow His example (v. 15). Here Christ's point was that the disciples should expect to follow His example of suffering (cf. 1 Peter 2:21); they had no right to expect better treatment from the world than He had received. **If they persecuted Me,** Jesus reiterated, **they will also persecute you.** Earlier in His ministry Jesus had told them, "A disciple is not above his teacher, nor a slave above his master. It is enough for the disciple that he become like his teacher, and the slave like his master. If they have called the head of the house Beelzebul, how much more will they malign the members of his household!" (Matt. 10:24–25). Believers identify with Jesus Christ in the "fellowship of His sufferings" (Phil. 3:10; cf. 2 Cor. 1:5; Gal. 6:17; Col. 1:24).

But the picture was not entirely bleak; the Lord went on to add, **If they kept My word, they will keep yours also.** As was the case with Jesus, the majority would reject the disciples' teaching and persecute them. But there would always be a minority (cf. Matt. 7:14; 22:14; Luke 13:24) who would accept the disciples' message. The joy of seeing those few come to faith in Christ far outweighs the sorrow caused by the hatred and hostility of the many who reject the gospel.

THE WORLD HATES BELIEVERS
BECAUSE IT DOES NOT KNOW GOD

But all these things they will do to you for My name's sake, because they do not know the One who sent Me. If I had not come and spoken to them, they would not have sin, but now they have

no excuse for their sin. He who hates Me hates My Father also. If I had not done among them the works which no one else did, they would not have sin; but now they have both seen and hated Me and My Father as well. But they have done this to fulfill the word that is written in their Law, 'They hated Me without a cause.'" (15:21–25)

The **things** that the hostile world **will do to** Christ's followers are not aimed solely at them; the persecution they face is ultimately for His **name's sake.** In the Beatitudes Jesus said, "Blessed are you when people insult you and persecute you, and falsely say all kinds of evil against you because of Me" (Matt. 5:11). In the Olivet Discourse He warned, "They will deliver you to tribulation, and will kill you, and you will be hated by all nations because of My name" (Matt. 24:9; cf. Mark 13:9; Luke 21:12). Speaking to Ananias about the apostle Paul, Jesus declared, "I will show him how much he must suffer for My name's sake" (Acts 9:16). "If you are reviled for the name of Christ," Peter wrote, "you are blessed, because the Spirit of glory and of God rests on you" (1 Peter 4:14). Suffering for the name of Jesus Christ is a repeated New Testament theme (see also Matt. 10:18, 22, 39; 19:29; Mark 8:35; 13:9–13; Luke 6:22; 21:12–17; Rom. 8:36; 2 Cor. 4:11; Rev. 2:3).

Ultimately, the world hates Jesus and His followers because it does **not know the One who sent** Him. Because "the mind set on the flesh is hostile toward God" (Rom. 8:7), "those who are in the flesh cannot please God" (v. 8). Unbelievers are "dead in [their] trespasses and sins" (Eph. 2:1), "alienated and hostile in mind" (Col. 1:21), and "darkened in their understanding, excluded from the life of God because of the ignorance that is in them, because of the hardness of their heart" (Eph. 4:18). All people are sinners by nature, born into a state of rebellion against God. They "suppress the truth in unrighteousness" (Rom. 1:18), and "even though they [know] God, they [do] not honor Him as God or give thanks, but [are] futile in their speculations, and their foolish heart [is] darkened" (v. 21). Therefore in judgment God "gave them over in the lusts of their hearts to impurity" (v. 24), to "degrading passions" (v. 26), and to "a depraved mind" (v. 28). All people are responsible for their sin, "because that which is known about God is evident within them; for God made it evident to them. For since the creation of the world His invisible attributes, His eternal power and divine nature, have been clearly seen, being understood through what has been made, so that they are without excuse" (vv. 19–20; cf. John 1:9).

But those who heard Jesus bore an even greater responsibility for rejecting the truth. **If I had not come and spoken to them,** Jesus said, **they would not have sin, but now they have no excuse for**

their sin. . . . If I had not done among them the works which no one else did, they would not have sin. The Lord was not speaking here of sin in general, but rather of the specific sin of willfully rejecting Him in the face of full revelation. That is the most serious sin of all, because it is the only one that is not forgivable. Having witnessed first-hand Jesus' miracles and heard His teaching—both of which testified unmistakably to His deity (cf. Matt. 7:28–29; John 7:46; 10:25, 37–38; 14:10–11)—the Pharisees' conclusion was, "This man casts out demons only by Beelzebul the ruler of the demons" (Matt. 12:24). Because they attributed His miraculous works to Satan instead of the Holy Spirit, Jesus pronounced their sin to be unforgivable:

> Therefore I say to you, any sin and blasphemy shall be forgiven people, but blasphemy against the Spirit shall not be forgiven. Whoever speaks a word against the Son of Man, it shall be forgiven him; but whoever speaks against the Holy Spirit, it shall not be forgiven him, either in this age or in the age to come. (Matt. 12:31–32)

While that specific sin can no longer be committed, since Jesus is not physically present on earth, the principle remains the same. Total rejection in the face of total revelation is unforgivable, since there is nothing left for God to show such people. In the sobering words of the writer of Hebrews,

> For in the case of those who have once been enlightened and have tasted of the heavenly gift and have been made partakers of the Holy Spirit, and have tasted the good word of God and the powers of the age to come, and then have fallen away, it is impossible to renew them again to repentance, since they again crucify to themselves the Son of God and put Him to open shame. (Heb. 6:4–6)

Despite their outward zeal (cf. Rom. 10:2), Jesus' Jewish opponents had **both seen and hated** Him **and** the **Father as well.** The truth is that those who reject Christ do not know God. That applies to the one who is outwardly religious no less than it does to the hardened atheist. All false religions are of demonic origin. Paul wrote to the Corinthians, "The things which the Gentiles sacrifice, they sacrifice to demons and not to God" (1 Cor. 10:20; cf. Lev. 17:7; Deut. 32:17; Ps. 106:37). Jesus said to the most zealous religious people of His day, "You are of your father the devil, and you want to do the desires of your father" (John 8:44).

Jesus repeatedly emphasized the truth that the one **who hates** Him **hates** the **Father also.** To those who were outraged because He called God His Father, Jesus replied, "He who does not honor the Son does not honor the Father who sent Him" (John 5:23). John 7:28 records that "Jesus cried out in the temple, teaching and saying, 'You both know

Me and know where I am from; and I have not come of Myself, but He
who sent Me is true, whom you do not know." In John 8:19 He said to His
Jewish opponents, "You know neither Me nor My Father; if you knew Me,
you would know My Father also." In verse 42 He added, "If God were your
Father, you would love Me, for I proceeded forth and have come from
God, for I have not even come on My own initiative, but He sent Me." Later
He said, "If I glorify Myself, My glory is nothing; it is My Father who glorifies Me, of whom you say, 'He is our God'; and you have not come to know
Him" (John 8:54–55). After warning the disciples that they would be persecuted, Jesus said of their persecutors, "These things they will do
because they have not known the Father or Me" (John 16:3). He prayed
to the Father, "O righteous Father, although the world has not known You,
yet I have known You" (John 17:25). Echoing the Lord's words, John
wrote in his first epistle, "Whoever denies the Son does not have the
Father" (1 John 2:23). The truth is that if men had understood who Jesus
was, "they would not have crucified the Lord of glory" (1 Cor. 2:8).

The world's hatred of Jesus, though reprehensible and inexcusable, was not outside of God's sovereign plan. **They have done this,**
Jesus declared, **to fulfill the word that is written in their Law, "They
hated Me without a cause."** The Lord quoted from two Davidic
psalms, 35:19 and 69:4. His point is that if David, a mere man, could be so
hated by his enemies, how much more the sinless Son of God? The world
hated Jesus because He exposed their sin and confronted them with the
reality of who He is. But in light of Jesus' words and works, there was and
is no valid **cause** to hate Him. That the world continues to do so graphically reveals the vileness of sin.

But for those who are have been delivered from sin by the power
of the cross, and who subsequently encounter opposition for their commitment to the Savior, there is supreme joy in the Lord's promise:

> Blessed are those who have been persecuted for the sake of righ-
> teousness, for theirs is the kingdom of heaven. Blessed are you when
> people insult you and persecute you, and falsely say all kinds of evil
> against you because of Me. Rejoice and be glad, for your reward in
> heaven is great; for in the same way they persecuted the prophets who
> were before you. (Matt. 5:10–12)

Holy Spirit–Empowered Witness (John 15:26–27)

16

"When the Helper comes, whom I will send to you from the Father, that is the Spirit of truth who proceeds from the Father, He will testify about Me, and you will testify also, because you have been with Me from the beginning." (15:26–27)

As He gathered with the disciples on the night before His death, Jesus knew they were filled with sorrow and fear. Their love for Him was so intense that they were convinced that they would rather die with Him than live without Him. When Jesus predicted that they would in actuality abandon Him (Matt. 26:31), Peter replied, "Even though all may fall away because of You, I will never fall away" (v. 33), and later, "Even if I have to die with You, I will not deny You." Echoing Peter's bravado, "all the [rest of the] disciples said the same thing too" (v. 35).

But, as Jesus foretold, the disciples would soon abandon Him, being overcome by their fear and sorrow (cf. John 16:32). Even now, their sense of impending loss was overwhelming. As a result, the Lord spent this final night with the disciples comforting them. Amazingly, though He Himself was about to endure unimaginable suffering, He selflessly concerned Himself with the anxious apprehensions of His frightened followers.

Jesus began by reassuring them of His continuing love (chap.

13), which He graphically illustrated by washing their feet. Then in chapter 14 He made a series of magnificent promises, which assured them that they would not lack the resources they needed after He was gone. But the Lord knew that despite His love for the disciples and the resources He promised them, they would still have to face the world's hostility. His promises to the disciples, then, were necessarily balanced with warnings about the persecution they would face in His name (15:18–25).

But the disciples would not have to face the world's opposition in their own strength. In these two verses Jesus reiterated His earlier promise (14:16–17, 26) that He would send the Holy Spirit to indwell and empower them. The Spirit's coming made certain that all of Jesus' promises would be fulfilled. The rest of the New Testament echoes this same truth, that the promises Christ made to His disciples (and by extension to all of His followers) would be ensured and enabled through the ministry of the Holy Spirit.

For example, Jesus promised to return and take His own to be with Him in heaven (14:1–6). Thus, believers can confidently look forward to eternal life with Christ in resurrected glory. Describing that same reality, Paul wrote in 2 Corinthians 5:1, "For we know that if the earthly tent which is our house is torn down, we have a building from God, a house not made with hands, eternal in the heavens." As a guarantee that He will do as He promised, God "gave to us the Spirit as a pledge" (2 Cor. 5:5). In the words of Ephesians 1:13–14:

> In Him, you also, after listening to the message of truth, the gospel of your salvation—having also believed, you were sealed in Him with the Holy Spirit of promise, who is given as a pledge of our inheritance, with a view to the redemption of God's own possession, to the praise of His glory.

Earlier that evening the Lord promised the disciples, "Truly, truly, I say to you, he who believes in Me, the works that I do, he will do also; and greater works than these he will do; because I go to the Father" (14:12). In His final words before His ascension, Jesus revealed the source of the power that would enable believers to do those works: "You will receive power when the Holy Spirit has come upon you" (Acts 1:8). It is the indwelling of the Holy Spirit that enables believers "to do far more abundantly beyond all that we ask or think, according to the power that works within [them]" (Eph. 3:20).

In John 14:13–14 Jesus promised that He would supply believers' needs when they pray in His name. But since they "do not know how to pray as [they] should . . . the Spirit Himself intercedes for [them] with groanings too deep for words" (Rom. 8:26; cf. Eph. 6:18).

Another comforting promise the Lord made to the disciples was that He and the Father would reside in them:

> "I will not leave you as orphans; I will come to you. After a little while the world will no longer see Me, but you will see Me; because I live, you will live also. In that day you will know that I am in My Father, and you in Me, and I in you. He who has My commandments and keeps them is the one who loves Me; and he who loves Me will be loved by My Father, and I will love him and will disclose Myself to him." Judas (not Iscariot) said to Him, "Lord, what then has happened that You are going to disclose Yourself to us and not to the world?" Jesus answered and said to him, "If anyone loves Me, he will keep My word; and My Father will love him, and We will come to him and make Our abode with him." (John 14:18–23)

That promise was fulfilled by the coming of the Holy Spirit, who, Jesus told the disciples, "abides with you and will be in you" (John 14:17), since He is the "Spirit of God" and the "Spirit of Christ" (Rom. 8:9). Furthermore it is the Spirit who confirms the believer's saving relationship with God. As Paul wrote in Romans, "The Spirit Himself testifies with our spirit that we are children of God, and if children, heirs also and fellow heirs with Christ" (8:16–17). As those in fellowship with Jesus Christ and His Father (cf. 1 John 1:3), believers have been promised a legacy of peace (John 14:27), love (John 13:1, 34), and joy (John 15:11)—all of which are fruits produced in their lives by the Holy Spirit (Gal. 5:22).

The legacy Christ gave the church also includes the power to evangelize the world. That, too, comes from the Spirit. As noted earlier, just before He ascended into heaven, Jesus promised the disciples, "You will receive power when the Holy Spirit has come upon you; and you shall be My witnesses both in Jerusalem, and in all Judea and Samaria, and even to the remotest part of the earth" (Acts 1:8). There can be no Christian witness apart from the Spirit; it is His ministry to convict the world of sin (John 16:8) and present Jesus Christ to it (John 15:26). No one can be saved without confessing Jesus as Lord (Rom. 10:9–10) and no one can do that without the Holy Spirit (1 Cor. 12:3).

It is the Holy Spirit's empowering of Christian witness to a lost world that is in view in this passage. Four important truths regarding the nature of Christian witness emerge from these two verses: it is to the world, about the Son, from the Father, and through believers.

CHRISTIAN WITNESS IS TO THE WORLD

Though not explicitly stated in verses 26 and 27, the obviously implied object of believers' testimony concerning Jesus Christ is the world of lost sinners. The immediate context of verses 26 and 27 makes that clear; both the preceding passage (vv. 18–25) and the following section (16:1–11) discuss the world and its hostility. This point may seem trite and obvious, yet many Christians never confront the world with the gospel. Jesus' command, "Go therefore and make disciples of all the nations, baptizing them in the name of the Father and the Son and the Holy Spirit, teaching them to observe all that I commanded you" (Matt. 28:19–20), goes unheeded. Christians must be bold with the truth of the gospel message, the content of which focuses on the person and work of Jesus Christ (a point that will be developed below).

In an age of postmodern relativism and ambiguity, nothing is more needed than the clear presentation to the unbelieving world of God's absolute truth, centering on the gospel of Jesus Christ. To be sure, this message will be generally met with hostility and opposition. Jesus Himself said it would be so. Yet, faithfulness to Christ demands that believers speak boldly and with conviction (cf. 2 Cor. 4:13–14), being enabled to do so through the Spirit's power. As Paul told the Ephesians,

> With all prayer and petition pray at all times in the Spirit … and pray on my behalf that utterance may be given to me in the opening of my mouth to make known with boldness the mystery of the gospel, for which I am an ambassador in chains; that in proclaiming it I may speak boldly, as I ought to speak. (Eph. 6:18–20)

Of course, if believers are to effectively confront the world system, they cannot be part of it. Though they are in the world, they must not be "of the world" (cf. John 15:19; 17:14). James warned, "Do you not know that friendship with the world is hostility toward God? Therefore whoever wishes to be a friend of the world makes himself an enemy of God" (James 4:4), while in his first epistle John noted that "if anyone loves the world, the love of the Father is not in him" (1 John 2:15). There can be no compromise with the satanic world system that is irrevocably and unalterably opposed to the kingdom of God. As Jesus declared, "He who is not with Me is against Me; and he who does not gather with Me, scatters" (Luke 11:23).

Despite the world's hostility, however, Christians must confront the lost with compassion and gospel love. As Paul counseled his protégé Timothy,

> The Lord's bond-servant must not be quarrelsome, but be kind to all, able to teach, patient when wronged, with gentleness correcting those who are in opposition, if perhaps God may grant them repentance leading to the knowledge of the truth, and they may come to their senses and escape from the snare of the devil, having been held captive by him to do his will. (2 Tim. 2:24–26)

The apostle Peter echoed this same mindset when he wrote these words of instruction: "But sanctify Christ as Lord in your hearts, always being ready to make a defense to everyone who asks you to give an account for the hope that is in you, yet with gentleness and reverence" (1 Peter 3:15).

CHRISTIAN WITNESS IS FROM THE FATHER

When the Helper comes, whom I will send to you from the Father, that is the Spirit of truth who proceeds from the Father (15:26*a*)

The ultimate witness to Jesus Christ is God **the Father** (cf. 5:37; 6:27; 8:18), who testified to the Son in several ways. First, God spoke in the Hebrew Scriptures (Heb. 1:1–2) and the theme of His revelation is the Lord Jesus Christ. In John 5:39 Jesus said to His opponents, "You search the Scriptures because you think that in them you have eternal life; it is these that testify about Me," while in Luke 24:44 He told the disciples, "These are My words which I spoke to you while I was still with you, that all things which are written about Me in the Law of Moses and the Prophets and the Psalms must be fulfilled." Revelation 19:10 notes that "the testimony of Jesus is the spirit of prophecy."

A second way the Father testified to the Son was through the divine works that Jesus did. In John 5:36 Jesus told His adversaries, "The works which the Father has given Me to accomplish—the very works that I do—testify about Me, that the Father has sent Me." "The works that I do in My Father's name," He declared in 10:25, "these testify of Me"; in verse 37 He challenged His opponents, "If I do not do the works of My Father, do not believe Me." Peter affirmed that Jesus was "attested . . . by God with miracles and wonders and signs which God performed through Him" (Acts 2:22; cf. 10:38).

The Father's direct statements also testified to the Son. At Christ's baptism, and again at the transfiguration, the Father's "voice out of the heavens said, 'This is My beloved Son, in whom I am well-pleased'" (Matt. 3:17; 17:5). Reflecting on his dramatic experience at the transfiguration, Peter would later write:

> For we did not follow cleverly devised tales when we made known to you the power and coming of our Lord Jesus Christ, but we were eye-witnesses of His majesty. For when He received honor and glory from God the Father, such an utterance as this was made to Him by the Majestic Glory, "This is My beloved Son with whom I am well-pleased"— and we ourselves heard this utterance made from heaven when we were with Him on the holy mountain. (2 Peter 1:16–18)

Finally, the Father testified to the Son by sending **the Helper . . . that is the Spirit of truth who proceeds from the Father.** In his first epistle John wrote, "It is the Spirit who testifies [about Jesus Christ], because the Spirit is the truth" (1 John 5:6). In Acts 5:32 the apostles declared to the Sanhedrin, "We are witnesses of these things [concerning Christ]; and so is the Holy Spirit, whom God has given to those who obey Him." The writer of Hebrews also connects the Holy Spirit with the apostles' testimony to Christ:

> How will we escape if we neglect so great a salvation? After it was at the first spoken through the Lord, it was confirmed to us by those who heard, God also testifying with them, both by signs and wonders and by various miracles and by gifts of the Holy Spirit according to His own will. (Heb. 2:3–4)

CHRISTIAN WITNESS IS ABOUT THE SON

He will testify about Me (15:26b)

The Holy Spirit's primary ministry to the lost world is to **testify about** Jesus. Likewise, the message of the church is not political activism, social reform, or psychological self-fulfillment but Jesus Christ. In his sermon on the day of Pentecost, Peter boldly declared, "This Jesus God raised up again, to which we are all witnesses" (Acts 2:32), a truth he repeated in his second recorded sermon (3:15). The apostles fearlessly declared to the Sanhedrin,

> The God of our fathers raised up Jesus, whom you had put to death by hanging Him on a cross. He is the one whom God exalted to His right hand as a Prince and a Savior, to grant repentance to Israel, and for-giveness of sins. And we are witnesses of these things; and so is the Holy Spirit, whom God has given to those who obey Him. (5:30–32; cf. 10:38–41; 13:31; 22:15, 20; 23:11; 26:16)

Paul wrote to the Corinthians, "I determined to know nothing among you except Jesus Christ, and Him crucified" (1 Cor. 2:2; cf. 15:15), and Peter described himself as a "witness of the sufferings of Christ" (1 Peter 5:1). The apostle John was exiled to "the island called Patmos because of the word of God and the testimony of Jesus" (Rev. 1:9). The Lord commended Antipas as "My witness, My faithful one" (Rev. 2:13), and the martyred tribulation saints are called "the witnesses of Jesus" (Rev. 17:6).

But despite the clear biblical emphasis on being witnesses of

Jesus Christ, much of today's evangelistic methodology focuses on meeting people's felt needs. It also downplays the essential biblical emphasis on the glory of the person and work of the Savior and the crucial importance of confronting unbelievers with their sin and its consequences unless they are rescued by faith in the atoning accomplishment of Jesus Christ. Any inadequate presentation of Christ and His death for sin can leave the sinner in his love of iniquity and ignorance of the truth of justification by faith and produce a false and temporary confession. Evangelism is as basic and unchanged as when Paul said

> And when I came to you, brethren, I did not come with superiority of speech or of wisdom, proclaiming to you the testimony of God. For I determined to know nothing among you except Jesus Christ, and Him crucified. I was with you in weakness and in fear and in much trembling, and my message and my preaching were not in persuasive words of wisdom, but in demonstration of the Spirit and of power, so that your faith would not rest on the wisdom of men, but on the power of God. (1 Cor. 2:1–5)

The preaching of Christ and the cross is still the power of God for salvation (1 Cor. 1:18–25).

In addition to the truth of Christ, repentance is at the heart of the biblical message of salvation. Christ's forerunner, John the Baptist, challenged his hearers to "repent, for the kingdom of heaven is at hand. . . . bear fruit in keeping with repentance," and told them, "I baptize you with water for repentance" (Matt. 3:2, 8, 11). From the outset of His public ministry, Jesus' message was, "Repent, for the kingdom of heaven is at hand" (Matt. 4:17). He rebuked the people of Chorazin and Bethsaida for refusing to repent (Matt. 11:20–21), and commended those of Nineveh because they did repent (Matt. 12:41). When they were sent out by the Lord Jesus, the Twelve "preached that men should repent" (Mark 6:12). When the scribes and Pharisees took Him to task for hobnobbing with the riffraff of society, Jesus replied, "I have not come to call the righteous but sinners to repentance" (Luke 5:32). The Lord shocked those who told Him of Pilate's massacre of some Galileans by bluntly telling them,

> Do you suppose that these Galileans were greater sinners than all other Galileans because they suffered this fate? I tell you, no, but unless you repent, you will all likewise perish. Or do you suppose that those eighteen on whom the tower in Siloam fell and killed them were worse culprits than all the men who live in Jerusalem? I tell you, no, but unless you repent, you will all likewise perish. (Luke 13:2–5)

Christ also described the rejoicing in heaven that takes place when sinners repent (Luke 15:7, 10). After His resurrection He declared that "repentance for forgiveness of sins would be proclaimed in His name to all the nations, beginning from Jerusalem" (Luke 24:47).

The early church obeyed the Lord's command and preached a message of repentance. At the conclusion of the first sermon in the church's history, Peter exhorted his hearers, "Repent, and each of you be baptized in the name of Jesus Christ for the forgiveness of your sins; and you will receive the gift of the Holy Spirit" (Acts 2:38). Peter sounded the same theme in his second recorded sermon: "Therefore repent and return, so that your sins may be wiped away, in order that times of refreshing may come from the presence of the Lord" (3:19). Standing before the Sanhedrin, the apostles boldly asserted of Jesus, "He is the one whom God exalted to His right hand as a Prince and a Savior, to grant repentance to Israel, and forgiveness of sins" (5:31). After hearing Peter's report of what took place at Cornelius's house, the believers in Jerusalem "glorified God, saying, 'Well then, God has granted to the Gentiles also the repentance that leads to life'" (11:18). Paul declared to the pagan philosophers at Athens, "Therefore having overlooked the times of ignorance, God is now declaring to men that all people everywhere should repent" (17:30). The apostle described his ministry as one of "solemnly testifying to both Jews and Greeks of repentance toward God and faith in our Lord Jesus Christ" (20:21), and his message was that people "should repent and turn to God, performing deeds appropriate to repentance" (26:20).

The Bible demands that sinners be broken over their sin and forsake all to come to Christ (Luke 9:23–24; 14:26–33). Many contemporary evangelism methods, however, by emphasizing meeting felt needs, make it sound like following Jesus is easy. (Some, proponents of the now popular "wider mercy" view, even argue that people do not have to know the gospel or believe in Jesus to be saved. But the Bible unequivocally teaches that salvation comes only through faith in Jesus Christ [John 3:36; 14:6; Acts 4:12; 1 Cor. 3:11; Gal. 1:8–9; 1 Tim. 2:5; 1 John 5:11–12; 2 John 9–11].) Jesus, in contrast, taught that it was hard for sinners to believe. He even went so far as to say that, humanly speaking, salvation is impossible (Luke 18:27).

A memorable illustration of the Lord's evangelistic methodology in action is His encounter with a rich synagogue ruler in Luke 18:18–27. This man seemed to be the ideal prospect for evangelism. Although he was an outwardly devout, religious man, he knew something was lacking in his life. That prompted his question, "Good Teacher, what shall I do to inherit eternal life?" (v. 18). This was no abstract theological question; he not only recognized his need, but also felt it deeply. This young man was also diligent in his pursuit of an answer. Mark records that, oblivious to what the crowd might think, he "ran up to [Jesus] and knelt before Him" (Mark 10:17). He also came to the right source, since Jesus Christ is the only source of eternal life (John 14:6; 1 John 5:20). Finally, he asked the right question, how he might personally take possession of eternal life.

But to his sorrow (Matt. 19:22) and the crowd's astonishment (v. 25), this seemingly surefire prospect went away unsaved. Proud and self-righteous, he treasured his earthly possessions more than the promise of heavenly riches. His shallow, superficial faith was not sufficient for him to confess his sin and forsake all to enter the kingdom of heaven; he wanted eternal life on his own terms, but they were not God's terms.

As this account reveals, far from seeking to remove barriers that might hinder the lost from coming to Him, Christ instead raised new ones. The Lord refused to ignore real spiritual issues for the sake of expediency. The church must not ignore them either. People are sinners, facing God's eternal judgment unless they repent and believe solely and submissively in Jesus Christ for salvation. Those truths cannot be watered down; the stumbling block of the cross cannot be removed (Gal. 5:11). Those who in any way tamper with the reality of sin and the true person and work of the Savior are purveyors of a false gospel (Gal. 1:8–9).

Christian Witness Is through Believers

and you will testify also, because you have been with Me from the beginning. (15:27)

Believers are the final link in the chain of witness. Thus Jesus, after describing the Holy Spirit's witness, told the disciples **you will testify also.** The two are inseparably linked, since it is the Spirit who enables believers to effectively testify to the world about Jesus Christ. So vital is the Spirit's empowering of Christian witness that the Lord instructed the disciples to remain in Jerusalem until the coming of the Spirit on the day of Pentecost (Luke 24:49). It was "in the power of the Spirit" that Paul "fully preached the gospel of Christ" (Rom. 15:19).

The apostles were qualified to testify about Christ because they had **been with** Him **from the beginning** of His earthly ministry. When the early church sought a replacement for Judas to fill the ranks of the apostles, Peter told those assembled,

> Therefore it is necessary that of the men who have accompanied us all the time that the Lord Jesus went in and out among us—beginning with the baptism of John until the day that He was taken up from us— one of these must become a witness with us of His resurrection. (Acts 1:21–22)

Christians today are not eyewitnesses of Jesus Christ as the apostles were, but they are called to point people to the truths about Him revealed in the Bible. They can also demonstrate the power of His resurrection life in their lives (cf. Rom. 6:4; Phil. 3:10).

God has chosen His people as a means to reach the elect among the lost. The blessed truth is that "whoever will call on the name of the Lord will be saved" (Rom. 10:13). But that can happen only when believers proclaim to them the saving truth of the gospel:

> How then will they call on Him in whom they have not believed? How will they believe in Him whom they have not heard? And how will they hear without a preacher? How will they preach unless they are sent? Just as it is written, "How beautiful are the feet of those who bring good news of good things!" However, they did not all heed the good news; for Isaiah says, "Lord, who has believed our report?" So faith comes from hearing, and hearing by the word of Christ. (vv. 14–17)

The Holy Spirit Convicts the World (John 16:1–11)

17

"These things I have spoken to you so that you may be kept from stumbling. They will make you outcasts from the synagogue, but an hour is coming for everyone who kills you to think that he is offering service to God. These things they will do because they have not known the Father or Me. But these things I have spoken to you, so that when their hour comes, you may remember that I told you of them. These things I did not say to you at the beginning, because I was with you. But now I am going to Him who sent Me; and none of you asks Me, 'Where are You going?' But because I have said these things to you, sorrow has filled your heart. But I tell you the truth, it is to your advantage that I go away; for if I do not go away, the Helper will not come to you; but if I go, I will send Him to you. And He, when He comes, will convict the world concerning sin and righteousness and judgment; concerning sin, because they do not believe in Me; and concerning righteousness, because I go to the Father and you no longer see Me; and concerning judgment, because the ruler of this world has been judged." (16:1–11)

The followers of Jesus Christ have always faced the world's hostility (a point that was detailed in chapter 15 of this volume). From the inception of the church, the apostles and those closely associated with them endured intense persecution. They were ridiculed, scorned, denounced, hunted, arrested, beaten, and imprisoned. Many even paid the ultimate price, giving their lives as martyrs (a transliteration of the Greek word meaning "witnesses") for the sake of their Savior. A brief survey of ancient Christian tradition reveals that Peter, Andrew, and James the son of Alphaeus were all crucified; Bartholomew was whipped to death and then crucified; James the son of Zebedee was beheaded, as was Paul; Thomas was stabbed with spears; Mark was dragged to death through the streets of Alexandria; and James the half brother of Jesus was stoned by order of the Sanhedrin. Philip was also stoned to death. Others, including Matthew, Simon the Zealot, Thaddeus, Timothy, and Stephen, were also killed for their unwavering commitment to the Lord. As Clement of Rome, a contemporary of the apostles who died around A.D. 100, observed, "Through envy and jealousy, the greatest and most righteous pillars [of the church] have been persecuted and put to death" (*First Epistle of Clement to the Corinthians*, 5).

In the generations that followed, persecution continued. Under the Roman emperors of the first three centuries, thousands of faithful believers were arrested, tortured, and killed. One notable example is that of Polycarp, the aged bishop of Smyrna. Around A.D. 160, he was arrested for being a Christian, and then tied to a stake and burned. When asked to deny Christ, Polycarp stood firm. "Eighty and six years have I served Him, and He never did me any injury," he replied resolutely. "How then can I blaspheme my King and my Savior?" (*Concerning the Martyrdom of the Holy Polycarp*, 9). (Much more on the hostility of Imperial Rome toward the church can be found in chapter 15 of this volume.)

The persecution of the true church again reached a fever pitch during the Protestant Reformation. Appalled by the moral and doctrinal corruption of the Roman Catholic Church and emboldened by the clear teachings of Scripture, the Reformers denounced the Catholic system of indulgences and the false gospel of works righteousness. The response from Rome was vitriolic and violent. According to Protestant historian John Dowling, the Roman Catholic Church put to death more than fifty million "heretics" between A.D. 606 (the birth of the papacy) and the mid-1800s (*History of Romanism* [New York: Edward Walker, 1845], 8:541). Commenting on Rome's murderous tactics, Martin Luther remarked, "If the art of convincing heretics by fire were the right one, then the executioners would be the most learned Doctors on earth" (*Address to the Christian Nobility of the German Nation*, in Henry Clay Vedder, *The Reformation in Germany* [New York: Macmillan, 1914], 119).

Godly leaders like John Huss (c. 1369–1415), Hugh Latimer (c. 1485–1555), William Tyndale (1495–1536), Patrick Hamilton (1504–1528), and George Wishart (1513–1546) were among those martyred for the faith. When the chain was put around John Huss, securing him to the stake where he would be burned, he said with a smile, "My Lord Jesus Christ was bound with a harder chain than this for my sake, and why then should I be ashamed of this rusty one?" When asked to recant, Huss declined, saying, "What I taught with my lips I now seal with my blood" (John Fox, *Fox's Book of Martyrs* [Philadelphia: J. J. Woodward, 1830], 634). He died singing a hymn as the flames engulfed his body.

In many places around the world today, believers continue to face intense persecution. Muslim controlled countries are especially hostile toward Christianity (currently especially in the Middle East and Africa), though other nations such as Communist states also remain antagonistic. While exact numbers are difficult to reconstruct, historians estimate the number of Christian martyrs in the last century to be in the tens of millions. A 1997 article in the *New York Times* reported that "more Christians have died this century simply for being Christians than in the first nineteen centuries after the birth of Christ" (A. M. Rosenthal, "Persecuting the Christians," *New York Times*, February 11, 1997, citing information from Nina Shea, *In the Lion's Den* [Nashville: Broadman & Holman, 1997]). In addition, an incalculable number of faithful believers have been arrested, beaten, or otherwise persecuted short of death—all on account of their loyalty to Jesus Christ.

The theme of persecution, which Jesus introduced in 15:18–25, continues into the opening section of chapter 16. But as He had done in 15:26–27, the Lord was quick to remind His disciples that they would not face the world's hostility alone. Their witness to the world would be accompanied and empowered by the witness of the Holy Spirit. The Spirit would confront the world, not only by testifying to Jesus, but also by convicting sinners of their true heart condition. Because the Helper was coming to them, the disciples could remain confident, knowing that though the world system would always oppose them, many within that system would be delivered from its darkness and transferred into the kingdom of light (cf. Col. 1:13).

Although the content of this section is similar to that of chapter 15, there is a subtle difference in emphasis. In chapter 15, Jesus instructed the disciples as to what they were to do (e.g., vv. 4, 9, 10, 12, 14, 17–20). But in chapter 16 He focused on what God would do for them through the indwelling power of the Holy Spirit (e.g., vv. 1–4, 7, 13–15). He would comfort, strengthen, and aid the disciples in the midst of their conflict with the world. As Leon Morris writes,

The work of the Holy Spirit in the church is done in the context of persecution. The Spirit is not a guide and a helper for those on a straight way perfectly able to manage on their own. He comes to assist men caught up in the thick of battle, and tried beyond their strength. Jesus makes it quite plain that the way before His followers is a hard and a difficult way. (*The Gospel According to John*, The New International Commentary on the New Testament [Grand Rapids: Eerdmans, 1979], 692)

It is the mission of both the Holy Spirit and believers to bear witness to Jesus (cf. 15:26–27). The Spirit testifies to believers that the gospel is true (1 John 2:20–21, 27; cf. 14:26; 16:13–14), and then empowers them as they proclaim it to the world (Acts 1:8). Though God uses Christians to proclaim the gospel, only the Holy Spirit is able to redeem lost sinners (Titus 3:5). He alone can convict unbelievers of their sin and need for a Savior.

In these verses, Jesus warned the disciples that they would face conflict with the world. But He comforted them with the promised coming of the Holy Spirit, and explained to them that the Spirit would not only help them, but would also work in unbelievers to convict them of sin. Thus, the passage can be outlined around three distinct but related sections: the conflict with the world, the comforting of the disciples, and the convicting by the Spirit.

THE CONFLICT WITH THE WORLD

These things I have spoken to you so that you may be kept from stumbling. They will make you outcasts from the synagogue, but an hour is coming for everyone who kills you to think that he is offering service to God. These things they will do because they have not known the Father or Me. But these things I have spoken to you, so that when their hour comes, you may remember that I told you of them. These things I did not say to you at the beginning, because I was with you. (16:1–4)

The phrase **these things** refers back to the Lord's warning about the world's hostility (15:18–25). He had **spoken** those words to the disciples **so that** they might **be kept from stumbling. Stumbling** translates a form of the verb *skandalizō;* the related noun literally refers to the bait stick in a trap. The term here refers figuratively to the disciples' being caught off guard like an animal ensnared in a trap. Had Jesus not warned them of the persecution they would inevitably face, the disciples might have become shocked and disillusioned so that their faith might have faltered.

The events that transpired later that evening showed the timeliness of the Lord's warning. Despite being told by Jesus to expect persecution, the disciples wilted at the first sign of it—even though it was aimed not at them, but at Him. On their way to Gethsemane from the upper room, Jesus told them, "You will all fall away because of Me this night, for it is written, 'I will strike down the shepherd, and the sheep of the flock shall be scattered'" (Matt. 26:31). Later that evening, when Jesus was arrested, His prediction came true:

> At that time Jesus said to the crowds, "Have you come out with swords and clubs to arrest Me as you would against a robber? Every day I used to sit in the temple teaching and you did not seize Me. But all this has taken place to fulfill the Scriptures of the prophets." Then all the disciples left Him and fled. (Matt. 26:55–56)

Some might question why the Lord warned the disciples against stumbling when He knew they would shortly do just that. It is true that Jesus, in His omniscience, knew what was going to happen. But the point is that the disciples were responsible for their actions. They had been given the resources they needed to stand firm and not stumble, including a warning that persecution was imminent. Yet they failed to utilize those resources, and when the moment of truth came, they capitulated under the pressure and fled. Their failure in face of the truth they were told was inexcusable. But it is easy to see how hard the transition was, and for them to shift their minds from the expectation of the promised kingdom and glory (cf. Luke 19:11) to a promise of rejection and hostility. This was another in a list of things hard for them to believe.

The Lord continued by describing some of the specific persecution the disciples would face in the coming **hour** (a term that in John's gospel refers especially to the events connected with Jesus' death, resurrection, and exaltation [cf. 2:4; 4:21, 23; 5:25, 28; 7:30; 8:20; 12:23, 27; 13:1; 16:25; 17:1]). To be made **outcasts from the synagogue** meant far more than merely being forbidden to attend religious services. Those who were excommunicated from the synagogue were cut off from all religious, social, and economic aspects of Jewish society. They were branded as traitors to their people and their God, and faced the likely consequence of losing both their families and their jobs. Not surprisingly, being unsynagogued was greatly feared (cf. 9:22; 12:42).

But even worse than such excommunication, some of Christ's followers would pay with their lives (as was noted earlier). In a bitter irony, the enemies of Christ sometimes **think that** by killing Christians they are **offering service to God** (the word translated **service** is used in Scripture to speak of religious service, or worship [cf. Rom. 9:4; 12:1; Heb. 9:1, 6]). This is true even today in nations where in the name of Allah militant

Islam stands violently opposed to Christianity. The folly of attempting to serve a false god by murdering God's people reveals the depths to which sinful darkness blankets the minds of the unconverted.

Before his conversion, none other than the apostle Paul was a zealous persecutor of Christians. After being rescued by Roman soldiers outside the temple, he told the mob that had been trying to kill him, "I persecuted this Way to the death, binding and putting both men and women into prisons" (Acts 22:4). In his defense before Herod Agrippa, Paul elaborated on that statement:

> So then, I thought to myself that I had to do many things hostile to the name of Jesus of Nazareth. And this is just what I did in Jerusalem; not only did I lock up many of the saints in prisons, having received authority from the chief priests, but also when they were being put to death I cast my vote against them. And as I punished them often in all the synagogues, I tried to force them to blaspheme; and being furiously enraged at them, I kept pursuing them even to foreign cities. (26:9–11)

Writing to the churches of Galatia, the apostle explained what had motivated his violent persecution of the church: "For you have heard of my former manner of life in Judaism, how I used to persecute the church of God beyond measure and tried to destroy it; and I was advancing in Judaism beyond many of my contemporaries among my countrymen, being more extremely zealous for my ancestral traditions" (Gal. 1:13–14; cf. Phil. 3:6; 1 Tim. 1:12–13).

After Paul's conversion the hater became the hated; the hunter the hunted; and the persecutor the persecuted. In virtually every city he visited, Paul faced opposition from Jews, Gentiles, or both, thereby fulfilling the Lord's prediction concerning him: "I will show him how much he must suffer for My name's sake" (Acts 9:16). In 2 Corinthians 11:22–27 the apostle summarized how he received the "brand-marks of Jesus" (Gal. 6:17) that he so proudly bore:

> Are they [the Judaizing false teachers] Hebrews? So am I. Are they Israelites? So am I. Are they descendants of Abraham? So am I. Are they servants of Christ?—I speak as if insane—I more so; in far more labors, in far more imprisonments, beaten times without number, often in danger of death. Five times I received from the Jews thirty-nine lashes. Three times I was beaten with rods, once I was stoned, three times I was shipwrecked, a night and a day I have spent in the deep. I have been on frequent journeys, in dangers from rivers, dangers from robbers, dangers from my countrymen, dangers from the Gentiles, dangers in the city, dangers in the wilderness, dangers on the sea, dangers among false brethren; I have been in labor and hardship, through many sleepless

nights, in hunger and thirst, often without food, in cold and exposure. (2 Cor. 11:22–27)

How could seemingly religious people commit such atrocities in the guise of worshiping God? **These things,** Jesus explained, **they will do because they have not known the Father or Me.** Far from serving God, such people do not in any sense know the true God; no one who hates Jesus Christ or His followers (1 John 4:20; 5:1) knows the Father (John 8:19; 1 John 3:1; cf. John 5:23; 14:7; 15:21). Failing to know God is willful, inexcusable ignorance (Rom. 1:18–32), and those who manifest it do not have eternal life (cf. Rom. 10:2–3).

In verse 4 Jesus gave another reason for His warning to the disciples. **These things I have spoken to you,** He told them, **so that when their hour comes, you may remember that I told you of them.** Persecution would surely come, since "all who desire to live godly in Christ Jesus will be persecuted" (2 Tim. 3:12; cf. Acts 14:22). Years later, in his first epistle, Peter echoed the Lord's prediction:

> Beloved, do not be surprised at the fiery ordeal among you, which comes upon you for your testing, as though some strange thing were happening to you; but to the degree that you share the sufferings of Christ, keep on rejoicing, so that also at the revelation of His glory you may rejoice with exultation. (1 Peter 4:12–13)

But rather than shatter the disciples' faith, the hostility they faced would actually deepen and strengthen their resolve as they saw the Lord's prediction fulfilled (cf. John 14:29).

Jesus had not needed to say **these** words of warning to the disciples **at the beginning, because** He **was with** them. During His ministry, the Lord not only protected His disciples, but also bore the brunt of the world's attacks—something He would shortly do again for the last time (18:8–9). Because Jesus had been there to receive the assaults Himself and to shield them, the disciples had not experienced the full force of the opposition they would now face in His absence. In such passages as Matthew 5:10–12 and 10:24–25, Jesus had referred to persecution in general terms. But now that His death was only hours away, the disciples would be left to face the full fury of the world's hatred. That reality is what prompted this explicit warning.

Jesus never glossed over the truth when it came to counting the cost of being His disciple. In Luke 9:23–24 He said, "If anyone wishes to come after Me, he must deny himself, and take up his cross daily and follow Me. For whoever wishes to save his life will lose it, but whoever loses his life for My sake, he is the one who will save it." Later He told a parable illustrating that truth:

For which one of you, when he wants to build a tower, does not first sit down and calculate the cost to see if he has enough to complete it? Otherwise, when he has laid a foundation and is not able to finish, all who observe it begin to ridicule him, saying, "This man began to build and was not able to finish." Or what king, when he sets out to meet another king in battle, will not first sit down and consider whether he is strong enough with ten thousand men to encounter the one coming against him with twenty thousand? Or else, while the other is still far away, he sends a delegation and asks for terms of peace. So then, none of you can be My disciple who does not give up all his own possessions. (Luke 14:28–33)

Christ does not offer His followers the way of comfort and ease, but a hard and difficult path. Though the gate is small and the road is narrow, it is certainly well worth the strenuous journey, for it alone "leads to life" and to eternal glory (Matt. 7:13–14). Thus Paul could write, in the midst of his multitudinous trials, "For momentary, light affliction is producing for us an eternal weight of glory far beyond all comparison" (2 Cor. 4:17).

THE COMFORTING OF THE DISCIPLES

But now I am going to Him who sent Me; and none of you asks Me, 'Where are You going?' But because I have said these things to you, sorrow has filled your heart. But I tell you the truth, it is to your advantage that I go away; for if I do not go away, the Helper will not come to you; but if I go, I will send Him to you. (16:5–7)

These verses present a sharp contrast between the complete self-lessness of Jesus and the utter selfishness of the disciples. As the cross loomed ever larger, they should have been comforting Him. He should have been their focus, since the time had come for Him to accomplish His mission and return to the Father who **sent** Him.

But **none of** them was even concerned enough about the Lord to ask Him, **"Where are You going?"** Though both Peter (13:36) and Thomas (14:5) had asked Him earlier where He was going, the Lord's point was that their questions had reflected a concern for themselves and not a concern for Him. Those earlier queries were more of a protest over His abandoning them than an expression of genuine interest in what He was about to experience. As R. C. H. Lenski explains:

Peter's question in 13:36 was of a different kind; it was only a selfish exclamation which would not hear of Jesus' going away alone. And the assertion of Thomas in 14:5 was nothing but an expression of discouragement and dullness of mind at the thought of Jesus' going away while leaving the disciples to follow later on a way that Thomas felt he did not know. (*The Interpretation of St. John's Gospel* [repr.; Peabody, Mass.: Hendrickson, 1998], 1078–79; cf. D. A. Carson, *The Gospel According to John*, The Pillar New Testament Commentary [Grand Rapids: Eerdmans, 1991], 532–33)

Because Jesus had **said these things** (about the coming persecution) **to** them, **sorrow** had **filled** the disciples' hearts. Their thoughts were not centered on what this moment meant for Jesus, but only on what it meant for them. But instead of being consumed with anxiety, they should have been filled with joy to know that Jesus' earthly mission was almost over and His return to heavenly glory near. As He had earlier chided them, "If you loved Me, you would have rejoiced because I go to the Father" (14:28).

In actuality, the disciples' sorrow was completely unwarranted. The **truth** is that **it** was **to** their **advantage that** Jesus **go away.** Obviously, apart from Jesus' propitiatory, sacrificial death on the cross, there would be no atonement for their sins. But beyond that, **if** Jesus did **not go away, the Helper** (the Holy Spirit) would **not come to** them. **But** if the Lord left, He would **send Him to** them. Jesus promised that when the Holy Spirit came, He would give them eternal life (7:37–39), indwell them (14:16–17), instruct them (and through them all believers [14:26]), empower them in their witness, and activate for them the promises of God (see 15:26–27 and the commentary on those verses in the previous chapter of this volume).

There are at least two reasons why the Holy Spirit did not come until after Christ's death, resurrection, and ascension. First, the Spirit's ministry is to reveal the person and works of Christ. That was not fully possible until after Christ finished His work of redemption on the cross and ascended to His full glory in heaven. Second, the Father gave the Spirit to the church to vindicate His Son's faithfulness in completing the work of salvation in His death and resurrection (cf. John 7:39; Gal. 3:14). In his sermon on the day of Pentecost, Peter, after referring to the death and resurrection Christ (Acts 2:23–32), declared, "Therefore having been exalted to the right hand of God, and having received from the Father the promise of the Holy Spirit, He has poured forth this which you both see and hear" (v. 33).

THE CONVICTING BY THE SPIRIT

And He, when He comes, will convict the world concerning sin and righteousness and judgment; concerning sin, because they do not believe in Me; and concerning righteousness, because I go

to the Father and you no longer see Me; and concerning judgment, because the ruler of this world has been judged. (16:8–11)

The Holy Spirit does not minister only to believers, but also to the unbelieving world. Though the word **convict** judicially implies a negative connotation, theologically the Spirit's convicting ministry is an exceedingly positive one. His goal is to bring sinners to a saving knowledge of Jesus Christ.

No one can be saved apart from the Spirit's convicting and regenerating work. The Bible teaches that all people are by nature rebels against God and hostile to Jesus Christ. They are "dead in [their] trespasses and sins" (Eph. 2:1); "by nature children of wrath" (v. 3); "darkened in their understanding, excluded from the life of God because of the ignorance that is in them, because of the hardness of their heart ... callous [having] given themselves over to sensuality for the practice of every kind of impurity with greediness" (Eph. 4:18–19); "and alienated and hostile in mind, engaged in evil deeds" (Col. 1:21); blinded by Satan so that they cannot understand spiritual truth (2 Cor. 4:4; cf. Luke 8:5, 12). In that condition, they are helpless; they are unable to believe the truth and are even guilty of suppressing it (Rom. 1:18–32). In John 6:44 Jesus declared, "No one can come to Me unless the Father who sent Me draws him." In a graphic description of fallen man's utter inability to seek God on his own, Paul wrote,

> There is none righteous, not even one; there is none who understands, there is none who seeks for God; all have turned aside, together they have become useless; there is none who does good, there is not even one. Their throat is an open grave, with their tongues they keep deceiving, the poison of asps is under their lips; whose mouth is full of cursing and bitterness; their feet are swift to shed blood, destruction and misery are in their paths, and the path of peace they have not known. There is no fear of God before their eyes. (Rom. 3:10–18)

The world hates Jesus Christ because sinfulness hates righteousness, imperfection hates perfection, and the "domain of darkness" hates the "kingdom of His beloved Son" (Col. 1:13; cf. John 3:19). It is the ministry of the Holy Spirit to penetrate hearts steeped in sin, overcome sinners' resistance to the gospel, and bring them through saving faith in the Lord Jesus Christ to fellowship with God.

To do that, the Spirit must break the power of sin that enslaves people (John 8:34), and the love of iniquity that keeps them in rebellion against God. Jesus had already told the disciples that the Spirit would testify about Him to the world (15:26). In addition to that outward testimony, the Spirit also convicts the hearts of sinners. **When He comes** on the day of Pentecost, Jesus said, the Spirit **will convict the world concerning sin and righteousness and judgment.**

The beginning of the Holy Spirit's saving ministry to the lost is revealed in this word **convict.** The word can describe convicting in a judicial sense, like a criminal who is convicted of wrongdoing (cf. its use in James 2:9 and Jude 15). Ultimately, those convicted in this sense will be sentenced to eternal punishment in hell. But in this context the word more likely refers to being convinced of the reality of sin and the need for salvation in Christ (cf. 1 Cor. 14:24). It is the Spirit's mission to present the truth about Jesus Christ to the world (15:26); those who reject the truth will be found guilty and judged by the Son and Father (5:22,27,30).

The Holy Spirit convicts **the world concerning** three things: **sin and righteousness and judgment.** The singular form of *hamartias* (**sin**) refers not to sin in general but specifically to the ultimate sin of refusing to **believe in** Jesus Christ. It is that sin that finally damns people, since all others are forgiven when a person believes savingly in Him (cf. Matt. 12:31–32). In John 3:18 Jesus said, "He who believes in Him (Christ) is not judged; he who does not believe has been judged already, because he has not believed in the name of the only begotten Son of God." In 5:40 He rebuked those who were "unwilling to come to [Him] so that [they might] have life." He solemnly warned the unbelieving Jews, "Unless you believe that I am He, you will die in your sins" (John 8:24). The sole issue that determines people's eternal destiny is how they react to the Spirit's convicting ministry concerning their own sin and the provision of forgiveness by grace through Jesus Christ.

Second, Jesus told the disciples, "the Holy Spirit convicts the world **concerning righteousness, because I go to the Father and you no longer see Me."** The **righteousness** here is that which belongs to Jesus Christ by nature as the holy Son of God. This is the flip side of the previous point; not only does the Spirit convict unbelievers of their sin, but also of the necessity of having the perfect righteousness of Christ (cf. Matt. 5:20, 48). When their wickedness is compared to His sinless holiness, their sin is seen more truly for the detestable evil that it is. And the sinner is face-to-face with the impossibility of salvation by any effort, work, or achievement he may do.

The Lord's statement, **because I go to the Father and you no longer see Me,** provides the supreme evidence of His righteousness: His acceptance into the Father's presence. Habakkuk 1:13 says of God, "Your eyes are too pure to approve evil, and You can not look on wickedness with favor." When the Father "highly exalted Him, and bestowed on Him the name which is above every name" (Phil. 2:9), He Himself testified to Christ's righteousness. Those who heed the Spirit's testimony about their utter sinfulness and Christ's perfect righteousness and respond to the gospel in genuine faith, are instantly clothed with His righteousness. Their sins are placed fully on Him and, in His death at the hands of God's holy justice, He paid the penalty in full (Phil. 3:9; cf. Rom. 3:21–22; 4:5, 13; 5:21; 10:10; 1 Cor. 1:30; 2 Cor. 5:21). God justifies sinners when He accounts their sins to have been paid for by Christ's death and Christ's righteousness is credited to them by His grace alone.

Finally, the Holy Spirit convicts the world **concerning judgment, because the ruler of this world has been judged.** The world's judgments are erroneous and evil, as was supremely demonstrated by its rejection of the Son of God. But while the world is incapable of judging righteously (cf. 7:24), the Spirit always does so. He convicts people of their false assessment of Jesus Christ.

The **ruler of this world** is Satan (12:31; 14:30; 1 John 5:19). He **has** already **been judged** and cast from heaven along with the rest of the angels who rebelled with him (Rev. 12:7–9; cf. Luke 10:18). He was totally defeated at the cross (Col. 2:15; Heb. 2:14; 1 John 3:8), when what appeared to be his hour of triumph was in reality the hour of his undoing. Though Satan has been defeated and judged, the final sentence against him will not be carried out until the end of the millennium (Rev. 20:10). In the meantime he goes about as the god of this age, seeking to capture and devour souls. The sobering warning to those who embrace the world system is that since its ruler will not escape judgment, neither will they, unless they repent. The Devil's fate guarantees the judgment of every unrepentant sinner.

There are only two possible responses to the convicting work of the Spirit: repentance or rejection. From those who reject the Spirit's conviction will come hostility to the followers of Christ. Their end is "eternal destruction, away from the presence of the Lord and from the glory of His power" (2 Thess. 1:9). Those who repent when the Spirit convicts them will spend eternity in the inexpressible glory and joy of heaven. Yet they will, in this life, face fiery trials of persecution without a fatal defection because "greater is He who is in [them] than he who is in the world" (1 John 4:4).

The Holy Spirit Reveals the Truth (John 16:12–15)

18

"I have many more things to say to you, but you cannot bear them now. But when He, the Spirit of truth, comes, He will guide you into all the truth; for He will not speak on His own initiative, but whatever He hears, He will speak; and He will disclose to you what is to come. He will glorify Me, for He will take of Mine and will disclose it to you. All things that the Father has are Mine; therefore I said that He takes of Mine and will disclose it to you." (16:12–15)

Although he lived in a time when books were laboriously written and copied by hand, Solomon still observed that "the writing of many books is endless" (Eccl. 12:12). In the modern era of high-speed printing presses, the trickle of books published each year has become a torrent. But of the countless millions of books that have been written, the Bible remains truly unique. It alone is the Word of God, inspired by the Spirit of God and invested with the power and authority of God. As such it is infallible, inerrant, authoritative, sufficient, and effective. Psalm 19:7–11 declares of God's Word,

> The law of the Lord is perfect, restoring the soul; the testimony of the Lord is sure, making wise the simple. The precepts of the Lord are right, rejoicing the heart; the commandment of the Lord is pure, enlightening the eyes. The fear of the Lord is clean, enduring forever; the judgments of the Lord are true; they are righteous altogether. They are more desirable than gold, yes, than much fine gold; sweeter also than honey and the drippings of the honeycomb. Moreover, by them Your servant is warned; in keeping them there is great reward.

The value of the Bible is unsurpassed. As the Word of God, it is to be believed (Ps. 119:42), obeyed (Ps. 119:11, 17, 67, 101, 105, 133), studied (Ps. 119:169; 2 Tim. 2:15), honored (Ps. 119:38, 82, 140, 162), and defended (Phil. 1:16; 1 Peter 3:15; Jude 3).

The Bible repeatedly claims to be inspired by God. The Old Testament refers to itself as the Word of God more than three thousand times—with the phrase "the word of the Lord," describing God's revelation through His spokesmen, appearing more than 250 times (e.g., Num. 30:1; 36:5; 1 Chron. 15:15; 2 Chron. 34:21; 35:6; Isa. 1:10; 28:14; Jer. 1:1–2; Ezek. 1:3; Dan. 9:2; Hos. 1:1; Joel 1:1; Amos 7:16; Jonah 1:1; Mic. 1:1; Zeph. 1:1; Hag. 1:1, 3; Zech. 1:1; Mal. 1:1). No wonder the prophet Amos declared, "Surely the Lord God does nothing unless He reveals His secret counsel to His servants the prophets" (Amos 3:7).

The New Testament writers also viewed the Old Testament as inspired by God, quoting from it more than three hundred times and clearly denoting it as Scripture (cf. Rom. 4:3 with Gen. 15:6; Rom. 9:17 with Ex. 9:16; Gal. 3:8 with Gen. 12:3). Paul told the Roman Christians, "For whatever was written in earlier times [the Old Testament] was written for our instruction, so that through perseverance and the encouragement of the Scriptures we might have hope" (Rom. 15:4). And Peter told the believers gathered in the upper room, "Brethren, the Scripture had to be fulfilled, which the Holy Spirit foretold by the mouth of David concerning Judas, who became a guide to those who arrested Jesus" (Acts 1:16). Not only did apostles regard the Old Testament as Scripture (cf. 3:18; 4:25; 8:32, 35; 17:2, 11; 18:24, 28; Rom. 1:2; 4:3; 9:17; 10:11; 11:2; 15:4; 1 Cor. 15:3–4; Gal. 3:8, 22; 4:30; 1 Tim. 5:18; 2 Tim. 3:16; James 2:8, 23; 1 Peter 2:6), they also declared that the Holy Spirit inspired those writings. Thus Peter wrote concerning the inspiration of the Old Testament, "No prophecy was ever made by an act of human will, but men moved by the Holy Spirit spoke from God" (2 Peter 1:21; cf. 2 Sam. 23:2; Neh. 9:30; Ezek. 11:5; Zech. 7:12; Mark 12:36; Acts 28:25; Heb. 1:1; 3:7; 9:8; 10:15; 1 Peter 1:10–11).

The New Testament also testifies to its own inspiration. In 1 Timothy 5:18 Paul wrote, "For the Scripture says, 'You shall not muzzle the ox while he is threshing,' and 'The laborer is worthy of his wages.'" The first quote is from the Old Testament (Deut. 25:4). But the second, which Paul also refers to as Scripture, is taken from Luke 10:7. Peter wrote concerning Paul's epistles, "Our beloved brother Paul, according to the wisdom given him, wrote to you, as also in all his letters, speaking in them of these things, in which are some things hard to understand, which the untaught and unstable distort, as they do also the rest of the Scriptures, to their own destruction" (2 Peter 3:15–16). Peter thus declared Paul's inspired writings to be Scripture.

Paul himself was conscious that what he wrote in his inspired letters was Scripture. "If anyone thinks he is a prophet or spiritual," he challenged the rebellious, unruly Corinthians, "let him recognize that the things which I write to you are the Lord's commandment" (1 Cor. 14:37; cf. 2 Cor. 13:2–3; 1 Thess. 2:13). Earlier in that letter Paul had written,

> Now we have received, not the spirit of the world, but the Spirit who is from God, so that we may know the things freely given to us by God, which things we also speak, not in words taught by human wisdom, but in those taught by the Spirit, combining spiritual thoughts with spiritual words. (2:12–13)

The book of Revelation similarly claims to be inspired by God. In its opening verse it declares itself to be "the Revelation of Jesus Christ, which God gave Him to show to His bond-servants, the things which must soon take place; and He sent and communicated it by His angel to His bond-servant John" (1:1). In the letter to the church at Ephesus, the Lord Jesus Christ said, "He who has an ear, let him hear what the Spirit says to the churches" (2:7). In 19:9 an angel declared, "These are true words of God," while in 21:5, God Himself reiterated that "these words are faithful and true."

The Bible, in its entirety, unambiguously claims to be the Word of God. But can that claim be verified? What supporting facts can be marshaled to demonstrate that the Bible is divinely inspired? In answering such questions, several lines of evidence can be surveyed.

First, consider the Bible's remarkable unity. Critics delight in pointing out "plot holes" (inconsistencies in the story lines) of movies, TV shows, and novels. But although the Bible was written over a period of about 1,600 years by forty or more human authors from widely diverse backgrounds—including kings, priests, physicians, fishermen, shepherds, theologians, statesmen, tax collectors, soldiers, scribes, and farmers—it contains no "plot holes." The specific facts and truths of the Bible are perfectly consistent from beginning to end, signifying the veracity of its claim to be authored by the all-knowing and true God.

A second argument for the Bible's veracity is its scientific accuracy. While it was not intended to be a scientific treatise, its descriptions of observable facts and natural processes are completely accurate. This is obvious, since the author is also the creator of all that exists and knows the way things truly are. For example, Isaiah 55:10 describes the hydrological cycle: "The rain and the snow come down from heaven, and do not return there without watering the earth" (cf. Job 36:27–28; Eccl. 1:7). It was not until the seventeenth century that William Harvey discovered the vital significance of the human body's circulatory system. Yet thousands of years earlier the Bible declared that the life of the flesh is in the blood (Gen. 9:4). In the ancient Mesopotamian world, the earth was believed to be flat. But Job 26:10 says that God "has inscribed a circle on the surface of the waters at the boundary of light and darkness," thus describing the earth as a circular globe. Similarly, Job 38:14 likens the earth to a cylindrical seal rolled over soft clay, indicating that it rotates on its axis, and Isaiah 40:22 declares that God "sits above the circle of the earth."

The Bible also records truths unknown until the advent of modern scientific discoveries. Genesis 22:17 compares the number of stars to the number of grains of sand on the beach, while Jeremiah said that there are so many stars that they cannot be counted (Jer. 33:22). Yet less than five thousand stars are visible to the naked eye—hardly an overwhelming, uncountable number. But using powerful modern telescopes, astronomers now estimate that there are at least 100 billion stars in our galaxy and billions more in numberless other galaxies.

The first and second laws of thermodynamics are foundational to all of science. But although they were not formulated until the beginning of the industrial revolution, both are implied by Scripture. The first law states that energy is conserved; that is, it can be neither created, nor destroyed. Genesis 2:2–3 gives the reason that energy cannot be created: God's creative activity has ceased, while His work of preserving His creation (Col. 1:17; Heb. 1:3) ensures that no energy can be destroyed.

The Bible also affirms the second law of thermodynamics, the principle that entropy, or disorder, is constantly increasing. Thus, everything in the universe is constantly deteriorating. The origin of the second law lies in the fall (Gen. 3:1–24). Adam's and Eve's disobedience not only plunged the human race into the ruin of sin, but also had a catastrophic effect on the physical universe. "The creation was subjected to futility," Paul wrote, "not willingly, but because of Him who subjected it, in hope … For we know that the whole creation groans and suffers the pains of childbirth together until now" (Rom. 8:20, 22). (For more examples of the Bible's scientific accuracy, see Henry M. Morris, *The Biblical Basis for Modern Science* [Grand Rapids: Baker, 1984]).

The Bible's historical accuracy, verified repeatedly by archaeological discoveries, offers further evidence of its truthfulness. One of the "assured results" of nineteenth-century rationalistic biblical higher criticism was that the Hittites, mentioned nearly fifty times in the Old Testament, had in fact never existed. Archaeological discoveries since then (including the unearthing of 10,000 clay tablets in the ruins of the Hittite capital city), however, have revealed vast amounts of information about their history, culture, religion, and language. The Hittite Empire, centered in Asia Minor, is now known to have been extensive, and powerful enough to have challenged Egypt militarily.

Unbelieving skeptics claim that the book of Daniel was written during the Maccabean period (second century B.C.), after many of the events it prophesies had already taken place. But there are several copies of Daniel among the Dead Sea Scrolls (discovered at Qumran), the earliest dating to only about half a century after the critics allege Daniel was written. Thus a second-century date for the book becomes untenable, since the community that produced the Dead Sea Scrolls clearly regarded Daniel as a prophet in their own writings—something they would not have done if a mere fifty years had elapsed since the book of Daniel was written. The only reasonable conclusion is that it was composed much earlier (in the sixth century B.C.). Commenting on Daniel's prophecies, Harvard-trained linguistic scholar Gleason Archer explains,

> The linguistic evidence from Qumran makes the rationalistic explanation for Daniel no longer tenable [i.e. that it was written late, in the second century]. It is difficult to see how any scholar can defend this view and maintain intellectual respectability. (Gleason L. Archer, *Encyclopedia of Bible Difficulties* [Grand Rapids: Zondervan, 1982], 24)

Summarizing the contribution archaeology has made to substantiating the Bible's historical accuracy, archaeologist J. A. Thompson writes,

> It is perfectly true to say that biblical archaeology has done a great deal to correct the impression that was abroad at the close of the [nineteenth] century and in the early part of [the twentieth] century, that biblical history was of doubtful trustworthiness in many places. If one impression stands out more clearly than any other today, it is that on all hands the overall historicity of the Old Testament tradition is admitted. In this connection the words of W. F. Albright may be quoted: "There can be no doubt that archaeology has confirmed the substantial historicity of Old Testament tradition." (*The Bible and Archaeology* [rev. ed., Grand Rapids: Eerdmans, 1987], 4–5)

An even more dramatic piece of evidence that the Bible is God's Word is fulfilled prophecy. No human can predict the events of the future, yet the Bible writers predicted future events with a detailed accuracy that is impossible to attribute to mere human insight, anticipation, or coincidence. Astronomical odds exist against their being fulfilled by chance; yet biblical prophecies come true. Among them are the hundreds of Old Testament predictions fulfilled in the coming of Jesus Christ. (For a detailed treatment of fulfilled prophecies in Scripture, see Josh McDowell, *Evidence That Demands a Verdict*, vol. 1 [San Bernardino, Calif.: Here's Life, 1986]; John Ankerberg et al., *The Case for Jesus the Messiah* [Eugene, Oreg., Harvest House, 1989; James E. Smith, *What the Bible Teaches about the Promised Messiah* [Nashville: Thomas Nelson, 1993]; and Alfred Edersheim, *The Life and Times of Jesus the Messiah* [Grand Rapids: Eerdmans, 1974], 2:710–41.)

But of all the evidence that demonstrates that the Bible is the Word of God, none is more significant than the testimony of the Lord Jesus Christ. The New Testament documents containing His testimony are the most well-attested documents from antiquity. There are far more early manuscripts of the New Testament in existence today than of any other ancient writing, and the time gap between them and the original documents is much shorter. Thus, "to be skeptical of the resultant text of the New Testament books is to allow all of classical antiquity to slip into obscurity, for no documents of the ancient period are as well attested bibliographically as the New Testament" (John Warwick Montgomery, *History and Christianity* [Downers Grove, Ill.: InterVarsity, 1974], 29; cf. F. F. Bruce, *The New Testament Documents: Are They Reliable?* [Downers Grove, Ill.: InterVarsity, 1973]).

As God incarnate who cannot err and only speaks truth, (cf. John 5:18; 8:58; 10:30–33), Jesus established the veracity and authority of Scripture. Quoting from it more than sixty times, He taught that the entire Old Testament is the infallible, authoritative Word of God. He declared that "the Scripture cannot be broken" (John 10:35), and that "it is easier for heaven and earth to pass away than for one stroke of a letter of the Law to fail" (Luke 16:17; cf. Matt. 5:18). Jesus was absolutely certain that "all things which are written through the prophets about the Son of Man will be accomplished" (Luke 18:31; cf. 24:44).

Christ also confirmed the historicity of numerous Old Testament people and events, including Moses' encounter with God at the burning bush (Mark 12:26), Moses' receiving of the Law (John 7:19), God's provision of manna for Israel (John 6:31–32), the bronze serpent by which the Israelites were healed of snakebite (John 3:14), Jonah's mission to Nineveh —including his having been swallowed by a large sea creature (Matt. 12:39–41), the queen of Sheba's visit to Solomon (Matt. 12:42), Elijah's ministry to the widow of Zarephath (Luke 4:25), and Daniel's prophecy of the seventy weeks (Matt. 24:15). Jesus also believed that Genesis 1–11 records actual historical events, in contrast to many people today who view those chapters as myth or allegory. He taught that Adam and Eve were created at the beginning of history (Mark 10:6)—not billions of years later as some contend. The Lord also affirmed the historicity and universality of the flood (Matt. 24:37–39), the destruction of Sodom (Luke 17:29), the death of Lot's wife (Luke 17:32), and the existence of the patriarchs (Matt.8:11; 22:32; John 8:56).

Either Jesus knew the Scripture was without error and said it was, or He did not know, and said it was when it is not; or He knew it was not free from error, and lied. In the first case, He is God; in the second case, He is not God; in the third case, He is the Devil!

But Jesus did more than just authenticate the revelation already given in the Old Testament. He also promised to reveal new truth to the disciples through the Holy Spirit, whose post-Pentecost ministry He had been discussing since 15:26. This passage, with its promise of further Spirit-given revelation, is the capstone of that section. It reveals the need, extent, and goal of the Holy Spirit's revelation.

THE NEED FOR THE HOLY SPIRIT'S REVELATION

"I have many more things to say to you, but you cannot bear them now. (16:12)

At first glance it seems surprising that after three years of intensive instruction Jesus would still **have many more things to say to** the disciples (cf. John 21:25). And if He did, why did He not take this opportunity to tell them what they still needed to know? The reason, as the Lord went on to explain, was that they could not **bear** those truths at that time. That was partly because they were overcome with sorrow because He was leaving them (16:6). A more important reason than their sorrow, however, was the disciples' inability to understand the significance of the cross, the resurrection, and the ascension before those events took place.

Like most of their fellow Jews, the disciples viewed the Messiah as a political and military deliverer. They expected Him to drive out the hated Romans, restore Israel's national sovereignty, and bring in the messianic kingdom with the fulfillment of all the Old Testament promises. They simply could not grasp the concept of a dying Messiah, who came not to vanquish the Romans, but to conquer sin and death.

For example after the transfiguration, "as they were coming down from the mountain, [Jesus] gave [Peter, James, and John] orders not to relate to anyone what they had seen, until the Son of Man rose from the dead. They seized upon that statement, discussing with one another what rising from the dead meant" (Mark 9:9–10). Later in that chapter Jesus was "teaching His disciples and telling them, 'The Son of Man is to be delivered into the hands of men, and they will kill Him; and when He has been killed, He will rise three days later." But they did not understand this statement, and they were afraid to ask Him" (vv. 31–32). On the way to Jerusalem for the last time, Jesus

> took the twelve aside and said to them, "Behold, we are going up to Jerusalem, and all things which are written through the prophets about the Son of Man will be accomplished. For He will be handed over to the Gentiles, and will be mocked and mistreated and spit upon, and after they have scourged Him, they will kill Him; and the third day He will rise again." But the disciples understood none of these things, and the meaning of this statement was hidden from them, and they did not comprehend the things that were said. (Luke 18:31–34)

Jesus predicted His resurrection in John 2:15–21. But it was not until "He was raised from the dead, [that] His disciples remembered that He said this; and ...believed the Scripture and the word which Jesus had spoken" (v. 22; cf. 20:9). John 12:16 says concerning the triumphal entry, "These things His disciples did not understand at the first; but when Jesus was glorified, then they remembered that these things were written of Him, and that they had done these things to Him."

Jesus also did not give the disciples further revelation because apart from the Spirit's indwelling, they lacked the power both to grasp and to live out the implications of that revelation. But after the Holy Spirit came on the day of Pentecost, the disciples were ready to receive the further revelation they needed.

THE EXTENT OF THE HOLY SPIRIT'S REVELATION

But when He, the Spirit of truth, comes, He will guide you into all the truth; (16:13a)

The agent of Christ's further revelation to the disciples would be **the Spirit of truth.** In addition to activating Christ' promises in the disciples, convicting the world of sin, and comforting Jesus' followers, the Spirit would also **guide** the disciples **into all the truth.** That promise, like the one in 14:26, refers to the Spirit's supernatural revelation concerning Christ's person and teaching. It serves as the Lord's preauthentication of the New Testament writers; the Holy Spirit, who inspired the Old Testament (see the discussion above), would also inspire the New. In 1 Corinthians 2:9–10 Paul wrote of the Spirit's inspiration of the New Testament writers,

Just as it is written, "Things which eye has not seen and ear has not heard, and which have not entered the heart of man, all that God has prepared for those who love Him." For to us God revealed them through the Spirit; for the Spirit searches all things, even the depths of God.

Only the Holy Spirit, since He is God, knows all that God knows, and thus is qualified to reveal divine truth to man.

Because it is impossible for **the Spirit of truth** to inspire error, the Bible is inerrant (cf. John 17:17). To argue otherwise is an affront to the holy nature of the God who inspired it. Inspiration includes all of Scripture (2 Tim. 3:16), and extends to the very words used by the writers (1 Cor. 2:13; cf. 2 Sam. 23:2). Thus, as R. C. Sproul illustrates, it is absurd to claim to believe in the Bible's inspiration while denying its inerrancy:

> On numerous occasions I have queried several Biblical and theological scholars in the following manner.—"Do you maintain the inerrancy of Scripture?"—"No"—"Do you believe the Bible to be inspired of God?"—"Yes"—"Do you think God inspires error?"—"No"—"Is all of the Bible inspired by God?"—"Yes"—"Is the Bible errant?"—"No!"—"Is it inerrant?"—"No!"— At that point I usually acquire an Excedrin headache. ("The Case for Inerrancy: A Methodological Analysis," in John Warwick Montgomery, ed. *God's Inerrant Word* [Minneapolis: Bethany, 1974], 257)

The Bible's inspiration also excludes all extrabiblical writings; the sixty-six books of the Bible alone comprise God's complete and final revelation to man. The Bible concludes with a solemn warning against tampering with or adding to Scripture:

> I testify to everyone who hears the words of the prophecy of this book: if anyone adds to them, God will add to him the plagues which are written in this book; and if anyone takes away from the words of the book of this prophecy, God will take away his part from the tree of life and from the holy city, which are written in this book. (Rev. 22:18–19; cf. Deut. 4:2; 12:32; Prov. 30:5–6)

Because Revelation describes the entire sweep of history from the end of the apostolic age to the eternal state, to add to it would be to add to Scripture:

> The predictive portions project from John's lifetime all the way into the eternal state. Any type of prophetic utterance would intrude into the domain of this coverage and constitute either an addition to or subtraction from Revelation's content. So the final book of the Bible is also the concluding product of NT prophecy. It also marks the close of the NT canon since the prophetic gift was the divinely chosen means for communicating the inspired books of the canon. (Robert L. Thomas,

> *Revelation 8-22: An Exegetical Commentary* [Chicago: Moody, 1995], 517)

Scripture was given "so that the man of God may be adequate, equipped for every good work" (2 Tim. 3:17); hence there is no need for any further revelation to supplant or supplement it.

The Lord's promise that the Spirit will **guide** believers **into all the truth** has primary reference to the writers of the New Testament. But it also extends in a secondary sense to the Holy Spirit's work of illumination (cf. 1 Cor. 2:10–16). He instructs and teaches believers from the inspired Scriptures, as John notes:

> But you have an anointing from the Holy One, and you all know.... As for you, the anointing which you received from Him abides in you, and you have no need for anyone to teach you; but as His anointing teaches you about all things, and is true and is not a lie, and just as it has taught you, you abide in Him. (1 John 2:20, 27)

That does not, of course, eliminate the need for the diligent study that is a prerequisite for "accurately handling the word of truth" (2 Tim. 2:15), especially since there are things "hard to understand, which the untaught and unstable distort" (2 Peter 3:16). But studying the Bible apart from being filled with the Spirit (Eph. 5:18) and walking in the Spirit (Gal. 5:16, 25) is fruitless.

THE GOAL OF THE SPIRIT'S REVELATION

for He will not speak on His own initiative, but whatever He hears, He will speak; and He will disclose to you what is to come. He will glorify Me, for He will take of Mine and will disclose it to you. All things that the Father has are Mine; therefore I said that He takes of Mine and will disclose it to you." (16:13b–15)

During His incarnation the Lord Jesus Christ did not act on His own initiative, but always did the Father's will (cf. John 5:19; 7:16; 8:26–29; 14:10). In the unfathomable unity of the Trinity, the Spirit likewise **will not speak on His own initiative, but whatever He hears, He will speak.** Like the Son, the Spirit always acts in complete harmony with the Father (cf. Rom. 8:26–27). Thus, the Holy Spirit's leading will always be consistent with God's revealed will in the Bible; He will never lead anyone to violate the principles of God's Word. When He speaks, He speaks through the Scriptures that He inspired. After all, to "be filled with the Spirit" (Eph. 5:18) begins with letting "the word of Christ richly dwell within you" (Col. 3:17; compare Eph. 5:18–6:9 with Col. 3:16–4:1) since the "sword of the Spirit"is"the word of God"(Eph.6:17).

Specifically, the Holy Spirit would **disclose to** the disciples **what is to come.** Like the Lord's earlier promise that the Spirit would guide the disciples into all the truth, that phrase refers primarily to the New Testament. The New Testament encompasses the entire sweep of history from Pentecost to the eternal state, as well as containing "everything pertaining to life and godliness"(2 Peter 1:3).

Having promised that the Spirit would reveal the truth to the disciples, the Lord then gave them the ultimate purpose of the Holy Spirit's revelation. **He will glorify Me,** Jesus said, **for He will take of Mine and will disclose it to you. All things that the Father has are Mine; therefore I said that He takes of Mine and will disclose it to you.** The Holy Spirit's ministry is to **glorify** Jesus Christ by disclosing the truth about Him, just as Christ glorified the Father by revealing Him. He does not point to Himself, but to the Son—a truth some Christian groups miss when they focus more on the gifts and blessings of the Holy Spirit than on the person and work of Jesus Christ.The Spirit

> would not present an independent message, differing from what [the disciples] had already learned from [Christ].They would be led further into the realization of his person and in the development of the principles he had already laid down. They would also be enlightened about coming events. He would unfold the truth as the disciples grew in spiritual capacity and understanding. (Merrill C.Tenney, *The Gospel of John*, in Frank E. Gaebelein, ed. The Expositor's Bible Commentary [Grand Rapids: Zondervan, 1981],9:158)

It is Christ's glory revealed on the pages of Scripture that the Holy Spirit uses to mold believers into the image of Jesus Christ:"But we all, with unveiled face, beholding as in a mirror the glory of the Lord, are being transformed into the same image from glory to glory, just as from the Lord,the Spirit" (2 Cor.3:18;cf.Rom.8:26–30).

If it is the Spirit's purpose to glorify Christ in revelation,how can it be any less our purpose to glorify Christ in proclamation?

Finally,it is the witness of the Holy Spirit that ultimately testifies to the truthfulness of Scripture.Though the coherent unity,scientific accuracy, historical verifiability,and fulfilled prophecy of the Bible all mark it as unique (as noted in the beginning of this chapter), in the end only the Holy Spirit can convince lost sinners of its divine inspiration.The Spirit therefore testifies to the truthfulness of Scripture in the hearts of men. Just as in regeneration (John 3:5–8),the Spirit must work in people's lives for them to change their views of both the Bible (the written Word) and Jesus Christ (the incarnate Word).That sovereign work in the heart and mind convinces men and women that the Bible is from God, that all its words are reliable, and that its message about Jesus Christ is indeed the good news of salvation.

The true believer loves the Word of God (cf. John 8:31–32; 14:15; 2 Thess. 2:10; 1 John 5:2–3) and believes it because of the work of the Spirit (1 Cor. 2:4–5, 14–16; cf. Matt. 16:16–17; John 6:64–70; Rom. 8:5–8; Gal. 1:15–16). Evidences confirm and validate that divine gift of confidence in Holy Scripture.

From Sorrow to Joy
(John 16:16–24)

19

"A little while, and you will no longer see Me; and again a little while, and you will see Me." Some of His disciples then said to one another, "What is this thing He is telling us, 'A little while, and you will not see Me; and again a little while, and you will see Me'; and, 'because I go to the Father'?" So they were saying, "What is this that He says, 'A little while'? We do not know what He is talking about." Jesus knew that they wished to question Him, and He said to them, "Are you deliberating together about this, that I said, 'A little while, and you will not see Me, and again a little while, and you will see Me'? Truly, truly, I say to you, that you will weep and lament, but the world will rejoice; you will grieve, but your grief will be turned into joy. Whenever a woman is in labor she has pain, because her hour has come; but when she gives birth to the child, she no longer remembers the anguish because of the joy that a child has been born into the world. Therefore you too have grief now; but I will see you again, and your heart will rejoice, and no one will take your joy away from you. In that day you will not question Me about anything. Truly, truly, I say to you, if you ask the Father for anything in My name, He will give it to you. Until now you have asked for nothing in My

name; ask and you will receive, so that your joy may be made full." (16:16–24)

Most people can endure a trial if they can see an end. Lack of hope is the ultimate agony of suffering, since "hope deferred makes the heart sick" (Prov. 13:12). In the midst of his trials Job lamented, "My days are swifter than a weaver's shuttle, and come to an end without hope.... Where now is my hope? And who regards my hope? ... He breaks me down on every side, and I am gone; and He has uprooted my hope like a tree" (Job 7:6; 17:15; 19:10). During a time of great personal turmoil, the psalmist challenged his heart with these words, "Why are you in despair, O my soul? And why have you become disturbed within me? Hope in God, for I shall again praise Him for the help of His presence" (Psalm 42:5; cf. Pss. 86:17; 119:76).

Because He is the "God of all comfort," God "comforts [His people] in all [their] affliction" (2 Cor. 1:3–4; cf. Pss. 23:4; 119:50, 52; Isa. 12:1; 40:1; 49:13; 51:3, 12; 61:2; 66:13; Matt. 5:4; Acts 9:31). God comforts His depressed children (2 Cor. 7:6) by affirming that suffering is for their spiritual good and also by reassuring them that their sorrow will only be temporary. Proverbs 23:18 promises, "Surely there is a future, and your hope will not be cut off" (cf. 24:14). Such promises ultimately point to heaven. Though this life may be full of trials, believers can hope with confidence in the eternal rest that awaits them after death (Rev. 21:1–4; cf. Heb. 4:9–11). Despite the many sufferings that the apostle Paul endured (2 Cor. 11:23–28), he expressed his hopeful perspective with these words, "For momentary, light affliction is producing for us an eternal weight of glory far beyond all comparison" (2 Cor. 4:17; cf. 1 Tim. 4:8–10).

During the seventy-year Babylonian captivity (Jer. 29:10; Dan. 9:2), God reminded the people of Israel that their ordeal would one day come to an end. " 'For I know the plans that I have for you,' declares the Lord, 'plans for welfare and not for calamity to give you a future and a hope' " (Jer. 29:11). In Jeremiah 31:17 He added, " 'There is hope for your future,' declares the Lord, 'and your children will return to their own territory.' " During the captivity, recalling God's compassion gave Jeremiah hope:

> This I recall to my mind,
> Therefore I have hope.
> The Lord's lovingkindnesses indeed never cease,
> For His compassions never fail.
> They are new every morning;
> Great is Your faithfulness.
> "The Lord is my portion," says my soul,
> "Therefore I have hope in Him." (Lam. 3:21–24)

During His incarnation, Jesus Christ modeled God's compassion for hurting, sorrowing people. In Matthew 15:32 "Jesus called His disciples to Him, and said, 'I feel compassion for the people, because they have remained with Me now three days and have nothing to eat; and I do not want to send them away hungry, for they might faint on the way.'" "Moved with compassion" at the plight of two blind men, "Jesus touched their eyes; and immediately they regained their sight and followed Him" (Matt. 20:34). Mark 1:41 records that again "moved with compassion, Jesus stretched out His hand and touched [a leper], and said to him, 'I am willing; be cleansed.'" Later in Mark's gospel, "Jesus . . . saw a large crowd, and He felt compassion for them because they were like sheep without a shepherd; and He began to teach them many things" (6:34). Luke 7:12–15 records the Lord's compassionate reaction to the tragedy of a widow who had just lost her only son:

> Now as He approached the gate of the city, a dead man was being carried out, the only son of his mother, and she was a widow; and a sizeable crowd from the city was with her. When the Lord saw her, He felt compassion for her, and said to her, "Do not weep." And He came up and touched the coffin; and the bearers came to a halt. And He said, "Young man, I say to you, arise!" The dead man sat up and began to speak. And Jesus gave him back to his mother.

Because of His perfect and complete love for the disciples (13:1), Jesus selflessly (cf. Phil. 2:3–8) spent much of this final night with them comforting them in their sorrow (cf. 14:1, 18–19, 27; 15:11). Actually, they should have been comforting Him as He faced the ordeal of the cross, now only a matter of hours away. They should also have been glad for Him, since He was returning to His place of glory at the Father's right hand (Acts 2:32–33; 5:31; 7:55–56; Rom. 8:34; Eph. 1:20; Col. 3:1; Heb. 1:3; 8:1; 10:12; 12:2; 1 Peter 3:22). Instead, characteristically viewing events from their own self-centered perspective, the disciples were overwhelmed with grief and a sense of impending loss (cf. 16:6).

Of course, they should have known better. On multiple occasions, Jesus had told them that He would one day die and rise again (Matt. 12:39–40; 16:21; 20:19; Mark 8:31; 9:31; Luke 9:22; 18:33; John 2:18–22). One day, "while they were gathering together in Galilee, Jesus said to them, 'The Son of Man is going to be delivered into the hands of men; and they will kill Him, and He will be raised on the third day'" (Matt. 17:22–23). While on the road to Jerusalem, Jesus similarly told His disciples, "Behold, we are going up to Jerusalem, and the Son of Man will be delivered to the chief priests and the scribes; and they will condemn Him to death and will hand Him over to the Gentiles. They will mock Him and spit on Him, and scourge Him and kill Him, and three days later

He will rise again" (Mark 10:33–34). Though Jesus frequently balanced the news that He would die with the fact that He would rise again, the disciples did not fully understand what the resurrection meant until after it took place. Thus, when He predicted His resurrection in John 2:19, it was not until after "He was raised from the dead, [that] His disciples remembered that He said this; and they believed the Scripture and the word which Jesus had spoken" (John 2:22; cf. Luke 24:8).

Though they had heard His repeated predictions (of both His death and resurrection), the disciples were not ready when the moment for Christ's passion actually came. Thus, as that fateful evening drew to a close, Jesus once again spoke words of comfort to the disciples. He reassured them that their sorrow would be short-lived, predicting that they would soon see Him again. When they reacted to that prediction with uncomprehending perplexity, Jesus illustrated His point with a parable. Then Jesus closed the section by promising the disciples fullness of joy.

THE LORD'S PREDICTION

"A little while, and you will no longer see Me; and again a little while, and you will see Me." (16:16)

The key to understanding this statement lies in correctly interpreting the two uses of the phrase **a little while.** That phrase refers earlier in John's gospel to the time remaining until Jesus' departure, whether that was several months (7:33), or several days (12:35) away. The first reference in this verse looks to the events set in motion by the death of Christ, which would culminate in His ascension. After that brief period, the disciples would **no longer see** Him.

Interpreters disagree over what the second **little while,** after which the disciples would again **see** Jesus, refers to specifically. Some view it as a reference to the second coming, connecting the Lord's illustration of a woman's pain in childbirth (v. 21) with His reference to the birth pangs preceding His return (Matt. 24:8). But the two references illustrate different truths. The birth pains associated with the second coming refer metaphorically to the cataclysmic events of the tribulation. On the other hand, the Lord used childbirth in this passage to show that the same event that initially produces sorrow can ultimately result in joy. Further, it is difficult to stretch the phrase **a little while** from the few days or months of its earlier uses into the more than two thousand years that have elapsed since Christ spoke these words.

Others believe that the Lord's second use of **a little while** points to the three days between His death and resurrection. (Those who hold this view would limit the first use of **a little while** to Christ's death on the cross.) The disciples, of course, were overjoyed and greatly comforted to see Him alive again. But the Lord was only with them for forty days (Acts 1:3) after His resurrection before leaving them again at the ascension. According to this view the disciples' grief would turn to joy, and then back into grief as Jesus left them again. That is hardly the permanent joy Jesus promised them (v. 22).

It seems most accurate to view the Lord's promise that He would see the disciples again primarily as a reference to the coming of His Spirit on the day of Pentecost (cf. 14:16–17, 26; 15:26; 16:7, 13). After accomplishing the work of redemption and ascending to heaven, Jesus sent His Spirit to be with the disciples (cf. 15:26 and the exposition of 16:5–7 in chapter 17 of this volume). Christ came to them through the ministry of the Holy Spirit, who is the "Spirit of Christ" (Rom. 8:9; cf. Gal. 4:6; Phil. 1:19; 1 Peter 1:11) and reveals Christ (John 16:13–15). The Lord's presence with His people through the Spirit is permanent, as His promise, "Lo, I am with you always" (Matt. 28:20), indicates. The sending of the Spirit was to take place after He had ascended to the Father's right hand; it was, He said, "because I go to the Father" (v. 17). This argues for the view just stated.

The Disciples' Perplexity

Some of His disciples then said to one another, "What is this thing He is telling us, 'A little while, and you will not see Me; and again a little while, and you will see Me'; and, 'because I go to the Father'?" So they were saying, "What is this that He says, 'A little while'? We do not know what He is talking about." Jesus knew that they wished to question Him, and He said to them, "Are you deliberating together about this, that I said, 'A little while, and you will not see Me, and again a little while, and you will see Me'? (16:17–19)

The disciples had not been heard from since Judas's question in 14:22, but Jesus' enigmatic statement in verse 16 startled them out of their silence. Unwilling to question Him openly (cf. Mark 9:31–32), perhaps because He had just told them, "I have many more things to say to you, but you cannot bear them now" (v. 12), **some of His disciples then said to one another, "What is this thing He is telling us, 'A little while, and you will not see Me; and again a little while, and you will see Me'; and, 'because I go to the Father'? . . . What is this that He says, 'A little while'? We do not know what He is talking about."** They had a difficult enough time coming to grips with the reality that

Jesus was about to die (see the exposition of 16:12 in chapter 18 of this volume); His words, **'A little while, and you will not see Me; and again a little while, and you will see Me,'** left them utterly bewildered. Adding to their confusion was the Lord's statement **because I go to the Father** (cf. vv. 5, 10; 7:33; 14:12, 28), seemed contradictory. The nineteenth-century Swiss commentator Frederic Louis Godet aptly summarized the disciples' perplexity: "Where for us all is clear, for them all was mysterious. If Jesus wishes to found the Messianic kingdom, why go away? If He does not wish it, why return?" (*Commentary on John's Gospel* [repr.; Grand Rapids: Kregel, 1978], 875).

With His omniscient insight in the hearts of men (cf. 1:47–48; 2:24–25; 4:17–18; 6:64; 21:17; Matt. 12:25; Luke 5:22; 6:8), **Jesus knew that** the disciples **wished to question Him.** Seeking both to alleviate their ignorance and comfort them in their sorrow, Jesus **said to them, "Are you deliberating together about this, that I said, 'A little while, and you will not see Me, and again a little while, and you will see Me'?"** The Lord took the initiative and moved to comfort the disciples by answering their unasked questions. His action is reminiscent of God's words through the prophet Isaiah: "It will also come to pass that before they call, I will answer; and while they are still speaking, I will hear" (Isa. 65:24).

THE ILLUSTRATIVE PARABLE

Truly, truly, I say to you, that you will weep and lament, but the world will rejoice; you will grieve, but your grief will be turned into joy. Whenever a woman is in labor she has pain, because her hour has come; but when she gives birth to the child, she no longer remembers the anguish because of the joy that a child has been born into the world. Therefore you too have grief now; but I will see you again, and your heart will rejoice, and no one will take your joy away from you. (16:20–22)

The solemn phrase *amēn amēn* (**truly, truly**) underscores the importance of what the Lord was about to **say to** the disciples (cf. v. 23; 1:51; 3:3, 5, 11; 5:19, 24, 25; 6:26, 32, 47, 53; 8:34, 51, 58; 10:1, 7; 12:24; 13:16, 20, 21, 38; 14:12; 21:18). Jesus' followers would soon **weep and lament** over His death (cf. 20:11; Luke 24:17–21) but **the world,** the Jewish leaders, and the apostate nation which had so bitterly opposed Him would **rejoice.**

But Christ's enemies' joy over His death would be short-lived. The Jewish leaders had mockingly promised to believe in Jesus if He came down from the cross (Matt. 27:42). But when He did the far greater miracle of rising from the dead, they refused to believe. Instead, they hastily concocted a scheme to cover up the resurrection, bribing the soldiers to spread the lie that Jesus' body had been stolen while they were sleeping (Matt. 28:11–15). Then the Jewish leaders tried desperately, but futilely, to suppress the apostles from preaching the resurrection (Acts 4:1–21; 5:17–18, 27–42).

While the world's joy over Christ's death would turn to dismay, just the opposite would be the case with the disciples. **Your grief,** Jesus assured them, **will be turned into joy.** The Lord was not saying that the event causing their sorrow would be replaced by an event producing joy but rather that the same event (the cross) that caused their mourning would be the cause of their joy. The dark shadows of sorrow and grief cast by the cross fled before the brilliant, glorious light of the resurrection and the coming of the Spirit on the day of Pentecost (Acts 2:4–47). That light also caused the disciples to view the cross in its proper perspective, making it an unending source of joy for them (cf. v. 22; Acts 13:52). As Paul exulted, "But may it never be that I would boast, except in the cross of our Lord Jesus Christ, through which the world has been crucified to me, and I to the world" (Gal. 6:14). The cross is foundational to all Christian joy, because it is the basis of redemption.

A vivid example of an event that initially causes pain but ultimately brings joy is childbirth. The reality that **a woman . . . in labor . . . has pain** stems from the Edenic curse that God pronounced on Eve in the aftermath of the fall. Genesis 3:16 records that "to the woman [God] said, 'I will greatly multiply Your pain in childbirth, in pain you shall bring forth children'" (cf. Ps. 48:6; Isa. 13:8; 21:3; 26:17; Jer. 4:31; 6:24; 22:23; 49:24; 50:43; Mic. 4:9–10; 1 Thess. 5:3). Yet after a woman **gives birth to the child, she no longer remembers the anguish** she has been through. The intense **anguish** and suffering of labor in giving birth fades in the face of the consuming joy **that a child has been born into the world.**

In the same way though the disciples would **have grief** in the short-term, they could take comfort in the Lord's promise, **I will see you again, and your heart will rejoice.** In verses 16 and 19 Jesus spoke of the disciples seeing Him; here He told them that He will see them. His knowledge of believers is more important than and foundational to their knowledge of Him. "You have come to know God," Paul wrote, "or rather to be known by God" (Gal. 4:9). The reality that **no one will take** the disciples' **joy away from** them indicates that more than just seeing Jesus after the resurrection is in view, since that lasted only forty days. The Lord's reference, as noted above, is to the coming of the Spirit on the day of Pentecost to permanently indwell them. The disciples' Spirit-produced joy (Gal. 5:22; cf. Rom. 14:17; 1 Thess. 1:6) would be permanent. Nothing can undo the work of grace wrought in believers' lives through the power of the cross.

THE BLESSED PROMISE

"In that day you will not question Me about anything. Truly, truly, I say to you, if you ask the Father for anything in My name, He will give it to you. Until now you have asked for nothing in My name; ask and you will receive, so that your joy may be made full." (16:23–24)

In the **day** when the disciples see the Lord again (v. 23) and their sorrow turns to joy, they **will not question** Him **about anything.** That further suggests that the **day** cannot be the resurrection (cf. the discussion of v. 16 above). The disciples undoubtedly asked many questions during the forty days between the resurrection and the ascension that the Lord spent "speaking of the things concerning the kingdom of God" (Acts 1:3; one of their questions is recorded in v. 6). But after the coming of the Holy Spirit on the day of Pentecost, they would no longer question Jesus.

Obviously Jesus, having ascended to heaven, would no longer be physically present for them to question. But more significantly, the disciples would have the indwelling Holy Spirit as their resident truth teacher. Jesus had just finished telling them, "When He, the Spirit of truth, comes, He will guide you into all the truth; for He will not speak on His own initiative, but whatever He hears, He will speak; and He will disclose to you what is to come" (v. 13; cf. 14:26). In his first epistle John wrote,

> But you have an anointing from the Holy One, and you all know.... As for you, the anointing which you received from Him abides in you, and you have no need for anyone to teach you; but as His anointing teaches you about all things, and is true and is not a lie, and just as it has taught you, you abide in Him. (1 John 2:20, 27).

The disciples would at long last understand why Jesus had to die (cf. Luke 9:44–45), His relationship with the Father would be clarified (cf. John 14:8–9), and they would realize why it was to their advantage for Him to go away and send the Spirit (John 16:7). All of this clarification of the cross and resurrection by the Holy Spirit is contained in the rest of the inspired New Testament.

The phrase **truly, truly** introduces another important truth (cf. the discussion of v. 20 above); namely, that if the disciples **ask the Father for anything in** Christ's name, **He** [the Father] **will give it to** them. This is the third time that evening that the Lord stated that truth (cf. 14:13; 15:16), underscoring its immense significance. As noted in the exposition of 14:13–14 in chapter 9 of this volume, to pray in Jesus' name is not to use His name as a formula, ritualistically tacked onto the end of a prayer to ensure its success. Rather, it is to pray for that which is consistent with Christ's person and will, and to affirm one's complete dependence on Him to supply every need, with the goal that He would be glorified in the answer. Such prayer was new to the disciples, who **until** that point had **asked for nothing in** Jesus' **name.** They had either asked Jesus Himself, or prayed to the Father. But now Jesus urged them, **Ask and you will receive,** and then added the blessed promise **so that your joy may be made full.** Answered prayer, based on the finished work of Jesus Christ and springing from an obedient life (15:10–11), is a powerful force in turning sorrow into joy.

Even in the face of His own unimaginable sufferings, Jesus compassionately countered the anxiety of His disciples with comfort and hope. He promised them that the pain of the moment would result in their profound joy; and also assured them that though He was going away, they would see Him again soon in the arrival of the Holy Spirit. Though He would shortly ascend to the Father, He would be with them "always, even to the end of the age" (Matt. 28:20).

Three Cardinal Christian Virtues
(John 16:25–33)

20

"These things I have spoken to you in figurative language; an hour is coming when I will no longer speak to you in figurative language, but will tell you plainly of the Father. In that day you will ask in My name, and I do not say to you that I will request of the Father on your behalf; for the Father Himself loves you, because you have loved Me and have believed that I came forth from the Father. I came forth from the Father and have come into the world; I am leaving the world again and going to the Father." His disciples said, "Lo, now You are speaking plainly and are not using a figure of speech. Now we know that You know all things, and have no need for anyone to question You; by this we believe that You came from God." Jesus answered them, "Do you now believe? Behold, an hour is coming, and has already come, for you to be scattered, each to his own home, and to leave Me alone; and yet I am not alone, because the Father is with Me. These things I have spoken to you, so that in Me you may have peace. In the world you have tribulation, but take courage; I have overcome the world." (16:25–33)

Because God is the God of truth (Ex. 34:6; 2 Sam. 7:28) who cannot lie (Titus 1:2; Heb. 6:18), it follows that His Word is also true and free from error—being absolutely right in all it commands and accurate in all it describes (Ps. 119:142; John 17:17). It is true not only when it speaks to spiritual and moral issues, but also in matters of science and history. The God who created this universe (Gen. 1:1; Acts 17:24–25) and who orchestrates human history for His purposes (Isa. 46:10; Acts 17:26) is the same God who has revealed Himself in the Scriptures. There is therefore a unified field of knowledge between the general revelation of the Creator God found in the natural world (cf. Ps. 19:1–6) and the revelation of His plan of salvation and judgment found in the Bible (cf. Ps. 19:7–10). Because God is its author, His Word reveals His perfection and carries His authority, meaning that the truth it reveals is absolute.

But postmodernism rejects that concept. One of the legacies of the rationalism crafted by the Enlightenment philosophers has been the artificial division of the realm of truth into two completely separate spheres. On the one hand is the world of facts, of objective, public knowledge that is binding on all and is verifiable rationally. On the other hand is the realm of values, which postmodernism views as private, subjective matters of personal preference, neither necessarily rational nor verifiable. The former realm encompasses science, history, and autonomous human reason. Religion, morality, and the arts are relegated to the private realm of values; they are seen as nothing more than culturally conditioned preferences, with no right to be considered either objective or universally binding.

This divided view of truth has created a profound intellectual schizophrenia in modern man. Scientific naturalism tells him he is nothing more than a sophisticated biochemical machine, with a mind that is nothing more than a "three-pound computer made of meat," as one scientist put it. But that notion does not find resonance in the human mind because men are made in the image of God, and cannot live consistently with such a materialistic, mechanistic view of themselves. They cannot stop behaving as though people have value and dignity, and the freedom to make choices—even though such beliefs contradict their naturalistic worldview. As Nancy Pearcey explains,

> The postmodern dilemma can be summed up by saying that ethics depends on the *reality* of something that materialistic science has declared to be *unreal*....This is the tragedy of the postmodern age: The things that matter most in life—freedom and dignity, meaning and significance—have been reduced to nothing but useful fictions. Wishful thinking. Irrational mysticism. (*Total Truth* [Wheaton: Crossway, 2005], 107, 110. Italics in original.)

The consequence of it all is a bleak world of hopelessness and despair. People yearn for the very significance, meaning, and purpose in their lives that their worldview cannot offer them. As a result, they resort to irrational "leaps of faith," searching desperately for some experience, feeling, intuition, or idea to believe in and to live for, to give them hope and meaning. But all they succeed in doing is hewing out for themselves "broken cisterns that can hold no water" (Jer. 2:13). The worldly pleasures they tirelessly pursue can never satisfy them (cf. Eccl. 2:1–26). Real hope, the experience of genuine love, and a true sense of purpose in life come only through believing in "the glorious gospel of the blessed God" (1 Tim. 1:11).

Faith, hope, and love are thus central to the Christian faith. It is that triad of Christian virtues (cf. 1 Cor. 13:13; 1 Thess. 1:3; 5:8) that underlies the closing words of the Lord Jesus Christ's final teaching time with His disciples. As He continued to comfort the disciples, Jesus reassured them of the Father's love for them, bolstered their sagging faith, and held out the hope of their ultimate victory over the trials and tribulations they would face.

LOVE

"These things I have spoken to you in figurative language; an hour is coming when I will no longer speak to you in figurative language, but will tell you plainly of the Father. In that day you will ask in My name, and I do not say to you that I will request of the Father on your behalf; for the Father Himself loves you, because you have loved Me." (16:25–27*a*)

During their time with Jesus, the disciples had often failed to understand Him. Several illustrations make this point. On one occasion, after He told them that "it is not what enters into the mouth that defiles the man, but what proceeds out of the mouth, this defiles the man" (Matt. 15:11), "Peter," speaking for the rest, "said to Him, 'Explain the parable to us'" (v. 15). That prompted the Lord's rebuke, "Are you still lacking in understanding also?" (v. 16). Matthew 16 records another example of their miscomprehension. On that occasion "the disciples came to the other side of the sea, but they had forgotten to bring any bread," an oversight that caused them to misunderstand Jesus' warning, "Watch out and beware of the leaven of the Pharisees and Sadducees" (vv. 5–6). Missing the point entirely, "they began to discuss this among themselves, saying, 'He said that because we did not bring any bread'" (v. 7). Rebuking them for their obtuseness, Jesus said to them,

> You men of little faith, why do you discuss among yourselves that you have no bread? Do you not yet understand or remember the five loaves of the five thousand, and how many baskets full you picked up? Or the seven loaves of the four thousand, and how many large baskets full you picked up? How is it that you do not understand that I did not speak to you concerning bread? But beware of the leaven of the Pharisees and Sadducees. (vv. 8–11)

It was only then that they "understood that He did not say to beware of the leaven of bread, but of the teaching of the Pharisees and Sadducees" (v. 12).

Again, "as they were coming down from the mountain [after the transfiguration], He gave [to Peter, James, and John] orders not to relate to anyone what they had seen, until the Son of Man rose from the dead. They seized upon that statement, discussing with one another what rising from the dead meant" (Mark 9:9–10). Speaking of His impending death, Jesus told the disciples, "The Son of Man is to be delivered into the hands of men, and they will kill Him; and when He has been killed, He will rise three days later" (Mark 9:31). But, typically, "they did not understand this statement, and they were afraid to ask Him" (v. 32).

Earlier in John's gospel, there is another time when the disciples failed to grasp the significance of the Lord's declaration. He said, "Destroy this temple, and in three days I will raise it up" (John 2:19). It was not until Jesus "was raised from the dead [that] His disciples remembered that He said this; and . . . believed the Scripture and the word which Jesus had spoken" (v. 22). Additionally, they failed to grasp the significance of the triumphal entry, "but when Jesus was glorified, then they remembered that these things were written of Him, and that they had done these things to Him" (John 12:16). Just a few moments earlier that very evening, the disciples had been baffled by Jesus' statements, " 'A little while, and you will not see Me; and again a little while, and you will see Me'; and, 'because I go to the Father.' " So they were saying, "What is this that He says, 'A little while'? We do not know what He is talking about" (16:17–18).

On some occasions the disciples' initial lack of understanding was due to the fact that the Lord had **spoken to** them **in figurative language.** *Paroimia* (**figurative language**) refers to veiled, pointed, enigmatic, cryptic sayings—statements for which the meaning is not immediately apparent, but must be diligently searched out. The purpose for such sayings was to judgmentally and mercifully (cf. Luke 12:47–48) veil the truth from unbelievers, who are spiritually blind as a result of their own unbelief and rebellion (cf. Matt. 15:14; 23:16–26; John 9:39–41; Eph. 2:1–3). When the disciples asked Him, "Why do You speak to them in parables?" (Matt. 13:10), Jesus replied,

> To you it has been granted to know the mysteries of the kingdom of heaven, but to them it has not been granted. For whoever has, to him more shall be given, and he will have an abundance; but whoever does not have, even what he has shall be taken away from him. Therefore I speak to them in parables; because while seeing they do not see, and while hearing they do not hear, nor do they understand. In their case the prophecy of Isaiah is being fulfilled, which says, "You will keep on hearing, but will not understand; you will keep on seeing, but will not perceive; for the heart of this people has become dull, with their ears they scarcely hear, and they have closed their eyes, otherwise they would see with their eyes, hear with their ears, and understand with their heart and return, and I would heal them." (vv. 11–15; cf. vv. 34–35)

Even the disciples, as noted above, failed to understand much of Jesus' teaching until He explained it to them (cf. Matt. 13:36–43). It was not until after Christ's death and the coming of the Spirit that things hard for the disciples to understand during His life became clear. They actually understood Jesus' ministry and teaching better then than they had when He was with them. In their post-Pentecost Spirit-empowered ministry, they unfolded the teachings of Christ and expounded the rich truths of His person and work.

Then Jesus promised them that **an hour** was **coming when** He would **no longer speak to** them **in figurative language.** The disciples, before the cross, were unable to fully grasp the profound significance of the Son's work of redemption. Nor did they comprehend the depth of the Father's love expressed in sending the Son to die as a sacrifice for sin (see the discussion of 16:12 in chapter 18 of this volume). But in that future **hour** (the coming of the Spirit at Pentecost), the veil would be lifted and Jesus would **tell** them **plainly of the Father.** The disciples would understand more fully Jesus' relationship to the Father (cf. Matt. 11:27; John 1:1–2, 18; 3:35; 5:17–20, 36–37, 43; 6:27, 46, 57; 8:16–19, 28, 38, 42, 54; 10:15, 17–18, 25, 30, 38; 12:49–50; 13:1; 14:6–12, 20, 28, 31; 15:9–10, 15; 16:15; 17:5, 21, 24–25; 20:21) and the Father's love for them (cf. John 14:21, 23; 16:27; Rom. 5:8; 8:15; Gal. 4:6; Heb. 1:1–3; 1 John 3:1; 4:10).

In that day, Jesus promised, **you will ask in My name, and I do not say to you that I will request of the Father on your behalf; for the Father Himself loves you, because you have loved Me.** That statement clarifies what it means to pray in Jesus' **name** (cf. the expositions of 14:13–14; 15:16; and 16:23–24 in previous chapters of this volume). It does not mean that believers ask Jesus to **request of the Father on** their **behalf,** as though the Father were indifferent to their requests. If that were all that praying in the name of Jesus meant, it would be an inestimable privilege. But the full privilege believers have is that of making their requests directly to the Father consistent with the will of the

Son. They have that privilege because **the Father Himself loves** them, **because** they **have loved** Christ—love that they demonstrate through their obedience to Him (John 3:36; 14:21, 23; Heb. 5:9; James 2:14–26; 1 Peter 1:1–2. For a thorough discussion of the relationship of obedience to saving faith, see my books *The Gospel According to Jesus*, rev. ed. [Grand Rapids: Zondervan, 1994], and *The Gospel According to the Apostles* [Nashville: Thomas Nelson, 1993, 2000]).

One of the horrendous falsehoods of Roman Catholicism is that God is indifferent and harsh, Jesus is committed to justice, but Mary is compassionate, as are the lesser saints. Thus, to appeal to them is best. That is a lie, since believers have direct access to their Father, who loves them because they are in Jesus Christ (1 John 4:10, 19), who also loves them perfectly (John 13:1). According to Paul it is "in Christ Jesus our Lord in whom we have boldness and confident access through faith in Him . . . . for through Him we both have our access in one Spirit to the Father" (Eph. 3:11–12; 2:18). The writer of Hebrews exhorted his readers,

> Therefore, since we have a great high priest who has passed through the heavens, Jesus the Son of God, let us hold fast our confession. For we do not have a high priest who cannot sympathize with our weaknesses, but One who has been tempted in all things as we are, yet without sin. Therefore let us draw near with confidence to the throne of grace, so that we may receive mercy and find grace to help in time of need. (Heb. 4:14–16)

> Therefore, brethren, since we have confidence to enter the holy place by the blood of Jesus, by a new and living way which He inaugurated for us through the veil, that is, His flesh, and since we have a great priest over the house of God, let us draw near with a sincere heart in full assurance of faith, having our hearts sprinkled clean from an evil conscience and our bodies washed with pure water. (Heb. 10:19–22)

The tearing of the veil in front of the Holy of Holies (Matt. 27:51) symbolized that the way into God's presence stands open through the death of Christ.

The biblical doctrine of the priesthood of all believers (1 Peter 2:9; Rev. 1:6) eliminates the need to go through intermediaries—such as Mary, the saints, or human priests—to obtain access to the Father. The great Reformer Martin Luther assaulted the Roman counterfeit when he wrote, "It says in 1 Peter 2:9, 'Ye are an elect race, a royal priesthood, and a priestly kingdom.' It follows that all of us who are Christians are also priests" ("The Pagan Servitude of the Church," in John Dillenberger, *Martin Luther: Selections from His Writings* [Garden City, N.Y.: Anchor, 1961], 345). That Christians have direct priestly access to the Father does not, however, obviate the need for Christ's intercession on their behalf as their Great High Priest (Isa. 53:12; Rom. 8:34; Heb. 7:25; cf. 1 John 2:1–2).

As noted above, the Father's motive for allowing believers access to Him is that He **loves** them. **Loves** translates a form of the verb *phileō*, which is the love of deep, caring affection. It is the love of emotion, which is consistent with *agapaō*, which is the love of the will. *Phileō* describes the love of parents for their children and children for their parents (Matt. 10:37) and of friends for each other (John 11:3, 36). God loves (*agapaō*) sinners (John 3:16), but expresses a special, fatherly affection (*phileō*) for His children—so much so that He sent His Son to die as the sacrifice for their sins (Rom. 5:8; 1 John 4:9–10). Because of that they can boldly and fearlessly enter His presence in complete confidence, as children for whom He cares deeply (cf. Rom. 8:15; Gal. 4:6).

FAITH

and have believed that I came forth from the Father. I came forth from the Father and have come into the world; I am leaving the world again and going to the Father." His disciples said, "Lo, now You are speaking plainly and are not using a figure of speech. Now we know that You know all things, and have no need for anyone to question You; by this we believe that You came from God." Jesus answered them, "Do you now believe? Behold, an hour is coming, and has already come, for you to be scattered, each to his own home, and to leave Me alone; and yet I am not alone, because the Father is with Me. (16:27*b*–32)

Despite whatever pessimism or skepticism they may have about ultimate truth, all people exercise a great measure of human faith in the mundane matters of everyday life. People trust that the food they eat, the water they drink, and the medicine they take is safe, that the planes they board will not crash during flight nor land in the wrong city, and that the houses they live in will not suddenly collapse. On a higher level, people believe in love, themselves, money, or even in some sort of nebulous higher power. Oliver Wendell Holmes's vague statement, "It's faith in something and enthusiasm for something that makes life worth living," is the flimsy credo of many, if not most, in this culture.

But in contrast to such aimless and contentless fatuity, the believer's faith is firmly rooted in the love of God manifested in the person of Jesus Christ and recorded in Scripture. The Lord's words **I came forth from the Father and have come into the world** express the central doctrines of the Christian faith. That He **came forth from the Father** (cf. Matt. 10:40; Mark 9:37; John 4:34; 5:24, 30; 6:38, 39, 44; 7:29, 33; 8:26, 29; 9:4; 12:44; 13:20; 16:5; 17:18, 21, 23) affirms Christ's deity (John 1:1, 14), and apart from embracing that doctrine, no one can be saved. (For a defense of the deity of Christ, see *John 1–11* [Chicago: Moody, 2006], chaps. 1, 15). Jesus warned those who rejected Him, "Therefore I said to you that you will die in your sins; for unless you believe that I am He [i.e., Yahweh of the Old Testament; cf. Ex. 3:14] you will die in your sins" (John 8:24). To reject the biblical truth that Jesus Christ is God in human flesh is to believe in another false and damning gospel (Gal. 1:6–9). It is to be satanically deceived and "led astray from the simplicity and purity of devotion to Christ" (2 Cor. 11:3) and to believe in "another Jesus" whom the apostles did not preach (v. 4). In his first epistle John wrote,

> Who is the liar but the one who denies that Jesus is the Christ? This is the antichrist, the one who denies the Father and the Son. Whoever denies the Son does not have the Father; the one who confesses the Son has the Father also. ... every spirit that does not confess Jesus is not from God. (1 John 2:22–23; 4:3)

In his second epistle the apostle added, "For many deceivers have gone out into the world, those who do not acknowledge Jesus Christ as coming in the flesh. This is the deceiver and the antichrist" (2 John 7). The church is to not embrace those who propagate such heretical teaching:

> Anyone who goes too far and does not abide in the teaching of Christ, does not have God; the one who abides in the teaching, he has both the Father and the Son. If anyone comes to you and does not bring this teaching, do not receive him into your house, and do not give him a greeting; for the one who gives him a greeting participates in his evil deeds. (vv. 9–11)

In contrast to the disciples, the Jewish authorities vehemently refused to believe that Jesus was sent by the Father (cf. John 8:14; 9:29) and placed themselves under the judgment of God.

The reason Christ came **into the world** was to do the work of redemption. Before His birth the angel told His earthly father, Joseph, "[Mary] will bear a Son; and you shall call His name Jesus, for He will save His people from their sins" (Matt. 1:21). The Lord defined His mission when He said, "The Son of Man has come to seek and to save that which was lost" (Luke 9:10), and, "The Son of Man did not come to be served, but to serve, and to give His life a ransom for many" (Matt. 20:28). A few days earlier at the triumphal entry, Jesus had said, "Now My soul has become troubled; and what shall I say, 'Father, save Me from this hour'? But for this purpose I came to this hour .... I did not come to judge the world, but to save the world" (John 12:27, 47).

The rest of the New Testament reiterates the truth that Christ came to redeem lost sinners. John wrote, "By this the love of God was manifested in us, that God has sent His only begotten Son into the world so that we might live through Him. . . . We have seen and testify that the Father has sent the Son to be the Savior of the world" (1 John 4:9, 14). "It is a trustworthy statement, deserving full acceptance," Paul affirmed, "that Christ Jesus came into the world to save sinners" (1 Tim. 1:15). To the Galatians he wrote, "But when the fullness of the time came, God sent forth His Son, born of a woman, born under the Law, so that He might redeem those who were under the Law, that we might receive the adoption as sons" (Gal. 4:4–5).

The Lord's statement, **I am leaving the world again and going to the Father,** completes a remarkably concise summary of the gospel in verse 28. Jesus, God the Son, was sent into the world by the Father to accomplish the work of redemption, and having done so, returned to His place of full glory with the Father. Jesus longed to return to the Father, and often spoke of it (e.g., John 7:33; 14:12, 28; 16:5, 10; 17:11, 13; cf. 13:3).

The **disciples'** reply, **"Lo, now You are speaking plainly and are not using a figure of speech,"** suggests that at long last they were beginning to understand. The plan of redemption was becoming clear; the time when the Lord would speak **plainly** to them (see the discussion of v. 25 above) was drawing near. Already He had spoken to them of His origin, His mission, His return to the Father, the Father's love for them, and their access to Him. Jesus had done so directly and without **using a figure of speech.** Their confident assertion, **Now we know that You know all things, and have no need for anyone to question You; by this we believe that You came from God,** is far more than an affirmation of their appreciation for the Lord's teaching. It is nothing less than a full affirmation of Christ's omniscience and hence His deity. It represents the apex of the disciples' recognition of Jesus as a member of the Godhead.

Yet the disciples' bold notion that all questions had been answered was premature, since the complete revelation of Christ's person and work awaited the coming of the Spirit at Pentecost. John Calvin notes, "The disciples certainly did not yet understand fully what Christ had been saying; but although they were not yet capable of this, the mere scent of it refreshed them" (*John,* The Crossway Classic Commentaries [Wheaton: Crossway, 1994], 386). William Hendriksen adds,

> The light is shining brightly now, more brightly, perhaps, than ever before. Within a few hours it will be obscured once more. Yet, the confession which is here made will linger on in the realm of the subconscious, until by and by, when the Lord arises in triumph from the tomb and (a little later) pours out his Spirit, it will bear the fruit of calm and steadfast assurance, and this fruit will abide forever. (*New Testament*

Commentary: The Gospel of John, vol. 2 [Grand Rapids: Baker, 1954], 340)

Knowing their hearts, **Jesus answered them, "Do you now believe?"** The Lord's poignant question underscored that the disciples' faith, though genuine (cf. 17:8), was still immature. The sad reality was that only a few hours later they would all forsake Him and **be scattered, each to his own home, and . . . leave** Him **alone** (Matt. 26:56; cf. v. 31; Zech. 13:7). But after the Spirit came, the disciples would courageously proclaim the truth about Jesus Christ (e.g., Acts 2:22–36; 3:12–26) despite fierce opposition (e.g., Acts 4:1–21; 5:17–40).

Although the disciples would **leave** Him **alone,** Jesus would **not** be **alone** at all, **because the Father** was ever **with** Him (cf. 8:29)— except when He was bearing sin on the cross. The reality that God "made Him who knew no sin to be sin on our behalf, so that we might become the righteousness of God in Him" (2 Cor. 5:21), caused Jesus to cry out, "My God, My God, why have You forsaken Me?" (Matt. 27:46). In that moment, "the Lord was pleased to crush Him" because He was "render[ing] Himself as a guilt offering" (Isa. 53:10). Thus "He Himself bore the sin of many, and interceded for the transgressors" (v. 12) such that many have been justified because He paid the penalty for their iniquities (v. 11).

HOPE

These things I have spoken to you, so that in Me you may have peace. In the world you have tribulation, but take courage; I have overcome the world. (16:33)

Understanding God's love and placing one's faith in Him—the **things** of which Christ had just **spoken to** the disciples—brings **peace** despite the hostility of the **world** and the relentless **tribulation** it brings. These words were spoken just one evening after our Lord had told the disciples how much tribulation there was to be in the world before His return:

And He said, "See to it that you are not misled; for many will come in My name, saying, 'I am He,' and, 'The time is near.' Do not go after them. When you hear of wars and disturbances, do not be terrified; for these things must take place first, but the end does not follow immediately." Then He continued by saying to them, "Nation will rise against nation and kingdom against kingdom, and there will be great earthquakes, and in various places plagues and famines; and there will be terrors and great signs from heaven. But before all these things, they will lay their hands on you and will persecute you, delivering you to the synagogues and prisons, bringing you before kings and governors for My name's sake. It will lead to an opportunity for your testimony. So make up your minds not to prepare beforehand to defend yourselves; for I will give you utterance and wisdom which none of your opponents will be able to resist or refute. But you will be betrayed even by parents and brothers and relatives and friends, and they will put some of you to death, and you will be hated by all because of My name. Yet not a hair of your head will perish. By your endurance you will gain your lives. But when you see Jerusalem surrounded by armies, then recognize that her desolation is near. Then those who are in Judea must flee to the mountains, and those who are in the midst of the city must leave, and those who are in the country must not enter the city; because these are days of vengeance, so that all things which are written will be fulfilled. Woe to those who are pregnant and to those who are nursing babies in those days; for there will be great distress upon the land and wrath to this people; and they will fall by the edge of the sword, and will be led captive into all the nations; and Jerusalem will be trampled under foot by the Gentiles until the times of the Gentiles are fulfilled." (Luke 21:8–24)

Still, in the midst of all that, believers will enjoy divine **peace.** That is more than enough reason to **take courage** and have hope. The believer's hope is in the Lord (Pss. 31:24; 38:15; 39:7; 42:5, 11; 43:5; 62:5; 71:5; 130:7; 146:5; Lam. 3:24; 1 Tim. 1:1), His Word (Pss. 119:49; 130:5; Rom. 15:4), the salvation He provides (Ps. 119:166; Eph. 1:18; 4:4; Titus 1:2), and the eternal glory that awaits in heaven (Col. 1:5, 27; 1 Thess. 5:8). That hope is made possible because Jesus Christ has **overcome the world** and conquered sin (John 1:29; Heb. 1:3; 9:26, 28; 1 Peter 2:24; 1 John 3:5; Rev. 1:5), death (John 14:19; 1 Cor. 15:26, 54–55; 2 Tim. 1:10), and Satan (Gen. 3:15; Col. 2:15; Heb. 2:14; 1 John 3:8). In Him, Christians too are overcomers (Rom. 8:37; 1 John 4:4; 5:4–5; Rev. 2:7, 11, 17, 26; 3:5, 12, 21; 21:7), for whom the Lord will work all things to their good (Rom. 8:28).

After the resurrection and the coming of the Spirit on the day of Pentecost, the disciples would be radically transformed from men of fear to men of courage. Though they abandoned Jesus on the night of His arrest, they would boldly stand before the Jewish leaders less than two months later. In Acts 2, the Twelve (with Matthias replacing Judas Iscariot) "were all filled with the Holy Spirit and began to speak with other tongues as the Spirit was giving them utterance" (v. 4). None other than Peter, who had denied Christ on three occasions (Mark 14:66–72), publicly took "his stand with the eleven, raised his voice and declared" to the crowds in Jerusalem that they should repent (v. 14; cf. v. 42). A little while later, he and John healed a lame man in the temple (Acts 3:6) and boldly preached the gospel there (vv. 11–26). They were quickly arrested and brought before the Sanhedrin. But instead of cowering in fear, they bravely proclaimed the truth to the same Jewish leaders who had crucified Jesus. "There is salvation in no one else," declared Peter of Christ. "For there is no other name under heaven that has been given among men by which we must be saved" (Acts 4:12). Noting his courage, the Jewish leaders were astonished. "Now as they observed the confidence of Peter and John and understood that they were uneducated and untrained men, they were amazed" (v. 13).

That same supernatural courage and boldness is reflected in the examples of Stephen (Acts 7:54–60), Philip (8:5, 26–30), Ananias (9:10–19), Barnabas (13:46), Silas (16:25), Apollos (18:25–26), and Paul (26:19–21). Filled with the Holy Spirit and marked by personal conviction, these men were not intimidated by the threats of the world. Instead, they bravely proclaimed the truth of the gospel and rejoiced when they were persecuted (cf. 5:41), being confident of the promise that "greater is He who is in you than he who is in the world" (1 John 4:4).

The peace and hope that characterized them is the same that has characterized true believers in every age. Being assured of what they believed and hoped for, and convinced of what they did not see (cf. Heb. 11:1), the saints of old "were stoned, they were sawn in two, they were tempted, they were put to death with the sword; they went about in sheepskins, in goatskins, being destitute, afflicted, ill-treated (men of whom the world was not worthy), wandering in deserts and mountains and caves and holes in the ground" (vv. 37–38). Believers today can find that same courage of conviction when their "faith and hope are in God" (1 Peter 1:21). They need not fear persecution or even death, because they know "the God of hope" (Rom. 15:13) and Jesus Christ, "the hope of glory" (Col. 1:27; cf. 1 Tim. 1:1). Having trusted in the death and resurrection of Christ, they are eternally secure in His love—knowing that "neither death, nor life, nor angels, nor principalities, nor things present, nor things to come, nor powers, nor height, nor depth, nor any other created thing, will be able to separate [believers] from the love of God, which is in Christ Jesus [their] Lord" (Rom. 8:38–39).

Significantly, Jesus' last words to His disciples in the upper room, before praying for them and departing for Gethsemane, were words of love, faith, and hope. In the face of their greatest trial in the next few days, the Lord reminded them of those three foundational truths—truths that would subsequently mark their ministries for the rest of their lives and also mark all the saints to follow them. Having done all He could to prepare them for what was about to take place, Jesus now turned in prayer to His Father, knowing that only He could truly protect the disciples in the following hours.

The Real Lord's Prayer (John 17:1)

21

Jesus spoke these things; and lifting up His eyes to heaven, He said, "Father, the hour has come; glorify Your Son, that the Son may glorify You" (17:1)

"A godly man cannot live without prayer," wrote the seventeenth-century English Puritan Thomas Watson. "A man cannot live unless he takes his breath, nor can the soul, unless it breathes forth its desires to God" (*The Godly Man's Picture* [repr.; Edinburgh: Banner of Truth, 1992], 88). Prayer expresses the soul's longing for God (Pss. 42:1–2; 63:1; 143:6); it is the cry (Pss. 34:15, 17; 86:3) of God's people to their gracious, compassionate (Ex. 34:6; 2 Chron. 30:9; Neh. 9:17; Ps. 103:8) heavenly Father (Matt. 6:6, 9; 7:11).

The Bible both commands prayer (e.g., Jer. 33:3; Matt. 6:5–13; Luke 6:28; 18:1; Rom. 12:12; Eph. 6:18; Phil. 4:6; Col. 4:2; 1 Thess. 5:17; 1 Tim. 2:1, 8; 1 Peter 4:7; Jude 20) and records examples of the prayers of godly people.

In the Old Testament Abraham prayed for his son Ishmael (Gen. 17:18), for Abimelech (Gen. 20:17), and for God to spare Sodom (Gen. 18:23–32). Abraham's servant prayed for guidance in finding a wife for Isaac (Gen. 24:12–14). When Rebekah was barren, Isaac prayed that the

Lord would open her womb (Gen. 25:21). Jacob prayed that God would protect him from Esau (Gen. 32:9–12). Moses prayed that God would spare rebellious Israel (Ex. 32:11–14, 31–32; Num. 14:13–19; Deut. 9:26–29), and for Miriam (Num. 12:13) and Aaron (Deut. 9:20). Moses' successor Joshua prayed after Israel's defeat at Ai (Josh. 7:7–9), and for the sun to stand still so Israel could inflict further punishment on her enemies (Josh. 10:12–14). Gideon prayed for a sign that would reveal God's will (Judg. 6:36–40). Both Naomi (Ruth 1:8) and Boaz (Ruth 2:12) prayed for Ruth. Hannah prayed for a son (1 Sam. 1:9–11) and Eli prayed for Hannah (1 Sam. 1:17). Hannah's son, Samuel, prayed that God would forgive the people of Israel and deliver them from their enemies (1 Sam. 7:5, 8), and promised to intercede for them after they foolishly demanded a king (1 Sam. 12:19–23). Job prayed in humble contrition (Job 42:1–6), and that God would forgive his friends for their foolish counsel (vv. 8–10). David offered a prayer of thanksgiving for God's promised blessings to him and his house (2 Sam. 7:18–29), pleaded with God to spare the son Bathsheba gave birth to after their adulterous affair (2 Sam. 12:16), begged God to spare Israel from judgment (2 Sam. 24:17), praised God for His blessings on the nation (1 Chron. 29:10–18), and prayed for his son and successor Solomon (1 Chron. 29:19). Solomon prayed for God's blessing on Israel (1 Kings 8:22–53), and for wisdom for himself (1 Kings 3:5–9). Confronting the false prophets on Mt. Carmel, Elijah prayed that God would reveal Himself as the only true God (1 Kings 18:36–37), and that it would rain after a three-and-one-half year drought (vv. 41–45; cf. Luke 4:25; James 5:17–18). Elisha prayed and a dead child was restored to life (2 Kings 4:33–35). Hezekiah prayed and God delivered His people from the invading Assyrians (2 Kings 19:1–36). God also spared the king's life in response to his prayer for mercy (2 Kings 20:1–6).

In perhaps the most unusual circumstances in which anyone ever prayed, Jonah cried out to God from the stomach of a large fish (Jonah 2:1–10). In the waning days of the southern kingdom (Judah), Jeremiah's prayer resulted in the comforting promise that God would one day restore the nation from captivity (Jer. 32:17–25). During the exile Ezekiel cried out to God to have mercy on His people (Ezek. 9:8; 11:13), as did Daniel in his magnificent prayer recorded in Daniel 9:3–19. After the exile Ezra (Ezra 8:21; 9:5–15) and Nehemiah (Neh. 1:4–11) prayed for the remnant who returned to their homeland. In addition to those specific prayers, virtually the entire book of Psalms consists of prayers of various types (e.g., praise, worship, confession, petition, and thanksgiving).

The New Testament also records the prayers of God's people. After His ascension Jesus' followers returned to Jerusalem, where they "were continually devoting themselves to prayer" (Acts 1:14; cf. 2:42). When faced with persecution by the Jewish leaders, the early church's response was to pray (4:24–31).The apostles defined their ministry when they told the congregation,"But we will devote ourselves to prayer and to the ministry of the word" (6:4). While "Peter was kept in the prison . . . prayer for him was being made fervently by the church to God" (12:5,12). Peter and John prayed for the believers in Samaria (8:14–15); Peter prayed before raising Tabitha from the dead (9:40) and before his vision and the coming of the messengers from Cornelius (10:9); the church at Antioch prayed before sending Paul and Barnabas on their missionary journey (13:1–3); and Epaphras labored in prayer for the Colossians (Col.4:12).

From his conversion (Acts 9:11) to the end of his life, Paul's ministry was marked by continual prayer (e.g., Acts 14:23; 16:25; 20:36; 21:5; 22:17; 27:35; 28:8, 15; Rom. 1:8–10; 10:1; 1 Cor. 1:4–8; 2 Cor. 13:7, 9; Eph. 1:16–23; 3:14–19; Phil. 1:3–4, 9–11; Col. 1:3, 9–14; 1 Thess. 1:2; 3:10; 2 Thess. 1:11–12; 2 Tim. 1:3; Philem. 4–6).The apostle also frequently asked others to pray for him and his ministry (e.g., Rom. 15:30; 2 Cor. 1:11; Eph. 6:18–19; Phil. 1:19; Col. 4:2–3; 1 Thess. 5:25; 2 Thess. 3:1; Philem. 22), as did the writer of Hebrews (Heb. 13:18).

But the supreme example of prayer in Scripture comes from the life of the Lord Jesus Christ. Curtis C. Mitchell writes, "Beyond doubt the greatest examples of correct prayer practice ever displayed were those demonstrated by Jesus Christ. So distinct was His prayer life that by simply observing it our Lord's disciples were motivated to request instruction on the subject (see Luke 11:1)" (*Praying Jesus' Way* [Old Tappan, N.J.: Revell, 1977], 15).

From beginning to end Jesus' earthly ministry was marked by frequent times of prayer. He prayed at His baptism (Luke 3:21), during His first preaching tour (Mark 1:35; Luke 5:16), before choosing the twelve apostles (Luke 6:12–13), before feeding the 5,000 (Matt. 14:19), after feeding the 5,000 (Matt. 14:23), before feeding the 4,000 (Matt. 15:36), before Peter's confession of Him as the Christ (Luke 9:18), at the transfiguration (Luke 9:28–29), for some children brought to Him (Matt. 19:13), after the return of the seventy (Luke 10:21), before giving the Lord's Prayer (Luke 11:1), before raising Lazarus from the dead (John 11:41–42), as He faced the reality of the cross (John 12:28), at the Last Supper (Matt. 26:26–27), for Peter (Luke 22:31–32), in Gethsemane (Matt. 26:36–42), from the cross (Matt. 27:46; Luke 23:34, 46), with the disciples He encountered on the road to Emmaus (Luke 24:30), and at the ascension (Luke 24:50–51).

But of all the prayers of Jesus, the one recorded here in the seventeenth chapter of John's gospel is the most profound and magnificent. Its words are plain, yet majestic; simple, yet mysterious. They plunge the reader into the unfathomable depths of the inter-Trinitarian communication between the Father and the Son, and their scope encompasses the entire sweep of redemptive history from election to glorification, including the themes of regeneration, revelation, illumination, sanctification, and preservation. The veil is drawn back and the reader is escorted by Jesus Christ into the Holy of Holies, to the very throne of God.

The value of its infinite richness is heightened by its uniqueness. There is no other chapter in the Bible like it. As one commentator explains:

> This chapter embraces the longest recorded prayer of our Lord while He was on earth. No doubt He prayed other prayers as lengthy as this, for we know He spent much time in prayer and in communion with His heavenly Father; but God did not see fit to give these other prayers to us as the Holy Ghost spoke to holy men. We have many of the sermons of Jesus, many of His parables; but only this one lengthy prayer. (Oliver Greene, *The Gospel According to John* [Greenville, S.C.: The Gospel Hour, 1966], 3:132)

The setting of this prayer (as Jesus comforted His disciples immediately before the cross), the substance of it (as a heartfelt petition from the Son to the Father), and the length and detail of it, as well as its theological richness, contribute to its unique and unsurpassed significance.

THE SETTING OF THIS PRAYER

Jesus spoke these things; and lifting up His eyes to heaven, He said, "Father, the hour has come;" (17:1*a*)

Jesus' prayer marks the end of the disciples' time with Jesus in the upper room. During the previous few hours, Jesus had served, comforted, and instructed His anxious followers. They had experienced John's fitting description of Jesus firsthand, that He "loved His own who were in the world, He loved them to the end" (13:1). The evening began with a footwashing, in which Jesus Himself "poured water into the basin, and began to wash the disciples' feet and to wipe them with the towel with which He was girded" (13:5). Remarkably, He even knowingly washed the feet of the one who would betray Him, Judas Iscariot.

Next there was the final meal, the Last Supper (cf. Matt. 26:26–29; Mark 14:22–25; Luke 22:19–20; 1 Cor. 11:23–26), during which Jesus revealed that Judas would betray Him (John 13:26–27; cf. Matt. 26:20–25), that He was about to die (John 13:31–35), and that Peter would deny Him (John 13:36–38; cf. Matt. 26:30–35). The disciples were understandably shocked and dismayed by what Jesus told them. Yet, the Lord was quick to console them, comforting them with the promise of future glory. "Do not let your heart be troubled," He said to them. "Believe in God, believe also in Me. In My Father's house are many dwelling places; if it were not so I would have told you; for I go to prepare a place for you" (14:1–2). The Lord further encouraged His followers with the promise of the Holy Spirit, the Helper who would come to them after He left. "The Helper, the Holy Spirit, whom the Father will send in My name," declared Jesus, "He will teach you all things, and bring to your remembrance all that I said to you" (14:26). Though the world would hate them, just as it hated Christ (15:18–16:4), the Spirit would strengthen and guide them in the truth (15:26–27; 16:5–15).

The words of Christ in the upper room also emphasized the vital, saving relationship that His disciples (and by extension, all believers) enjoyed with Him. Using the imagery of a vine and its branches, Jesus emphasized the abiding and life-giving nature of His love (15:1). Those who truly believe in Him share in that love, resulting in spiritual fruit (15:5), powerful prayer (15:7), a God-exalting life (15:8), heartfelt obedience (15:10; cf. 14:15), supernatural joy (15:11), and a sincere love for others (15:12). Jesus' remarkable words, "You did not choose Me but I chose you, and appointed you that you would go and bear fruit, and that your fruit would remain, so that whatever you ask of the Father in My name He may give to you" (15:16), comforted the disciples by confirming their genuine, saving relationship to Him.

Though they would grieve for a short time, Jesus assured them that their sadness was only temporary. With solemn certainty, He told them, "Truly, truly, I say to you, that you will weep and lament, but the world will rejoice; you will grieve, but your grief will be turned into joy" (16:20). The disciples, of course, did not understand that Jesus would rise from the dead only three days after the horrifying events that were about to take place (16:18; cf. John 2:22). They did not realize that His death was a necessary part of God's plan, and had been for the Messiah all along (cf. Isa. 53:1–12; Dan. 9:26). Their thinking, in keeping with the mainstream Jewish understanding of their day, had no place for a crucified Christ (cf. 1 Cor. 1:23). The Messiah, they thought, would come, overthrow Rome, and establish His earthly kingdom. When Jesus triumphantly entered Jerusalem just a few days before, the disciples must have been overwhelmed and overjoyed (12:12–19). Though their Master was still disliked by the religious leaders (11:16, 47–53), His popularity with the people seemed to be growing (cf. 12:9–11). The crowds had jubilantly hailed Him as their king, even laying down palm branches before Him, and greeting Him with shouts of "Hosanna!" as He entered the city (12:12–18). Surely, the disciples must have reasoned, the kingdom was finally at hand.

Now, just a few days later, they were shocked to hear Jesus tell them the unthinkable—He was leaving them (13:33; 14:18; 16:16). Rather than conquering Rome, He was going away. Rather than building up a kingdom, He was laying down His life (15:14). In the upcoming hours, He would be betrayed (18:2), arrested (18:12), put on trial (18:19), abandoned (18:25–27; cf. 16:32), falsely accused (18:38; 19:4), beaten (19:1), mocked (19:5), and crucified (19:16). The disciples' great expectations quickly turned to shock, heartbreak, and despair.

It is in this context, after **Jesus spoke** the **things** recorded in the previous three chapters, that He graciously and fervently prayed for His disciples. As they left the upper room and started their journey through the city and across the Kidron Valley to Gethsemane, the disciples would have been unable to separate this prayer from the solemn instruction they had just received in the upper room. In fact, much of what Jesus had just told them is repeated in His prayer to the Father:

> This prayer clearly belongs with the farewell discourses because it reiterates and sums up various of the themes found in these discourses: (1) the departure of Jesus (vv. 11,13); (2) the joy of the disciples (v. 13); (3) the hatred of the world (v. 14); (4) the division of the world and the disciples (v. 16); (5) the truth (v. 17); and (6) the indwelling of Christ in the believers (v. 23). (Ben Witherington III, *John's Wisdom* [Louisville: Westminster John Knox Press, 1995], 268)

The Lord had told His disciples what to expect (14:29), and warned them of the persecution they too would face on His behalf (15:18). He had comforted them with the promise of heaven (14:2) and of the Holy Spirit's coming (14:16–17). He had assured them of His love for them, and of their saving relationship with Him (15:1–11). He had instructed them with regard to their love for one another (15:12, 17), and even modeled that love in washing their feet (13:1–20). Now He would model that sacrificial love once again—this time by publicly praying for them, entrusting their safekeeping to His Father.

The Lord had promised them peace, joy, strength, provision, answered prayer, spiritual power through the Holy Spirit, and intimate fellowship both with Himself and the Father. All of those promises culminated in Christ's concluding promise that the disciples would triumph over the world: "These things I have spoken to you, so that in Me you may have peace. In the world you have tribulation, but take courage; I have overcome the world" (16:33). It is no coincidence that this prayer immediately follows that exultant declaration. Having stated His victory over the world, Jesus immediately turned in submissive dependence to the One who would ensure His triumph. "To transform the victory which was announced into a present reality, nothing less was needed than the action of the omnipotence of God. It is to Him that Jesus turns" (Frederic Godet, *Commentary on John's Gospel* [repr.; Grand Rapids: Kregel, 1978], 883).

The circumstances were certainly dismal from a human perspective, just hours before the cross. Yet Jesus' prayer was anything but pessimistic. Instead, it was a confident declaration of undying faith and certain glory. In the words of Leon Morris,

> We so often understand this prayer as though it were rather gloomy. It is not. It is uttered by One who has just affirmed that he has overcome the world (16:33), and it starts from this conviction. Jesus is looking forward to the cross, but in a mood of hope and joy, not one of despondency. (Leon Morris, *The Gospel According to John*, The New International Commentary on the New Testament [Grand Rapids: Eerdmans, 1995], 634)

Jesus began His prayer by **lifting up His eyes to heaven,** a familiar posture (cf. 11:41; Ps. 123:1; Mark 6:41; 7:34) acknowledging God's throne in heaven. It also reflected the confidence of His pure heart (Matt. 5:8; Eph. 3:12; cf. the guilt-stricken tax collector's unwillingness to lift up his eyes to heaven [Luke 18:13]). By addressing God as **Father** (cf. vv. 5, 11, 21, 24, 25; Matt. 11:25–26; 26:39, 42; Luke 10:21; 23:34, 46; John 11:41; 12:28), Jesus acknowledged His submission to and dependence on Him, while simultaneously underscoring His equality with God as His Son (cf. John 5:18). In contrast to the common Jewish practice of referring to God with a plural pronoun, "our Father," Jesus addressed Him as "My Father" (e.g., Matt. 7:21; 10:32–33; 11:27; 12:50; 16:17; 18:10, 19; 20:23; 26:39, 42; Luke 22:29; John 5:17; 6:32, 40; 8:19, 38, 49, 54; 10:18, 29, 37; 14:7, 20, 21, 23; 15:1, 8, 15, 23, 24; 20:17). Gerald Borchert explains the cultural significance of that personal title:

> Jesus came into a Jewish world that had developed a remote view of God, one that needed angels to carry messages. The people had ceased to use the name of God for fear of taking his name in vain, just like the Prodigal Son, who could speak of "heaven" but not use the name of God (cf. Luke 15:18, 21). Into this context of speaking of God by means of surrogate titles Jesus came and called God his Father. (Gerald L. Borchert, *John 12–21*, The New American Commentary [Nashville: Broadman & Holman, 2002], 187)

In addressing this prayer to His Father, Jesus emphasized the intimate fellowship He shared with God. That kind of a personal, familial relationship with God was completely foreign to the Jews of Jesus' day. Yet through Christ, anyone who believes in Him is granted that same spiritual intimacy with God (17:20, 26).

That Jesus referred to God as His Father is significant for another reason. On the one hand, He was "making Himself equal with God" (John 5:18) by claiming to be the Son of God. But on the other hand, He was demonstrating His distinctness from the Father, since He was clearly not praying to Himself. That twofold reality underscores an important theological truth—that the Son is equal to the Father yet distinct from Him. Thus, while He is equal to the Father in essence, even sharing in His eternal glory (17:5), He is not a mere mode or manifestation of the Father. Rather, the Son is a distinct person within the Godhead. By calling God His Father, Jesus was underscoring the fundamental reality of the Trinity.

Earlier in John's gospel the point had been emphasized that Christ's hour had not yet come (2:4; 7:6, 30; 8:20). But now He opened His prayer with the dramatic declaration that **the hour has come.** The phrase refers to the consummation of His earthly ministry, encompassing His death, resurrection, and ascension.

The unfolding drama of redemptive history had reached its apex. Plans made in eternity past were finding their culmination in time. The hour had come in which the Son of Man would offer Himself as the perfect and only atoning sacrifice for sin. The hour had come when the sinless One would be made sin for believers that they "might become the righteousness of God in Him" (2 Cor. 5:21). The hour had come when Christ would cancel "the certificate of debt consisting of decrees against us, which was hostile to us" taking "it out of the way, having nailed it to the cross" (Col. 2:14). This was the hour when the Old Testament prophecies of Messiah's death would be fulfilled; when the serpent's head would be bruised (Gen. 3:15); when the suffering Servant, "a man of sorrows and acquainted with grief" (Isa. 53:3), would be "pierced through for our transgressions ... crushed for our iniquities" and have "the chastening for our well-being [fall] upon Him [so that] by His scourging we are healed" (v. 5). It was the hour when the shadows of the Old Testament sacrifices (cf. Heb. 10:1) would give way to the glorious reality of the final sacrifice —the Lamb of God (John 1:29; Heb. 10:14). It was the hour of Christ's triumph over the prince of this world and the kingdom of darkness (John 12:31; 16:11; Col. 2:14; Heb. 2:14). It was the climactic hour when God, through Christ's sacrifice, would defeat sin, death, and Satan, and redeem a people for Himself.

With the hour of supreme suffering and even greater victory at hand, and with His terrified and heartbroken disciples still surrounding Him (cf. 18:1), the Lord lifted His eyes to heaven and prayed. Though the words of this prayer would be magnificent in any context, the palpable imminence of the cross makes Christ's plea as poignant as it is profound.

THE SUBSTANCE OF THIS PRAYER

"glorify Your Son, that the Son may glorify You." (17:1b)

Having acknowledged that the time of His death was near, Jesus immediately requested that the Father would **glorify** the **Son, so that the Son may glorify** the Father. This short phrase (which will be discussed in more detail in the following chapter of this commentary) provides a fitting summary to all that had taken place in Jesus' life and ministry, and to all that was to follow both in this prayer and in the events of His passion. His prevailing focus had always been on glorifying His Father, perfectly submitting to the Father's will in everything, even to the end.

Throughout His ministry, Jesus was continually "seeking the glory of the One who sent Him" (John 7:18; cf. 13:31–32). The events of His birth brought glory to God (Luke 2:14, 20); as did His teaching (Matt. 5:16; John 15:8); His miracles (Matt. 9:8; 15:31; Mark 2:12; Luke 5:25–26; 7:16; 13:13; 17:15; 18:43); and His death and resurrection (John 12:23–28). In absolutely everything, the Son had submitted to the Father's will. "For I have come down from heaven," He explained to the crowds, "not to do My own will but the will of Him who sent Me" (John 6:38; cf. Matt. 12:50; John 4:34; 5:30). Even during His passionate prayers in Gethsemane, when the temptation to abandon the cross was at its peak, Jesus submitted to the plan of God. "My Father, if it is possible, let this cup pass from Me," He prayed, "yet not as I will, but as You will" (Matt. 26:39; cf. v. 42).

Just as the Son had glorified the Father, so the Father had glorified the Son. Thus, Jesus could say to His opponents, "The Father who sent Me, He has testified of Me" (John 5:37), and later, "It is My Father who glorifies Me, of whom you say, 'He is our God'" (John 8:54). At His baptism, the Father audibly affirmed His approval of the Son (cf. Matt. 3:13–17). This occurred a second time at His transfiguration (cf. Luke 9:35; 2 Peter 1:17–18), and a third time shortly before His passion (John 12:28). The Father further demonstrated that Jesus was truly His Son through His miracles (John 2:11; 9:3; 10:38; 11:40); as Jesus said regarding Lazarus's death, "This sickness is not to end in death, but for the glory of God, so that the Son of God may be glorified by it" (John 11:4). Even the events of Jesus' death and resurrection would result in the glory of the Son (Luke 24:46; John 12:23; 13:32)—glory that He has shared with the Father since eternity past (John 1:1, 14) and that will be visibly displayed to the world at His future return (Matt. 16:27; Mark 8:38; Luke 21:27).

It is fitting that His ministry would climax in a majestic prayer that emphasized the very thing that characterized His entire life. The theme of God's glory, stated in verse 1, is echoed throughout this passage. Just as the Son glorified the Father through His faithfulness on earth (17:4), so the Father would glorify the Son together with Himself, with the very glory that the Son shared with Him since before time began (17:5). The disciples too would be those who glorified the Father by bringing glory to the Son (17:10); they, along with all who would believe in the Son, would share in His glory (17:22), eternally praising Him for the glory that He received from the Father (17:24). Furthermore, the plan of salvation would certainly be fulfilled in the cross since God's glorious reputation, His name, was at stake (cf. 17:6,11,12,26).

The prayer itself falls readily into three sections, as Jesus prays for Himself (vv. 1–5), His disciples (vv. 6–19), and His church (vv. 20–26). But throughout all three sections, the focal point is the glory of God, being manifested through the cross. As Frederic Godet explains,

> ... when Jesus prays for Himself [in vv. 1–5] , it is not His own person that He has in view, it is *the work of God* ...; when He prays for His apostles [in vv. 6–19], He commends them to God as agents and continuers of this work; and when He extends His regard to all believers present or future [in vv. 20–26], it is as if to the *object* of this work, in other terms because these souls are the theatre where the glory of His Father is to shine forth; for His work and the glory of the Father are for Him one and the same thing. (*Commentary on John's Gospel*, 883)

Ironically, it was through the cross, the most shameful of deaths, that the Son of God displayed infinite glory. What seemed to be the worst possible outcome for Jesus, at least in the minds of His disciples, was in reality His ultimate victory. By looking at the cross from the standpoint of God's glory, the Lord saw triumph where His followers saw nothing but tragedy.

Jesus' prayer highlights His absolute confidence in and submission to the perfect will of God, even though He knew perfectly what it would cost Him. Therefore He prayed that the Father's will would be done, that the master plan of redemption would be accomplished, and that the Father would bring to reality all the promises He had made to His disciples. Knowing the will of God did not cause Jesus to fatalistically forego praying. On the contrary, it prompted Him to ask the Father to do what He had said He would do (cf. Daniel's prayer in Dan. 9:4–19, which was prompted by his understanding from Jeremiah's prophecy that Israel's captivity would last for seventy years [Dan. 9:2–3]). Not only did Jesus impart the truth to His disciples, but He also prayed that God would energize it in their lives. Teaching the truth must always be coupled with prayer; a lesson that the disciples themselves would later put into practice (Acts 6:4).

The prayer recorded in this chapter also forms a transition between Jesus' earthly ministry and His heavenly ministry of intercession (Heb. 7:25). The book of Hebrews reveals the rich theological truths regarding the Lord's intercessory work as the mediator of the new covenant (cf. Heb. 4:14–10:25); here we have a personal glimpse of Him in His role as the Great High priest interceding for His people. (This prayer is, in fact, often referred to as the High Priestly Prayer of Christ.) Significantly, as was noted earlier, this is the only place in Scripture where the words of a lengthy prayer of Christ have been recorded. Though shorter prayers can be found (cf. Matt. 11:25–27), there is no parallel in Scripture to the prayer recorded here.

Yet, in spite of its unique character and profundity, Jesus' words are simple and straightforward. No amount of study could ever exhaust the truths revealed in this prayer; and yet a basic understanding and appreciation of the text comes just from reading and meditating on it. One might expect the words of an inter-Trinitarian prayer to be utterly incomprehensible. But that is not the case. As James Montgomery Boice rightly observes:

> This prayer contains the simplest of sentences, though the ideas are profound. It is proof that the difficulty we have in understanding God's truth is not in the complexity of the truth itself or in the language with which it is conveyed (as if it were logarithms or German philosophy) but in our own ignorance, sin, and spiritual lethargy. (James Montgomery Boice, *The Gospel of John* [Grand Rapids: Zondervan, 1985], 1103)

Because He was consumed with the glory of God, as the substance of His prayer makes clear, Jesus viewed the cross from an eternal perspective. He was not dispassionate or stoic (cf. Luke 22:42), but fully dependent on His Father's care and wholly submissive to His will. Perfectly aware of the pain and suffering that awaited Him, He also knew of the triumphant glory that would result. Thus, "for the joy set before Him [He] endured the cross, despising the shame," knowing that He would soon victoriously sit "down at the right hand of the throne of God" (Heb. 12:2).

THE SIGNIFICANCE OF THIS PRAYER

Spoken by Jesus just hours before the cross, the significance of this passage is difficult to overstate. Here the words of the second member of the Trinity are recorded, as He speaks to His Father about the nature of their communion, about the outworking of their eternal plan of salvation, and about the way in which the disciples and all believers fit into that plan. In hearing this prayer, the disciples were allowed to listen in on the most holy and profound of conversations. In reading this prayer, believers today are similarly ushered into the Holy of Holies, where they find their Great High Priest—even in the moments before His death—interceding on their behalf. Some refer to it as the "Holy of Holies of sacred Scripture."

Though the church has always cherished and meditated on this prayer, and though individual Christians have studied it in great detail, its rich truths have never been exhausted. Hundreds of sermons have been preached on it, thousands of pages written about it, and millions of lives changed by it. And the words of the Lord remain as relevant and meaningful today as they were when He first uttered them.

> Its primary characteristic is *timelessness*. Though uttered within a few hours of Calvary, it contains thoughts and expressions which must have been familiar to our Lord at any moment during the centuries which have followed. As we study it, therefore, we are listening to words which have been uttered many times on our behalf, and will be uttered until we are with Him, where He is, beholding the glory of the divine Son, superadded to that of the Perfect Servant. (F. B. Meyer, *Gospel of John* [Grand Rapids: Zondervan, 1952], 296. Emphasis in original.)

In light of the fact that this prayer is the longest and, arguably, most significant of Jesus' recorded prayers, it is ironic that the title, "The Lord's Prayer" has traditionally been used elsewhere, in reference to the instruction on prayer in Matthew 6:9–13 (cf. Luke 11:2–4). Yet Matthew 6:9–13 does not actually record a prayer of Jesus, but rather is a model given by Jesus to His disciples for how they should pray—a disciple's prayer would be a better title. (Jesus, after all, could never have asked God for forgiveness—cf. Matt. 6:12.). If one wishes to read an actual prayer of the Lord, at least a prayer of any length, this passage is the only place to turn. From that perspective, the prayer recorded in John 17 is the true Lord's Prayer.

As Jesus prayed this prayer shortly before the cross, He rejoiced, knowing that the redemption that had been predetermined in eternity past was about to find its terminus in time and space. Jesus understood that the hour had finally come for the fulfillment of that which God had promised from before time began. He was ready to face the cross—with triumph and resolve. The cost would be immense, but the glorious result would be eternal.

Jesus' Prayer and the Eternal Plan of God
(John 17:1*b*–5)

22

"Father, the hour has come; glorify Your Son, that the Son may glorify You, even as You gave Him authority over all flesh, that to all whom You have given Him, He may give eternal life. This is eternal life, that they may know You, the only true God, and Jesus Christ whom You have sent. I glorified You on the earth, having accomplished the work which You have given Me to do. Now, Father, glorify Me together with Yourself, with the glory which I had with You before the world was." (17:1*b*–5)

Though unthinkable to the disciples, the death of the Messiah was an essential and deliberate part of God's eternal plan. Even though Jesus had told them clearly that "the Son of Man is going [up to Jerusalem to be killed] as it has been determined" (Luke 22:22), they did not fully understand what He meant (Mark 9:32; Luke 9:45). Moreover, they objected to what little they did understand—as this startling scene from Matthew's gospel demonstrates:

> From that time Jesus began to show His disciples that He must go to Jerusalem, and suffer many things from the elders and chief priests and scribes, and be killed, and be raised up on the third day. Peter took Him aside and began to rebuke Him, saying, "God forbid it, Lord! This shall

never happen to You." But He turned and said to Peter, "Get behind Me, Satan! You are a stumbling block to Me; for you are not setting your mind on God's interests, but man's." (Matt. 16:21–23)

It was not until after the resurrection that the disciples finally understood why Christ's death was necessary—in order that He might be the perfect substitute for sin, reconciling sinners to God through the cross (2 Cor. 5:18–21). Only then did the disciples come to realize that His death had been central to the divine plan all along. On the day of Pentecost, none other than Peter announced that Jesus Christ was "delivered over by the predetermined plan and foreknowledge of God [being] nailed to a cross by the hands of godless men" (Acts 2:23). His sentiments were echoed in the apostolic prayer of Acts 4:27–28: "For truly in this city [Jerusalem] there were gathered against Your holy servant Jesus, whom You anointed, both Herod and Pontius Pilate, along with the Gentiles and the peoples of Israel, to do whatever Your hand and Your purpose predestined to occur" (Acts 4:27–28). In fact, the reason the Old Testament prophets had been able to predict the Messiah's death with such vivid accuracy was because it had been part of the divine plan from the beginning (Acts 3:18; cf. Gen. 3:15; Isa. 53:1–12; Dan. 9:26; 1 Peter 1:20–21).

The salvation plan of God was formed in eternity past, before the beginning of time, when He purposed to save a remnant of the human race He would yet create and whom He knew would rebel against Him (Eph. 1:4–5; cf. Matt. 25:34). The plan itself was guaranteed by the promise of God. As Paul explains in Titus 1:2, salvation is "the hope of eternal life, which God, who cannot lie, promised long ages ago." The phrase "long ages ago" literally means, "before time began," indicating that redemption has always been part of God's sovereign plan (cf. Heb. 13:20). In eternity past, He made a promise to save those whom He had chosen; the fulfillment of which is absolutely certain since "it is impossible for God to lie" (Heb. 6:18; cf. Num. 23:19; 1 Sam. 15:29; John 14:6, 17; 15:26). But to whom was that promise made, since there was no one but God before time began?

The answer to that question is introduced in 2 Timothy 1:9, which states that God "has saved us and called us with a holy calling, not according to our works, but according to His own purpose and grace which was granted to us in Christ Jesus from all eternity." (The phrase "from all eternity" is identical in Greek to the phrase translated "long ages ago" in Titus 1:2. In both cases, the literal rendering is "from before time began.") God's promise to save His own was made in eternity past "according to His own purpose and grace," independent of any outside influence. Because there was no one beside the triune God, it was a promise He necessarily made to Himself.

More specifically, as Jesus' beautiful prayer in this chapter indicates, this divine promise was made from one member of the Trinity to another—from the Father to the Son. As a tangible expression of His infinite love for the Son, the Father promised Him a bride (cf. Rev. 19:7–8), a company of redeemed sinners who would honor and glorify the Son forever. In eternity past, the Father recorded their names in the book of life (Rev. 13:8; 17:8), and pledged them to His Son as a gift of His love. Thus, Jesus could pray, "Father, glorify Me together with Yourself, with the glory which I had with You before the world was. I have manifested Your name to the men whom You gave Me out of the world; they were Yours and You gave them to Me" (17:5–6). A few verses later, Jesus again underscored that believers are a gift from the Father, given out of His love and for the purpose of His Son's glory: "Father, I desire that they also, whom You have given Me, be with Me where I am, so that they may see My glory which You have given Me, for You loved Me before the foundation of the world" (v. 24).

Earlier in the gospel of John, Jesus had already made reference to the fact that believers are given to Him by His Father. After He fed the five thousand, He told the crowds, "All that the Father gives Me will come to Me, and the one who comes to Me I will certainly not cast out.... This is the will of Him who sent Me, that of all that He has given Me I lose nothing, but raise it up on the last day" (John 6:37, 39). He further taught that "No one can come to Me unless the Father who sent Me draws him" (v. 44). According to God's sovereign design, the Father draws to the Son those whom He has chosen to redeem, in keeping with His eternal promise. The Son, in return, receives and protects all those whom the Father draws. Because they are a gift to Him from the Father, He would never refuse them or allow them to be lost. He will raise them all to eternal glory.

Sinners, then, are saved not because they are inherently worthy of salvation, or wise enough on their own to choose it (cf. Eph. 2:1–10), but because the Father lovingly draws them for the purpose of giving them as a gift to the Son. In response to the Father's love, the Son eagerly receives all those who are drawn because they are a gift from His beloved Father. The Son opens His arms to sinners, not because they either deserve to be embraced or seek such, but because He is exceedingly glad to receive the gift His Father prepared for Him from before time began, and then sought and saved.

Romans 8:29–30 provides additional insight into the glorious salvation purposes of God: "For those whom He foreknew, He also predestined to become conformed to the image of His Son, so that He would be the firstborn among many brethren; and these whom He predestined, He also called; and these whom He called, He also justified; and these whom He justified, He also glorified." When the Father, in eternity past, decided to redeem sinners, He did so with the ultimate intent of conforming them into the image of His Son (cf. Phil. 3:20–21; 1 John 3:2). Because they will be like Christ in their glorified state, the redeemed will forever be a supreme tribute to the Son—reflecting His perfect goodness and proclaiming His eternal greatness.

First Corinthians 15:24–28 foretells the remarkable conclusion to God's sovereign plans. There Paul writes,

> Then comes the end, when He [Christ] hands over the kingdom to the God and Father, when He has abolished all rule and all authority and power. For He must reign until He has put all His enemies under His feet. The last enemy that will be abolished is death. For He has put all things in subjection under His feet. But when He says, "All things are put in subjection," it is evident that He is excepted who put all things in subjection to Him. When all things are subjected to Him, then the Son Himself also will be subjected to the One who subjected all things to Him, so that God may be all in all.

The day is coming when Jesus Christ, the true Lord of Lords, will reclaim the universe that rightfully belongs to Him. He will reign by His Father's authority until He subjects every enemy to Himself, including death (vv. 25–26). When that takes place, at the end of time, the Son will hand His kingdom back over to His Father (v. 24), and will Himself "be subjected to the One [the Father] who subjected all things to Him, so that God may be all in all" (v. 28). The Son will give everything, including Himself and those who are in Him, back to His Father. Thus, the Father's love gift to the Son will be reciprocated by the Son, and the redemptive purposes of God, which were formed in eternity past, will be fully and finally realized. God will be "all in all" (v. 28) and salvation history will be complete.

The humbling but marvelous reality is that believers are secondary within the scope of God's eternal plan. The Father's primary concern is the honor of the Son whom He loves and desires to see glorified. That is why, in eternity past, He promised to redeem a segment of sinful humanity whom He would give to the Son to worship and exalt Him forever.

The Son's primary concern, likewise, is the honor and glory of the Father. Because of His perfect love for the Father, He receives the Father's gift with infinite joy—gladly embracing every sinner whom the Father draws. Moreover, He considered the Father's gift so precious that He "emptied Himself, taking the form of a bond-servant, and being made in the likeness of men. Being found in appearance as a man, He humbled Himself by becoming obedient to the point of death, even death on a cross" (Phil. 2:7–8). He did this that the eternal purposes of God might be fulfilled in Him (cf. Eph. 3:11)—purposes that will finally culminate when He gives all things back to His Father at the end of the age (1 Cor.

15:25–28). (For a further discussion of this subject, see my foreword, "Divine Immutability and the Doctrines of Grace," in Steven J. Lawson, *Foundations of Grace* [Orlando, Fla.: Reformation Trust, 2006], 7–20.)

It is with these eternal purposes in mind that Jesus came to His Father in prayer on the night before His death. He knew that the Father had predetermined to redeem a people whom He would give to the Son as His bride. He also knew that the redeemed would reflect His glory (John 17:22; Phil. 3:20–21; 1 John 3:2), bear His image (Rom. 8:29), and praise, glorify, and serve Him through all eternity. Likewise, He knew that their names were written in the Book of Life (Phil. 4:3; Rev. 3:5; 13:8; 17:8; 20:15; 21:27), and that He had come into the world to pay the redemptive price to purchase them from the slave market of sin (1 Cor. 6:20; 7:23; Titus 2:14; 1 Peter 1:18; Rev. 5:9). He was fully aware that **the hour** had **come** for Him to do all that had been planned from before the foundation of the world.

Thus when Jesus asked the Father, **glorify Your Son,** He was asking that the eternal plan of redemption be consummated exactly as it had been sovereignly ordained. Significantly, this was Jesus' only request for Himself in His entire prayer (cf. v. 5)—that the Father would grant Him the glory that would be His through His death, resurrection, ascension, and coronation, just as it had been planned in eternity past. The fact that the Son shares the Father's glory affirms His deity, since God will not give His glory to another (Isa. 42:8; 48:11).

The Lord's request was a sincere affirmation of the promise His Father had made to Him in eternity past. The plan had always been that the Son would be glorified through the redemption of sinners. Thus Jesus' request for glorification was a prayer that God's eternal purposes would be fulfilled in the cross exactly as God had decreed. Ironically, what would appear to men to be a moment of supreme shame would in actuality be the moment of Christ's highest honor—as God's marvelous plan of redemption was perfectly realized. In fact, it is through the cross that all of God's saving purposes are made possible. Jesus will forever bear the scars of the cross (John 20:27), thus being forever marked with the honor of His accomplishment there.

But Jesus was not merely seeking His own glory; His perfectly righteous request was that by His sacrifice **the Son** might **glorify** the Father (cf. Rom. 6:4). As Leon Morris explains,

> This part of the prayer is often said to be Jesus' prayer for himself. As he prays that he may be glorified (vv. 1, 5) there is perhaps something in this. But this is not prayer "for" himself in the way we usually understand this. Since his glorification is to be seen in the cross it is a prayer rather that the Father's will may be done in him. If we do talk about this as Jesus' prayer for himself we should at least be clear that there is no self-

seeking in it. (Leon Morris, *The Gospel According to John*, The New International Commentary on the New Testament [Grand Rapids: Eerdmans, 1995], 635)

The cross displayed God's glory like no other event in history, revealing His righteousness, justice, and holiness in requiring the "precious blood" of His Son, "a lamb unblemished and spotless" (1 Peter 1:19) as a propitiation for His holy wrath against sin (Rom. 3:25). At the same time, it dramatically demonstrated His grace, mercy, and love in the sending of His only Son to die for the sins of the utterly undeserving (Eph. 2:1–10; cf. 1 John 4:9–10). "What God has accomplished in Jesus Christ," notes Thomas Schreiner, "displays both the justice and love of God because God's holiness is vindicated in the cross, while at the same time his love is displayed in the willing and glad sacrifice of his Son" (Thomas R. Schreiner, "Penal Substitution View," in *The Nature of the Atonement: Four Views*, ed. James Beilby and Paul R. Eddy [Downers Grove, Ill.: InterVarsity, 2006], 92). The cross further displayed God's power as He defeated sin, death, and Satan (Heb. 2:14; cf. 1 Cor. 15:54–58). Finally, the cross made clear the wisdom of God's eternal plan of redemption—"the wisdom which none of the rulers of this age has understood; for if they had understood it they would not have crucified the Lord of glory" (1 Cor. 2:8).

In these opening expressions, Jesus referenced four facets of the saving purposes of God, each of which centered on His glory-producing work of redemption at the cross—the right He possesses (to offer eternal life); the relationship He offers (which is eternal life); the requirement He meets (to pay for eternal life); and the reverence He deserves (having made eternal life available). As His prayer indicates, Jesus was fully aware that, like everything else, the next few hours of time had been sovereignly determined since eternity past and would have infinite ramifications into eternity future.

THE RIGHT HE POSSESSES

even as You gave Him authority over all flesh, that to all whom You have given Him, He may give eternal life. (17:2)

In keeping with God's eternal plan of salvation, the Son was given **authority over all flesh** (mankind) to grant eternal life **to all** those **whom** the Father had **given Him.** That authority, being granted to Him by His Father, was made possible through the cross. Though He submitted to His captors and allowed Himself to be nailed to a cross by wicked men, in reality it was He who had the authority. In dying for the sins of those who would believe in Him, He was given the right to grant eternal life to them.

> Jesus, the Son of Man who is about to be glorified and thus will fulfill his earthly mission, here anticipates his exalted, authoritative position subsequent to his crucifixion and resurrection. This authority enables him to bestow eternal life on all those whom God has given to him (cf. 6:39–40). God's granting of authority to Jesus (cf. 1:12; 5:27) marks the inbreaking of a new era (cf. Isa. 9:6–7; Dan. 7:13–14). All authority in heaven and on earth has been given to Jesus (Matt. 28:18), including the authority to judge (John 5:27). (Andreas Köstenberger, *John*, Baker Exegetical Commentary on the New Testament [Grand Rapids: Baker, 2004], 486)

Though His authority extends over all creation (cf. Matt. 28:18), it is clear that redemption applies only to those who have been chosen for Him by the Father. Only those whom the Father has given Him (vv. 6, 9, 24; 6:37, 39; cf. Acts 13:48; Rom. 8:29–30; Eph. 1:4–5; 2 Thess. 2:13; Titus 1:1; 1 Peter 1:1–2) will receive eternal life. Christ's authority to grant them that life is another aspect of His victory over the world through His death (cf. 16:33). That Jesus Christ is the source of eternal life is a central theme of John's gospel (cf. 3:15–16, 36; 4:14; 5:21, 24, 40; 6:27, 33, 35, 40, 47, 48, 51, 54, 68; 10:10, 28; 11:25; 14:6 and the apostle's purpose statement for writing his gospel in 20:31), and one he reiterates in his first epistle (1 John 5:20).

Throughout His ministry, Christ manifested the divine authority His Father had given Him in a multitude of ways (cf. Matt. 11:27; 28:18). His teaching was characterized by divine authority (Matt. 7:29; Mark 1:22; Luke 4:32); as were His healings (Mark 5:38–43; Luke 4:39; 9:1; John 11:43), exorcisms (Matt. 10:1; Mark 3:15; Luke 4:36), and other miracles (cf. Mark 8:26–27; Matt. 21:19; John 21:3–11). He claimed the right to violate traditional Jewish customs (cf. Matt. 5:21–22, 27–28; 15:1–9; Luke 6:1–11; John 5:9–17), to cleanse the temple (cf. Matt. 21:12–13; Mark 11:15–17; John 2:14–16), to forgive sins and offer salvation in His own name (Matt. 9:6, 8; Mark 2:10; Luke 5:24), to receive worship from others (Matt. 14:33; 15:25; 28:9), and even to judge the world (Mark 13:26–27; John 5:22–23). It was because His authority clashed with that of the Jewish religious leaders that they were so often angered by Him, and ultimately plotted His death.

His death, too, was under His own authority. As He declared in John 10:17–18, "For this reason the Father loves Me, because I lay down My life so that I may take it again. No one has taken it away from Me, but I lay it down on My own initiative. I have authority to lay it down, and I have authority to take it up again. This commandment I received from My Father." As the time of His crucifixion approached, Jesus did not relinquish the authority that His Father had given to Him. Rather, He anticipated the full authority He would have as a result of the cross. Following His resurrection, He knew that He would ascend to heaven where His Father would seat "Him at His right hand in the heavenly places, far above all rule and authority and power and dominion, and every name that is named, not only in this age but also in the one to come. And He [would] put all things in subjection under His feet, and [would give] Him as head over all things to the church" (Eph. 1:20–22).

The fact that Jesus Christ alone was given the authority to grant eternal life, through His death on the cross, also underscores the exclusivity of the gospel message. It is only through Him that eternal life can be received. As Jesus had said earlier that evening, "I am the way, and the truth, and the life; no one comes to the Father but through Me" (John 14:6). Though many may claim to offer eternal life (Matt. 7:13–14; 24:5), only the Son has actually been given the authority to grant it. As John the Baptist explained, "The Father loves the Son and has given all things into His hand. He who believes in the Son has eternal life; but he who does not obey the Son will not see life, but the wrath of God abides on him" (John 3:35–36).

THE RELATIONSHIP HE OFFERS

This is eternal life, that they may know You, the only true God, and Jesus Christ whom You have sent. (17:3)

In contrast to the pluralistic claims of contemporary religious culture, eternal life comes only to those who **know** (the Greek word implies not mere intellectual knowledge, but a deep, intimate love relationship; cf. v. 25; 10:14–15, 27) **. . . the only true God** (Jer. 10:10; 1 Thess. 1:9; 1 John 5:20; cf. 1 Cor. 8:6) and that is possible only through **Jesus Christ whom** He has **sent** (cf. 5:23, 36, 37; 10:36; 1 John 4:10, 14). As Peter boldly declared to the Jewish leaders, "There is salvation in no one else, for there is no other name under heaven that has been given among men by which we must be saved" (Acts 4:12; cf. 1 Tim. 2:5).

The essence of **eternal life** is participation in the blessed, everlasting life of Christ (cf. 1:4) through union with Him (Rom. 5:21; 6:4, 11, 23; 1 Cor. 15:22; 2 Cor. 5:17; Gal. 2:20; Col. 3:3–4; 2 Tim. 1:1, 10; Jude 21). It is the life of God in the soul of man (Gal. 2:20). Because believers have Christ's life in them, they also possess His peace (John 14:27; 16:33; cf. Phil. 4:7), love (John 15:10; cf. Rom. 5:5), and joy (John 15:11). The life that God predetermined to give the redeemed is a life of shared communion with Him.

Eternal life refers to a quality of life, and not just a quantity of life. It is much more than living forever; it is enjoying intimate fellowship with God both now and forever. It cannot be reduced merely to endless existence, since the unredeemed in hell will also live forever (cf. Matt. 25:46 where the same word, *aiōnios*, describes both the eternal life of the righteous and the eternal punishment of the wicked).

Because eternal life is a quality of life, it is not only a future possession, but also a present reality. In John 5:24 Jesus said, "Truly, truly, I say to you, he who hears My word, and believes Him who sent Me, has eternal life, and does not come into judgment, but has passed out of death into life." "These things I have written to you who believe in the name of the Son of God," John wrote, "so that you may know that you have eternal life" (1 John 5:13). Thus, believers enjoy eternal life even now as they experience the rich blessings that come through their personal and intimate fellowship with Christ (John 15:1–11; 1 Cor. 1:9; Eph. 1:3; Phil. 3:8–11; 1 John 1:3; 5:20). Of course, they will most fully experience that life in the age to come (Eph. 2:6–7), when they see Christ face-to-face (1 Cor. 13:12) and worship Him in the perfect, unending glory and joy of heaven (Rom. 8:19–23, 29; 1 Cor. 15:49; Phil. 3:20–21; 1 John 3:2; Rev. 22:3–4).

THE REQUIREMENT HE MEETS

I glorified You on the earth, having accomplished the work which You have given Me to do. (17:4)

In God's perfect plan, and in keeping with His perfect justice, the Son had to come to earth in order to save those whom the Father had given Him (Luke 19:10). As was noted earlier, the Father's gift was so precious to the Son that He was willing to do whatever was necessary to receive it (cf. Phil. 2:1–11).

The Lord Jesus Christ **glorified** the Father during His time **on the earth** by **having** perfectly **accomplished the work which** the Father gave Him to do (cf. 4:34; 5:30; 6:38; 15:10). That work culminated in the cross, which He viewed here in an anticipatory way. Jesus was certain that the eternal promise of God would be perfectly accomplished, and that nothing could prevent the Father's purposes from being realized. But His statement did more than merely reveal His own confidence in the plans of the Father. It also served as an example to the disciples—reminding them to trust in God's sovereign working and take comfort in knowing that He was in control.

Additionally, this verse implies the truth of Christ's impeccability (sinlessness). "Which one of you convicts Me of sin?" Jesus boldly challenged

His adversaries (John 8:46). Paul described Him in 2 Corinthians 5:21 as "Him who knew no sin." The writer of Hebrews declared that though He was "tempted in all things as we are," Jesus was "yet without sin" (Heb. 4:15), and went on to characterize Him as "holy, innocent, undefiled, separated from sinners" (Heb. 7:26). Peter referred to Him as "a lamb unblemished and spotless" (1 Peter 1:19) and declared that He "committed no sin" (1 Peter 2:22). John said simply, "In Him [Christ] there is no sin" (1 John 3:5). Most significant of all was the Father's affirmation, "This is My beloved Son, in whom I am well-pleased" (Matt. 3:17; 17:5). Only by living a sinless life could Jesus be an acceptable sacrifice for sin.

When John the Baptist hesitated to baptize Him, Jesus told him, "Permit it at this time; for in this way it is fitting for us to fulfill all righteousness" (Matt. 3:15). It was imperative for Him to live a life of perfect obedience, fulfilling all of God's righteous requirements. Only One who was perfectly holy, just as God is holy (Lev. 19:2), could be the final sacrifice for sin (cf. Heb. 10:1–18). Through His death and resurrection, Jesus conquered death and provided eternal life to all who believe in Him. But in addition, His perfect life of obedience, the fullest expression of which was His willingness to die on the cross (Luke 22:42), is imputed to believers at justification (cf. Rom. 5:18–21). Though Jesus was sinless, God treated Him as if He had committed the sins of everyone who would believe in Him, so that believers, though unrighteous, could be treated as if they had lived Christ's perfect life. Again, 2 Corinthians 5:21 succinctly summarizes that glorious truth: "He [the Father] made Him [Christ] who knew no sin to be sin on our behalf, so that we might become the righteousness of God in Him." Christ's willingness to be a sin-bearing sacrifice on the cross was the ultimate demonstration of His complete commitment to obey the Father, as well as the ultimate expression of His love for sinners (cf. John 15:13).

THE REVERENCE HE DESERVES

Now, Father, glorify Me together with Yourself, with the glory which I had with You before the world was. (17:5)

Having accomplished everything according to the predetermined plan of God, Jesus knew that He would be exalted to the place where He had been before His incarnation—at the glorious right hand of His Father (cf. Mark 16:19; Eph. 1:20). With that exaltation in sight, Jesus expressed His desire to return to the glory of heaven. Therefore He asked the Father to **glorify** Him, **together with** the Father, **with the glory** He had shared with the Father **before the world was.** The apostle John described the eternal fellowship Christ had enjoyed with the Father in the prologue to his gospel:"In the beginning was the Word [the Son], and the Word was with (lit.'face-to-face with') God, and the Word was God. He was in the beginning with God" (John 1:1–2). After an earthly life of submission and humiliation during the incarnation, Jesus was ready to return to the full glory that awaited Him at the Father's right hand. It was time for His coronation, which Paul described in Philippians 2:9–11:

> For this reason also, God highly exalted Him, and bestowed on Him the name which is above every name, so that at the name of Jesus every knee will bow, of those who are in heaven and on earth and under the earth, and that every tongue will confess that Jesus Christ is Lord, to the glory of God the Father.

Jesus looked beyond the humiliation and suffering in obedience, His death on the cross (Phil. 2:5–8), to the glory that awaited Him upon His return to heaven. The glory He would receive was rightfully His, both by His divine title (as the second member of the Trinity) and by His perfect submission (since He had submitted to His Father perfectly). He also knew that His death would bring eternal life to all who would believe in Him, thus causing joy in heaven (Luke 15:7, 10) and adding voices to the eternal choir of those who will praise and worship Him forever. The contemplation of those marvelous realities enabled Him to rejoice in the cross, even though He despised the shame of bearing sin (Heb. 12:2) and the horror of being forsaken by the Father (Matt. 27:46).

As those on the other side of the cross, removed from it by nearly two thousand years, believers must never lose sight of the glory and honor Christ deserves because of His redemptive work. What He endured on the cross is now the anthem of Christian praise and worship. And it will be for all of eternity, as believers forever praise the Lamb who was slain (Rev. 5:9). Though the Gospels record His earthly life and ministry —including the agony and suffering of His passion—it must always be remembered that He is no longer on the cross or in the tomb. He is even now the glorified Son of God, seated at His Father's right hand in power and glory (Rev. 1:13–20; cf. Dan. 7:13–14). The joy of seeing and praising Him in triumph awaits all those who love Him, while all who reject Him will be rejected by Him (Matt. 7:23; 25:41).

The glorious truth is that the cross made eternal life possible for all who sincerely believe in Jesus Christ (Rom. 10:9–10), and even before the cross all who genuinely repented of sin and trusted the forgiveness and mercy of God as their only hope (cf. Isa. 55:6–7). Were it not for the cross, there would be no salvation from sin for anyone in any age, no gospel of grace, no hope for this life, and no eternal destiny but hell. Without the cross, the eternal plan of salvation that God promised from before the beginning of time would never have come to fruition. The contemplation of those truths should cause everyone who knows and loves the Lord Jesus Christ to say with the apostle Paul,"But may it never be that I would boast, except in the cross of our Lord Jesus Christ, through which the world has been crucified to me, and I to the world" (Gal.6:14).

Jesus Prays for His Disciples—Part 1: As Those Whom the Father Had Given Him (John 17:6–10)

23

I have manifested Your name to the men whom You gave Me out of the world; they were Yours and You gave them to Me, and they have kept Your word. Now they have come to know that everything You have given Me is from You; for the words which You gave Me I have given to them; and they received them and truly understood that I came forth from You, and they believed that You sent Me. I ask on their behalf; I do not ask on behalf of the world, but of those whom You have given Me; for they are Yours; and all things that are Mine are Yours, and Yours are Mine; and I have been glorified in them. (17:6–10)

The doctrines of divine sovereignty (that God elected sinners for salvation in eternity past) and human responsibility (that sinners are held accountable for how they respond to the gospel) are both clearly taught in Scripture, and play an important role in this passage.

Without apology or excuse, the Bible teaches that the Father "chose [believers] in Him [Jesus Christ] before the foundation of the world" (Eph. 1:4; cf. Col. 3:12; Titus 1:1; 2 John 1). In eternity past, they were "predestined" for justification (Rom. 8:29), adoption (Eph. 1:5), and a heavenly inheritance (Eph. 1:11). Based on no merit or work of their own

(Eph. 2:8; Titus 3:5), God "saved [believers] and called [them] with a holy calling, not according to [their] works, but according to His own purpose and grace which was granted [them] in Christ Jesus from all eternity" (2 Tim. 1:9). Thus, they are "beloved by the Lord, because God has chosen [them] from the beginning for salvation" (2 Thess. 2:13). Credit for their salvation is wholly based on the Father's gracious electing choice, made possible through the Son's sacrificial death. The reality is that they would have remained "dead in [their] trespasses and sins" (Eph. 2:1), if God had not imparted spiritual life to them (v. 4). The Lord Himself declared that "No one can come to Me unless the Father who sent Me draws him" (John 6:44), underscoring the sinner's utter inability to come to saving faith unless God sovereignly initiates that work in his or her heart. Salvation is never the result of human morality, wisdom, or willpower, but of God's gracious purposes. As Paul told the Romans, salvation "does not depend on the man who wills or the man who runs, but on God who has mercy. . . . [And] He has mercy on whom He desires, and He hardens whom He desires" (Rom. 9:16, 18). Though Paul preached the gospel to thousands, only "as many as had been appointed to eternal life believed" (Acts 13:48). No one outside of those whom God has preselected for salvation will ever embrace Jesus Christ as Savior (cf. Rom. 3:10–12; 9:11; 1 Thess. 1:3–4; 1 Peter 1:2).

At the same time, the Bible contains numerous entreaties to all unsaved people to believe in the Lord (e.g., Isa. 55:1; Matt. 11:28–30; John 5:40; 7:37–39; Rev. 22:17). The gospel call, "Believe in the Lord Jesus, and you will be saved" (Acts 16:31), goes out as an open invitation to every sinner. The gracious offer is the same for everyone everywhere: "If you confess with your mouth Jesus as Lord, and believe in your heart that God raised Him from the dead, you will be saved" (Rom. 10:9). In fact, God's expressed desire (which is different than His sovereign decree) is for "all men to be saved and to come to the knowledge of the truth" (1 Tim. 2:4). That desire is made manifest in the gospel call, which extends to all people (Matt. 28:19), and which reveals the grace of God by offering salvation to anyone who believes in Jesus Christ (cf. Titus 2:11). The truth is that "many are called, but few are chosen" (Matt. 22:14), meaning that while the gospel is a plea to all men everywhere to repent (Acts 17:30), only the elect will embrace it in faith. Yet those who reject the gospel do so willingly and without excuse (cf. Rom. 1:20), having been given ample opportunity to respond by their patient Creator and Judge (2 Peter 3:9; cf. Rev. 2:21). On the basis of their own willful sins (Rev. 20:12–13; cf. Matt. 16:27), which evidence the fact that their names were never written in the Book of Life (Rev. 20:15; cf. 13:8; 17:8), they will be justly condemned and sent to eternal destruction (cf. 20:14; Matt. 25:46; 2 Thess. 1:9).

In this way, Scripture presents the dual realities that God is absolutely sovereign in choosing who will be part of His redeemed people, and also that sinners who reject the gospel bear personal responsibility for refusing God's offer of salvation. To be sure, there is an element of mystery (from the human perspective) in how those two truths work together in the mind of God. But believers should not go beyond what has been revealed in Scripture in trying to reconcile what their finite minds are incapable of comprehending (cf. Deut. 29:29; 1 Cor. 4:6); if both truths are set forth in God's Word, then both should be embraced. Furthermore, sinful human beings dare not accuse God of unfairness in only electing some sinners to salvation—since, if God were fair, all sinners would experience His wrath (cf. Romans 3:23; 6:23). No one has the right to question the eternal saving purposes of God. Anticipating any such reactions, the apostle Paul responded firmly with these words:

> You will say to me then, "Why does He still find fault? For who resists His will?" On the contrary, who are you, O man, who answers back to God? The thing molded will not say to the molder, "Why did you make me like this," will it? Or does not the potter have a right over the clay, to make from the same lump one vessel for honorable use and another for common use? What if God, although willing to demonstrate His wrath and to make His power known, endured with much patience vessels of wrath prepared for destruction? And He did so to make known the riches of His glory upon vessels of mercy, which He prepared beforehand for glory, even us, whom He also called, not from among Jews only, but also from among Gentiles. (Rom. 9:19–24)

Believers will praise God for all eternity because He graciously chose them and redeemed them through the work of the Son. They did nothing to earn their salvation, and therefore all the glory goes to God. But those who reject the gospel and are condemned to hell will have no one to blame but themselves. Having willfully suppressed the truth in unrighteousness, they will receive the penalty they rightly deserve for their rebellion. The seventeenth-century English Puritan Richard Baxter graphically illustrated this point in his classic work, *The Saints' Everlasting Rest:*

> [Salvation] was dear to Christ, but free to us. . . . Here is all free; if the Father freely give the Son, and the Son freely pay the debt; and if God freely accept that way of payment, when he might have required it of the principal; and if both Father and Son freely offer us the purchased life on our cordial acceptance; and if they freely send the Spirit to enable us to accept; what is here, then, that is not free? O the everlasting admiration that must surprise the saints to think of this freeness! . . . What an astonishing thought it will be [in heaven] to think of the

immeasurable difference between our deservings and receivings! Between the state we should have been in, and the state we are in! To look down upon hell, and see the vast difference from that to which we are adopted! What pangs of love will it cause within us to think, "Yonder was the place that sin would have brought me to; but this is it that Christ hath brought me to! Yonder death was the wages of my sin, but this eternal life is the gift of God, through Jesus Christ my Lord.... But no thanks to us, nor to any of our duties and labors, much less to our neglects and laziness; we know to whom the praise is due and must be given for ever.... So then let DESERVED be written on the door of hell; but on the door of heaven and life, THE FREE GIFT. (in *The Practical Works of Richard Baxter* [repr.; Grand Rapids: Baker, 1981], 14–15)

The eternal saving purposes of God had always been Jesus' primary concern during His earthly ministry (Luke 5:31–32; 19:10; John 3:16–17; 4:34–38). Now, as the cross drew near, the Lord articulated those purposes in this magnificent prayer to His Father—voicing them audibly so that His disciples could hear. The Lord knew that what had been planned in eternity past would be fulfilled in the next few hours of time (cf. vv. 1–5). He also knew that His disciples would abandon Him at the critical moment (John 13:36–38; 16:32), that their faith would be shaken (cf. Luke 22:31–32), and that their hearts would be deeply grieved (John 16:22). Though His own suffering would far outweigh theirs, Jesus sacrificially served them (as He had done throughout His entire ministry [cf. Mark 10:44–45] including that evening [John 13:1, 12], and would ultimately do on the cross [15:13]) by praying for them. In fact, of the twenty-six verses that comprise Jesus' prayer in John 17, fourteen center specifically on the disciples (vv. 6–19) with an additional seven (vv. 20–26) focusing on those who would believe in Christ in the future through their extended ministries.

Having prayed that the Father would glorify the Son (in vv. 1–5), Jesus then interceded for His disciples (vv. 6–19). This section of His High Priestly Prayer may be discussed under two headings: His prayer for them as those whom the Father had given Him (vv. 6–10); and His specific requests for them in light of His imminent departure (vv. 11–19). The first of those headings will be discussed below, with the second being addressed in the following chapter.

The frightening realization that Christ was leaving them was a paralyzing thought to the disciples. They had depended on Him for everything. He had been their teacher (John 13:13), their protector (Matt. 12:1–5), and the supplier of all their needs (cf. Luke 22:35). But now He was going away. They were about to be left alone and, from their viewpoint, thrown back on their own resources. Understanding their fears, Jesus spent much of His time with the disciples on the evening before

His death comforting them. He reassured them that He would continue to love them and provide for their needs (see the exposition of chapters 13–16 in previous chapters of this volume). Now, having given the disciples those marvelous promises, Jesus prayed that the Father would ensure those promises. As one commentator explains:

> By far the largest part of Jesus' prayer relates to the disciples. He was much more concerned about them than about himself. He was sure of the suffering that was inevitable and the victory that was certain. The disciples, however, were a variable quantity; in themselves they were likely to fail.... Nevertheless, he prayed for them with confidence that they would be kept by the Father's power and presented for a future ministry. (Merrill C. Tenney, "The Gospel of John," in *The Expositor's Bible Commentary*, ed. Frank E. Gaebelein [Grand Rapids: Zondervan, 1981], 9:163)

Jesus' confidence was founded, not in the resolve of the eleven, but in the will and power of the Father. But before launching into His specific requests for the disciples (in vv. 11–19), the Lord explained why He knew the Father would honor His requests (in vv. 6–10).

Verse 6 serves as an important transition statement from Christ's prayer for His own glory (in vv. 1–5) to His prayer for the disciples (in vv. 6–19). Of note in this verse is the interplay between the human side and the divine side of salvation. Christ subsequently expanded on each of those topics, as He established the disciples' believing response on the one hand (in vv. 7–8), and God's sovereign election on the other (in vv. 9–10). The verse itself provides a thesis statement of sorts for the verses that follow, introducing the reasons why Jesus knew the Father would ensure His previous promises to the disciples (in chapters 13–16) and answer His subsequent requests for them (in vv. 11–19).

The Lord defined those for whom He was praying first of all as those to whom He had **manifested** the Father's **name.** The phrase connects back to verse 4, indicating that part of Christ's earthly mission was to make known the Father's name to the disciples. **Manifested** translates a form of the verb *phaneroō,* which means "to reveal," "to make known," or "to show." The aorist tense denotes that this was an accomplished fact, one that Christ had perfectly finished according to the Father's plan. The concept of God's **name** encompasses all that He is: His character, nature, and attributes. Psalm 9:10 reads, "Those who know Your name will put their trust in You, for You, O Lord, have not forsaken those who seek You." In Psalm 20:7 David exulted, "Some boast in chariots and some in horses, but we will boast in the name of the Lord, our God," while in Psalm 22:22 he declared, "I will tell of Your name to my brethren" (cf. 5:11; 8:1; 48:10;

75:1; 115:1; 119:55; 1 Kings 8:33, 35, 43, 44, 48; 1 Chron. 17:24; 2 Chron. 6:20; Neh. 1:11; Isa. 26:8, 13; Mic. 6:9).

The supreme manifestation of the name of God was the Lord Jesus Christ, God in human flesh. So perfectly and completely did Jesus reveal God's nature and character that He could make the shocking statements, "He who sees Me sees the One who sent Me" (John 12:45) and, "He who has seen Me has seen the Father" (14:9; cf. 1:18). The New Testament writers declare Him to be "the image of the invisible God, the firstborn of all creation" (Col. 1:15), in whom "all the fullness of Deity dwells in bodily form" (2:9), "who ... existed in the form of God" (Phil. 2:6) and "is the radiance of His glory and the exact representation of His nature" (Heb. 1:3).

The name of God was so sacred to the Jews that they refused to pronounce it. Instead, they took the consonants from the tetragrammaton (YHWH; cf. Ex. 3:14–15) and added the vowels from the word *adonai* ("Lord"). When they read the Hebrew text of the Old Testament, they pronounced the resulting word ("Yahweh," rendered "Jehovah" in older English translations) "Adonai," in order to avoid speaking God's name aloud. Jesus, however, not only manifested God's name, He spoke it. And even more shockingly, He took it for Himself (cf. John 8:24, 58 and the exposition of those verses in *John 1–11*, The MacArthur New Testament Commentary [Chicago: Moody, 2006]). In so doing, Jesus so outraged His Jewish opponents, who thought it blasphemy, that they sought to kill Him (John 5:18; 8:59; 10:31–33), and eventually succeeded (John 19:7).

Nonetheless through His death, Jesus Christ opened the way to personal, loving fellowship with God. As He Himself said, "I am the way, the truth, and the life; no one comes to the Father but through Me" (John 14:6). And earlier, using the metaphor of a sheepfold, He declared, "I am the door; if anyone enters through Me, he will be saved, and will go in and out and find pasture" (John 10:9). Those who have placed their faith in Him have their sins forgiven, and enjoy an intimate relationship with the Father, whom they have the privilege of calling Abba (Rom. 8:15; Gal. 4:6), which endearingly means, "Papa" or "Daddy."

Christ further described the disciples to the Father as **the men whom You gave Me out of the world** (cf. 15:19). The truth that believers are a gift from the Father to the Son has already been seen as an important theme in this prayer (cf. vv. 2, 9, 24). The **world** is the evil, godless, satanically ruled system composed of all the unredeemed and all that opposes God and His kingdom (cf. 7:7; 12:31; 14:17, 19, 30, 31; 16:11; 2 Cor. 4:4; Eph. 6:12; 1 John 5:19). Christians are no longer part of the world, having been "rescued ... from the domain of darkness, and transferred ... to the kingdom of His beloved Son" (Col. 1:13). Earlier that evening Jesus had told the disciples, "If the world hates you, you know that it has hated Me before it hated you. If you were of the world, the world would love its own; but because you are not of the world, but I chose you out of the world, because of this the world hates you" (15:18–19). Since they are no longer part of it, and indeed have been crucified to it (Gal. 6:14), believers are not to be conformed to the world (Rom. 12:2) or walk in it as they once did (Eph. 2:2; cf. 1 John 2:15–17). Instead, they are called to overcome it (1 John 5:4–5) by keeping themselves unstained by it (James 1:27) and avoiding friendship with it (James 4:4).

Christ's statement **they were Yours and You gave them to Me** is a forceful affirmation that even before their conversion the disciples belonged to God. Earlier in John's gospel the Lord had declared, "All that the Father gives Me will come to Me, and the one who comes to Me I will certainly not cast out" (6:37; cf. v. 39; 17:2, 9, 24). God told the apostle Paul that He had "many people in this city [Corinth]" who belonged to Him even though they were not yet saved (Acts 18:10; cf. 13:48). As was discussed earlier, God elected believers to salvation in eternity past (Eph. 1:4), and wrote their names in the Book of Life (Phil. 4:3; Rev. 13:8; 17:8; 20:12, 15; 21:27; 22:19; cf. Dan. 12:1; Luke 10:20). Having chosen to redeem them, the Father gave them to the Son as gifts of His love (see the fuller discussion of this glorious reality in the previous chapter of this volume). Thus, as earlier demonstrated, the disciples (and by extension all believers —cf. v. 20) were infinitely precious to the Son, not because of anything intrinsically valuable in them, but because they were promised to Him by His Father before time began (cf. 2 Tim. 1:9; Titus 1:1). As the next few hours would prove, Jesus considered the Father's gift so precious He was willing to die to receive it.

In addition to recognizing that they were a gift from His Father, the Lord also described the disciples as those who **have kept** the Father's **word.** That statement introduces the element of obedience essential to salvation (cf. Phil. 2:12–13). That obedience, of course, is not a meritorious work that contributes something to salvation (cf. Gal. 2:15–16), but is rather the inevitable result of genuine saving faith (cf. Eph. 2:8–10). Thus, to say that the disciples had obeyed the Father's Word is merely another way of expressing that their faith was genuine. The New Testament inseparably joins saving faith and obedience, so much so that obedience is often used as a synonym for faith (e.g., John 3:36; Acts 6:7; Rom. 1:5; 16:26; 1 Peter 1:2). It is also the sure mark of sincere love for Jesus Christ (John 14:15, 21, 24; 15:10, 14). (Interestingly, Jesus used forms of this same Greek word for "keep" (*tereō*) in vv. 11, 12, 15 when He asked the Father to keep the disciples. Thus, the Lord asked the Father to keep those who keep His Word.)

The disciples, then, were among those who kept the Word that had been revealed to them. From the heart, they had responded in genuine faith to the truth they had received. At the same time, Scripture recognizes that they had done so because they were a gift from the Father to the Son, having been among those whom He sovereignly chose in eternity past and called effectually in time for salvation. The rest of this section (vv. 7–10) builds on those inseparable twin truths. Having summarized them in verse 6, Jesus continued to explain why He knew the Father would grant His requests regarding the disciples: because they had believed in Him as the Son (vv. 7–8) and because they were a gift to Him from the Father (vv. 9–10).

BECAUSE THEY HAD BELIEVED IN HIM AS THE SON

Now they have come to know that everything You have given Me is from You; for the words which You gave Me I have given to them; and they received them and truly understood that I came forth from You, and they believed that You sent Me. (17:7–8)

Though they had been with Jesus for several years, it was not until **now** that His disciples were beginning to truly understand the mission His Father had given Him. It would still be a few days until Christ arose, when they would begin to fully grasp the reasons Jesus had to die. Yet they clearly believed that Jesus was whom He claimed to be (Matt. 16:16; Mark 8:29; Luke 9:20), that He came from the Father, and that He alone spoke the words of eternal life (cf. John 6:68–69). As Jesus had already stated in verse 6, they had kept His Word and thus had proven to be His true disciples (cf. John 8:31).

The content of the disciples' faith offers further proof of its genuineness. Though before the cross there was still much that they did not grasp, they sincerely believed the truths they did understand (in contrast to the false faith of many others—cf. John 2:23–25; 6:64, 66). The eleven had **come to know** first of all, as Jesus said to the Father, **that everything You have given Me is from You** (a statement that again highlights His intimacy with and dependence on the Father). The disciples believed that Jesus worked by the power of God and did everything according to His Father's will. This was in contrast to the Jewish religious leaders, who accused Jesus of operating through the power of Satan (Matt. 12:24). Such conclusions, as Christ Himself pointed out, were not only blasphemous and unforgivable (cf. Matt. 12:24–32) but foolish, since Satan would never empower someone to further the work of God (vv. 25–29). The disciples, of course, knew the truth. They had seen Jesus' miracles, which were marked by divine compassion (Matt. 14:14; 15:32; 20:34; Mark 1:41; 6:34; 9:35–36; Luke 7:13–14); they had heard Jesus' sermons, which pierced the heart with divine authority (Matt. 7:29; 13:54;

22:33; Mark 1:22; 6:2; 11:18; Luke 4:32; John 7:46); they had seen Jesus pray, knowing that He spent long hours in communion with His Father (Matt. 14:23; Mark 1:35; Luke 5:16; 6:12; 9:18,28; 11:1–4); they had watched Jesus' minister to sinners, and yet never sin Himself (Matt. 9:11; 11:19; Luke 5:29–32; 15:2; 1 Peter 2:22; 3:18; 1 John 2:29; 3:5); they had even witnessed the Father's visible and audible approval of His Son (Matt. 17:5; Mark 9:7; Luke 9:35; John 12:28; cf. Matt. 3:17). They knew that He came from God, and as a result they followed Him wholeheartedly (Matt. 19:27; cf. Mark 8:34; Luke 9:57–62; John 12:25–26).

The disciples likewise believed that **the words which** the Father **gave** to Jesus were true (cf. v. 14; 7:16; 8:28; 12:49; 14:10, 24). Jesus had **given** those words **to them; and they received them,** by both affirming them and subsequently acting upon them (cf. James 1:22). They **truly understood** Christ's divine origin, **that** He **came forth from** the Father (cf. 16:30). **They** also **believed** in His divine mission, **that** the Father had **sent** Him into the world (cf. vv. 18, 21, 23, 25; 3:34; 4:34; 5:24, 30, 36, 37; 6:38, 39, 44, 57; 7:16, 28, 29, 33; 8:16, 18, 26, 29, 42; 9:4; 11:42; 12:44, 45, 49; 13:20; 14:24; 15:21; 16:5; 20:21). They had come to realize what John's prologue articulates: that He is the Son of God (John 1:1; cf. 16:30), equal in essence and eternally coexistent with the Father (1:1–2), the Creator of all things (1:3), and the source of eternal life and spiritual light (1:4). They recognized the glory of the Word made flesh, and knew that it was "glory as of the only begotten from the Father, full of grace and truth" (1:14). Soon they would also understand the wonders of His death and resurrection (cf. 16:20). Those realizations were revolutionary for the disciples:

> The response of these men did not seem like very much. But for them to see the source of these things was a spiritual miracle more wonderful than the miracle of a man born physically blind being enabled, for the first time, to see the wonder of a tree, the glory of a sunset, the mobile mystery of a human face. (John Phillips, *Exploring the Gospel of John* [Grand Rapids: Kregel, 1989], 321–22)

After Pentecost, the proof of their faith would be demonstrated in dramatic ways, as they boldly proclaimed Jesus as Lord to all who would listen. Though they suffered severe persecution and (for nearly all of them) martyrdom, the disciples would not abandon what they knew to be true. Even the threat of death could not undermine the undying conviction that God had placed within them (cf. Acts 4:13; 5:41). The saving faith they were given was enduring by its very nature (cf. 1 Peter 1:3–9; 1 John 2:19).

Through their obedience, they demonstrated that they were among those whom the Father had elected as a love gift for His Son. Their works did not save them, but they did evidence that true saving faith was alive in their hearts. James Montgomery Boice posed the question,

> How does one tell who are the elect of God? How do we judge who are Christians and who are not? ... There is only one answer, the answer given by the Lord Jesus Christ [speaking] of those who were truly his disciples [in John 17:6–8]. According to these verses, the only way to tell whether one is a Christian or not is to see whether he or she believes and continues in the words of the Lord Jesus Christ. (*The Gospel of John* [Grand Rapids: Baker, 1999], 1276)

The Bible teaches that God will certainly bring to glorification all those whom He predestined in eternity past (cf. John 6:37, 39; 10:28; Rom. 8:29–30; Eph. 1:13–14; Phil. 1:6; 1 Thess. 5:23, 24; 1 Peter 1:5; Jude 1, 24). It also teaches that those whom God has truly chosen will respond in faith to the gospel, and will also persevere in the truth to the end (cf. Matt. 24:13; 1 Cor. 15:1–2; Col. 1:21–23; Heb. 2:1; 3:14; 4:14; 6:11–12; 10:39; 2:Peter 1:10). On the one hand, this perseverance requires diligent effort on the part of believers (Phil. 2:12; 1 Tim. 4:7–8; Heb. 5:9). On the other hand, it is a work that God ultimately does through believers (Phil. 2:13; Heb. 13:21). In fact, all of the Christian life (including the desire to pursue godliness) is a result of God's grace (cf. 1 Cor. 15:10; 2 Cor. 3:5). (Note the discussion in the following chapter of this commentary regarding God's power to protect the faith of those who are His.)

As those who had received, believed, and persevered in the truth, the disciples proved themselves to be among God's elect. Of the Twelve only Judas Iscariot was not chosen, betraying the Lord "so that the Scripture would be fulfilled" (John 17:12; cf. 13:21–30).

BECAUSE THEY WERE GIVEN TO HIM FROM THE FATHER

I ask on their behalf, I do not ask on behalf of the world, but of those whom You have given Me; for they are Yours; and all things that are Mine are Yours, and Yours are Mine; and I have been glorified in them (17:9–10)

Because they had responded with belief, and demonstrated the genuineness of that faith through their continued obedience, the disciples showed evidence of what Jesus had always known to be true of them and said earlier—that they had been chosen out of the world by the Father as a gift for Him. This then provides the second and ultimate reason why Jesus was confident that the Father would grant His prayer for the disciples; the Father would be sure to protect and purify them because they were His gift to His Son (cf. vv. 11, 15, 17). By reiterating that He was asking exclusively on **behalf** of **those whom** the Father had **given** Him, Jesus made it clear that He did **not ask on behalf of the world.** Rather, He was asking on behalf of His own who remained in the world after He had left (vv. 11–12).

It is true that God shows a kind of love to all people in the world (what theologians call common grace), even to those who reject the gospel (cf. Mark 10:21). He pleads with sinners to repent (Ezek. 18:23, 32; Acts 17:30), extends the gospel invitation to them (Isa. 55:1; cf. Matt. 11:28–30), "causes His sun to rise on the evil and the good, and sends rain on the righteous and the unrighteous" (Matt. 5:45; cf. Ps. 145:9; Acts 14:17). But Christ's intercessory work as High Priest is only for those who belong eternally to Him because they have been given by the Father. In fact, the only recorded instance in the New Testament of Christ praying for the unregenerate is His cry from the cross, "Father, forgive them; for they do not know what they are doing" (Luke 23:34). That prayer is a model for believers, who are to "love [their] enemies and pray for those who persecute [them]" (Matt. 5:44; 2 Tim. 2:26). But the unredeemed world was not His interest in this prayer. His attention was on those whom the Father had given to Him and for whom He was about to die to provide atonement—that they would be protected from the world especially during the immediate events surrounding His arrest, trial, and crucifixion.

Jesus' statement **they are Yours; and all things that are Mine are Yours, and Yours are Mine** underscored His confidence in the fact that the eleven belonged to God. Like the disciples, all believers belong to the Father, having been adopted into His family through the Son (cf. Rom. 8:14–17; Gal. 3:26; 4:5–7) and sealed and cleansed by the Holy Spirit (Eph. 1:13–14; 4:30; Titus 3:5). "Do you not know," Paul wrote to the Corinthians, "that your body is a temple of the Holy Spirit who is in you, whom you have from God, and that you are not your own? For you have been bought with a price: therefore glorify God in your body" (1 Cor. 6:19–20; cf. 7:23). Christians are God's chosen ones (Matt. 22:14; John 13:18; Col. 3:12; 2 Thess. 2:13; 2 Tim. 2:10; Titus 1:1; 1 Peter 1:1–2; 2:9), His children (John 1:12; Eph. 5:1; Phil. 2:15; 1 Peter 1:14; 1 John 3:1–2), His subjects (Luke 6:20; John 3:3, 5; Acts 14:22; Col. 1:13; 1 Thess. 2:12), His slaves (Acts 4:29; Rom. 1:1; 1 Cor. 7:22; Phil. 1:1; Col. 4:12; 2 Tim. 2:24; 1 Peter 2:16), and His sheep (Ps. 100:3; John 10:7–16, 26–28; 1 Peter 5:2–4).

Christ's statement **all things that are . . . Yours are Mine** is nothing less than a claim to deity and full equality with the Father. It again emphasized the intimate unity that the Son shares with the Father (vv. 3, 6–7, 21, 23–24, 26; cf. 16:15). For a mere creature to claim that **all things** of God's were his would be blasphemous presumption. Only one who is Himself God could legitimately claim to be the owner of and ruler over all things. Martin Luther grasped the significance of this claim:

> Everyone may say this, that all we have is God's. But this is much greater, that he turns it around and says, all that is thine is mine. This no creature is able to say before God. . . . The word: all that is thine is mine, leaves nothing whatever excluded. Are all things his, then the eternal deity is also his; otherwise he could not and dared not use the word at all. (cited in R. C. H. Lenski, *The Interpretation of St. John's Gospel* [Minneapolis: Augsburg, 1943], 1133–34).

Since the Father and the Son have **all things** in common, believers also belong to Christ (1 Cor. 3:23; 15:23; 2 Cor. 10:7; Gal. 3:29; 5:24). Those who belong to the Father belong to the Son, and vice versa.

The Lord further noted that He had been **glorified in them.** Even now, their faith in Him as the Son of God brought Him glory. Here then Christ gives testimony that the gift of faith given to the disciples enabled them to recognize and to confess Him even in His state of self-humiliation. After His ascension, Christ's glory would continue to be displayed on earth through His followers even in His absence. That request was in perfect harmony with the Father's purpose—to give the Son a redeemed humanity who would glorify Him forever.

The supreme goal of everything a Christian does is to bring God glory. Paul exhorted the Corinthians, "Whether, then, you eat or drink or whatever you do, do all to the glory of God" (1 Cor. 10:31). In his second letter to them, he added, "Therefore we also have as our ambition, whether at home [on earth] or absent [in heaven], to be pleasing to Him" (2 Cor. 5:9; cf. Rom. 14:7–8). Jesus commanded His followers, "Let your light shine before men in such a way that they may see your good works, and glorify your Father who is in heaven" (Matt. 5:16; cf. Phil. 2:15). Believers are to reflect Christ's glory in a world of darkness. Paul made that glorious truth crystal clear when he wrote, "God, who said, 'Light shall shine out of darkness,' is the One who has shone in our hearts to give the Light of the knowledge of the glory of God in the face of Christ. But we have this treasure in earthen vessels, so that the surpassing greatness of the power will be of God and not from ourselves" (2 Cor. 4:6–7). The desire to glorify Christ will continue into all of eternity, as believers join with angels in magnifying and exalting the Son forever (cf. Rev. 4:8–11; 5:11–14; 19:6; 22:3–4).

That the disciples (and all other believers) could be changed from rebellious lovers of this world into sanctified worshipers and glorifiers of God is the miracle of God's grace in salvation. Though regeneration takes place at a moment in time, it is a miracle that was planned in eternity past and that has unending implications for eternity future. All believers (including the eleven disciples) were chosen and claimed by the Father before the world began and promised to the Son as a tangible expression of His infinite love. That is the divine side of salvation. The human side is persevering faith and obedience, by which the disciples had demonstrated that they truly belonged to God.

Believers at all times can be likewise assured that they are truly saved. Objectively, that assurance comes from the Bible's promise that anyone who sincerely embraces Jesus Christ as Lord and Savior will be saved (Rom. 10:9–10). Subjectively, that confidence stems from the fruit of enduring faith and continuing obedience in a person's life no matter what the temptation or test. Hear the powerful words of Peter:

> Blessed be the God and Father of our Lord Jesus Christ, who according to His great mercy has caused us to be born again to a living hope through the resurrection of Jesus Christ from the dead, to obtain an inheritance which is imperishable and undefiled and will not fade away, reserved in heaven for you, who are protected by the power of God through faith for a salvation ready to be revealed in the last time. In this you greatly rejoice, even though now for a little while, if necessary, you have been distressed by various trials, so that the proof of your faith, being more precious than gold which is perishable, even though tested by fire, may be found to result in praise and glory and honor at the revelation of Jesus Christ; and though you have not seen Him, you love Him, and though you do not see Him now, but believe in Him, you greatly rejoice with joy inexpressible and full of glory, obtaining as the outcome of your faith the salvation of your souls. (1 Peter 1:3–9; cf. John 10:27; 15:10, 14; 1 John 3:21–24; 4:20; 5:4; cf. Rev. 14:12).

Like the eleven, all true disciples of Christ abide in His Word (John 8:31) and lovingly obey His commands (John 14:15). Such behavior is only possible because their hearts have been changed by God, who has drawn them to the Son (John 6:44) and regenerated them through the Spirit (Titus 3:5). Thus the apostle John could write,

> By this we know that we have come to know Him, if we keep His commandments. The one who says, "I have come to know Him," and does not keep His commandments, is a liar, and the truth is not in him; but whoever keeps His word, in him the love of God has truly been perfected. By this we know that we are in Him: the one who says he abides in Him ought himself to walk in the same manner as He walked. (1 John 2:3–6)

Ensuring the preservation of the disciples' faith is a divine work that the Lord does by His power (cf. John 6:37–40). Nothing can separate His own from His love (Rom. 8:31–39) and He is willing and "able also to save forever those who draw near to God through Him, since He always lives to make intercession for them" (Heb. 7:25).

In the face of His absence in sin-bearing, though only for a few hours, Jesus proceeded to ask the Father to take up the protection of those whom He had given to Him. Yet, in making that request, Jesus expressed absolute certainty that the Father would do what He asked. His confidence was not in the disciples' steadfastness or ingenuity, but in the love and power of His Father (cf. John 10:28–30). He knew that what the Father had promised in eternity past He would certainly accomplish and ensure in the present.

Jesus Prays for His Disciples—Part 2: As Those Whom He Is about to Leave (John 17:11–19)

24

I am no longer in the world; and yet they themselves are in the world, and I come to You. Holy Father, keep them in Your name, the name which You have given Me, that they may be one even as We are. While I was with them, I was keeping them in Your name which You have given Me; and I guarded them and not one of them perished but the son of perdition, so that the Scripture would be fulfilled. But now I come to You; and these things I speak in the world so that they may have My joy made full in themselves. I have given them Your word; and the world has hated them, because they are not of the world, even as I am not of the world. I do not ask You to take them out of the world, but to keep them from the evil one. They are not of the world, even as I am not of the world. Sanctify them in the truth; Your word is truth. As You sent Me into the world, I also have sent them into the world. For their sakes I sanctify Myself, that they themselves also may be sanctified in truth. (17:11–19)

Through Jesus Christ, every believer has been granted direct access to the very throne room of God. Each can "draw near with confidence to the throne of grace [and] receive mercy and find grace to help in time of need" (Heb. 4:16). Though formerly His enemies, they have been reconciled to God (2 Cor. 5:17–18), having been adopted into His family "through faith in Jesus Christ" (Gal. 3:26; cf. 4:5–6; Rom. 8:15–17). Because they are His children, the glorious God of the universe graciously, willingly, and lovingly responds to their prayers, no matter how small or feeble they may seem (cf. the exposition of 16:26–27 in chapter 20 of this volume).

In addition to personal prayers, believers also have the prayers of others, who intercede on their behalf. The apostle Paul emphasized the need for that kind of intercession in the closing paragraphs of his epistle to the Ephesians:

> With all prayer and petition pray at all times in the Spirit, and with this in view, be on the alert with all perseverance and petition for all the saints, and pray on my behalf, that utterance may be given to me in the opening of my mouth, to make known with boldness the mystery of the gospel, for which I am an ambassador in chains; that in proclaiming it I may speak boldly, as I ought to speak. (Eph. 6:18–20)

Having just warned his readers about the reality of spiritual warfare (Eph. 6:10–17), Paul stressed the critical importance of making supplication "for all the saints" (v. 18). "Pray for us" is a recurring theme throughout his letters (1 Thess. 5:25; 2 Thess. 3:1; Heb. 13:18; cf. Col. 4:2–3; 1 Tim. 2:7–8). Like Paul, the venerable Spurgeon acutely understood the importance of intercessory prayer. He addressed his congregation with these dramatic words:

> Oh! may God help me, if you cease to pray for me! Let me know the day, and I must cease to preach. Let me know when you intend to cease your prayers, and I shall cry, "O my God, give me this day my tomb, and let me slumber in the dust." (Charles Spurgeon, "Prayer—the Forerunner of Mercy," in *The New Park Street Pulpit* [Pasadena, Tex.: Pilgrim, 1981], 3:255–56)

The intercession of Christians for each other is an essential element of the church's spiritual life, and the New Testament contains numerous examples of it (e.g., Acts 12:5; 20:36; 21:5; 2 Cor. 1:11; 9:14; Eph. 1:16; 6:18–19; Phil. 1:4; Col. 4:12).

But other Christians are not the only ones who intercede on behalf of the believer. The Holy "Spirit also helps our weakness; for we do not know how to pray as we should, but the Spirit Himself intercedes for us with groanings too deep for words" (Rom. 8:26). The skewed perspectives, human imperfections, and spiritual limitations that plague Christians in this life keep them from praying as they ought to pray—in absolute consistency with God's will. But the indwelling Spirit intercedes on behalf of each Christian, faithfully bringing his needs before God even when he is confused as to what those needs truly are. The Spirit's prayers are always answered "because He intercedes for the saints according to the will of God" (v. 27).

Yet, beyond all of that there is another who prays for believers— none other than the Lord Jesus Christ, who is "seated at the right hand of God" (Col. 3:1) and "always lives to make intercession for [His people]" (Heb. 7:25). Like the Spirit, the blessed Christ intercedes continually for His own, often in response to the accusations of Satan (1 John 2:1; Rev. 12:10), and always in accord with the will of God. His mediatorial work of intercession is as real and indispensable as His work of atonement. It was the death of the Lord Jesus Christ that gave believers eternal life; it is His intercessory work for them that sustains that life, bringing them from justification, through sanctification, to glorification (cf. Rom. 8:30). His intercession is the guarantee that undergirds Christ's promise, "All that the Father gives Me will come to Me, and the one who comes to Me I will certainly not cast out.... For this is the will of My Father, that everyone who beholds the Son and believes in Him will have eternal life, and I Myself will raise him up on the last day" (John 6:37, 40).

Christ's prayer in this chapter provides a priceless preview of His current intercessory work, which did not formally begin until after His ascension. In entrusting His followers to His Father, interceding on their behalf just a few hours before the cross, Jesus vividly displayed the profound depths of both His communion with God and His compassion for His own. As one commentator observes, the sublime magnificence of this aspect of the prayer

> surpasses all literature in its setting forth the identity of being and power and love in the twofold personality of the God-Man. We are brought by it to the mercy-seat, into the heaven of heavens, to the very heart of God; and we find there a presentation of the most mysterious and incomprehensible love to the human race, embodied in the Person, enshrined in the words, of the only begotten Son. (H. R. Reynolds, *St. John*, The Pulpit Commentary, ed. H. D. M. Spence and Joseph S. Exell [Grand Rapids: Eerdmans, 1981], 17:340)

This petition marks the transition from His earthly to His heavenly ministry. After completing His work of redemption on the cross and triumphing over sin, death, and the forces of hell, Jesus ascended to heaven. There, He continually "intercedes for us" (Rom. 8:34) while seated "at the right hand of God" (Col. 3:1; Heb. 10:12; 1 Peter 3:22; cf. Matt. 22:44; 26:64; Acts 2:33–34; 5:31; 7:55–56; Eph. 1:20; Heb. 1:3; 8:1; 12:2).

The prayer itself has been divided into three sections. In the first section (vv. 1–5) Jesus prayed for His glory; in the last section (vv. 20–26)

He prayed for all believers. But between those first and last sections, the Lord prayed specifically for the eleven disciples—as those whom the Father had given Him (vv. 6–10), and as those whom He was about to leave (vv. 11–19).

All twelve disciples had been present in the upper room when Jesus humbly washed their feet (13:5), and when they ate a final meal together (13:12). But not all twelve were true disciples (cf. 6:66; 8:31). One of them, Judas the son of Simon Iscariot, was a traitor (13:21)—a characteristic that he had hidden from everyone else except Christ (13:11). In fact, when Jesus mentioned that someone would betray Him, none of the other disciples even suspected Judas (13:22). After exposing Judas as the betrayer, He said to him, "What you do, do quickly" (13:27). But even then, the other disciples did not know "for what purpose He had said this to him. For some were supposing because Judas had the money box, that Jesus was saying to him, 'Buy the things we have need of for the feast'; or else, that he should give something to the poor" (13:28–29).

With Judas gone, only the eleven remained. (After the events of the resurrection and ascension, Matthias would be chosen as Judas's replacement [Acts 1:26].) It was to them that Jesus spoke the profound words of the upper room discourse (in chapters 14–16). And it was for them that Jesus specifically prayed in verses 6–19.

A quick survey of the behavior of those eleven men underscores the necessity of Jesus' prayer on their behalf. First among the apostles was Peter (Matt. 10:2–4; Mark 3:16–19; Luke 6:14–16; Acts 1:13), whose characteristic outspokenness (cf. Matt. 16:21–23) had earned him a dire rebuke from the Lord earlier that evening. After impetuously promising that he would die for Jesus, he heard this chilling reply: "Will you lay down your life for Me? Truly, truly, I say to you, a rooster will not crow until you deny Me three times" (John 13:38). Peter, who had been concerned about who would betray his Master (13:24), must have been profoundly distraught by the Lord's prediction about him. This, compounded by the realization that Jesus was going away, surely weighed heavy on his heart as he heard the Lord's intercession on his behalf.

The other disciples were similarly distraught at the thought of Christ's absence. Their own weakness and seeming lack of readiness would have been an inescapable concern. None of them appear particularly savvy or resourceful. They were not highly educated (Acts 4:13), nor did they have much in the way of material resources, since they had given up everything to follow Jesus (Mark 10:28). Many of the disciples were common fishermen (Peter, Andrew, James, and John were for sure [cf. Matt. 4:18–21], and possibly Thomas, Philip, and Nathanael [Bartholomew] were as well [cf. John 21:2–3]). Others came from even less prestigious backgrounds. Matthew had been a tax collector (Matt. 9:9) and was thereby despised by the Jews; while Simon had been a political revolutionary (as his name "the Zealot" indicates; Luke 6:15; Acts 1:13), and was thereby despised by the Romans.

They were ordinary men, with ordinary weaknesses. Peter was impetuous (as noted above); Thomas was a skeptic (John 20:25); and James and John were hotheaded "sons of thunder" (Mark 3:17; cf. Mark 9:38; Luke 9:52–54). Like Philip (John 6:5–7; 14:8), the rest lacked spiritual perception. Like Thaddeus (cf. John 14:22), they all failed to understand Christ's role in His first coming (as the Suffering Servant). Like the sons of Zebedee (Matt. 20:21–22), they all evidenced pride and a desire to hold a preeminent position (Matt. 20:24). And like Peter (John 13:38), whose name meant "rock" (Matt. 16:18), they all became cowards when the Lord was arrested (John 16:32). In fact, their spiritual resolve was such that when they were supposed to be praying, at the moment of Christ's supreme agony (Luke 22:44), Jesus found them sleeping (v. 46).

From a human perspective, this ragamuffin group of followers was anything but extraordinary or impressive (cf. 1 Cor. 1:16–31). Yet they were called to continue Jesus' work in the world after He was gone—having been given the responsibility of taking the gospel throughout the world (Matt. 28:18–20; cf. Acts 1:8), and shepherding the church through their teaching and oversight (cf. Acts 2:42; 6:4). They played a vital role in the future of the Christian faith, because God had chosen them to tell the world of redemption through His Son (cf. Eph. 2:20).

It is no wonder, then, that Jesus interceded for them, and that the bulk of His prayer concentrates on these eleven men. His confidence was not in their resolve or resourcefulness (of which they had little), but in the power and love of His Father. Jesus knew that the Father would hear and answer His prayers, not because the eleven were inherently capable, but because they were part of those whom the Father had promised Him from before the foundation of the world. The striking reality of prayer is that it is not designed to change God's will, but to call for its fulfillment. Furthermore, the Lord purposely prayed aloud so that His disciples could hear Him and be strengthened and encouraged.

Soon Jesus would **no longer** be **in the world** to protect and care for His disciples, although **they themselves** would remain **in the world.** His use of the present tense is indicative of the fact that, after the events of the next few hours transpired, His earthly mission would be completed. The time was no longer future, it had arrived. He was going away but they were staying behind. Though they surely wished to go with Him (cf. 14:1–6), it was critical that, for the time being, they remain and take the gospel to the world (cf. Matt. 28:18–20; John 17:18; Acts 1:7–8). Since in the plan of God there would have been no church, and no subsequent generations of believers, if the disciples had not been left as witnesses to the gospel, this intercession on their behalf is weighty. It is a means God used for activating His will.

And the **world,** where the disciples would remain, was certain to be hostile to them. It was, after all, a place of hateful rebellion against God and against His Son (John 1:11; 7:7; 15:18–19; 16:33; cf. Luke 21:12–19). Once Jesus left, antagonism toward Him (under the direction of Satan—cf. John 14:30; 16:11) would be redirected toward the disciples. They were therefore in desperate need of the Father's protection from the world around them. The world, in spiritual darkness and confusion (John 1:5; 3:19; 8:12; 9:39; 12:46), gave residence to sins and temptations of every kind—from the "doctrines of demons" (1 Tim. 4:1) to the abominable acts of the heathen that were too disgraceful even to mention (cf. Eph. 5:12). Thus, as they went forth to proclaim the gospel, the disciples also needed the Father's sanctifying, purifying power and grace.

Having established the reasons why He knew the Father would answer His prayer (in vv. 6–10), Jesus now made those two requests on behalf of His disciples: that they would receive spiritual protection (in vv. 11*b*–16) and sanctifying purity (in vv. 17–19) from the Father.

THE REQUEST FOR SPIRITUAL PROTECTION

Holy Father, keep them in Your name, the name which You have given Me, that they may be one even as We are. While I was with them, I was keeping them in Your name which You have given Me; and I guarded them and not one of them perished but the son of perdition, so that the Scripture would be fulfilled. But now I come to You; and these things I speak in the world so that they may have My joy made full in themselves. I have given them Your word; and the world has hated them, because they are not of the world, even as I am not of the world. I do not ask You to take them out of the world, but to keep them from the evil one. They are not of the world, even as I am not of the world. (17:11*b*–16)

Jesus began the requests for His disciples by addressing God as **Holy Father** (a title for God found only here). The emphasis on God's holiness sets the stage for the rest of this section (in vv. 11–19), which targets the holiness of the disciples in the midst of the hostile and wicked world. Their relationship to God was a sanctifying one. They were unholy men, but through the Son they had been brought into a purifying relationship with Holy God.

Jesus' first petition, **keep them** (which is reiterated in v. 15), is a request for the disciples' spiritual security. God's **name** represents all that

He is, though in this case there is a marked emphasis on His holiness (since Jesus just referred to Him as "Holy Father"). Jesus asked the Father to guard the disciples according to His holy character and attributes. That request is all-encompassing, and extends to all believers, as A. C. Gaebelein explains:

> That keeping means everything. Keeping from falling away, from evil doctrines, from being overcome by sorrow, or in tribulation and suffering, keeping them in life and in death. From this first petition of our Lord's prayer we learn the absolute security of a true believer. If a true believer, one who belongs to Christ, who has been given by the Father to the Son, for whom the Son of God intercedes, can be lost, it would mean the loss of Christ's glory, the loss of a part of the travail of His soul. (*The Gospel of John* [Wheaton: Van Kampen Press, 1936], 320)

The Lord again emphasized His perfect oneness with the Father by noting that the name of the Father is also **the name which** the Father has **given** the Son. God's holy character was reflected perfectly in Him. "No one has seen God at any time," John wrote earlier in his gospel. "[But] the only begotten God who is in the bosom of the Father, He has explained Him" (John 1:18). Jesus had provided the disciples with a perfect picture of who God is and what He expects.

The Father's protection was essential for the disciples for at least two reasons. First, it secured their glorification, as it does for all believers. Christians "are protected by the power of God through faith for a salvation ready to be revealed in the last time" (1 Peter 1:5). Romans 8:29–30 reveals that God's providential care forges an unbroken chain leading from eternity past to eternity future: "For those whom He foreknew, He also predestined to become conformed to the image of His Son, so that He would be the firstborn among many brethren; and these whom He predestined, He also called; and these whom He called, He also justified; and these whom He justified, He also glorified."

Second, the Father's protection also secured their unity with one another—**that they** would **be one even as** Christ and the Father **are.** That unity the Lord had in mind is the spiritual unity that all believers possess, namely, the life of God in their regenerated souls, secured to them forever by His power and presence. The emphasis here is not on a fluctuating, visible unity in the church, but on the real, constant unity that is invisible. The Lord is praying for the essential oneness of believers that they share in common eternal life. This prayer is answered every time a sinner is regenerated.

The unity of invisible eternal life implanted in Christ's followers is the foundation for a visible unity that crosses all organizational lines and that produces an effective gospel and testimony to the lost (cf. the exposition of 13:35 in chapter 8 of this volume). It is produced by the Holy Spirit (Eph. 4:3), who indwells every believer (Rom. 8:9). Practically, this spiritual unity of divine life produces a common love for the Lord (1 John 4:19–21), commitment to His Word (Eph. 4:13), affection for His people (Col. 3:14), and separation from all that is ungodly and worldly (1 John 2:15–17).

During His earthly ministry, Jesus had been **keeping them in** the Father's **name which** He had **given** Him. In fact, He **guarded** the disciples so well that **not one of them perished but the son of perdition.** The Lord had taught them, empowered them, and shielded them from the attacks of the hostile Jewish authorities (cf. Matt. 12:2–8; 15:2–9). Soon, in Gethsemane, He would do so again (John 18:4–9). Jesus used two different Greek words for "keeping" (*tēreō*) and "guarded" (*phulassō*). The first speaks of protection by means of restraint, and carries the idea of preserving or watching over. It is often used in John's gospel to refer to keeping God's words or commandments. The second refers to protection from outside dangers. It is an act of safeguarding, used in Luke to picture the strong man who guards his house (Luke 11:21). Taken together, the words give a picture of complete deliverance from all perils, and lasting security. The Son asks the Father to secure His disciples, knowing that it is the Father's will (John 6:39). The omniscient Son always prayed in perfect agreement with His Father (John 5:30). The work of securing His people is a Trinitarian work. In John 5:17–19 Jesus

> answered [His Jewish opponents], "My Father is working until now, and I Myself am working." For this reason therefore the Jews were seeking all the more to kill Him, because He not only was breaking the Sabbath, but also was calling God His own Father, making Himself equal with God. Therefore Jesus answered and was saying to them, "Truly, truly, I say to you, the Son can do nothing of Himself, unless it is something He sees the Father doing; for whatever the Father does, these things the Son also does in like manner."

In Ephesians 1:13–14 Paul wrote,

> In Him [Christ], you also, after listening to the message of truth, the gospel of your salvation—having also believed, you were sealed in Him with the Holy Spirit of promise, who is given as a pledge of our inheritance, with a view to the redemption of God's own possession, to the praise of His glory.

The loss of Judas, **the son of perdition,** was not due to Jesus failing to keep him. He knew all along that he was a false disciple (6:70–71). Far from catching Jesus by surprise, Judas's apostasy took place **so that the Scripture would be fulfilled** (see the discussion of 13:18 in chapter 7 of this volume; cf. Pss. 41:9; 109:8; Acts 1:20). Judas, of course, was still personally responsible for his wicked actions (cf. Matt. 26:24 and Mark 14:21). As Leon Morris rightly notes:

> The reference to the fulfilling of Scripture brings out the divine purpose. This does not mean that Judas was an automaton. He was a responsible person and acted freely. But God used that man's evil act to bring about his own purpose. There is a combination of the human and the divine, but in this passage it is the divine aspect rather than the human that receives stress. In the end God's will was done in the handing over of Jesus to be crucified. (Leon Morris, *The Gospel According to John*, The New International Commentary on the New Testament [Grand Rapids: Eerdmans, 1995], 645)

(For further discussion of the interplay between human responsibility and divine sovereignty, see the introduction to the previous chapter of this volume.) Yet, what Judas (and Satan—John 13:27) intended for evil, God in His perfect purposes worked together for good (cf. Gen. 50:20; Rom. 9:17). God would use the most horrific event in human history— the murder of His Son—as the means by which He would atone for the sins of His elect.

The prophetic Scriptures fulfilled in Jesus were certainly much broader than just those that reference Judas. The Old Testament foretold that the Christ would be a descendant of Abraham (Gen. 22:18), from the tribe of Judah (Gen. 49:10), of the family of Jesse (Isa. 11:1), in the line of David (Jer. 23:5). He would be born in Bethlehem (Mic. 5:2), have a forerunner (Isa. 40:3; Mal. 3:1), begin His ministry in Galilee (Isa. 9:1; cf. Matt. 4:12–17), be anointed by the Spirit (Isa. 11:2; cf. Matt. 3:16–17), have a ministry of miracles (Isa. 35:5–6; cf. Matt. 9:35), and bring healing and life to His people (Isa. 61:1–2; cf. Luke 4:18). At the end of His ministry, He would enter Jerusalem on a donkey (Zech. 9:9; Luke 19:35–37). Then, having been fully rejected by the Jewish leaders (Ps. 118:22; cf. 1 Peter 2:7), He would be falsely accused (Isa. 53:7; Matt. 27:12), made to suffer (Isa. 53:5–6; cf. Matt. 26:67), and crucified with thieves (Isa. 53:12; cf. Matt. 27:38). Moreover, His garments would be divided (Ps. 22:18; cf. John 19:23–24), His side pierced (Zech. 12:10; cf. John 19:34), and His body buried in a rich man's tomb (Isa. 53:9; cf. Matt. 27:57ff.). All of this took place just as it had been foretold by the Old Testament.

Hence, after His resurrection, Jesus could rebuke two of His followers on the road to Emmaus for not understanding that the Old Testament Scriptures revealed the necessity of His suffering and death (Luke 24:25–26). As Luke records, "Then beginning with Moses and with all the prophets, He explained to them the things concerning Himself in all the Scriptures" (v. 27). Jesus knew that Judas's betrayal had been part of the divine plan all along. Judas did not defect because Jesus failed to protect him. Rather, Judas fell because he had never been a true disciple of Christ in the first place and was void of spiritual life; and because his role in Jesus' death was part of God's sovereignly predetermined plan.

Confident of the Father's protective care for the disciples, the Lord looked to His return to the Father. **But now I come to You,** Jesus acknowledged, **and these things I speak in the world so that they may have My joy made full in themselves.** For the third time that evening, Jesus spoke of the joy that was His legacy to His followers (cf. 15:11; 16:20–24). Understanding the Father's protection (cf. Rom. 8:33–39) and Christ's intercession inevitably produced joy in the hearts of the listening disciples. This had to have been a stunningly wonderful experience for the disciples—to hear their Lord praying as He did for them to the Father to guarantee their eternal glory and remove all fear that they might fail and perish. Elsewhere, Jesus had earlier prayed that the disciples would share in the fullness of His life (John 10:10; 11:25–26) and in His peace (14:27); now He prayed for their fullness of joy. All of this concern and care for His own is enriching because it reveals His love for them (John 13:1; Rom 8:35–39).

The Lord's use of the personal possessive pronoun, **My,** indicates that this was not just any kind of arbitrary happiness. It was His joy—both that which was based in Him, and which He Himself experienced. It was the joy that was "set before Him" (Heb. 12:2); joy that was not founded on immediate circumstances but on the eternal purposes of God. It was joy that came not from momentary happiness, but from the knowing that the Father was pleased with His perfect obedience (cf. 2 Cor. 4:17–18). The disciples would share in that joy by experiencing the eternal life that Jesus made possible through His death (cf. 16:22; 17:3, 18). All believers, in the generations that have followed the eleven, have shared in that same joy.

Having spoken only divine truth, Jesus had **given them** God's **word,** which the world rejected (5:38). In the past, God had spoken through His prophets; but now He had spoken through His Son (Heb. 1:1–2; cf. John 1:1, 18). Yet, just as the world had rejected the message of the prophets beforehand, so it also rejected the message of the Son (cf. Mark 6:1–12). As John had earlier written about Jesus, "He came to His own, and those who were His own did not receive Him" (John 1:11). The Lord Himself rebuked His opponents with these words, "The Father who sent Me, He has testified of Me. You have neither heard His voice at any time nor seen His form. You do not have His word abiding in you, for you do not believe Him whom He sent" (John 5:37–38). And later, "If you believed Moses, you would believe Me, for he wrote about Me. But if you do not believe his writings, how will you believe My words?" (5:46–47).

In contrast to the world, which rejected the message of Christ, the disciples had received and believed His word (John 17:8). Because of that the world **hated them,** just as it had hated Jesus. After all, **they** were **not of the world, even as** Jesus was **not of the world** (8:23). Because the disciples had been born again from above (3:3, 5), their citizenship was no longer in the world but in heaven (Phil. 3:20)—making them aliens and strangers on this earth (cf. 1 Peter 1:1; 2:11).

Though they were not part of the world, Christ did not request that they be removed from the world. He plainly said to the Father, **I do not ask You to take them out of the world.** Jesus' earlier promise to them was not that they would be taken out of the world, but that in Him they would triumph over it (cf. 16:33). Like the disciples, true believers today are in the world, without being part of its evil system. James declared forcefully, "You adulteresses, do you not know that friendship with the world is hostility toward God? Therefore whoever wishes to be a friend of the world makes himself an enemy of God" (James 4:4; cf. 1:27). The apostle John commanded believers, "Do not love the world nor the things in the world. If anyone loves the world, the love of the Father is not in him" (1 John 2:15).

Paul explained to the Corinthians that he "did not at all mean [that they should not associate] with the immoral people of this world, or with the covetous and swindlers, or with idolaters, for then you would have to go out of the world" (1 Cor. 5:10). On the contrary, believers are to reach the lost world with the truth of the gospel (cf. Matt. 5:13–16). That is their primary reason for remaining here; it is the one thing they could not do better in heaven. The glorious truth is that "whoever will call on the name of the Lord will be saved" (Rom. 10:13). But as Paul goes on to ask, "How then will they call on Him in whom they have not believed? How will they believe in Him whom they have not heard? And how will they hear without a preacher?" (v. 14). Far from taking believers out of the world, God "has committed to us the word of reconciliation. Therefore, we are ambassadors for Christ" (2 Cor. 5:19–20).

Though He does not ask for them to be removed from the world, He does reiterate the basic request of verse 11, that while they live on the earth the Father would **keep them from the evil one.** There is nothing that Satan (the prince of this world—Eph. 2:2) would like better than to destroy saving faith; to snatch a soul from the safety of Christ's and the Father's hands (10:28–29) would be his desire. He tried to destroy Job's faith, but after all the calamities that Satan brought upon him, Job's response showed that the faith God gives cannot be destroyed. It is by divine power an enduring faith:

> Then Job answered the Lord and said, "I know that You can do all things, and that no purpose of Yours can be thwarted. 'Who is this that hides counsel without knowledge?' Therefore I have declared that which I did not understand, things too wonderful for me, which I did not know. 'Hear, now, and I will speak; I will ask You, and You instruct me.' I have heard of You by the hearing of the ear; but now my eye sees You; therefore I retract, and I repent in dust and ashes." (Job 42:1–6)

Satan also sought to destroy Peter's faith. Jesus warned him, "Simon, Simon, behold, Satan has demanded permission to sift you like wheat; but I have prayed for you, that your faith may not fail; and you, when once you have turned again, strengthen your brothers" (Luke 22:31–32). It is true that Peter failed miserably when he denied the Lord, but his faith endured. He repented (cf. Matt. 26:75), Jesus restored him (John 21:15–19), and he was the powerful evangelist for Christ in the early church (Acts 2–12). The Lord's intercession for His people guarantees that none of them will be reclaimed by Satan.

As He concluded His first request for the disciples, Jesus reiterated the fact that **they are not of the world, even as** He is **not of the world.** On the one hand, that meant they would face the persecution of the world—for they would be treated by unbelievers just as Christ Himself was treated. Yet, on the other hand, it also meant they would enjoy the protection of the Father, for they would likewise be treated by the Father in the same manner as Christ. Verse 16 is therefore more than just a restatement of verse 14. It is a reiteration by the Son, before the Father, of the solidarity that those whom He was leaving in the world shared with Him.

THE REQUEST FOR SANCTIFYING PURITY

Sanctify them in the truth; Your word is truth. As You sent Me into the world, I also have sent them into the world. For their sakes I sanctify Myself, that they themselves also may be sanctified in truth. (17:17–19)

Having prayed for their spiritual protection from the world, Jesus continued by asking the Father to sanctify and purify the disciples as they prepared to preach the truth to the world. It was not enough that they be safeguarded from outside evils. They must also be internally conformed more and more to the Son. Though they had already been cleansed (referring to salvation—John 15:3), they still needed to occasionally have their feet washed from the filth of this world (John 13:10; cf. Heb. 12:1–2; 1 John 2:1–2). The Evil One would aggressively try to derail this work of sanctification, but the Father Himself guaranteed it through the Word of truth (v. 17), empowered by the Spirit of truth (14:17; 15:26; 16:13).

Jesus therefore asked His Father to **sanctify them in the truth,** to set them apart from sin. The instrument of sanctification is God's revealed, inscripturated **word,** contained in Old and New Testaments, the totality of which **is truth.** God's Word and truth are synonymous.

> "Thine own word is truth" certifies the inerrancy and infallibility of the Word excepting no portion of it. The holy garment of the Word is seamless; it has no rents of error—or call them mistakes—which hands today must sew up. "Thine own word" signifies all of it, the Word of the Old Testament on which Jesus placed his approval again and again, plus the revelation that Jesus added in person with the promise of its perfect preservation through the Paraclete (14:26; 16:13). (R. C. H. Lenski, *The Interpretation of St. John's Gospel* [Minneapolis: Augsburg, 1943], 1149)

Throughout His ministry, Jesus put a premium on the written Word of God. He saw the Old Testament Scriptures as the "word of God" (cf. Matt. 15:6; 22:31), and repeatedly affirmed their inerrancy (Matt. 5:18; John 10:35) and historical accuracy (cf. Jesus' testimony to the historicity of various Old Testament characters such as Jonah [Matt. 12:40]; Noah [Matt. 24:38]; Moses [Mark 12:26]; Abel [Luke 11:51]; Lot [Luke 17:29]; and Lot's wife [Luke 17:32]). As He told the Pharisees, "It is easier for heaven and earth to pass away than for one stroke of a letter of the law to fail" (Luke 16:17). He further saw the Old Testament as being perfectly fulfilled in Him (Matt. 5:17; Luke 24:27; John 5:39; 13:18; cf. Acts 13:27), such that those who rejected Him simultaneously rejected the Scriptures (John 5:46–47). During His ministry, Jesus viewed His own words as words from God (John 7:16; 8:26–28, 38; 12:49; 14:10, 24), as He revealed the Father through everything He said and did (John 1:18; 6:69; cf. Heb. 1:1–2; 1 John 1:1–3). As He was about to depart, while in the upper room with His disciples, He promised the eleven that through them the rest of His word would be revealed (John 14:26; 15:26–27; 16:12–15). That promise is fulfilled by the New Testament.

Thus, in referring to the **word** that is **truth,** Jesus was speaking not only of His immediate words (as if the red letters in Scripture comprised the only true words), but of the entirety of Scripture. His revelation was in perfect harmony with that of the Old Testament; and His disciples were authorized by Him to record the revelation He would give them through His Spirit. All of it, from Genesis to Revelation, is truth (cf. Pss. 19:7; 119:160). And all of it is necessary for the believer's sanctification (cf. Eph. 5:26; 2 Tim. 3:16–17). As the apostle Peter would instruct the

Christians of Asia Minor many years later, "Like newborn babies, long for the pure milk of the word, so that by it you may grow in respect to salvation" (1 Peter 2:2). "Your word I have treasured in my heart," wrote the psalmist, "that I may not sin against You" (Ps. 119:11). It is "the word of His grace," Paul told the Ephesian elders, "which is able to build you up and to give you the inheritance among all those who are sanctified" (Acts 20:32).

Only sanctified believers are ready to be **sent into the world** as the Father **sent** Christ **into the world.** These words, directed at the eleven, served as a preview of the Great Commission the Lord would give these same disciples following His resurrection (Matt. 28:18–20; cf. Acts 1:7–8). Having been set apart from the world and transformed by God's grace, the disciples would be the heralds of that same grace to the very world that hated them. In the same way that they were disciples of Jesus, they were to "make disciples" of Christ in "all the nations, baptizing them in the name of the Father and the Son and the Holy Spirit, teaching them to observe all that [Christ] commanded [them]" (Matt. 28:19–20). Just as Jesus had been sent to the world by His Father, so now the disciples were being sent to the world by Jesus. Through their witness, the world would be exposed to the gospel and many would come to saving faith.

But no such salvation would even be possible, if it were not for the sacrificial death of the Son. The Lord returned to that thought in verse 19, acknowledging that what He was about to endure at the cross would make salvation possible both for the eleven and for those who would be saved through their extended ministries. **For** the disciples' **sakes** Jesus would **sanctify** Himself; that is, He would set Himself apart to righteously obey the Father's will by dying on the cross. It was only because He atoned for their sins **that they themselves also** would be **sanctified in truth** (cf. Heb. 10:10; 13:12). Having been justified through their faith in Him (cf. Rom. 5:1, 8), they would be daily conformed more and more into His perfect image (Rom. 8:29; cf. Phil. 2:12–13; 3:21).

As He always did, Jesus prayed consistently with the will of the Father. He asked the Father to do what He had predetermined in eternity past to do—to pour out His love, grace, mercy, and power on those whom He had chosen and given to Jesus. It is on that basis that Christ appealed to the Father to protect and secure the disciples. Guarded by the Father, interceded for by Christ, and indwelt by the Holy Spirit, these men, along with the apostle Paul (1 Cor. 15:8), would provide the solid foundation upon which all believers in the ages to come would rest (Eph. 2:20).

Jesus Prays for All Believers—Part 1: That They Would Be Presently United in Truth (John 17:20–23)

25

"I do not ask on behalf of these alone, but for those also who believe in Me through their word; that they may all be one; even as You, Father, are in Me and I in You, that they also may be in Us, so that the world may believe that You sent Me. The glory which You have given Me I have given to them, that they may be one, just as We are one; I in them and You in Me, that they may be perfected in unity, so that the world may know that You sent Me, and loved them, even as You have loved Me." (John 17:20–23)

As noted in the previous chapter of this volume, the unity Christ prayed for is not an outward, organizational unity, but the inward, spiritual unity based on believers' life in Christ. Because of their union with Jesus Christ—since "the one who joins himself to the Lord is one spirit with Him" (1 Cor. 6:17)—all believers are one with each other as well (Gal. 3:28). In the words of the Westminster Confession of Faith, "The catholic or universal Church, which is invisible, consists of the whole number of the elect, that have been, are, or shall be gathered into one, under Christ the head thereof; and is the spouse, the body, the fullness of him that filleth all in all" (25.1).

285

How does that spiritual unity manifest itself in practice? In Philippians 2:2 Paul listed four marks of the unity that characterizes the true church.

First, unity results in believers "being of the same mind." That does not mean that they share all the same likes and dislikes. Nor does it entail complete agreement on all the secondary doctrinal issues that godly men differ over. Rather, it signifies that true believers are controlled by a deep knowledge of the Word of Christ that is energized in them by the power of the Spirit (cf. Col. 3:16). Because they walk in the Spirit, they maintain the same spiritual attitude.

Second, unity results in believers "maintaining the same love"; that is, they love each other equally. That does not mean that they have the same emotional commitment to everyone, which is impossible. The love in view here is *agapē* love, the love not of emotional attraction, but of will and choice. It is expressed when believers are "devoted to one another in brotherly love; [and] give preference to one another in honor" (Rom. 12:10). It has been "poured out within our hearts through the Holy Spirit who was given to us" (Rom. 5:5).

Third, unity results in believers being "united in spirit." The Greek word literally means "one-souled." It refers to a passionate, common commitment to the same spiritual goals. By definition it excludes such divisive attitudes as personal ambition, selfishness, hatred, envy, jealousy, and the countless other manifestations of the evil fruit of self-love.

Finally, unity results in believers being "intent on one purpose." Because they are of the same mind, love each other, and are united in spirit they have the same goal—advancing the kingdom of God. But believers can interrupt their spiritual unity by fleshly behavior and need to be exhorted to have "one mind striving together for the faith of the gospel" (Phil. 1:27).

But in our obsessively tolerant age, the opposite extreme poses a far more serious threat to true spiritual unity. In the name of love, many work hard to achieve a superficial, false, sinful unity that is broad enough to embrace false Christians and even those who deny the central truths of the Christian faith. Genuine biblical love, however, cannot be divorced from biblical truth (Eph. 4:15). Far from compromising it, God's people are called to "contend earnestly for the faith which was once for all handed down to the saints" (Jude 3). The true church of Jesus Christ cannot unite with those who deny the essential truths of the gospel (2 John 7–11), or who affirm a false gospel (Gal. 1:6–9). "Do not be bound together with unbelievers," Paul commanded the Corinthians, "for what partnership have righteousness and lawlessness, or what fellowship has light with darkness? Or what harmony has Christ with Belial, or what has a believer in common with an unbeliever?" (2 Cor. 6:14–15). True unity is the reality among true Christians.

As He concluded His magnificent High Priestly Prayer, the unity of His followers was very much on the heart of the Lord Jesus Christ. Having prayed for His glory (vv. 1–5) and for His disciples (vv. 6–19), the Savior expanded His prayer to include all future believers—those who would come to Him through the power of the Word (v. 17), the witness of the disciples (v. 18), and the sacrifice of the cross (v. 19). The Lord made two requests on their behalf: that they would be united in the truth, and that they would be reunited with Him in eternal glory. The first of those requests is the subject of this chapter.

The Lord's first request may be examined under four headings: the root of true unity, the request for true unity, the representation of true unity, and the result of true unity.

THE ROOT OF TRUE UNITY

"I do not ask on behalf of these alone, but for those also who believe in Me through their word; (17:20)

The opening words of verse 20 introduce the third thing for which Christ said He was not praying. In verse 9 He made it clear that He was not interceding on behalf of the unbelieving world (see the discussion of this point in chapter 23 of this volume), while in verse 15 He said that He was not asking for the disciples to be removed from the world. His words **I do not ask on behalf of these alone** introduce another group distinct from the then-living disciples for whom He had just prayed (vv. 6–19). Jesus looked ahead through the centuries and prayed for all the believers who were to come in the future. Although the vast majority had not yet been born, they nevertheless were and had been for eternity on the heart of the Savior. He knew them all, since their names have "been written from the foundation of the world in the book of life" (Rev. 13:8; cf. 3:5; 17:8; 20:12, 15; 21:27; Phil. 4:3). Christ's intercession for us, which began with this prayer 2,000 years ago, continues to this day, "since He always lives to make intercession for [us]" (Heb. 7:25).

Jesus further identified these future believers as those who would **believe in** Him (John 1:12; 3:15–16, 36; 6:40, 47; 7:37–38; 11:25–26; 20:31; Acts 13:38–39; 16:31; Rom. 10:9–10; Gal. 3:22), reminding all again that salvation comes through faith alone, "not as a result of works, so that no one may boast" (Eph. 2:9; cf. Rom. 3:20–30; Gal. 2:16; 3:8, 11–14, 24). The Lord's reference to believing in Him again preserves the biblical balance concerning salvation. On the one hand, only those given by the Father to

Christ will come to Him (v. 6; cf. 6:44). But on the other hand, their salvation does not take place apart from personal faith (cf. Rom. 10:9–10). In much the same way, the reality that the Lord will draw those whom He chooses to Himself (John 6:44; Acts 2:39; 11:18; 13:48; 16:14) does not obviate the church's responsibility to evangelize the lost (Matt. 28:19–20; Luke 24:47; Acts 1:8).

The apostles and their associates were the human authors of the New Testament (John 14:26; 16:13–15; cf. Eph. 2:20), therefore all who would be saved in the future would come to Christ **through** their **word.** Some would hear that message directly from the apostles' own preaching (e.g., Acts 2:14–42; 3:11–26; 4:8–12; 5:30–32; 13:14–41; 16:11–14; 17:22–34; 18:4–11). Most, however, would hear the apostolic message through the written Word of their Spirit-inspired writings. The early church was reading the truths of Scripture when reading "the apostles' teaching" (Acts 2:42; cf. Jude 17). Through the centuries all who have preached the true gospel have preached the apostles' word. As Paul wrote in Romans 10:17, "Faith comes from hearing, and hearing by the word of Christ" (lit., "a speech about Christ")—the apostolic message of salvation.

The disciples at that point hardly seemed ready to turn the world upside down (cf. Acts 17:6). One of them, Judas Iscariot, had turned traitor, and was at that moment preparing to lead those who would arrest Jesus to Gethsemane (18:1–3). Their brash, bold, seemingly fearless leader, Peter, would soon cower before the accusations of a servant girl, and repeatedly deny the Lord (John 18:17; cf. vv. 25–27). The rest of the disciples would abandon Jesus after His arrest and flee for their lives (Matt. 26:56).

But Christ's prayer ensures that the apostles' ministry would be successful. In His omniscience, Jesus knew that they would fulfill their role in redemptive history. The gospel would prevail, despite the apostles' weakness, the world's hatred, and Satan's opposition. Empowered by the Holy Spirit (Acts 1:8; 2:1–4), those early disciples would begin the chain of witnesses that continues unbroken down to the present day (cf. 2 Tim. 2:2). All of the church's evangelistic success is the result of the Lord's request in verse 20 for those who would believe in the future. This request guaranteed the successful establishment of the church, and the success of its evangelistic ministry from apostolic times to the present. "I will build My church," Jesus declared, "and the gates of Hades will not overpower it" (Matt. 16:18).

THE REQUEST FOR TRUE UNITY

that they may all be one; (17:21*a*)

Despite their outward denominational differences, all true Christians are spiritually united by regeneration in their belief that salvation is by grace alone through faith alone, in Christ alone, and their commitment to the absolute authority of Scripture. All those who savingly believe in the Lord Jesus Christ "are one body in Christ, and individually members one of another" (Rom. 12:5). D. A. Carson notes that the unity for which Christ prayed "is not achieved by hunting enthusiastically for the lowest common theological denominator, but by common adherence to the apostolic gospel, by love that is joyfully self-sacrificing, by undaunted commitment to the shared goals of the mission with which Jesus' followers have been charged" (*The Gospel According to John,* The Pillar New Testament Commentary [Grand Rapids: Eerdmans, 1991], 568). By the power of God, believers, united in spiritual life, are also united in purpose, share the same mission, proclaim the same gospel, and manifest the same holiness.

The actual fulfillment of Christ's prayer began with the birth of the church on the day of Pentecost. Suddenly, sovereignly, supernaturally, believers were united by the Spirit into the body of Christ and made one positionally (Acts 2:4). All who have been saved since then have immediately received the baptism of the Holy Spirit, by which they were placed into the body of Christ (1 Cor. 12:13). Consequently, there is an extraordinary, supernatural unity in the universal church; it is the "the unity of the Spirit," not created by believers, but preserved by them (Eph. 4:3). In Ephesians 4:4–6 Paul lists seven features of that Holy Spirit–created unity.

First, there is "one body," the body of Christ, which is comprised of all believers since the church's inception on the day of Pentecost.

Second, there is "one Spirit," the Holy Spirit, apart from whom no one can believe savingly in Jesus Christ (1 Cor. 12:3). The Spirit is also the agent by which Christ baptizes believers into His body (1 Cor. 12:13; cf. Matt. 3:11).

Third, there is "one hope," in the promised eternal inheritance guaranteed to every believer by the Holy Spirit (Eph. 1:13–14).

Fourth, there is "one Lord," Jesus Christ, who is the sole head of the body (Col. 1:18; cf. Acts 4:12; Rom. 10:12).

Fifth, there is "one faith," the "faith which was once for all handed down to the saints" (Jude 3); the body of doctrine revealed in the New Testament.

Sixth, there is "one baptism." This probably refers to water baptism, the believer's public confession of faith in Jesus Christ. (Holy Spirit baptism is implied in v. 5.)

Finally, there is "one God and Father of all who is over all and through all and in all." The one true God is the sovereign ruler of everything, including the church.

THE REPRESENTATION OF TRUE UNITY

even as You, Father, are in Me and I in You, that they also may be in Us, . . . The glory which You have given Me I have given to them, that they may be one, just as We are one; I in them and You in Me, that they may be perfected in unity (17:21b–23a)

The unity of nature Christ prayed for reflects that of the Father and the Son, which is expressed in Christ's words **You, Father, are in Me and I in You.** Because of His unity with the Father, Jesus claimed in John 5:16ff. to have the same authority, purpose, power, honor, will, and nature as the Father. That startling claim to full deity and equality with God so outraged His Jewish opponents that they sought to kill Him (5:18; cf. 8:58–59; 10:31–33; 19:7).

The unique intra-Trinitarian relationship of Jesus and the Father forms the pattern for the unity of believers in the church. This prayer reveals five features of that unity the church imitates.

First, the Father and the Son are united in motive; they are equally committed to the glory of God. Jesus began His prayer by saying, "Father, the hour has come; glorify Your Son, that the Son may glorify You" (v. 1), as He had done throughout His ministry (v. 4). In verse 5 He added, "Now, Father, glorify Me together with Yourself, with the glory which I had with You before the world was." Finally, in verse 24 Jesus expressed to the Father His desire that believers would one day "be with Me where I am, so that they may see My glory which You have given Me." In John 7:18 Jesus declared that He was constantly "seeking the glory of the One who sent Him." He did not need to seek His own glory (8:50), because the Father glorified Him (8:54). Both Jesus and the Father were glorified in the raising of Lazarus (11:4). In John 12:28 Jesus prayed, "'Father, glorify Your name.' Then a voice came out of heaven: 'I have both glorified it, and will glorify it again.'" Shortly before His High Priestly Prayer, Jesus had said to the disciples, "Now is the Son of Man glorified, and God is glorified in Him; if God is glorified in Him, God will also glorify Him in Himself, and will glorify Him immediately" (13:31–32). Jesus promised to answer the prayers of His people "so that the Father may be glorified in the Son" (14:13).

The church is also united in a common commitment to the glory of God. "Whether, then, you eat or drink or whatever you do," Paul wrote, "do all to the glory of God" (1 Cor. 10:31).

Second, the Father and the Son are united in mission. They share the common goal of redeeming lost sinners and granting them eternal life, as Christ made clear earlier in this prayer:

> Even as You gave Him authority over all flesh, that to all whom You have given Him, He may give eternal life. This is eternal life, that they may know You, the only true God, and Jesus Christ whom You have sent. I glorified You on the earth, having accomplished the work which You have given Me to do.... I have manifested Your name to the men whom You gave Me out of the world; they were Yours and You gave them to Me, and they have kept Your word. (vv. 2–4, 6)

God chose in eternity past to give believers to Christ as a gift of His love, and Christ came to earth to die as a sacrifice for their sins and redeem them. That the church lives to pursue the one goal of evangelizing the lost is clear from Jesus' words in verse 18: "As You sent Me into the world, I also have sent them into the world" (cf. Matt. 28:19–20).

Third, the Father and the Son are united in truth. "The words which You gave Me," Jesus said, "I have given to them" (v. 8), while in verse 14 He added, "I have given them Your word." Earlier that evening Jesus had told the disciples, "The words that I say to you I do not speak on My own initiative, but the Father abiding in Me does His works" (14:10; cf. 3:32–34; 7:16; 8:28, 38, 40; 12:49).

The church is also unified in its commitment to proclaiming the singular truth of God's Word. In Romans 15:5–6 Paul prayed, "Now may the God who gives perseverance and encouragement grant you to be of the same mind with one another according to Christ Jesus, so that with one accord you may with one voice glorify the God and Father of our Lord Jesus Christ" (cf. Acts 2:42, 46; Phil. 1:27). Far from dividing the church, a commitment to proclaiming sound doctrine is what defines it.

Fourth, the Father and the Son are united in holiness. In verse 11 Jesus addressed the Father as "Holy Father," and in verse 25 as "righteous Father." The utter holiness of God is expressed throughout the Old and New Testaments. God's holiness is His absolute separation from sin. In Habakkuk 1:13 the prophet declared, "Your eyes are too pure to approve evil, and You can not look on wickedness with favor." In Isaiah's vision of God the angelic beings cried out, "Holy, Holy, Holy, is the Lord of hosts, the whole earth is full of His glory" (Isa. 6:3; cf. Rev. 4:8). The writer of Hebrews described Jesus as "holy, innocent, undefiled, separated from sinners" (Heb. 7:26). In Revelation 4:8 the heavenly chorus unceasingly cries out, "Holy, holy, holy is the Lord God, the Almighty, who was and who is and who is to come."

When they see believers united in the pursuit of holiness, unbelievers will be drawn to Christ. In Hebrews 12:14 the writer of Hebrews exhorted his readers, "Pursue peace with all men, and the sanctification without which no one will see the Lord." If a church tolerates sin, it not only obscures the glory of Christ it is called to radiate, but also faces the discipline of the Lord of the church (Rev. 2:14–16, 20–23).

Finally, the Father and the Son are united in love. In verse 24 Jesus affirmed that the Father had "loved [Him] before the foundation of the world." In John 5:20 Jesus said, "For the Father loves the Son, and shows Him all things that He Himself is doing" (cf. 3:35). Both at His baptism (Matt. 3:17) and at the transfiguration (Matt. 17:5), the Father declared Jesus to be His beloved Son. Similarly, love is the glue that binds believers together in unity (Col. 3:14; cf. 2:2), and it is that love for one another that is the church's ultimate apologetic to the lost world (John 13:34–35).

Though not to the same infinite divine extent, the spiritual life and power that belongs to the Trinity belongs also in some way to believers and is the basis for the church's unity. This is what the Lord meant when He said, **The glory which You have given Me I have given to them, that they may be one, just as we are one; I in them and You in Me, that they may be perfected in unity.** That stunning truth describes believers as those to whom the Son has given glory—that is, aspects of the very divine life that belongs to God. The church's task is to so live as to not obstruct that glory (Matt. 5:16).

The Result of True Unity

"so that the world may believe that You sent Me. . . . so that the world may know that You sent Me, and loved them, even as You have loved Me." (17:21c, 23b)

The observable unity of the church authenticates two important realities. First, it gives evidence to **the world** so that it **may believe that** the Father **sent** the Son. That familiar phrase summarizes the plan of redemption, in which God sent Jesus on a mission of salvation "to seek and to save that which was lost" (Luke 19:10). It is so used throughout John's gospel (e.g., 3:34; 4:34; 5:23, 24, 30, 36, 37, 38; 6:29, 38, 39, 44, 57; 7:16, 18, 28, 29, 33; 8:16, 18, 26, 29, 42; 9:4; 10:36; 11:42; 12:44, 45, 49; 13:20; 14:24; 15:21; 16:5; 17:3, 8, 18, 25; 20:21). Jesus prayed that the visible unity of His church would convince many in the world concerning His divine mission of redemption. The church's unity is the foundation of its evangelism; it demonstrates that Christ is the Savior who transforms lives (cf. John 13:35).

The church's unity also authenticates the Father's love for believers. When unbelievers see believers' love for each other, it offers proof to them that the Father has **loved** those who have believed in His Son. The loving unity of the church made visible is used by God to produce a desire on the part of unbelievers is produced to experience that same love. On the other hand, where there are carnal divisions, strife, backbiting, and quarreling in the church, it drives unbelievers away. Why would they want to be part of such a hypocritical group that is at cross-purposes with itself? The effectiveness of the church's evangelism is devastated by dissension and disputes among its members.

It must be the goal of everyone who is part of the body of Christ through faith in Him to do their part in maintaining the full visibility of the unity that believers possses, as Paul wrote:

> Therefore I, the prisoner of the Lord, implore you to walk in a manner worthy of the calling with which you have been called, with all humility and gentleness, with patience, showing tolerance for one another in love, being diligent to preserve the unity of the Spirit in the bond of peace. (Eph. 4:1–3)

Jesus Prays for All Believers—Part 2: That They Would One Day Be Reunited in Glory (John 17:24–26)

26

"Father, I desire that they also, whom You have given Me, be with Me where I am, so that they may see My glory which You have given Me, for You loved Me before the foundation of the world. O righteous Father, although the world has not known You, yet I have known You; and these have known that You sent Me; and I have made Your name known to them, and will make it known, so that the love with which You loved Me may be in them, and I in them." (17:24–26)

I once visited an isolated eastern city in the former Soviet Union, where I met with fifteen hundred impoverished Christians. They were the descendants of exiles, and they and their ancestors had suffered terribly under Soviet oppression for three quarters of a century. Their poverty was so severe that they had to work hard every day just to put food on the table. The subject that was most on their heart was their future in the glory of heaven. I had the privilege of teaching them about that from Scripture for several hours, and many were so overcome that they wept with joy.

Their response was strikingly different from that of many Christians in the West, who have things so good that they do not know what it is to long for heaven. As a result, they live as if going to heaven would be an unwelcome intrusion into their busy schedules—an interruption of their career goals, or vacation plans. They do not want to see heaven until they have enjoyed all the pleasures the world has to offer. When they have seen it all and done it all, or when age or sickness hinder their ability to enjoy those pleasures, then they will be ready for heaven. While it is true that, as the old spiritual put it, "Everybody talkin' 'bout heaven ain't goin' there," it is also true that everybody going to heaven is not talking about it.

When the church loses its focus on heaven, it becomes self-indulgent and self-centered, materialistic and worldly, spiritually weak and lethargic. The pleasures and comforts of this present world consume too much of its time and energy. Believers forget that this world is not their true home, that they are "aliens and strangers" (1 Peter 2:11; cf. Heb. 11:13) here, that their "citizenship is in heaven" (Phil. 3:20), and that "here we do not have a lasting city, but we are seeking the city which is to come" (Heb. 13:14). The church is increasingly in danger not of being so heavenly minded that it is no earthly good, but rather of being so earthly minded that it is no heavenly good.

A worldly minded church is the result of a disobedient church. The Lord Jesus Christ commanded His followers, "Store up for yourselves treasures in heaven, where neither moth nor rust destroys, and where thieves do not break in or steal; for where your treasure is, there your heart will be also" (Matt. 6:20–21). "Therefore if you have been raised up with Christ," Paul wrote, "keep seeking the things above, where Christ is, seated at the right hand of God" (Col. 3:1). The apostle John warned believers,

> Do not love the world nor the things in the world. If anyone loves the world, the love of the Father is not in him. For all that is in the world, the lust of the flesh and the lust of the eyes and the boastful pride of life, is not from the Father, but is from the world. The world is passing away, and also its lusts; but the one who does the will of God lives forever. (1 John 2:15–17)

Godly men have always longed for heaven. In the Old Testament David expressed his heart's yearning for heaven when he wrote, "In Your presence is fullness of joy; in Your right hand there are pleasures forever" (Ps. 16:11). In the New Testament Paul wrote to the Philippians of his "desire to depart and be with Christ, for that is very much better" (Phil. 1:23), while in 2 Corinthians 5:8 he declared his preference "to be absent from the body and to be at home with the Lord." In his triumphant epitaph, Paul wrote to Timothy,

> For I am already being poured out as a drink offering, and the time of my departure has come. I have fought the good fight, I have finished the course, I have kept the faith; in the future there is laid up for me the crown of righteousness, which the Lord, the righteous Judge, will award to me on that day; and not only to me, but also to all who have loved His appearing. (2 Tim. 4:6–8)

Like David and Paul, all Christians should long for heaven, since everything precious to them is there. Their Father is there. Jesus taught believers to pray, "Our Father who is in heaven, hallowed be Your name" (Matt. 6:9; cf. vv. 1, 14, 32; 5:48; 18:14; 23:9; Luke 11:13). Their fellow believers who have died are there. The writer of Hebrews described the "general assembly and church of the firstborn who are enrolled in heaven, and …the spirits of the righteous made perfect" (Heb. 12:23). Their names are recorded there. In Luke 10:20 Jesus told the disciples, "Do not rejoice in this, that the spirits are subject to you, but rejoice that your names are recorded in heaven" (cf. Phil. 4:3; Rev. 3:5; 13:8; 17:8; 20:12, 15; 21:27). As noted earlier, their citizenship is there (Phil. 3:20). Their inheritance is there. Peter described it as "an inheritance which is imperishable and undefiled and will not fade away, reserved in heaven for you" (1 Peter 1:4). Their holiness is there (Rev. 21:27; 22:3, 14–15). Their eternal reward is there. In Matthew 5:12 Jesus exhorted believers, "Rejoice and be glad, for your reward in heaven is great," while in 6:19–21 He spoke of believers' treasure being in heaven.

Most important of all, their Savior is there, "standing at the right hand of God" (Acts 7:55, 56; cf. Rom. 8:34; Col. 3:1; Heb. 1:3; 8:1; 10:12; 12:2; 1 Peter 3:22). He has gone there to prepare a place for them (John 14:1–3), so they can be with Him forever, sharing rich fellowship with Him and worshiping Him. Jesus Himself is the glory of heaven.

The reality that believers will be reunited in heaven with Christ and each other is the subject of the last part of the Lord's High Priestly Prayer. Verses 24–26 describe the fellowship of future glory, the focus of future glory, and the foretaste of future glory.

THE FELLOWSHIP OF FUTURE GLORY

"Father, I desire that they also, whom You have given Me, be with Me where I am, (17:24*a*)

This passionate plea that those **whom** the Father has **given** to Him might **be with** Him in His eternal glory in heaven is the final petition of Christ's prayer.

Humanly speaking, there is nothing to warrant such a staggering, overwhelming privilege. Christians, as Paul reminded the Corinthians, are "not many wise according to the flesh, not many mighty, not many noble" (1 Cor. 1:26). Even worse, they were God's enemies (Rom. 5:10),

> dead in [their] trespasses and sins, in which [they] formerly walked according to the course of this world, according to the prince of the power of the air, of the spirit that is now working in the sons of disobedience. Among them [they] too all formerly lived in the lusts of [their] flesh, indulging the desires of the flesh and of the mind, and were by nature children of wrath, even as the rest. (Eph. 2:1–3)

They were "separate from Christ, excluded from the commonwealth of Israel, and strangers to the covenants of promise, having no hope and without God in the world" (Eph. 2:12), having "sinned and fall[en] short of the glory of God" (Rom. 3:23).

But the marvelous truth of redemption is that

> God, being rich in mercy, because of His great love with which He loved us, even when we were dead in our transgressions, made us alive together with Christ (by grace you have been saved), and raised us up with Him, and seated us with Him in the heavenly places in Christ Jesus, so that in the ages to come He might show the surpassing riches of His grace in kindness toward us in Christ Jesus. (Eph. 2:4–7)

God, Paul wrote to the Christians at Rome,

> demonstrates His own love toward us, in that while we were yet sinners, Christ died for us. Much more then, having now been justified by His blood, we shall be saved from the wrath of God through Him. For if while we were enemies we were reconciled to God through the death of His Son, much more, having been reconciled, we shall be saved by His life. (Rom. 5:8–10)

Not only does God forgive repentant sinners, but He also adopts them as His children (Rom. 8:15; Gal. 4:5; Eph. 1:5). That truth that prompted the apostle John to exclaim in wonder, "See how great a love the Father has bestowed on us, that we would be called children of God; and such we are" (1 John 3:1). The glorification of believers in heaven is the ultimate goal of the plan of salvation: "For those whom He foreknew, He also predestined to become conformed to the image of His Son, so that He would be the firstborn among many brethren; and these whom He predestined, He also called; and these whom He called, He also justified; and these whom He justified, He also glorified" (Rom. 8:29–30).

Jesus' request was in perfect harmony with God's purpose in choosing believers before the foundation of the world (Eph. 1:4), inscribing their names in the Book of Life, and giving them to the Son as gifts of

His love (John 6:37, 39). True prayer is always consistent with God's will. Jesus taught His followers to pray to God, "Your kingdom come. Your will be done, on earth as it is in heaven" (Matt. 6:10).

But the Lord's request was more than merely a plea that the Father's will be done; it also expressed His **desire** (*thelō;* "to wish," "to desire," "to want"). It is not difficult to understand believers wanting to be with Him; but it staggers the imagination to realize that He wants them to be with Him.

The phrase **they . . . whom You have given Me** expresses again the reason that believers are special to Christ: they are a love gift to Him from the Father. It is the Lord's most affectionate way of referring to believers when addressing the Father (vv. 2, 6, 9; cf. 6:37, 39, 10:29; 18:9). The church is His bride (Rev. 19:7; cf. 2 Cor. 11:2; Eph. 5:22–24), betrothed to Him by His Father.

Christ's specific request for those given Him by the Father, that they might **be with Me where I am,** further expressed His desire for eternal fellowship with them. He wants all of those chosen for Him in eternity past to be with Him where He now is—heaven. In John 14:3 Jesus revealed His purpose in bringing believers to heaven: "If I go and prepare a place for you, I will come again and receive you to Myself, that where I am, there you may be also." In John 12:26 He promised, "If anyone serves Me, he must follow Me; and where I am, there My servant will be also."

The Lord's use of the present tense, **where I am,** obviously does not refer to His location in Jerusalem on the way to Gethsemane. Such a request would have been pointless, since the disciples were already with Him. Further, in this section of His prayer, Christ looked beyond the eleven disciples to all who would believe in Him in the future through their ministry. Jesus was not speaking of where He was at that moment, but where He would soon be. He was so certain that He would be returning to heaven that He spoke of that future event in the present tense, as if it had already happened (cf. v. 11).

What will make heaven so glorious for believers is not its gates of pearl, or streets of gold, but the presence of the Lamb. Their supreme joy will be to "dwell in the house of the Lord forever" (Ps. 23:6), experiencing perfect, intimate, holy fellowship with Him and all the saints forever.

THE FOCUS OF FUTURE GLORY

so that they may see My glory which You have given Me, (17:24*b*)

Jesus also asked the Father that His followers might **see** His **glory which** the Father had **given** Him. It is true that in Christ's incarnation "we saw His glory, glory as of the only begotten from the Father" (John 1:14). But that glory was veiled in His flesh (Phil. 2:5–8). Only in heaven will it be fully manifested to His people when they "see Him just as He is" (1 John 3:2; cf. 1 Cor. 13:12; Phil. 2:9–11).

In God's gracious plan believers will not only see Christ's glory, but also share it: "For our citizenship is in heaven," Paul wrote to the Philippians, "from which also we eagerly wait for a Savior, the Lord Jesus Christ; who will transform the body of our humble state into conformity with the body of His glory, by the exertion of the power that He has even to subject all things to Himself" (Phil. 3:20–21; cf. Rom. 8:29; 1 Cor. 15:49; 1 John 3:2). Throughout all eternity the song of the redeemed as they behold the glory of the Lord Jesus Christ will be, "Worthy is the Lamb that was slain to receive power and riches and wisdom and might and honor and glory and blessing ... To Him who sits on the throne, and to the Lamb, be blessing and honor and glory and dominion forever and ever" (Rev. 5:12–13).

This request complements the statement the Lord made back in verse 22: "The glory which You have given Me I have given to them." In the incarnation, Christ had manifested "His glory, glory as of the only begotten from the Father" (John 1:14; cf. 2:11). Believers also receive Christ's glory through His indwelling of them through the Holy Spirit (vv. 23, 26; 14:20, 23). In that sense they have His glory—His attributes and essence—within them.

But the glory of which Christ speaks here is the visible manifestation of the fullness of His glory that believers will one day see in heaven. In the incarnation, Christ's glory was partially veiled (cf. Phil. 2:7). But when Jesus returned to heaven, the Father restored that fullness of glory to Him, as He had requested in verse 5: "Now, Father, glorify Me together with Yourself, with the glory which I had with You before the world was."

Believers will enter the fullness of Christ's glorious presence when they die (or at the rapture, if they are alive at that time). To see God after death has always been the hope of the saints. In Psalm 11:7 David expressed his confidence that "the upright will behold His face," while in Psalm 17:15 he wrote, "As for me, I shall behold Your face in righteousness; I will be satisfied with Your likeness when I awake." Jesus pronounced the pure in heart "Blessed ... for they shall see God" (Matt. 5:8). John wrote that one day believers "will see Him just as He is" (1 John 3:2), while Revelation 22:3–4 reveals that in heaven, "There will no longer be any curse; and the throne of God and of the Lamb will be in it, and His bond-servants will serve Him; they will see His face, and His name will be on their foreheads." So overwhelming will the manifestation of Christ's glory be that the only possible response will be praise:

Then I looked, and I heard the voice of many angels around the throne and the living creatures and the elders; and the number of them was myriads of myriads, and thousands of thousands, saying with a loud voice, "Worthy is the Lamb that was slain to receive power and riches and wisdom and might and honor and glory and blessing." And every created thing which is in heaven and on the earth and under the earth and on the sea, and all things in them, I heard saying, "To Him who sits on the throne, and to the Lamb, be blessing and honor and glory and dominion forever and ever." And the four living creatures kept saying, "Amen." And the elders fell down and worshiped. (Rev. 5:11–14)

All of the blessings believers will one day experience in heaven flow from the reality that the Father **loved** the Son **before the foundation of the world.** From all eternity the Father and Son enjoyed perfect fellowship (John 1:1), love, and shared glory (17:5). As indicated throughout this prayer, based on that mutual love, the Father chose a people (Eph. 1:4), gave them to the Son, and prepared an eternal kingdom for them (Matt. 25:34) where they will behold His glory forever.

THE FORETASTE OF FUTURE GLORY

"O righteous Father, although the world has not known You, yet I have known You; and these have known that You sent Me; and I have made Your name known to them, and will make it known, so that the love with which You loved Me may be in them, and I in them." (17:25–26)

The closing verses of this magnificent prayer exude Christ's confidence that the **righteous Father** (cf. v. 11; Deut. 32:4; Pss. 7:9; 11:7; 50:6; 71:19; 116:5; Isa. 5:16; 45:21; Rom. 3:22, 25; Rev. 15:3) would grant His requests (cf. John 11:42). God is **righteous** in everything He does (Ps. 145:17); His judgments (Pss. 19:9; 119:7; Rom. 2:5), deeds (Ps. 103:6), ordinances (Ps. 119:62), and Word (Ps. 119:123) are righteous.

Jesus reiterated the point He had made earlier in verse 9. His requests were not for **the world,** which **has not known** the Father and hence has no right to receive His special care or the Son's intercession. Apart from faith in Jesus Christ, sinners face only eternal judgment. In John 3:18 Jesus warned, "He who does not believe has been judged already, because he has not believed in the name of the only begotten Son of God," while in 3:36 John the Baptist added, "He who believes in the Son has eternal life; but he who does not obey the Son will not see life, but the wrath of God abides on him."

Not only had Jesus perfectly **known** the Father from all eternity

(Matt. 11:27; John 1:1, 18; 7:29; 8:55; 10:15), but He had also **made** His **name known to** His followers, who had **known that** the Father had **sent** Him (v. 6; Matt. 11:27; John 1:18; 15:15; 1 Tim. 2:5). The Lord's mission was to lead lost sinners into a personal relationship with God (Luke 19:10), which comes only through the knowledge of Him (John 17:3, cf. 14:6). Jesus initially makes the Father known at the moment of salvation, continues to **make** Him **known** to believers through the process of sanctification, and finally ushers them into the Father's heavenly presence at their glorification. His goal is **that** even now they might experience **the love with which** the Father **loved** Christ, and by knowing "the love of Christ which surpasses knowledge, that [they might] be filled up to all the fullness of God" (Eph. 3:19). God's love is poured out on believers at salvation (Rom. 5:5), continues in them as Christ indwells them (cf. John 14:23), and is fulfilled perfectly in them in heaven.

Christ's requests in this the greatest prayer ever prayed may be summed up in seven words. The Lord prayed for believers' preservation ("Holy Father, keep them in Your name," v. 11); jubilation ("that they may have My joy made full in themselves," v. 13); liberation ("keep them from the evil one," v. 15); sanctification ("sanctify them in the truth; Your word is truth," v. 17); unification ("that they may all be one," v. 21); association ("Father, I desire that they also, whom You have given Me, be with Me where I am," v. 24); and glorification ("that they may see My glory," v. 24).

Jesus' Betrayal and Arrest
(John 18:1–11)

27

When Jesus had spoken these words, He went forth with His disciples over the ravine of the Kidron, where there was a garden, in which He entered with His disciples. Now Judas also, who was betraying Him, knew the place, for Jesus had often met there with His disciples. Judas then, having received the Roman cohort and officers from the chief priests and the Pharisees, came there with lanterns and torches and weapons. So Jesus, knowing all the things that were coming upon Him, went forth and said to them, "Whom do you seek?" They answered Him, "Jesus the Nazarene." He said to them, "I am He." And Judas also, who was betraying Him, was standing with them. So when He said to them, "I am He," they drew back and fell to the ground. Therefore He again asked them, "Whom do you seek?" And they said, "Jesus the Nazarene." Jesus answered, "I told you that I am He; so if you seek Me, let these go their way," to fulfill the word which He spoke, "Of those whom You have given Me I lost not one." Simon Peter then, having a sword, drew it and struck the high priest's slave, and cut off his right ear; and the slave's name was Malchus. So Jesus said to Peter, "Put the sword into the sheath; the cup which the Father has given Me, shall I not drink it?" (18:1–11)

Of all the false views of our Lord's earthly life and ministry, one of the most pernicious is the portrayal of His death as that of an unwitting, unwilling victim. Pseudoscholars who advocate this view see Jesus merely as a Jewish sage or philosopher, a teacher of morality and ethics. Others imagine that He was a revolutionary seeking to overthrow Rome's rule. In either case, so the story goes, things went horribly wrong. Jesus ran afoul of the Jewish and Roman authorities, and quite unintentionally managed to get Himself executed. (Incredibly some, who either have not read the gospel accounts or refuse to believe them, even argue that the Jewish authorities tried to save Jesus from the Romans.)

But in truth Jesus was no victim. In John 10:17–18 He declared, "I lay down My life so that I may take it again. No one has taken it away from Me, but I lay it down on My own initiative. I have authority to lay it down, and I have authority to take it up again." On the contrary, His death was according to the plan and will of God. Isaiah wrote concerning Messiah's sacrificial death, "The Lord has caused the iniquity of us all to fall on Him....the Lord was pleased to crush Him, putting Him to grief" (Isa. 53:6, 10). In His sermon on the day of Pentecost, Peter said that Jesus was "delivered over [to death] by the predetermined plan and foreknowledge of God" (Acts 2:23; cf. 3:18; 4:27–28; 13:27; Matt. 26:24; Luke 22:22; 24:44–46).

As God incarnate, Jesus was always in absolute control of all the events of His life. That control extended even to the circumstances surrounding His death. Far from being an accident, Jesus' sacrificial death was the primary reason that He took on human life in the first place; it is the pinnacle of redemptive history. Earlier in John's gospel He had said, "Now My soul has become troubled; and what shall I say, 'Father, save Me from this hour'? But for this purpose I came to this hour" (12:27). Instead of being taken by surprise by His execution, the Lord had repeatedly predicted it (e.g., Matt. 16:21; 17:22–23; 20:17–19; Luke 24:6–7, 26). Underscoring the crucial importance of Christ's death, the Gospels devote about one-fifth of their material to the last few days of His life. John devotes nine chapters (12–20)—nearly half of his account of Christ's life—to the events of Passion Week.

In keeping with his purpose of portraying Jesus as the incarnate Son of God (20:31), John depicts His majesty and glory—even as He is betrayed and arrested to be executed. The apostle skillfully demonstrates that the shameful, debasing things done to Christ failed to detract from His person, but rather offered decisive proof of His glory. B. F. Westcott observes,

> In comparing the narrative of St. John with the parallel narratives of the Synoptists, it must be observed generally that here, as everywhere, St. John fixes the attention of the reader upon the ideas which the several

events bring out and illustrate. The Passion and Resurrection are for him revelations of the Person of Christ. The objective fact is a "sign" of something which lies deeper. . . . It [the account of the Passion and Resurrection] is . . . like the rest of the Gospel, an interpretation of the inner meaning of the history which it contains. (*The Gospel According to St. John* [repr.; Grand Rapids: Eerdmans, 1978], 249)

Thus unlike Matthew, Mark, and Luke, John makes no mention of Jesus' agonized prayer to the Father (cf. Matt. 26:39; Mark 14:36; Luke 22:42–44). John's different emphasis does not contradict the picture of Christ given in the other gospels, but supplements it (see the discussion of that point in the introduction to John's gospel in *John 1–11*, The MacArthur New Testament Commentary [Chicago: Moody, 2006]).

In his account of Christ's betrayal and arrest, John presents four preeminent features that demonstrate His majesty and glory: His supreme courage, power, love, and obedience.

CHRIST'S SUPREME COURAGE

When Jesus had spoken these words, He went forth with His disciples over the ravine of the Kidron, where there was a garden, in which He entered with His disciples. Now Judas also, who was betraying Him, knew the place, for Jesus had often met there with His disciples. Judas then, having received the Roman cohort and officers from the chief priests and the Pharisees, came there with lanterns and torches and weapons. So Jesus, knowing all the things that were coming upon Him, went forth. (18:1–4*a*)

His final teaching time with the eleven remaining disciples was now over, and having **spoken these words** (chaps. 13–17), Jesus **went forth with His disciples.** The point made here is not that they left the upper room, but that they left Jerusalem. They had already abandoned the upper room, so that the last part of Jesus' farewell discourse, and His High Priestly Prayer, took place as He and the disciples passed through the streets of Jerusalem (see the exposition of 14:31 in chapter 12 of this volume). As the little group left the city behind, they crossed **over the ravine of the Kidron,** east of and a few hundred feet below the temple mount. The **ravine** was actually a wadi, through which water flowed during the winter rainy season. In its first mention in Scripture, the Kidron Valley had been part of another scene of betrayal and treachery, as David fled Jerusalem after Absalom's rebellion (2 Sam. 15:23). Asa (1 Kings 15:13), Josiah (2 Kings 23:4–12), and Hezekiah (2 Chron. 29:16; 30:14) had burned idols there in connection with their reforms.

Across the familiar valley was the western slope of the Mount of Olives, where **there was a garden.** John does not name that place, but Matthew 26:36 and Mark 14:32 call it Gethsemane. The name literally means "oil press," suggesting that this was an olive orchard (such orchards were common on the Mount of Olives; hence its obvious designation). That Jesus **entered** the garden **with His disciples** and later left it (v. 4) suggests that it was an identifiable, perhaps even a walled private garden, owned by a wealthy family of Jerusalem who allowed the Lord's use of it.

Gethsemane was well known to **Judas . . . who was betraying Him,** because **Jesus had often met there with His disciples.** Luke's account states that it was Jesus' custom to visit the Mount of Olives (Luke 22:39). That had been true throughout His ministry whenever He was in Jerusalem (cf. John 8:1). It was on the Mount of Olives that Jesus had given the detailed teaching on the signs of His return known as the Olivet Discourse (Matt. 24:3). He had also spent all the previous nights of Passion Week there (Luke 21:37; cf. Mark 11:19). In addition, the Lord had frequently visited Bethany (Matt. 21:17; 26:6; John 11:1; 12:1), located two miles from Jerusalem (John 11:18) on the southeast slope of the Mount of Olives.

Christ went to Gethsemane because it was a secluded place where He could pour out His heart to the Father in private. But more significant on this night, He went there because He knew that is where Judas would look for Him. Thus, the Lord sovereignly arranged the time and place of His betrayal. All His enemies' previous attempts to seize Him had been unsuccessful, because His hour had not yet come (cf. John 2:4; 7:30; 8:20). But now, in the outworking of God's eternal plan, the time had come for Him to offer His life (cf. Luke 22:53).

The Lord had another reason for choosing this specific place to allow His enemies to seize Him. Jerusalem was teeming with pilgrims, many of whom had fervently hailed Him as the Messiah just a few days earlier. His arrest could have sparked an insurrection by the passionately nationalistic crowds. That is exactly what the Jewish leaders feared would happen, hence "they plotted together to seize Jesus by stealth and kill Him. But they were saying, 'Not during the festival, otherwise a riot might occur among the people'" (Matt. 26:4–5; cf. 21:46; Luke 19:47–48). Neither did Jesus want to be the catalyst for a revolt of the populace, since He did not come as a military conqueror seeking to overthrow the Romans (cf. John 6:15)—He came to die as a sacrifice for sin (Matt. 1:21; John 1:29). Further, the disciples may well have been killed in the ensuing melee, and the Lord wanted to protect them (cf. the discussion of v. 9 below).

Meanwhile Judas's evil plans were about to come to fruition. A few days earlier he had approached the Jewish authorities and offered to betray the Lord (cf. chapter 1 of this volume). Then earlier that evening Judas, having been dismissed by Jesus, left to make the final arrangements for the betrayal (see chapters 6 and 7 of this volume). Now, **having received the Roman cohort and officers from the chief priests and the Pharisees,** Judas led this "large crowd" (Matt. 26:47) to Gethsemane, where he knew Jesus would be waiting.

A Roman cohort at full strength numbered from 600 to 1,000 men. It is unlikely, however, that the full cohort stationed in Jerusalem to keep order during the Passover season would have been sent to arrest Jesus. More likely this was a smaller detachment known as a *maniple,* which consisted of about 200 men. In any case, enough of the soldiers from the cohort were sent to warrant their commanding officer accompanying them (v. 12). John's reference to the larger unit of which this detachment was a part was a figure of speech. In much the same way, to say that the fire department put out a fire does not imply that the entire department was involved. For the Romans to send such a large detachment to deal with one potentially troublesome individual was not unusual; they detailed 470 soldiers to take Paul from Jerusalem to Caesarea (Acts 23:23). Like the Jewish authorities, the Romans feared that Christ's arrest might touch off a riot. The legionnaires were there to serve as backup for the **officers from the chief priests and the Pharisees.** These members of the temple police force (cf. 7:32) evidently made the actual arrest (since Jesus was taken first to the Jewish authorities, not the Roman governor). Luke adds that some of the chief priests were also present, no doubt to supervise the temple police (Luke 22:52).

The large procession, with Judas in the lead (Luke 22:47), arrived **there with lanterns and torches and weapons** to seize Jesus. The mention of this seemingly minor detail offers evidence that the author was an eyewitness (see the introduction to John in *John 1–11*). The **lanterns and torches** would not have been necessary to light the way to Gethsemane; since it was Passover, which was celebrated when there was a full moon, there would have been ample light. Evidently, they anticipated that Jesus would attempt to flee, and that they would have to search for Him on the mountainside.

But the Lord had no intention of hiding or fleeing. Instead with majestic calmness, absolute self-control, and supreme courage, **Jesus, knowing all the things that were coming upon Him, went forth** out of the garden **and** met those who came to arrest Him. John's note that Jesus knew **all the things that were coming upon Him** emphasizes both His omniscience and His complete mastery of the situation. The Lord's voluntary surrender stresses again that He willingly laid down His life (John 10:17–18).

Though the apostle John does not record it, Judas, in history's most cynical act of hypocrisy, brazenly approached Jesus and kissed him (Matt. 26:49; Mark 14:45; Luke 22:47)—the prearranged signal by which he would point Him out (Mark 14:44). Nothing more clearly symbolizes the depravity of his heart and the depth of his sin than Judas's using a disciple's kiss as a traitor's sign.

In addition to being a recognized gesture of respect and affection, this kind of kiss was a sign of homage in that culture. Of the varieties of the kiss (feet, hand, head, hem of the garment), Judas chose the one that declared the deepest homage and love. The kiss on the cheek with an embrace was appropriate for an intimate friend. Thus the treachery of Judas is the most despicable.

CHRIST'S SUPREME POWER

and said to them, "Whom do you seek?" They answered Him, "Jesus the Nazarene." He said to them, "I am He." And Judas also, who was betraying Him, was standing with them. So when He said to them, "I am He," they drew back and fell to the ground. (18:4b–6)

Jesus, the intended victim, took charge of the situation and **said to them, "Whom do you seek?" They** (most likely the leaders), probably stating their official orders, **answered Him, "Jesus the Nazarene."** The Lord **said to them, "I am He."** The word "He" is not in the original Greek, so that as He had done before on a number of occasions (e.g., 8:24, 28, 58), Jesus was claiming for Himself the name of God from Exodus 3:14—"I AM."

Before relating the crowd's startling response to Jesus' words, John inserts the parenthetical statement that **Judas also, who was betraying Him, was standing with them.** This seemingly insignificant detail stresses yet again Jesus' absolute mastery of the circumstances. John wants to make it clear that Judas was merely one of those who experienced what was about to happen. Judas had absolutely no power over Jesus (cf. 19:11); he was jolted to the ground with the rest of those present.

Christ demonstrated His divine dominance in a stunning manner. Immediately after **He said to them, "I am He," they drew back and fell to the ground.** All Jesus had to do was speak His name—the name of God—and His enemies were rendered helpless. This amazing demonstration of His power clearly reveals that they did not seize Jesus. He went with them willingly, to carry out the divine plan of redemption that called for His sacrificial death.

Illustrating the foolishness of unbelief, some argue that no supernatural power is in view here. Jesus' sudden appearance out of the shadows, they maintain, startled those in the front of the column. They then lurched backward and knocked the ones behind them down, who in turn knocked others down, until the whole column went down. But the temple police and the Roman soldiers were prepared for trouble (cf. Matt. 26:55). They would surely have been spread out, both to defend themselves against an attack by Jesus' followers, and to cut off any escape attempt on His part. The notion that hundreds of experienced police officers and highly trained soldiers would stand so close together in one long line that they could be toppled over like dominoes is ludicrous.

The Bible speaks repeatedly of the power of God's spoken word. He spoke, and the heavens and earth were created (Gen. 1:3, 6, 9, 11, 14, 20, 24, 26; cf. Ps. 33:6); Satan and mankind were judged (Gen. 3:14–19); the rebellious generation of Israelites died in the wilderness (Num. 26:65); and Israel went into exile for seventy years (2 Chron. 36:21). When the Lord Jesus Christ returns, He will execute judgment on His enemies "with the sword which [comes] from [His] mouth" (Rev. 19:21; cf. v. 15; 1:16; 2:16). John's account highlights Christ's divine power; at His word His enemies were thrown backward to the ground.

CHRIST'S SUPREME LOVE

Therefore He again asked them, "Whom do you seek?" And they said, "Jesus the Nazarene." Jesus answered, "I told you that I am He; so if you seek Me, let these go their way," to fulfill the word which He spoke, "Of those whom You have given Me I lost not one." (18:7–9)

After His stunning display of His divine power, Jesus **again asked** His dazed would-be captors, **"Whom do you seek?"** Picking themselves up off the ground, they parroted their orders and replied, **"Jesus the Nazarene." "I told you that I am He,"** Jesus reminded them, and then commanded them, **"if you seek Me, let these go their way."** By making His captors twice state that their orders were only to arrest Him, the Lord forced them to acknowledge that they had been given by their superiors no authority to arrest the disciples. His demand that they leave the eleven alone was backed up by the awesome power He had just displayed.

Why did Jesus shield the disciples from arrest? The Lord is the good shepherd, who protects His sheep. He is not like the hired hand who fled when he saw the wolf approaching (John 10:12–13). Jesus kept the disciples from being arrested **to fulfill the word which He spoke, "Of those whom You have given Me I lost not one"** (cf. 6:39, 40, 44; 10:28; 17:12). This is a startling statement, meaning that He kept them from being arrested so they would not be lost. Each was a gift from the Father to the Son. And He had already said,

> All that the Father gives Me will come to Me, and the one who comes to Me I will certainly not cast out. For I have come down from heaven, not to do My own will, but the will of Him who sent Me. This is the will of Him who sent Me, that of all that He has given Me I lose nothing, but raise it up on the last day. For this is the will of My Father, that everyone who beholds the Son and believes in Him will have eternal life, and I Myself will raise him up on the last day. (John 6:37–40)

He will not lose one! The implication is that if they had been arrested, their faith would have failed and they would have lost their salvation. The Lord knew that the trauma of being arrested, imprisoned, or perhaps even executed could shatter the disciples' faith. Therefore He made certain that they would not be taken.

Does that mean that salvation can be lost? That faith can fail? If left up to us, of course. But we will never be lost nor will saving faith fail, precisely because our Lord keeps us secure. He never allows anything to come upon us that would be more than our faith could handle.

Like the disciples, all believers are weak and vulnerable apart from the Lord's protection. Martin Luther, no stranger to spiritual conflict, expressed that truth in his magnificent hymn, "A Mighty Fortress Is Our God":

> Did we in our own strength confide,
> Our striving would be losing,
> Were not the right Man on our side,
> The Man of God's own choosing:
> Dost ask who that may be?
> Christ Jesus, it is He;
> Lord Sabaoth His name
> From age to age the same;
> And He must win the battle.

Believers can be confident that God will always keep His promise never to allow them to be tempted beyond their ability to endure (1 Cor. 10:13). Their eternal security does not rest in their own strength, but in Christ's constant intercession (Heb. 7:25; 1 John 2:1–2) and unceasing love (Rom. 8:35–39) for them. "For if while we were enemies we were reconciled to God through the death of His Son," Paul wrote, "much more, having been reconciled, we shall be saved by His life" (Rom. 5:10).

CHRIST'S SUPREME OBEDIENCE

Simon Peter then, having a sword, drew it and struck the high priest's slave, and cut off his right ear; and the slave's name was Malchus. So Jesus said to Peter, "Put the sword into the sheath; the cup which the Father has given Me, shall I not drink it?" (18:10–11)

Sensing what was about to happen, the disciples cried out, "Lord, shall we strike with the sword?" (Luke 22:49). Without waiting for the Lord's reply, **Simon Peter,** emboldened by the awesome display of Christ's divine power he had just seen, impulsively (and needlessly) charged to the Lord's defense. **Having a sword** (Gk. *machaira,* a short sword or dagger; one of the two disciples had with them according to Luke 22:38), Peter **drew it.** Rather than allow Jesus to be arrested, and feeling invincible in the wake of the Lord's display of "flattening" power, he intended to hack his way through the entire detachment. His first target was **the high priest's slave, Malchus.** (Although all four Gospels mention the incident, only John notes that it was Peter who attacked Malchus. Perhaps since Peter was already dead by the time John wrote, John did not need to protect him from reprisals.) Peter aimed for Malchus's head, but missed (or Malchus managed to duck) **and cut off his right ear.** Peter's reckless act threatened to start a battle that could wind up getting the disciples either killed or arrested—the very thing Jesus was trying to prevent.

The Lord moved immediately to defuse the situation. Sharply rebuking him, **Jesus said to Peter,** in effect, "Stop! No more of this" (Luke 22:51). **"Put the sword into the sheath.** For all those who take up the sword shall perish by the sword" (Matt. 26:52). He was not an earthly king, who needed His followers to fight to protect Him (John 18:36). Had He chosen to, Jesus could have called on far more powerful defenders than the disciples (Matt. 26:53).

Then the Lord "touched [Malchus's] ear and healed him" (Luke 22:51). This was a further display of Christ's divine power in the span of just a few minutes. Upon seeing Him create an ear, the crowd should have fallen at His feet again and worshiped Him. But blinded by and hardened in their sin, they arrested Him (v. 12), demonstrating again the truth of what John had written earlier in his gospel: "But though He had performed so many signs before them, yet they were not believing in Him" (12:37).

Peter's brave but impetuous act revealed his continued failure to understand the necessity of Jesus' death. After his ringing affirmation that Jesus was the Christ (Matt. 16:16), the Lord immediately spoke to the disciples about His death (v. 21). Shocked, "Peter took Him aside and began to rebuke Him, saying, 'God forbid it, Lord! This shall never happen to You'" (v. 22). Now that the moment had arrived, Peter still did not get it, so Jesus reminded him (and the rest of the disciples), **"The cup which the Father has given Me, shall I not drink it?"** The **cup** of which the Lord spoke was the cup of divine judgment (cf. Pss. 11:6; 75:8; Isa. 51:17, 22; Jer. 25:15; Ezek. 23:31–34; Matt. 26:39; Rev. 14:10; 16:19), which He would drain completely on the cross when God "made Him who knew no sin to be sin on our behalf, so that we might become the righteousness of God in Him" (2 Cor. 5:21). It was to that saving sacrifice that Christ's supreme courage, power, love, and obedience would lead.

Jesus' Trial; Peter's Denial (John 18:12–27)

28

So the Roman cohort and the commander and the officers of the Jews, arrested Jesus and bound Him, and led Him to Annas first; for he was father-in-law of Caiaphas, who was high priest that year. Now Caiaphas was the one who had advised the Jews that it was expedient for one man to die on behalf of the people. Simon Peter was following Jesus, and so was another disciple. Now that disciple was known to the high priest, and entered with Jesus into the court of the high priest, but Peter was standing at the door outside. So the other disciple, who was known to the high priest, went out and spoke to the doorkeeper, and brought Peter in. Then the slave-girl who kept the door said to Peter, "You are not also one of this man's disciples, are you?" He said, "I am not." Now the slaves and the officers were standing there, having made a charcoal fire, for it was cold and they were warming themselves; and Peter was also with them, standing and warming himself. The high priest then questioned Jesus about His disciples, and about His teaching. Jesus answered him, "I have spoken openly to the world; I always taught in synagogues and in the temple, where all the Jews come together; and I spoke nothing in secret. Why do you question Me? Question those who have heard what I spoke to them; they know what I said." When He had said this, one of the officers standing nearby struck Jesus, saying, "Is that the way You answer the high priest?" Jesus answered him, "If I have spoken wrongly, testify of the wrong; but if rightly, why do you strike Me?" So Annas sent Him bound to Caiaphas the high priest. Now Simon Peter was standing and warming himself. So they said to him, "You are not also one of His disciples, are you?" He denied it, and said, "I am not." One of the slaves of the high priest, being a relative of the one whose ear Peter cut off, said, "Did I not see you in the garden with Him?" Peter then denied it again, and immediately a rooster crowed. (18:12–27)

Throughout his gospel, John portrays the majesty and glory of the Lord Jesus Christ. The prologue declares Him to be God the Son (1:1), who enjoys intimate fellowship with the Father (1:2) and is self-existent (1:4), the Creator (1:3), and the Word who became flesh and manifested God's glory (1:14). John the Baptist, the greatest man who had lived up to his time (Matt. 11:11), acknowledged that Jesus was superior to him (1:15, 27). The apostle John also records Jesus' omniscience (1:48; 2:24–25; 16:30), sinlessness (8:46), eternity (1:1–2), union with the Father (10:30, 38; 12:45), and miraculous signs (2:1–11; 4:46–54; 5:1–9; 6:1–13, 16–21; 9:1–7; 11:1–45; 21:6–11).

Even in his account of Jesus' betrayal and arrest, John portrays Jesus' dignity, courage, and complete mastery of the situation (see the exposition of 18:1–11 in the previous chapter of this volume). The present passage finds the Lord in the custody of His enemies, on trial for His life. But even in such seemingly degrading circumstances, John still managed to exalt Him. The apostle did so by juxtaposing the accounts of the Lord's initial hearing before Annas and Peter's denials. Both scenes took place at the same time and John, under the Spirit's inspiration, wove them into one dramatic narrative.

The interplay of the two dramas brings into sharp focus opposite truths that are foundational to all of Christian doctrine: the glory of Christ and the sinfulness of man. Those truths are evident from the contrast between Christ's faithfulness and Peter's faithlessness; His courage and Peter's cowardice; His sacrificial love and Peter's self-preserving lies.

The drama unfolds in four acts: it opens with the first act of Jesus' trial, followed by act one of Peter's denial. The scene then shifts to the second act of Jesus' trial, and then concludes with the second and final act of Peter's denial.

JESUS' TRIAL: ACT ONE

So the Roman cohort and the commander and the officers of the Jews, arrested Jesus and bound Him, and led Him to Annas first; for he was father-in-law of Caiaphas, who was high priest that year. Now Caiaphas was the one who had advised the Jews that it was expedient for one man to die on behalf of the people. (18:12–14)

As noted in the previous chapter of this volume, the arresting party consisted of both Jews and Gentiles. The detachment from **the Roman cohort** that was stationed in Jerusalem during Passover season was accompanied by the cohort's **commander,** the Roman tribune (Gk. *chiliarchos*; commander of a thousand"). The **officers of the Jews** (members of the temple police force) were also accompanied by some of their superiors (Luke 22:52). The presence of high-ranking officials reveals the explosiveness of the situation. Both the Romans and the Jews feared that arresting Jesus might spark a riot by the militantly nationalistic crowds that had hailed Him as the Messiah only a few days earlier.

Jesus had just displayed His supernatural power by saying His divine name (after which the entire multitude collapsed on the ground) and restoring Malchus's severed ear (18:6; Luke 22:51). Incredibly, the soldiers and temple policemen acted as if nothing miraculous had happened and mechanically carried out their orders. Their stubborn obtuseness graphically illustrates the terrible power of sin and Satan to blind the minds and harden the hearts of the unregenerate (2 Cor. 4:4). They are literally "dead in [their] trespasses and sins" (Eph. 2:1).

Having formally **arrested** Jesus, the soldiers and police **bound Him.** This probably was standard procedure when making an arrest, but it also suggests a deeper significance. Just as Isaac (Gen. 22:9) and the Old Testament sacrifices (Ps. 118:27) were bound to the altar, so also was the Lamb of God, the ultimate sacrifice.

After seizing Jesus, they **led Him to Annas first.** This preliminary hearing, recorded only by John, marked the first of the three phases of Jesus' religious trial before the Jewish authorities. The second phase was before Caiaphas and the Sanhedrin (Matt. 26:57–68; Mark 14:53–65; Luke 22:54); the third was after sunrise the next morning as the authorities confirmed the decision reached at the earlier hearing (Matt. 27:1; Mark 15:1; Luke 22:66–71). The Lord's civil trial also had three phases: before Pilate (Matt. 27:2, 11–14; Mark 15:1–5; Luke 23:1–5; John 18:28–38); before Herod (Luke 23:6–12); and then before Pilate again (Matt. 27:15–26; Mark 15:6–15; Luke 23:13–25; John 18:39–19:16). (For further information about Jesus' trials, see Robert L. Thomas and Stanley N. Gundry, *A Harmony of the Gospels* [Chicago: Moody, 1979], 329–37.)

Although he no longer held office at the time, **Annas** was the most powerful figure in the Jewish hierarchy. He had been the high priest from A.D. 6 to A.D. 15, when he was removed from office by Valerius Gratus, Pilate's predecessor as governor. He could still properly carry the title of high priest (vv. 15, 16, 19, 22), in much the same way that former presidents of the United States are still referred to as president after they leave office. Annas's title, however, was more than a mere courtesy. Many Jews, resentful of the Romans' meddling in their religious affairs, still considered Annas to be the true power (especially since according to the Mosaic law high priests served for life; cf. Num. 35:25).

Further, after his removal from office, five of Annas's sons and one of his grandsons served as high priest. He was also the **father-in-law of Caiaphas, who was high priest that year** (i.e., at that time; John is not implying that the high priests served for only one year). Thus, Leon Morris concurs, "There is little doubt but that ... the astute old man at the head of the family exercised a good deal of authority. He was in all probability the real power in the land, whatever the legal technicalities" (*The Gospel According to John,* The New International Commentary on the New Testament [Grand Rapids: Eerdmans, 1979], 749). The New Testament places the beginning of John the Baptist's ministry "in the high priesthood of Annas and Caiaphas" (Luke 3:2; cf. Acts 4:6), as though they jointly held the office.

Annas was a proud, ambitious, and notoriously greedy man. Evidently a significant source of his income came from the concessions in the temple. He received a share of the proceeds from the sale of sacrificial animals; frequently those brought by the people would be rejected and those for sale at the temple (for exorbitant prices) would be approved as an offering. Annas also profited from the fees the money changers charged to exchange foreign currency into the Jewish money that alone could be used to pay the temple tax (cf. 2:14). So infamous was his greed that the outer courts of the temple, where those transactions took place, became known as the Bazaar of Annas (see Alfred Edersheim, *The Life and Times of Jesus the Messiah* [repr.; Grand Rapids: Eerdmans, 1974], 1:371–72).

Annas had a special hatred for Jesus, who had twice disrupted his business operations by cleansing the temple (John 2:13–16; Matt. 21:12–13). Perhaps he had Jesus brought to him because he "wanted to be the first to gloat over the capture of this disturbing Galilean" (William Barclay, *The Gospel of John,* vol. 2 [Louisville: Westminster John Knox, 2001], 264).

John's parenthetical note that **Caiaphas was the one who had advised the Jews that it was expedient for one man to die on behalf of the people** refers to the incident recorded in 11:49–52:

> But one of them, Caiaphas, who was high priest that year, said to them, "You know nothing at all, nor do you take into account that it is expedient for you that one man die for the people, and that the whole nation not perish." Now he did not say this on his own initiative, but being high priest that year, he prophesied that Jesus was going to die for the nation, and not for the nation only, but in order that He might also gather together into one the children of God who are scattered abroad.

Joseph **Caiaphas** had been appointed high priest in A.D. 18 by Valerius Gratus, the same Roman prefect who had deposed his father-in-law Annas three years earlier. He remained in office until A.D. 36 when the Romans removed him. Caiaphas's tenure as high priest was one of the longest in the first century, which reveals his cunning and opportunistic nature. That he proposed killing Jesus to preserve his and the Sanhedrin's power (cf. 11:48) demonstrates his utter ruthlessness.

With Jesus in the custody of His enemies, the scene now shifts to Peter.

PETER'S DENIAL: ACT ONE

Simon Peter was following Jesus, and so was another disciple. Now that disciple was known to the high priest, and entered with Jesus into the court of the high priest, but Peter was standing at the door outside. So the other disciple, who was known to the high priest, went out and spoke to the doorkeeper, and brought Peter in. Then the slave-girl who kept the door said to Peter, "You are not also one of this man's disciples, are you?" He said, "I am not." Now the slaves and the officers were standing there, having made a charcoal fire, for it was cold and they were warming themselves; and Peter was also with them, standing and warming himself. (18:15–18)

Despite his show of bravado in attacking and wounding Malchus, **Peter** had fled along with the rest of the disciples after Jesus' arrest (Matt. 26:56). But he had managed to regain his composure and now **was following Jesus** and the arresting party—albeit at a distance (Matt. 26:58; Mark 14:54; Luke 22:54). Peter was not alone; **another disciple** had also mastered his fear and turned back with him. Some identify this unnamed disciple as Joseph of Arimathea or Nicodemus, but neither is a likely candidate. Neither one was with the Lord in the upper room (Matt. 26:20; Mark 14:17–18; Luke 22:14) and hence not in Gethsemane either (cf. Matt. 26:36; "them" in the context of vv. 30–36 refers to the eleven remaining disciples who had been in the upper room). It is unlikely that there would have been time for either Joseph or Nicodemus to have found out about Jesus' arrest and joined Peter. Further, Joseph of Arimathea was still not openly a disciple of Jesus (John 19:38). Thus, it is unlikely that he would have followed Him into the high priest's courtyard—especially not with Peter, who was known to be one of Christ's disciples.

The other disciple with Peter was most likely John, who never names himself in his gospel but instead describes himself as the disciple whom Jesus loved (see introduction, "The Authorship of John's Gospel," in *John 1–11*, The MacArthur New Testament Commentary [Chicago: Moody, 2006]). That identification receives support from 20:2–8, the only other passage in John's gospel where the phrase "other disciple" occurs. There the "other disciple" is clearly identified as the disciple whom Jesus loved (20:2). The disciple whom Jesus loved (John) is also associated with Peter in 13:23–24 and 21:20–21.

Some object that a simple Galilean fisherman such as John could hardly be **known** (the Greek word suggests more than a casual acquaintance) **to the high priest.** But it must be remembered that "fishermen were entrepreneurs, not common laborers at the bottom of the social spectrum" (D. M. Smith, cited in Andreas J. Köstenberger, *John*, Baker Exegetical Commentary on the New Testament [Grand Rapids: Baker, 2004], 513 n. 14). John's father's fishing business was large enough for him to have hired servants working for him (Mark 1:19–20). According to the apocryphal gospel of the Hebrews, the apostle John used to deliver fish to the high priest's house while he was still working for his father (Köstenberger, *John*, 513 n. 14).

It is also possible that John, through his mother, Salome (cf. Matt. 27:56 with Mark 15:40), was of priestly descent. She apparently was the sister of Jesus' mother, Mary (cf. John 19:25 with Mark 15:40). Since Mary was related to Elizabeth (Luke 1:36; probably through her mother; she was of the line of David through her father [Luke 3:23–38]), who was from a priestly family (Luke 1:5), Salome would be too. The early church historian Eusebius (*Ecclesiastical History* III.31.3) cites a letter from Polycrates, a late second-century bishop of Ephesus (where John spent his last years), in which Polycrates states that John had been a priest.

Whatever the case may be, John was sufficiently well known that he was allowed to enter **with Jesus into the court of the high priest.** Peter, however, was not, and was left **standing at the door outside.** Realizing what had happened, **the other disciple, who was known to the high priest, went out and spoke to the doorkeeper** (the feminine form of the noun indicates that this was a woman, as v. 17 confirms. That a woman was on duty at the entrance indicates that this incident did not take place in the temple complex, where only men manned such posts.), **and brought Peter in.** That John was able to vouch for Peter shows again that he was well known in the high priest's household. Peter's desire to be with Jesus overcame his fear, and he entered the courtyard.

But as he did, **the slave-girl who kept the door said** something **to Peter** that jolted him. **"You are not also** (in addition to John) **one of this man's disciples, are you?"** she demanded. The question in the Greek text expects a negative answer. Following her cue, Peter tersely blurted out, **"I am not."** Why he should deny being a disciple of Jesus is not immediately apparent. After all, John, who was known to be one of Jesus' disciples, had just been admitted without incident. It may be that Peter was not accustomed to associating with the rich and powerful. Perhaps the unfamiliar setting he found himself in caused him to lose his nerve and burst out a cowardly denial when he was caught off guard by the servant girl's unexpected challenge. Whatever the reason may have been, this and his subsequent denials proved that the Lord knew Peter better than he knew himself (cf. 13:37–38). The tragic story of Peter's multiple denials "is a warning to all who would claim self-confidently that they would follow Jesus 'wherever he leads them.' Boasting of our abilities is an invitation to failure. That is exactly what Peter discovered" (Gerald L. Borchert, *John 12–21*, The New American Commentary [Nashville: Broadman & Holman, 2002], 230).

No doubt desperate to avoid any further questions, Peter hurried across the courtyard toward the place where some of the high priest's **slaves** and **officers** of the temple guard (probably part of the arresting party) **were standing.** The detail that they had **made a charcoal fire, for it was cold and they were warming themselves,** again reflects eyewitness testimony. More significant, it shows that this initial hearing took place at night, since it would not likely have been cold enough at Passover to have a fire during the day. Trying to blend in and be as inconspicuous as possible, **Peter was also with them, standing and warming himself.** He was taking a risk that someone else would recognize him in the firelight (which is exactly what did happen; Mark 14:66–67; Luke 22:55–56). But standing all alone in the courtyard would only have called further attention to himself—which was the last thing he wanted to do. In a bitter irony Peter, like Judas a little while earlier in Gethsemane (18:5), wound up standing with the enemies of Jesus.

Leaving Peter in that vulnerable position, the scene now shifts indoors to the dramatic confrontation between Annas and Jesus.

JESUS' TRIAL: ACT TWO

The high priest then questioned Jesus about His disciples, and about His teaching. Jesus answered him, "I have spoken openly to the world; I always taught in synagogues and in the temple, where all the Jews come together; and I spoke nothing in secret. Why do you question Me? Question those who have heard what I spoke to them; they know what I said." When He had said this, one of the officers standing nearby struck Jesus, saying, "Is that the way You answer the high priest?" Jesus answered him, "If I have spoken wrongly, testify of the wrong; but if rightly, why do you strike Me?" So Annas sent Him bound to Caiaphas the high priest. (18:19–24)

Jesus' trial before the Jewish authorities was a sham, since His fate had already been determined. Back in chapter 11 "the chief priests and the Pharisees convened a council, and were saying, 'What are we doing? For this man is performing many signs'" (vv. 47–48). The chilling conclusion they arrived at (proposed by Caiaphas; vv. 49–50) was that Jesus had to die, "so from that day on they planned together to kill Him" (v. 53). Thus none of the three phases of the Lord's trial before the Jewish authorities was an impartial attempt to truly determine His guilt or innocence. Instead, their purpose was to put a veneer of legality on His murder.

This informal hearing before Annas was no exception. Rather than bringing charges against the Lord and producing evidence to substantiate them as in any legal proceeding, Annas **questioned Jesus about His disciples, and about His teaching.** This blatant attempt to get the Lord to incriminate Himself was illegal. Just as the Fifth Amendment to the United States Constitution does today, Jewish law protected the accused from being forced to testify against himself. It was Annas's responsibility to inform Jesus of the charges against Him. Instead, he asked vague, general questions, hoping to uncover a crime to justify the death sentence that had already been decided on.

Jesus, however, was well aware of the law. Therefore He **answered him, "I have spoken openly to the world; I always taught in synagogues and in the temple, where all the Jews come together; and I spoke nothing in secret."** The Lord had no ulterior motive, no secret plan, no hidden agenda known only to an inner cadre of followers. He had openly preached the saving gospel of the kingdom (Matt. 11:1–5; Mark 1:14, 38–39; 4:17; Luke 4:18–21, 43–44; 8:1; 20:1) and offered salvation to those who accepted it (Matt. 11:28–30; John 10:9; 14:6). Jesus' challenge, **"Why do you question Me? Question those who have heard what I spoke to them; they know what I said,"** was not an act of insolent defiance, but a demand that the requirements of the law for legitimate accusers and accusations be observed. The Lord unmasked Annas's hypocrisy, and challenged him to present his case and call his witnesses.

Embarrassed by his master's loss of face (and likely seeking to curry Annas's favor), **one of the officers standing nearby struck Jesus, saying, "Is that the way You answer the high priest?"** To strike a prisoner, especially one not accused of a crime, was illegal. Years later when Paul stood before the Sanhedrin, he too was illegally struck, in his case by order of the high priest (Acts 23:2). Angered at this egregious violation of the law, Paul retorted, "God is going to strike you, you whitewashed wall! Do you sit to try me according to the Law, and in violation of the Law order me to be struck?" (v. 3). After one of the bystanders rebuked him for reviling the high priest (v. 4), Paul humbly apologized (v. 5).

Jesus, however, maintained a majestic calm; "while being reviled, He did not revile in return; while suffering, He uttered no threats, but kept entrusting Himself to Him who judges righteously" (1 Peter 2:23). The Lord **answered** the one who struck Him, **"If I have spoken wrongly, testify of the wrong; but if rightly, why do you strike Me?"** Christ's logic was impeccable. If He was wrong about the proper legal procedure, they should have corrected Him instead of hitting Him. But if (as He did) the Lord spoke accurately, what justifiable reason was there for striking Him? Once again Jesus demanded a fair trial—which His opponents had no intention of giving Him.

Realizing that he was getting nowhere with his questioning of Jesus, **Annas sent Him bound to Caiaphas the high priest.** Only **Caiaphas,** the reigning **high priest,** could bring legal charges against Jesus before Pilate.

As they led Jesus away, the focus shifted back to the courtyard, where the final act in the drama of Peter's denial was about to play out.

PETER'S DENIAL: ACT TWO

Now Simon Peter was standing and warming himself. So they said to him, "You are not also one of His disciples, are you?" He denied it, and said, "I am not." One of the slaves of the high priest, being a relative of the one whose ear Peter cut off, said, "Did I not see you in the garden with Him?" Peter then denied it again, and immediately a rooster crowed. (18:25–27)

While Jesus was being questioned by Annas, Peter, still **standing and warming himself** next to the fire in the courtyard, was interrogated by Annas's subordinates. Becoming suspicious of this stranger, **they said to him, "You are not also one of His disciples, are you?"** Here was a chance for Peter to redeem himself and be courageously honest. Once again, however, **he denied it, and said, "I am not."** But the repeated questioning of Peter by the others had aroused the suspicions of **one of the slaves of the high priest.** Making a bad situation for Peter far worse, this individual was **a relative of the one whose ear Peter cut off** (Malchus) earlier that evening in Gethsemane. He challenged Peter with the most specific (and dangerous) accusation of all: **"Did I not see you in the garden with Him?"** Being a disciple of Jesus was not a crime as of yet, but assaulting a man with a sword was. Panic-stricken, Peter emphatically **denied** for the third time any knowledge of Jesus.

At that very moment, two things happened that drew the two dramas concerning Jesus and Peter together. **Immediately** after Peter's third denial, **a rooster crowed.** At that very moment "the Lord turned and looked at Peter. And Peter remembered the word of the Lord, how He had told him, 'Before a rooster crows today, you will deny Me three times'" (Luke 22:61). Overwhelmed with shame, guilt, and grief at his sins of denial, Peter "went out and wept bitterly" (v. 62).

Jesus Before Pilate—Part 1: Phase One of the Civil Trial (John 18:28–38)

29

Then they led Jesus from Caiaphas into the Praetorium, and it was early; and they themselves did not enter into the Praetorium so that they would not be defiled, but might eat the Passover. Therefore Pilate went out to them and said, "What accusation do you bring against this Man?" They answered and said to him, "If this Man were not an evildoer, we would not have delivered Him to you." So Pilate said to them, "Take Him yourselves, and judge Him according to your law." The Jews said to him, "We are not permitted to put anyone to death," to fulfill the word of Jesus which He spoke, signifying by what kind of death He was about to die. Therefore Pilate entered again into the Praetorium, and summoned Jesus and said to Him, "Are You the King of the Jews?" Jesus answered, "Are you saying this on your own initiative, or did others tell you about Me?" Pilate answered, "I am not a Jew, am I? Your own nation and the chief priests delivered You to me; what have You done?" Jesus answered, "My kingdom is not of this world. If My kingdom were of this world, then My servants would be fighting so that I would not be handed over to the Jews; but as it is, My kingdom is not of this realm." Therefore Pilate said to Him, "So You are a king?" Jesus answered, "You say

correctly that I am a king. For this I have been born, and for this I have come into the world, to testify to the truth. Everyone who is of the truth hears My voice." Pilate said to Him, "What is truth?" And when he had said this, he went out again to the Jews and said to them, "I find no guilt in Him." (18:28–38)

The trials of the Lord Jesus Christ are history's most egregious miscarriage of justice. In them the friend of sinners (Luke 7:34) faced the hatred of sinners; the Judge of all the earth (Gen. 18:25) was arraigned before petty human judges; the exalted Lord of glory (1 Cor. 2:8) was humiliated by being mocked, spit upon, and beaten; the Holy and Righteous one (Acts 3:14) was treated as a vile sinner; the One who is the truth (John 14:6) was impugned by evil liars.

But shining forth out of the satanic darkness of His trials is the absolute innocence of Jesus Christ. The evil efforts of His accusers are turned upside down so as to actually confirm His blamelessness. During His earthly ministry, He challenged His opponents, "Which one of you convicts Me of sin? If I speak truth, why do you not believe Me?" (John 8:46; cf. 14:30). In the Old Testament, Isaiah prophesied concerning Him,

> His grave was assigned with wicked men,
> Yet He was with a rich man in His death,
> Because He had done no violence,
> Nor was there any deceit in His mouth. (Isa. 53:9)

The angel who foretold His birth called Him "the holy Child" (Luke 1:35); His betrayer lamented that he had "sinned by betraying innocent blood" (Matt. 27:4); one of the criminals crucified with Him declared of Him, "This man has done nothing wrong" (Luke 23:41); and the Roman centurion in charge at His execution said of Him, "Certainly this man was innocent" (v. 47). Paul said that He "knew no sin" (2 Cor. 5:21); the writer of Hebrews affirmed that He "has been tempted in all things as we are, yet without sin" (Heb. 4:15), and is "holy, innocent, undefiled, separated from sinners" (7:26); and Peter wrote that He "committed no sin, nor was any deceit found in His mouth" (1 Peter 2:22).

The cast of characters in the gospel accounts of Jesus' trials includes most of the rulers and important men in Israel. Annas, the former high priest and still the real power behind the scenes, was there. So was Caiaphas, the current high priest and son-in-law of Annas. Along with them were the members of the Sanhedrin, the ruling body (under the Romans) of Israel. Pilate, the Roman governor, played a major role; Herod Antipas, ruler of Jesus' home region of Galilee, had a cameo role; and the extras included various unnamed false witnesses along with the crowds that would scream for Him to be crucified. But throughout the six phases (three religious, three civil) of His trials, the Lord Jesus Christ occupies center stage.

John did not record the second and third phases of the Lord's religious trial, though he mentioned that Annas sent Jesus to Caiaphas (18:24). The Sanhedrin had met at Caiaphas's house during the night (Matt. 26:57–68) and decided that Jesus should die (Matt. 26:66). Then in a nod to legality (since Jewish law did not permit capital trials to be held at night), the Sanhedrin reconvened after daybreak and formally pronounced sentence (Matt. 27:1). John picked up the story at that point, noting that **they led Jesus from Caiaphas into the Praetorium,** Pilate's headquarters (probably either at Fort Antonius or Herod's palace) where he stayed when he visited Jerusalem (Pilate's permanent headquarters were in Caesarea).

The Jewish leaders' motive for bringing Jesus before Pilate was obvious. Out of envy, jealousy, and hatred, they had been plotting to kill Him for a long time (cf. 5:18; 7:1; 11:53). Their murderous designs had been frustrated until now because "His hour had not yet come" (7:30; 8:20). At last, in God's timing, with the help of the traitor Judas Iscariot, they had managed to seize Jesus. After giving Him a sham trial, they had sentenced Him to death. But having done so, they were powerless to carry out that sentence; the Romans did not permit them to execute anyone (18:31). That was standard Roman policy in the territories they ruled; they did not want nationalists executing those who were loyal to Rome.

Early Jewish sources differ as to when Rome removed the right of capital punishment from the Jews. The first-century Jewish historian Josephus states that it was in A.D. 6 when Judea became a Roman province. The Talmud (second century), however, dates it about forty years before the destruction of the temple (i.e., about A.D. 30). Perhaps, as F. F. Bruce suggests, "it may be that the remembrance persisted of a situation around A.D. 30 when the deprivation of this right was of special significance" (*The Gospel of John* [Grand Rapids: Eerdmans, 1983], 351).

By way of further setting the scene, John noted that **it was early.** *Prōi*, **early,** refers technically to the fourth watch of the night (3:00–6:00 A.M.), though it can also be used in a more general sense. Roman officials often began their duties at dawn and finished by late morning, so there is no reason why the Jewish leaders could not have brought Jesus to Pilate before 6:00 A.M. Their goal was to have him rubber-stamp their decision to kill Jesus, and carry out the execution before the crowds were aware of what was happening.

When they arrived at Pilate's headquarters, the Jewish leaders remained outside and **did not enter into the Praetorium so that**

they would not be defiled, but might eat the Passover. They had ceremonially cleansed themselves in preparation for the Passover meal they would eat later that day (Friday; for a discussion of how Jesus and the disciples could have eaten the Passover meal on Thursday night, see the exposition of 13:1 in chapter 6 of this volume), and could not risk a defilement that would bar them from that important meal. Most likely, the defilement they feared was contamination from a dead body, which would render them unclean for seven days (Num. 19:11, 14, 16). That concern stemmed from the common Jewish belief that Gentiles disposed of aborted or stillborn babies by throwing them down the drains (Leon Morris, *The Gospel According to John,* The New International Commentary on the New Testament [Grand Rapids: Eerdmans, 1979], 763, n. 59). Thus, the Mishnah declared all Gentile homes to be unclean (Morris, *John,* 763, n. 58). Entering the colonnade or courtyard outside Pilate's residence, however, would not defile them.

Illustrative of the twisted devotion of religious legalists, the Jewish leaders expected to please God through their legalism expressed in physical separation from a Gentile house, while at the same time illegally murdering God's Son. They fastidiously avoided any superficial ceremonial defilement, but cared nothing about the profound moral defilement they incurred from rejecting and condemning the Holy Son of God to death. "The Jews take elaborate precautions to avoid ritual contamination in order to eat the Passover, at the very same time they are busy manipulating the judicial system to secure the death of him who alone is the true Passover" (D. A. Carson, *The Gospel According to John,* The Pillar New Testament Commentary [Grand Rapids: Eerdmans, 1991], 589).

John's account of this phase of Jesus' trial unfolds in three acts: the accusation, the interrogation, and the adjudication.

THE ACCUSATION

Therefore Pilate went out to them and said, "What accusation do you bring against this Man?" They answered and said to him, "If this Man were not an evildoer, we would not have delivered Him to you." So Pilate said to them, "Take Him yourselves, and judge Him according to your law." The Jews said to him, "We are not permitted to put anyone to death," to fulfill the word of Jesus which He spoke, signifying by what kind of death He was about to die. (18:29–32)

In deference to their religious scruples, **Pilate went out to** meet the Jews outside his residence. Their refusal to enter the Praetorium forced him to shuttle back and forth from inside the building, where Jesus was, to outside, where His accusers stood.

Pontius **Pilate** had been appointed the fifth governor of Judea by Emperor Tiberius in A.D. 26 and held that position for about ten years. Both the Gospels and extrabiblical sources portray him as proud, arrogant, and cynical (cf. 18:38), but also as weak and vacillating. His tenure as governor was marked by insensitivity and brutality (cf. Luke 13:1). Reversing the policy of his predecessors, Pilate had sent troops into Jerusalem carrying standards bearing images that the Jews viewed as idolatrous. When many of them vehemently protested against what they saw as a sacrilege, Pilate ordered them to stop bothering him on pain of death. But they called his bluff, and dared him to carry out his threat. Unwilling to massacre so many people, Pilate gave in and removed the offending standards. The story highlights his poor judgment, stubborn arrogance, and vacillating weakness. Pilate further angered the Jews when he took money from the temple treasury to build an aqueduct to bring water to Jerusalem. His soldiers beat and slaughtered many Jews in the riots that followed.

But the incident that led to Pilate's downfall involved not the Jews, but their hated rivals the Samaritans. A group of them planned to climb Mt. Gerizim in search of golden objects allegedly hidden on its summit by Moses. Viewing the Samaritans as insurrectionists, Pilate ordered his troops to attack, and many of the pilgrims were killed. The Samaritans complained about Pilate's brutality to his immediate superior, the governor of Syria. He removed Pilate from office and ordered him to Rome to be judged by Emperor Tiberius. But Tiberius died while Pilate was en route to Rome. Nothing is known for certain about Pilate after he reached Rome. Some accounts claim he was banished; others that he was executed; still others that he committed suicide.

Pilate's question, **"What accusation do you bring against this Man?"** formally opened the legal proceedings. The Jewish leaders had undoubtedly already communicated with him about this case, since Roman troops took part in Jesus' arrest. They evidently expected him to rubber-stamp their judgment and sentence Jesus to death. Instead, exercising his prerogative as governor, he ordered a fresh hearing over which he would preside. But the last thing the Jewish leaders wanted was a trial. They wanted a death sentence; they wanted Pilate to be an executioner, not a judge. They knew that their charge against Jesus, that He was guilty of blasphemy because He claimed to be God incarnate, would not stand up in a Roman court.

The Jews' peremptory reply, **"If this Man were not an evildoer, we would not have delivered Him to you,"** was not only insulting, but also skirted the issue. Their false (cf. 8:46), blasphemous assertion that He was **an evildoer** was an assault on His character, but not an accusation of a specific legal violation. Quite unintentionally, their utter inability to bring one legitimate charge against Him affirmed Jesus' innocence. Still, they made it clear that they expected Pilate simply to confirm their decision and sentence Jesus to death.

Stung by their haughty, disrespectful, disdainful treatment of him, Pilate fired back a barb of his own. **"Take Him yourselves,"** he taunted them, **"and judge Him according to your law."** Pilate knew full well that they wanted him to execute Jesus. But as **the Jews** were forced to acknowledge **to him, "We are not permitted to put anyone to death."** Though he would soon cave in to their demands, Pilate initially stood his ground. "If [the Jews] expected a capital sentence to be handed down they were going to have to speak up and convince him, since, as they themselves conceded, they could not legally proceed without him" (Carson, *John,* 591).

But there was a deeper significance to the exchange between Pilate and the Jews. The wicked scheming of the Jewish leaders and the cowardly connivance of Pilate merely served **to fulfill the word of Jesus which He spoke, signifying by what kind of death He was about to die.** Jesus had predicted that Gentiles would be involved in His death. "Behold," He told the disciples,

> we are going up to Jerusalem, and the Son of Man will be delivered to the chief priests and the scribes; and they will condemn Him to death and will hand Him over to the Gentiles. They will mock Him and spit on Him, and scourge Him and kill Him, and three days later He will rise again. (Mark 10:33–34)

The Lord had also predicted the form His execution would take. In 3:14; 8:28; and 12:32 He spoke of being "lifted up," which He said "to indicate the kind of death by which He was to die" (12:33; cf. Ps. 22:6–18). Had the Jews executed Him, they would have thrown Him down and stoned Him (as they did Stephen; Acts 7:58–60). But the Lord's prediction was about to be fulfilled, as He was "lifted up" on the cross, a distinctively Roman kind of execution. God providentially controlled the events of Jesus' trial to ensure that His prophetic words would come to pass.

THE INTERROGATION

Therefore Pilate entered again into the Praetorium, and summoned Jesus and said to Him, "Are You the King of the Jews?" Jesus answered, "Are you saying this on your own initiative, or

did others tell you about Me?" Pilate answered, "I am not a Jew, am I? Your own nation and the chief priests delivered You to me; what have You done?" Jesus answered, "My kingdom is not of this world. If My kingdom were of this world, then My servants would be fighting so that I would not be handed over to the Jews; but as it is, My kingdom is not of this realm." Therefore Pilate said to Him, "So You are a king?" Jesus answered, "You say correctly that I am a king. For this I have been born, and for this I have come into the world, to testify to the truth. Everyone who is of the truth hears My voice." Pilate said to Him, "What is truth?" (18:33–38*a*)

Leaving the Jewish leaders standing outside, **Pilate entered again into the Praetorium, and summoned Jesus.** Luke 23:2 provides the background to his question, **"Are You the King of the Jews?"** Realizing that they had to come up with a charge that would impress a Roman judge, the Jewish leaders "began to accuse [Jesus], saying, 'We found this man misleading our nation and forbidding to pay taxes to Caesar, and saying that He Himself is Christ, a King.'" The charges, of course, were completely false; Jesus had actually said the opposite: "Render to Caesar the things that are Caesar's; and to God the things that are God's" (Matt. 22:21). Their goal was to portray Him as an insurrectionist, bent on overthrowing Roman rule and establishing His own.

Pilate could not overlook such a threat to Roman power. His question, **"Are You the King of the Jews?"** was in effect asking Jesus whether He was pleading guilty or not guilty to the charge of insurrection. "Pilate's question seeks to determine whether or not Jesus constituted a political threat to Roman imperial power" (Andreas J. Köstenberger, *John*, Baker Exegetical Commentary on the New Testament [Grand Rapids: Baker, 2004], 527). In all four gospel accounts this is the first question Pilate asks Jesus, and in all four the pronoun "You" is emphatic. The Greek text literally reads, "You, are You the King of the Jews?" Pilate was incredulous; from a human perspective, Jesus did not look like a king. And if He was a king, where were His followers and His army? And how was He a threat to Rome?

Jesus could not answer Pilate's question with an unqualified "Yes" or "No" without first defining exactly what His kingship entails. His counterquestion, **"Are you saying this on your own initiative, or did others tell you about Me?"** was intended to clarify the issue. If Pilate was **saying this on** his **own initiative,** he would be asking if Jesus was a king in the political sense (and hence a threat to Rome). Jesus' answer in that case would be no; He was not a king in the sense of a military or political leader. He had earlier rejected the crowd's attempt to make Him such a king (6:15). But neither could the Lord deny that as the Messiah He was Israel's true king.

Pilate's sharp retort, **"I am not a Jew, am I?"** reflects both his disdain for the Jewish people, and his growing exasperation with the frustrating, puzzling ethnic case set before him. His further elaboration, **Your own nation and the chief priests delivered You to me,** makes it clear that the governor was merely repeating the charge leveled against Jesus by the Jewish leaders; the accusation was theirs, not Rome's. Exactly why they had done so still eluded Pilate. He knew perfectly well that the Jews would not have handed over to him someone hostile to Rome unless they stood to gain from doing so.

Attempting once again to get to the bottom of things, Pilate asked the question that he should have asked at the outset: **what have You done?** Unlike Jewish practice (see the discussion of 18:19 in the previous chapter of this volume), Roman legal procedure allowed the accused to be questioned in detail (Köstenberger, *John*, 527). Pilate understood that the Jewish leaders had handed Jesus over to him because of envy (Matt. 27:18). What he still did not understand was what Jesus had done to provoke such vehement hostility from them and what, if any, crime He had committed.

Since it was now clear that Pilate was merely repeating the charge of the Jewish leaders, **Jesus answered** his question. He was a king, but not a political ruler intent on challenging Rome's rule. **"My kingdom is not of** (Greek *ek;* "out from the midst of") **this world,"** He declared. Its source was not the world system, nor did Jesus derive His authority from any human source. As noted earlier, He had rejected the crowd's attempt to crown Him king. He also passed up an opportunity to proclaim Himself king at the triumphal entry, when He rode into Jerusalem at the head of tens of thousands of frenzied hopefuls.

To reinforce His point, Jesus noted that **if His kingdom were of this world, then** His **servants would be fighting so that** He **would not be handed over to the Jews.** No earthly king would have allowed himself to have been captured so easily. But when one of His followers (Peter) attempted to defend Him, Jesus rebuked him. The messianic kingdom does not originate from human effort, but through the Son of Man's conquering of sin in the lives of those who belong to His spiritual kingdom.

Christ's kingdom is spiritually active in the world today, and one day He will return to physically reign on the earth in millennial glory (Rev. 11:15; 20:6). But until then His Kingdom exists in the hearts of believers, where He is undisputed King and sovereign Lord. He was absolutely no threat either to the national identity of Israel, or to the political and military identity of Rome.

That the Lord spoke of being handed over to the **Jews** is significant. Far from leading them in a revolt against Rome, Jesus spoke of the Jews (especially the leaders) as His enemies. He was a king, but since He disavowed the use of force and fighting, He was clearly no threat to Rome's interests. The Lord's statement rendered the Jews' charge that He was a revolutionary bent on overthrowing Rome absurd.

Jesus' description of His kingdom had left Pilate somewhat confused. If His kingdom was not an earthly one, then was Jesus really a king at all? Seeking to clarify the issue, **Pilate said to Him, "So You are a king?"** Jesus' answer was clear and unambiguous: **"You say correctly that I am a king."** The Lord boldly "testified the good confession before Pontius Pilate" (1 Tim. 6:13). Unlike earthly kings, however, Jesus was not crowned a king by any human agency. **For this I have been born,** He declared, **and for this I have come into the world.** Jesus had not only **been born** like all other human beings, but also had **come into the world** from another realm—heaven (cf. 3:13, 31; 6:33; 8:23; 17:5). Taken together, the two phrases are an unmistakable reference to the preexistence and incarnation of the Son of God.

Jesus' mission was not political but spiritual. It was **to testify to the truth** by "proclaiming the gospel of the kingdom" (Matt. 4:23). Christ proclaimed the truth about God, men, sin, judgment, holiness, love, eternal life, in short, "everything pertaining to life and godliness" (2 Peter 1:3). What people do with the message of truth Jesus proclaimed determines their eternal destiny; as He went on to declare, **"Everyone who is of the truth hears** (the Greek word includes the concept of obedience; cf. Luke 9:35) **My voice."** Jesus is "the way, and the truth, and the life; no one comes to the Father but through [Him]" (14:6). In 10:27 He added, "My sheep hear My voice and I know them, and they follow Me." Only those who continue in His Word are truly His disciples; only those who are truly His disciples will know and be set free by the truth (8:31–32).

Jesus' words were an implied invitation to Pilate to hear and obey the truth about Him. But they were lost on the governor, who abruptly ended his interrogation of Christ with the cynical, pessimistic remark, **"What is truth?"** Like skeptics of all ages, including contemporary postmodernists, Pilate despaired of finding universal truth. This is the tragedy of fallen man's rejection of God. Without God, there cannot be any absolutes; without absolutes, there can be no objective, universal, normative truths. Truth becomes subjective, relative, pragmatic; objectivity gives way to subjectivity; timeless universal principles become mere personal or cultural preferences. All fallen mankind has accomplished by forsaking God, "the fountain of living waters," is "to hew for themselves cisterns, broken cisterns that can hold no water" (Jer. 2:13). Pilate's flippant retort proved that he was not one of those given by the Father to the Son, who hear and obey Christ's voice.

The Adjudication

And when he had said this, he went out again to the Jews and said to them, "I find no guilt in Him." (18:38*b*)

Having finished interrogating Jesus, Pilate pronounced his verdict. **He went out again to the Jews and said to them, "I find no guilt in Him."** He understood enough to realize that Jesus posed no threat to Roman rule. He made it clear that Jesus was innocent of the charges of sedition and insurrection leveled against Him by the Jewish leaders (Luke 23:2).

No valid indictment of Him at the beginning; no conviction of Him at the end. The Lord of glory was maligned, hated, and falsely accused, but nevertheless found to be perfect, faultless, and innocent.

Jesus Before Pilate—Part 2: Phase Three of the Civil Trial (John 18:39–19:16)

30

"But you have a custom that I release someone for you at the Passover; do you wish then that I release for you the King of the Jews?" So they cried out again, saying, "Not this Man, but Barabbas." Now Barabbas was a robber. Pilate then took Jesus and scourged Him. And the soldiers twisted together a crown of thorns and put it on His head, and put a purple robe on Him; and they began to come up to Him and say, "Hail, King of the Jews!" and to give Him slaps in the face. Pilate came out again and said to them, "Behold, I am bringing Him out to you so that you may know that I find no guilt in Him." Jesus then came out, wearing the crown of thorns and the purple robe. Pilate said to them, "Behold, the Man!" So when the chief priests and the officers saw Him, they cried out saying, "Crucify, crucify!" Pilate said to them, "Take Him yourselves and crucify Him, for I find no guilt in Him." The Jews answered him, "We have a law, and by that law He ought to die because He made Himself out to be the Son of God." Therefore when Pilate heard this statement, he was even more afraid; and he entered into the Praetorium again and said to Jesus, "Where are You from?" But Jesus gave him no answer. So Pilate said to Him, "You do not speak to me? Do You not know

**that I have authority to release You, and I have authority to cruci-
fy You?" Jesus answered, "You would have no authority over Me,
unless it had been given you from above; for this reason he who
delivered Me to you has the greater sin." As a result of this Pilate
made efforts to release Him, but the Jews cried out saying, "If
you release this Man, you are no friend of Caesar; everyone who
makes himself out to be a king opposes Caesar." Therefore when
Pilate heard these words, he brought Jesus out, and sat down on
the judgment seat at a place called The Pavement, but in Hebrew,
Gabbatha. Now it was the day of preparation for the Passover; it
was about the sixth hour. And he said to the Jews, "Behold, your
King!" So they cried out, "Away with Him, away with Him, crucify
Him!" Pilate said to them, "Shall I crucify your King?" The chief
priests answered, "We have no king but Caesar." So he then
handed Him over to them to be crucified.** (18:39–19:16)

Through the centuries the debate has raged over who was
responsible for the death of Jesus Christ. Some blame the Romans, since
they are the ones who sentenced and executed Him (Matt. 20:19; John
19:10, 16, 18). Others argue that the Jews (particularly their leaders) were
responsible, since "they asked Pilate that He be executed" (Acts 13:28).
One of the disciples on the road to Emmaus lamented that "the chief
priests and our rulers delivered [Christ] to the sentence of death, and
crucified Him" (Luke 24:20). "This Man," Peter told the crowds in
Jerusalem on the day of Pentecost, "you nailed to a cross by the hands of
godless men and put Him to death" (Acts 2:23). Shortly afterward Peter
again laid the blame for Christ's death at the feet of his countrymen:

> The God of Abraham, Isaac and Jacob, the God of our fathers, has glo-
> rified His servant Jesus, the one whom you delivered and disowned in
> the presence of Pilate, when he had decided to release Him. But you
> disowned the Holy and Righteous One and asked for a murderer to be
> granted to you, but put to death the Prince of life, the one whom God
> raised from the dead, a fact to which we are witnesses. (Acts 3:13–15)

Peter and John boldly declared to the Sanhedrin that Jesus was the one
"whom you crucified" (Acts 4:10) and, "The God of our fathers raised up
Jesus, whom you had put to death by hanging Him on a cross" (5:30; cf.
10:39). Stephen accused the same Sanhedrin of being Christ's "betrayers
and murderers" (Acts 7:52). The Jewish people themselves accepted
responsibility for Christ's death when they cried out, "His blood shall be
on us and on our children!" (Matt. 27:25).

The truth is that humanly speaking the Romans played a part
while the Jews were the instigators who bear the greatest blame for

Christ's death. But the real responsibility does not rest solely with either of them; What put Him on the cross was God's own determination to punish His Son for all the sins of all who would ever be saved. John the Baptist hailed Him as the "Lamb of God who takes away the sin of the world!" (John 1:29). The writer of Hebrews said that He "has been manifested to put away sin by the sacrifice of Himself" (Heb. 9:26). In his first epistle John wrote that "He Himself is the propitiation for our sins; and not for ours only, but also for those of the whole world" (1 John 2:2) and "He appeared in order to take away sins" (3:5). Our sins put Him on the cross.

Jesus Christ was no victim. Neither the Romans nor the Jews had the power to take His life. For that matter, neither did all the sinners for whom He died. "No one has taken [My life] away from Me," He said, "but I lay it down on My own initiative. I have authority to lay it down, and I have authority to take it up again. This commandment I received from My Father" (John 10:18). He told Pilate, "You would have no authority over Me, unless it had been given you from above" (see the discussion of v. 11 below). His Jewish adversaries sought to kill Him, but were unsuccessful "because His hour had not yet come" (7:30; 8:20).

Ultimately, Christ died not because of any human intentions, schemes, or actions, but because of the will of His Father. In the same sermon in which he indicted Israel for killing Jesus, Peter nonetheless affirmed that He had been "delivered over by the predetermined plan and foreknowledge of God" (Acts 2:23). In another sermon Peter reminded the people that "the things which God announced beforehand by the mouth of all the prophets, that His Christ would suffer, He has thus fulfilled" (Acts 3:18). The early church prayed, "For truly in this city there were gathered together against Your holy servant Jesus, whom You anointed, both Herod and Pontius Pilate, along with the Gentiles and the peoples of Israel, to do whatever Your hand and Your purpose predestined to occur" (Acts 4:27–28). In an example of God's using the wrath of sinful men to praise Him (Ps. 76:10), Paul declared, "Those who live in Jerusalem, and their rulers, recognizing neither Him nor the utterances of the prophets which are read every Sabbath, fulfilled these by condemning Him" (Acts 13:27). In his magnificent prophecy of Christ's death, Isaiah said, "It was the will of the Lord to crush him; he has put him to grief" (Isa. 53:10 ESV). Speaking of His death, Jesus said, "The Son of Man is going as it has been determined" (Luke 22:22; cf. Matt. 26:24). "He [God] made Him who knew no sin to be sin on our behalf," said Paul in 2 Corinthians 5:21.

But God's sovereign control of events does not relieve individuals of responsibility for their actions. This passage gives the account of the last phase of Christ's civil trial (John omits the Lord's hearing before Herod Antipas [Luke 23:7–12]). As was the case with the first phase of that trial (18:28–38), it was presided over by Pontius Pilate, the Roman governor of Judea.

As he did throughout his gospel, John presented the majesty and dignity of the Lord Jesus Christ—even as He was beaten, unjustly sentenced to death, and led away to be crucified. The apostle did so by contrasting Him with the weak and vacillating Pilate, who lost his composure, his control over events, and was pressured into sentencing an innocent man to die. The story of Pilate's downfall reveals his failed proposals to dispose of the case, his fatal panic as events spiraled out of control, and produced his final pronouncement of the death sentence on the Lord Jesus Christ.

PILATE'S FAILED PROPOSALS

"But you have a custom that I release someone for you at the Passover; do you wish then that I release for you the King of the Jews?" So they cried out again, saying, "Not this Man, but Barabbas." Now Barabbas was a robber. Pilate then took Jesus and scourged Him. And the soldiers twisted together a crown of thorns and put it on His head, and put a purple robe on Him; and they began to come up to Him and say, "Hail, King of the Jews!" and to give Him slaps in the face. Pilate came out again and said to them, "Behold, I am bringing Him out to you so that you may know that I find no guilt in Him." Jesus then came out, wearing the crown of thorns and the purple robe. Pilate said to them, "Behold, the Man!" So when the chief priests and the officers saw Him, they cried out saying, "Crucify, crucify!" Pilate said to them, "Take Him yourselves and crucify Him, for I find no guilt in Him." The Jews answered him, "We have a law, and by that law He ought to die because He made Himself out to be the Son of God." (18:39–19:7)

Pilate had already tried unsuccessfully to rid himself of this explosive case. In 18:31 he had half mockingly said to the Jewish leaders, "Take Him yourselves, and judge Him according to your law." The Jews refused since, as they were forced to admit, "We are not permitted to put anyone to death." Pilate then tried to transfer the case to Herod Antipas, who ruled Jesus' home region of Galilee (Luke 23:7). But Herod merely mocked Jesus and then sent Him back to Pilate, leaving the latter still caught on the horns of a dilemma. On the one hand, he had formally pronounced Jesus to be innocent (18:38; cf. 19:4, 6). According to the proud tradition of Roman justice, Pilate should have released Him. But to do so would have infuriated the Jewish leaders, and possibly touched off a riot that could have cost him his position as governor (see the discussion of v. 12 below).

Desperate to extricate himself from the tense, dangerous situation, Pilate came up with another plan. There was **a custom that** the governor **release someone** (i.e., a prisoner held by the Romans) as a goodwill gesture **at the Passover.** There is no clear reference to this practice outside of Scripture (some scholars see an allusion to it in the Talmud), but "the testimony of the Evangelists [gospel writers] is evidence enough for the historicity of the practice" (F. F. Bruce, *The Gospel of John* [Grand Rapids: Eerdmans, 1983], 355).

Pilate accordingly said to the crowd, **"Do you wish then that I release for you the King of the Jews?"** By referring to Jesus by that title, Pilate again mocked the Jewish leaders, who vehemently rejected Jesus as their king. The governor's offer appeared to be a logical solution to his problem. By now people had gotten wind of what was happening and a large crowd had assembled outside the Praetorium (Matt. 27:17). Pilate knew that many in that crowd had hailed Jesus as their messianic King earlier in the week. He hoped to play them off against their leaders and force the latter to agree to Jesus' release.

Unfortunately, Pilate underestimated both the chief priests' resolve and the crowd's fickleness. The sight of Jesus, a bound, helpless prisoner of the Romans, made it clear that He was not going to meet their messianic expectations and drive out their oppressors. That allowed the persistent chief priests to manipulate the crowd (while Pilate was temporarily preoccupied with a message from his wife; Matt. 27:19) into crying out, **"Not this Man, but Barabbas"** (Matt. 27:20; Mark 15:11). **Barabbas,** as John's footnote indicates, **was a robber.** He was no common, petty thief, however. Matthew calls him a "notorious prisoner" (Matt. 27:16), while Mark (15:7) and Luke (23:19) note that he was a murderer (cf. Acts 3:14) and an insurrectionist. The specific insurrection he was involved in is unknown, but such uprisings, precursors of the wholesale revolt of A.D. 66–70, were common at that time. Ironically, the same Jewish leaders who had demanded that Pilate condemn Jesus as an insurrectionist now demanded the release of the notorious insurrectionist Barabbas.

Pilate was rapidly running out of options. Almost plaintively, he asked the crowd, "Then what shall I do with Jesus who is called Christ?" With one voice "they all said, 'Crucify Him!'" (Matt. 27:22). In a last desperate attempt to appease them (Luke 23:16, 22), he **then took Jesus and scourged Him.** By brutally punishing a man whom he had already declared innocent, Pilate plunged further down into the abyss of injustice.

Scourging was a hideously cruel form of punishment. The victim was stripped, bound to a post, and beaten by several torturers in turn.

Jewish law set the maximum number of blows at forty (Deut. 25:3), and in practice the Jews gave a maximum of thirty-nine (to avoid accidently exceeding forty blows; cf. 2 Cor. 11:24). The Romans, however, were not bound by any such restrictions. The punishment would continue until the torturers were exhausted, the commanding officer decided to stop it, or, as was often the case, the victim died. The whip consisted of a short wooden handle to which several leather thongs, each with jagged pieces of bone or metal attached to the end, were fastened. As a result, the body could be so torn and lacerated that the muscles, bones, veins, or even internal organs were exposed. So horrible was this punishment that Roman citizens were exempt from it (cf. Acts 22:25). The scourging He endured left Jesus too weak to carry the crosspiece of His cross all the way to the execution site (Matt. 27:32). Pilate hoped that this brutalizing of Jesus short of death would satisfy the bloodthirsty mob.

Not content with savagely beating Jesus, Pilate's **soldiers twisted together a crown of thorns and put it on His head.** This further indignity, a mock crown in imitation of the wreaths worn on occasion by Caesar, added to the Lord's suffering. The sharp spikes would have cut deeply into His head, increasing His pain and bleeding. They also **put a purple robe on Him** (probably one of the soldiers' cloaks), in mocking imitation of the royal robes worn by kings. Matthew records that the soldiers also put a reed in His right hand, mimicking the scepter carried by sovereigns. Having thus outfitted Jesus in the caricature of a king, they continued their sadistic game by "[kneeling] down before Him and [mocking] Him, saying, 'Hail, King of the Jews!'" (Matt. 27:29). In an ugly mockery of and disdain for Him, **they** also **began to come up to Him . . . and to give Him slaps in the face.** Matthew records that they also spat on Him, seized the reed from His hand, and beat Him over the head with it (Matt. 27:30).

Meanwhile, **Pilate came out** of the Praetorium **again,** implying that he had looked on approvingly as his soldiers abused Jesus, **and said to** the crowd, **"Behold, I am bringing Him out to you so that you may know that I find no guilt in Him."** Once again, Pilate affirmed Jesus' innocence (cf. 18:38), the pronouncement of which heightens the injustice that he had just allowed to be inflicted on the Lord. At that point **Jesus . . . came out,** still **wearing the crown of thorns and the purple robe** the soldiers had dressed Him in.

Theatrically, sarcastically, **Pilate said to them, "Behold, the Man!"** Jesus, bleeding from His scourging and the crown of thorns, His face bruised and swollen from being beaten by Pilate's soldiers, looked like anything but a king. Pilate hoped this beaten and pathetic figure would satiate their bloodlust and elicit sympathy from the multitude. His designation of Jesus as **the Man** instead of "your King" as in verse 14 (cf.

v. 15; 18:39) stressed to the Jews his view that Jesus posed no danger either to them or to Rome.

Once again, Pilate misjudged the depth of the Jewish leaders' contempt for Jesus. The sight of the Lord's bruised and bleeding body merely whetted their appetite. Like sharks sensing blood in the water, **when the chief priests and the officers saw Him, they cried out saying, "Crucify, crucify!"**

That was enough for Pilate. Disgusted with the Jews' callous attitude and wanting simply to be rid of Jesus, **Pilate said to them, "Take Him yourselves and crucify Him, for I find no guilt in Him."** The emphatic pronouns **Him** and **yourselves** underscore Pilate's exasperation. He in effect said to them, "*You* take *Him* and crucify Him; I want nothing more to do with Him." The statement is a non sequitur; the governor is in reality saying, "Take this man and crucify Him, because I find Him not guilty." Whether Pilate was officially granting them the right to execute Jesus or merely mocking them again is not clear; perhaps he knew the Jews did not crucify people. But that Pilate would even mention granting them the right of capital punishment—one of the most jealously guarded prerogatives of Roman rule—is yet another sign that he was losing control.

Pilate may have been through with the Jews, but they were not through with him. Realizing that they now had the upper hand, **the Jews answered him, "We have a law, and by that law He ought to die."** They knew that Pilate was still trying to evade the issue and pass the buck back to them, and they would have none of it. They reminded Pilate that they had already judged Jesus according to Jewish law and found Him guilty and deserving of death. Part of the genius of the Roman form of occupation throughout the empire was to grant autonomy in civil matters to the conquered nations. Roman provincial governors were expected to maintain control while upholding local laws insofar as they did not conflict with Rome's priorities. The Jews demanded again that Pilate acknowledge their legal rights and order Jesus to be executed.

The specific charge that the Jews brought against Jesus, that **He made Himself out to be the Son of God,** at last revealed their true motives. Having tried unsuccessfully to get Jesus condemned on political grounds as an insurrectionist, they now wanted Pilate to sentence Him based on Jewish religious law. Evidently they had in mind Leviticus 24:16: "Moreover, the one who blasphemes the name of the Lord shall surely be put to death; all the congregation shall certainly stone him. The alien as well as the native, when he blasphemes the Name, shall be put to death." Because they rejected Jesus' claim to be God incarnate, the chief priests held Him guilty of blasphemy for making it (cf. Matt. 26:63–65). This was an especially sensitive issue for Pilate, who had himself offended

Jewish sensibilities regarding idolatry (see the discussion of 18:29–32 in the previous chapter of this volume). To do so again might provoke the Jews to riot, or to complain to his superiors. Either would be fatal to his future as governor.

PILATE'S FATAL PANIC

Therefore when Pilate heard this statement, he was even more afraid; and he entered into the Praetorium again and said to Jesus, "Where are You from?" But Jesus gave him no answer. So Pilate said to Him, "You do not speak to me? Do You not know that I have authority to release You, and I have authority to crucify You?" Jesus answered, "You would have no authority over Me, unless it had been given you from above; for this reason he who delivered Me to you has the greater sin." As a result of this Pilate made efforts to release Him, but the Jews cried out saying, "If you release this Man, you are no friend of Caesar; everyone who makes himself out to be a king opposes Caesar." (19:8–12)

As the situation deteriorated, Pilate's fear increased. But **when** he **heard** the Jewish leaders' **statement** that Jesus claimed to be the Son of God, **he was even more afraid.** Pilate may have been cynical (cf. 18:38), but he was also, like many Romans, superstitious. The thought that Jesus might be a man with divine powers, or perhaps a god or son of a god in human form (cf. Acts 14:11) filled him with fear. If that were the case, he had just scourged and beaten someone who might use his supernatural powers to take vengeance on him. Fueling Pilate's superstitious fear that he might have incurred the wrath of the gods was his wife's dream about Jesus and subsequent warning to him (Matt. 27:19).

Taking Him with him, Pilate **entered into the Praetorium again and said to Jesus, "Where are You from?"** His question had nothing to do with Jesus' earthly residence; Pilate already knew that He was a Galilean (Luke 23:6–7). The governor's question concerned Jesus' nature: was He from earth, or the realm of the gods? **But Jesus gave him no answer.** There are several possible reasons for the Lord's silence. It fulfilled Isaiah's prophecy concerning Him: "He was oppressed and He was afflicted, yet He did not open His mouth; like a lamb that is led to slaughter, and like a sheep that is silent before its shearers, so He did not open His mouth" (Isa. 53:7). Further, Jesus had already told Pilate that He was a king from another realm (18:36–37). Certainly Jesus' silence was judgmental, in the sense that Pilate had heard the truth and rejected it, and now would receive no further answer from Him. The Bible teaches that when men persist in rejecting God, He will reject them (cf. Judg. 10:13; 2 Chron. 15:2; 24:20; Ps. 81:11–12; Hos. 4:17; Matt. 15:14).

Irritated by Jesus' silence **Pilate said to Him, "You do not speak to me?"** He was insulted at the Lord's apparent lack of respect for his dignity and power. **"Do You not know,"** he boasted, **"that I have authority to release You, and I have authority to crucify You?"** He may have had the right, but he did not have the courage to do either one. But as Leon Morris notes,

> The question is illuminating. In the last resort it was Pilate alone who could say "Crucify" or "Release," and this frank recognition of it makes nonsense of all the shifts to which he resorted in the attempt to avoid making a decision. Ultimately he could not avoid responsibility and these words show that deep down he must have realized this. (*The Gospel According to John*, The New International Commentary on the New Testament [Grand Rapids: Eerdmans, 1979], 796–97)

Pilate's arrogant boast was not true. Breaking His silence, **Jesus answered, "You would have no authority over Me, unless it had been given you from above"** (i.e., from God). Although he was a responsible moral agent and accountable for his actions, Pilate did not have ultimate control over events related to the Son of God. Nothing that happens—even the death of Jesus Christ—is outside of the sovereignty of God. Faced with opposition and evil, Jesus took comfort in the Father's sovereign control of events (cf. 6:43–44, 65).

Although Pilate was culpable for his actions, there was one who bore even greater guilt—the one **who delivered** Him **to** Pilate, Jesus declared, **has the greater sin.** The Lord was not referring to Judas, who did not deliver Him to Pilate, but to the Jews, who did. The reference is particularly to Caiaphas, who more than anyone else was responsible for handing Jesus over to the Roman governor. He was more guilty than Pilate for at least two reasons. First, he had seen the overwhelming evidence that Jesus was the Messiah and Son of God; Pilate had not. Further, it was Caiaphas who, humanly speaking, had put Pilate in the position he was in. As D. A. Carson notes, "Pilate remains responsible for his spineless, politically–motivated judicial decision; but he did not initiate the trial or engineer the betrayal that brought Jesus into court" (*The Gospel According to John*, The Pillar New Testament Commentary [Grand Rapids: Eerdmans, 1991], 602).

Despite the additional charge of blasphemy, the governor remained unconvinced that Jesus was guilty of anything worthy of death. Therefore **Pilate made efforts to release Him,** either by further attempts at reasoning with the crowd, or by preparing to pronounce Him innocent. But his attempts were brought to an abrupt halt. Realizing that they had failed to convince Pilate of Jesus' guilt and afraid that the governor was going to set Him free, **the Jews cried out saying, "If you release this Man, you are no friend of Caesar; everyone who makes himself out to be a king opposes Caesar."** Here is yet another corrupt, hypocritical irony, since the Jews' hatred of all Roman rule certainly indicated that they themselves were anything but friends of Caesar.

This was the last straw for Pilate; the Jews' implied threat finally overwhelmed him. He could not risk having them report to the emperor that he had released a revolutionary, especially one who made **himself out to be a king** in opposition to **Caesar.** Several of Pilate's foolish acts had already infuriated the Jews and caused turmoil in Palestine. Rome's eye was on him, and he dared not risk another upheaval. The emperor at that time, Tiberius, was noted for his suspicious nature and willingness to exact ruthless punishment on his subordinates. Pilate feared for his position, his possessions, even for his life. He felt that he had no choice now but to give in to the Jews' wishes and pronounce the sentence they demanded.

PILATE'S FINAL PRONOUNCEMENT

Therefore when Pilate heard these words, he brought Jesus out, and sat down on the judgment seat at a place called The Pavement, but in Hebrew, Gabbatha. Now it was the day of preparation for the Passover; it was about the sixth hour. And he said to the Jews, "Behold, your King!" So they cried out, "Away with Him, away with Him, crucify Him!" Pilate said to them, "Shall I crucify your King?" The chief priests answered, "We have no king but Caesar." So he then handed Him over to them to be crucified. (19:13–16)

After hearing the **words** that the Jews had shouted at him, Pilate **brought Jesus out** from inside the Praetorium. In preparation for formally passing sentence on Him, he **sat down on the judgment seat at a place called The Pavement, but in Hebrew, Gabbatha.** Ironically, Pilate rendered judgment on the One to whom the Father had granted all judgment (John 5:22), and who will one day pass eternal sentence on him.

The supreme moment to which all of redemptive history pointed had arrived, so John carefully, dramatically set the scene. It was **the day of preparation for the Passover.** The time **was about the sixth hour;** or late morning, approaching noon. This statement presents an apparent difficulty, because according to Mark's account, Jesus was crucified at the third hour (9:00 A.M.). But as Andreas Köstenberger writes,

"Since people related the estimated time to the closest three-hour mark, any time between 9:00 A.M. and noon may have led one person to say an event occurred at the third (9:00 A.M.) or the sixth hour (12:00 noon)" (*John*, Baker Exegetical Commentary on the New Testament [Grand Rapids: Baker, 2004], 538). D. A. Carson cautions against "insisting on a degree of precision in both Mark and John which, in days before watches, could not have been achieved" (*John*, 605).

In one final sarcastic statement, Pilate taunted the Jews again, saying to them, **"Behold, your King!"** This was his way of mocking them, suggesting that this beaten, bloody, helpless man was all the king they deserved. Enraged, they **cried out, "Away with Him, away with Him, crucify Him!"** Either in continued mockery, or perhaps seeking one final time to escape his dilemma, **Pilate said to them, "Shall I crucify your King?"** In a chilling act of appalling hypocrisy, **the chief priests answered, "We have no king but Caesar."** Though said with blatant duplicity, the irony was that there was truth in their statement; having rejected their messianic King, they were left with only Caesar as their king. In yet one more bitter irony, those who had falsely accused Jesus of blasphemy committed an act of blasphemy of their own, since God alone was Israel's true King (cf. Judg. 8:23; 1 Sam. 8:7; Ps. 149:2; Isa. 33:22).

All options exhausted, Pilate acknowledged defeat and **handed** Jesus **over to them to be crucified.** John is not saying that the Jews took physical custody of Jesus; Roman soldiers would perform the actual crucifixion. Rather, the sense is that Pilate "delivered Jesus to their [the Jews'] will" (Luke 23:25).

Pilate's dilemma, expressed in his question, "Then what shall I do with Jesus who is called Christ?" (Matt. 27:22) is the same one facing every person. There are only two alternatives: to stand with His rejecters and crucifiers and face eternal damnation (Heb. 6:6), or to acknowledge Him as Lord and Savior (Rom. 10:9) and be saved. Pilate's futile attempts to evade the issue reveal clearly that there is no middle ground for, as Jesus declared, "He who is not with Me is against Me; and he who does not gather with Me scatters" (Matt. 12:30). In the end, pride and fear of man led to Pilate's downfall, and he sided with the crucifiers of Christ to the damnation of his soul. He stands in history as a monumentally tragic figure. Privileged to converse privately with the Savior, he found no value in the opportunity. It was likely the worst experience of his life. He belongs in Judas's category.

The Crucifixion of Jesus Christ
(John 19:17–30)

31

They took Jesus, therefore, and He went out, bearing His own cross, to the place called the Place of a Skull, which is called in Hebrew, Golgotha. There they crucified Him, and with Him two other men, one on either side, and Jesus in between. Pilate also wrote an inscription and put it on the cross. It was written, "JESUS THE NAZARENE, THE KING OF THE JEWS." Therefore many of the Jews read this inscription, for the place where Jesus was crucified was near the city; and it was written in Hebrew, Latin and in Greek. So the chief priests of the Jews were saying to Pilate, "Do not write, 'The King of the Jews'; but that He said, 'I am King of the Jews.'" Pilate answered, "What I have written I have written." Then the soldiers, when they had crucified Jesus, took His outer garments and made four parts, a part to every soldier and also the tunic; now the tunic was seamless, woven in one piece. So they said to one another, "Let us not tear it, but cast lots for it, to decide whose it shall be"; this was to fulfill the Scripture: "They divided My outer garments among them, and for My clothing they cast lots." Therefore the soldiers did these things. But standing by the cross of Jesus were His mother, and His mother's sister, Mary the wife of Clopas, and Mary Magdalene. When Jesus

then saw His mother, and the disciple whom He loved standing nearby, He said to His mother, "Woman, behold, your son!" Then He said to the disciple, "Behold, your mother!" From that hour the disciple took her into his own household. After this, Jesus, knowing that all things had already been accomplished, to fulfill the Scripture, said, "I am thirsty." A jar full of sour wine was standing there; so they put a sponge full of the sour wine upon a branch of hyssop and brought it up to His mouth. Therefore when Jesus had received the sour wine, He said, "It is finished!" And He bowed His head and gave up His spirit. (19:17–30)

The crucifixion of the Lord Jesus Christ is the climax of redemptive history, the focal point of the plan of salvation. It was because God "loved us and sent His Son to be the propitiation for our sins" (1 John 4:10; cf. John 15:13) that Jesus Christ went to the cross (John 12:27). It was there as the Lamb of God (John 1:29; cf. Rev. 5:12; 13:8) that He poured out His life as a sacrifice for sin (Rom. 3:25–26; Heb. 1:3; 9:12, 26; 10:12; 1 Peter 2:24; 3:18; 1 John 2:2; 3:5).

But while the cross was the supreme expression of God's redeeming love, it was also the ultimate manifestation of man's depravity; the most egregious sin against divine light, love, and grace. Jesus "endured such hostility by sinners against Himself" (Heb. 12:3) for several reasons. First, He was God incarnate, and "the mind set on the flesh is hostile toward God" (Rom. 8:7). This was also hell's hour (Luke 22:53), the time when the serpent would bruise His heel (Gen. 3:15). Still ultimately, Jesus suffered according to God's sovereign plan; "it was the will of the Lord to crush him; he has put him to grief" (Isa. 53:10 ESV; cf. Rom. 8:32). At the cross the sovereign God used the evil schemes of wicked men (cf. Gen. 50:20; Ps. 76:10) to bring about His purpose: the redemption of lost sinners. Because God is "rich in mercy, because of His great love with which He loved us" (Eph. 2:4) He "did not spare His own Son, but delivered Him over for us all" (Rom. 8:32).

The theme of the cross runs throughout John's gospel. Sin dooms mankind to spiritual death, which results in eternal separation from God in the never-ending punishment of hell. In 8:24 Jesus solemnly warned, "Unless you believe that I am He, you will die in your sins." In 3:36 John the Baptist added, "He who believes in the Son has eternal life; but he who does not obey the Son will not see life, but the wrath of God abides on him" (cf. Rom. 1:18; 5:9; 1 Thess. 1:10). The only remedy for sin and its eternal consequences is the atoning sacrifice of Jesus Christ at the cross. Because "without shedding of blood there is no forgiveness" (Heb. 9:22), Christ "has been manifested to put away sin by the sacrifice of Himself" (v. 26). Thus Jesus said, "I, if I am lifted up from the earth, will draw all men to Myself" (12:32). Those who look to Him in saving faith will be redeemed from slavery to sin, forgiven, and granted eternal life (1:12; 3:15–18; 5:24; 6:35, 40, 47; 11:25–26; 12:46). It was to persuade sinners of the truth that salvation comes only through believing in the person and work of Christ that John wrote his gospel (20:31).

The unjust, unfair, sham trials of the Lord Jesus Christ were over. Although he declared repeatedly that Jesus was innocent of any crime, Pilate, cowed by the Jewish leaders' threat to report him to Rome (19:12), caved in to their demands and "handed Him over to them to be crucified" (19:16).

As he related the story of the crucifixion, John, as was the case throughout his gospel, was concerned to present Jesus Christ in all His majesty and glory. In keeping with that theme, John does not focus on features of Christ's physical suffering (as none of the Gospels do), or the wickedness of the crucifixion (as for instance Matthew does). Instead, John zeroes in on four aspects of the cross that emphasize the magnificence of Christ's person: the specific fulfillments of prophecy, the superscription written by Pilate, the selfless love of Jesus, and His supernatural knowledge and sovereign control of events.

The Specific Fulfillments

They took Jesus, therefore, and He went out, bearing His own cross, to the place called the Place of a Skull, which is called in Hebrew, Golgotha. There they crucified Him, and with Him two other men, one on either side, and Jesus in between. . . . Then the soldiers, when they had crucified Jesus, took His outer garments and made four parts, a part to every soldier and also the tunic; now the tunic was seamless, woven in one piece. So they said to one another, "Let us not tear it, but cast lots for it, to decide whose it shall be"; this was to fulfill the Scripture: "They divided My outer garments among them, and for My clothing they cast lots." Therefore the soldiers did these things. (19:17–18, 23–25a)

These verses seem at first glance to be mere historical narrative, a straightforward description of Jesus' crucifixion. But the factual details are actually rich in fulfillment of Old Testament prophecies, both verbal and typological. Jesus Christ fulfilled all the redemptive promises contained in the Old Testament. "For as many as are the promises of God," Paul wrote, "in Him they are yes" (2 Cor. 1:20). Some of those promises are stunningly and specifically fulfilled in the narrative here. These prove the divine authorship of Old Testament Scripture and the New Testament claims for Christ.

After Pilate pronounced sentence on Him (19:16; cf. Luke 23:24), his soldiers **took Jesus, therefore, and He went out.** The Synoptic Gospels say that Jesus was led away by the soldiers (Matt. 27:31; Mark 15:20; Luke 23:26), suggesting that the Lord went willingly, without resistance. By so doing He fulfilled Isaiah's prophecy that Messiah would go to His death "like a lamb that is led to slaughter" (Isa. 53:7), and not be forcibly driven like most prisoners. F.F. Bruce comments,

> In stating that Jesus "went out, carrying His cross" ... [John] is ... emphasizing that, as at His arrest in the garden, Jesus is still in command of the situation. He is "taken" to the place of execution, it is true, but he is no reluctant victim, compelled to go whither he would not: he goes with his executioners of his own volition and carries the cross for himself. (*The Gospel of John* [Grand Rapids: Eerdmans, 1983], 366)

Thus, Jesus was "not a helpless victim but the Shepherd-King laying down his life for his sheep (10:11, 15, 17; 15:13)" (Gerald L. Borchert, *John 12–21*, The New American Commentary [Nashville: Broadman & Holman, 2002], 261).

As the soldiers led Him away, Jesus was **bearing His own cross,** which was standard Roman procedure. The condemned prisoner was forced to carry the crosspiece on his shoulders as he was led through the streets to the execution site. The sight of a beaten, bloodied, terrified prisoner carrying part of the instrument of his own execution illustrated that crime does not pay. Since the time of the church fathers, interpreters have seen in Christ's bearing His cross an allusion to Isaac who, like Jesus, carried on his back the wood that would have been used in his sacrifice (Gen. 22:6).

In keeping with Old Testament law (Num. 15:36) and Roman practice, executions took place outside the city. Therefore Jesus **went out** of Jerusalem to the place of execution. That too fulfilled Old Testament typology. According to the Mosaic law, the sin offerings were to be taken outside the camp of Israel. Exodus 29:14 reads, "But the flesh of the bull and its hide and its refuse, you shall burn with fire outside the camp; it is a sin offering." Leviticus adds, "the rest of the bull [the sin offering], he [the priest] is to bring out to a clean place outside the camp where the ashes are poured out, and burn it on wood with fire; where the ashes are poured out it shall be burned. ... But the bull of the sin offering and the goat of the sin offering, whose blood was brought in to make atonement in the holy place, shall be taken outside the camp, and they shall burn their hides, their flesh, and their refuse in the fire" (4:12; 16:27). Noting the theological significance of Jesus, the final sin offering, being executed outside the city, the author of Hebrews wrote, "For the bodies of those animals whose blood is brought into the holy place by the high priest as an offering for sin, are burned outside the camp. Therefore Jesus also, that He might sanctify the people through His own blood, suffered outside the gate" (Heb. 13:11–12).

The execution site was **the place called the Place of a Skull, which is called in Hebrew, Golgotha,** or in Latin, Calvary. Some believe the site was so named because it was a place where skulls could be found lying around. There is no evidence that such was the case, however, and to leave parts of corpses unburied would violate Jewish law (Deut. 21:23). A strange theory, embraced by several of the church fathers, holds that the site received its name because Adam's skull was found there. Needless to say, there is no evidence for that view either. Most likely, the name indicates that the site resembled a skull. The exact location is uncertain; the two most commonly suggested locations are the traditional site, west of Jerusalem at the Church of the Holy Sepulchre, and Gordon's Calvary, north of the city.

Crucifixion was regarded as the most horrible, shameful form of execution, one reserved for slaves, bandits, prisoners of war, and insurrectionists. It was such a terrible punishment that no Roman citizen could be crucified except by authorization of the emperor himself (Andreas J. Köstenberger, *John*, Baker Exegetical Commentary on the New Testament [Grand Rapids: Baker, 2004], 543). Crucifixion originated in Persia, and had come down to the Romans through the Phoenicians and Carthaginians. The Romans had perfected the art of prolonging the victim's agony as he was slowly tortured to death. Most hung on their crosses for days, before succumbing to exhaustion, dehydration, shock, or suffocation, when the victim could no longer raise himself into a position where he could breathe.

John, however, like the writers of the Synoptic Gospels (Matt. 27:35; Mark 15:24; Luke 23:33), does not dwell on the Lord's physical suffering. Instead of describing the process of crucifixion in gruesome detail, John simply states, **There they crucified Him.** The infinitely greater suffering for Jesus lay in His bearing sin and being separated from the Father (Matt. 27:46).

Jesus' crucifixion fulfilled several Old Testament prophecies. The first comes from an incident during Israel's wilderness wandering. After they complained against Moses, "The Lord sent fiery serpents among the people and they bit the people, so that many people of Israel died" (Num. 21:6). Acknowledging their guilt, "the people came to Moses and said, 'We have sinned, because we have spoken against the Lord and you; intercede with the Lord, that He may remove the serpents from us.' And Moses interceded for the people" (v. 7). In response to Moses' intercession, "the

Lord said to Moses,'Make a fiery serpent, and set it on a standard; and it shall come about, that everyone who is bitten, when he looks at it, he shall live.' And Moses made a bronze serpent and set it on the standard; and it came about, that if a serpent bit any man, when he looked to the bronze serpent, he lived" (vv. 8–9).

In John 3:14 Jesus referred to that incident as a typological prediction of His own death: "As Moses lifted up the serpent in the wilderness, even so must the Son of Man be lifted up." In 8:28 Jesus again spoke of being lifted up in His death: "When you lift up the Son of Man, then you will know that I am He, and I do nothing on My own initiative, but I speak these things as the Father taught Me." The Lord predicted the manner of His death a third time when He declared, "And I, if I am lifted up from the earth, will draw all men to Myself" (12:32). As John explained, "He was saying this to indicate the kind of death by which He was to die" (v. 33; cf. 18:31–32). It was obvious, then, that the Lord could not be put to death by the Jews. The Jewish form of execution (when the Romans permitted it) was stoning, which involved throwing a person down, not lifting him up. The crucifixion of Jesus Christ by the Romans specifically fulfilled both the picture of Numbers 21 and the predictions of the Lord Himself.

An even more graphic picture of Christ's crucifixion comes from Psalm 22. Remarkably David, who had no knowledge of crucifixion, penned a vivid description of Christ's crucifixion centuries before it happened. The Lord's cry of abandonment and despair, "'Eli, Eli, lama sabachthani?' that is, 'My God, My God, why have You forsaken Me?'" (Matt. 27:46) is a direct quote of the opening words of this psalm. Verses 6–8 reflect the derision hurled at Jesus as He hung on the cross:

> But I am a worm and not a man, a reproach of men and despised by the people. All who see me sneer at me; they separate with the lip, they wag the head, saying, "Commit yourself to the Lord; let Him deliver him; let Him rescue him, because He delights in him."

The parallel with Matthew 27:39–43 is striking:

> And those passing by were hurling abuse at Him, wagging their heads and saying, "You who are going to destroy the temple and rebuild it in three days, save Yourself! If You are the Son of God, come down from the cross." In the same way the chief priests also, along with the scribes and elders, were mocking Him and saying, "He saved others; He cannot save Himself. He is the King of Israel; let Him now come down from the cross, and we will believe in Him. He trusts in God; let God rescue Him now, if He delights in Him; for He said, 'I am the Son of God.'"

The psalm likens those heaping abuse on Jesus to "strong bulls" (v. 12), ravening and roaring lions (v. 13), scavenging dogs (v. 16), and wild oxen (v. 21).

David also depicted the physical torment the Lord would endure. He suffered exhaustion (v. 14): the unnatural position of His body caused His bones to be out of joint (v. 14) and put stress on His heart (v. 14). Verse 15 speaks of His failing strength and raging thirst; verse 16 of the nails through His hands and feet (cf. Zech. 12:10); and verse 17 of His taut, emaciated body.

The actions of **the soldiers** after **they had crucified Jesus** also fulfilled the words of Psalm 22. The execution squad normally consisted of four soldiers under the command of a centurion (Matt. 27:54). By custom the clothes of the condemned man were divided among the four soldiers. Therefore this group **took His outer garments** (head covering, belt, sandals, outer robe) **and made four parts, a part to every soldier.** Mark notes that they divided the items up by "casting lots for them to decide what each man should take" (Mark 15:24). But Jesus' **tunic** (worn next to the skin) **was seamless, woven in one piece.** They were unwilling to ruin this garment, **so they said to one another, "Let us not tear it, but cast lots for it, to decide whose it shall be."**

Though the soldiers acted from purely selfish motives, their actions furthered the sovereign plan of God and validated biblical accuracy by fulfilling prophecy. As John notes, what they did **was to fulfill the Scripture** (Ps. 22:18): **"They divided My outer garments among them, and for My clothing they cast lots." Therefore the soldiers did these things.** "Once again we see his [John's] master-thought that God was over all that was done, so directing things that His will was accomplished, and not that of puny man. It was because of this that the soldiers acted as they did" (Leon Morris, *The Gospel According to John,* The New International Commentary on the New Testament [Grand Rapids: Eerdmans, 1979], 810).

Jesus was not crucified alone; **with Him** were **two other men, one on either side, and Jesus in between.** They were robbers (Matt. 27:38), and may have been accomplices of Barabbas. John's statement does more than reveal that he was an eyewitness to the crucifixion; it too records the fulfillment of prophecy. Isaiah 53:12 predicted that Messiah would be "numbered with the transgressors." And so Jesus was, even though He was innocent of any crime or wrongdoing (8:46); even though no valid charge was ever brought against Him or proven true at His trials before the Jewish authorities, and the testimony of the false witnesses against Him was not consistent (Mark 14:56, 59); even though Pilate officially pronounced Him not guilty six times (18:38; 19:4, 6; Luke 23:4, 14, 22). But despite the injustice meted out to Him, John in magnificent irony reveals not a humiliated Christ dying with criminals, but an exalted Christ fulfilling prophecy. God used the most wicked, sinful act in history to bring about the greatest good—the redemption of lost sinners. And the first trophy of grace won by Christ on the cross was one of the very men crucified alongside Him (Luke 23:39–43).

THE SUPERSCRIPTION

Pilate also wrote an inscription and put it on the cross. It was written, "JESUS THE NAZARENE, THE KING OF THE JEWS." Therefore many of the Jews read this inscription, for the place where Jesus was crucified was near the city; and it was written in Hebrew, Latin and in Greek. So the chief priests of the Jews were saying to Pilate, "Do not write, 'The King of the Jews'; but that He said, 'I am King of the Jews.'" Pilate answered, "What I have written I have written." (19:19–22)

It was customary that a criminal being led away to be crucified be preceded by a man carrying a placard. On that placard would be written the crime for which the condemned man was to be executed. Often it would be affixed to the man's cross. But since Jesus was innocent, there was no crime to put on the placard. Pilate therefore decided to give a parting shot to the Jewish leaders, taking revenge on them for blackmailing him into ordering Jesus' death. He **wrote an inscription and put it on** Jesus' **cross** above His head (cf. Matt. 27:37; Luke 23:38). The inscription read, **"JESUS THE NAZARENE, THE KING OF THE JEWS."** The Romans usually crucified prisoners in public places, such as alongside highways, so that the public would see the price to be paid for resisting or challenging Rome's authority. Therefore **many of the Jews read this inscription, for the place where Jesus was crucified was near the city.** To make certain that everyone could read it, Pilate commanded that the inscription be **written in Hebrew, Latin and in Greek,** the three languages commonly spoken in first-century Palestine.

As the governor had correctly anticipated, **the chief priests of the Jews were** infuriated at being so openly mocked and began **saying to Pilate, "Do not write, 'The King of the Jews'; but that He said, 'I am King of the Jews.'"** The superscription was an affront to them for several reasons. First and foremost, although they certainly were not loyal to Caesar as they had pretended to be (19:15), the chief priests vehemently rejected Jesus as their king. That the inscription identified Him as **the NAZARENE** (i.e., from Nazareth) made the insult worse. Nazareth was an insignificant Galilean village, whose rustic inhabitants were looked down upon with scorn and contempt by the sophisticated Judeans. When Philip excitedly reported to Nathanael, "We have found Him of whom Moses in the Law and also the Prophets wrote—Jesus of Nazareth, the son of Joseph" (John 1:45), the latter replied incredulously, "Can any good thing come out of Nazareth?" (v. 46). The idea that a victimized man from such a town—especially one dying a criminal's death on a cross—could be their king was ludicrous. Worse, it was a direct affront both to the leaders and the nation. Pilate was expressing his contempt for the Jewish people, implying that such an individual was the only kind of king they deserved (cf. the discussion of 19:14 in chapter 30 of this volume).

Accordingly, the chief priests demanded that Pilate change the wording on the inscription. **"Do not write, 'The King of the Jews,'"** they insisted, **"but that He said, 'I am King of the Jews.'"** They wanted the governor to change the wording so that Christ would appear to be an imposter. But Pilate, no doubt relishing their discomfiture, bluntly refused. He dismissed them with the curt reply, **"What I have written I have written."**

Here again is an example of God using sinful men to accomplish His sovereign purposes. Neither Pilate nor the Jewish leaders believed that Jesus was the king of Israel. Yet the animosity between them ensured that the governor would write an inscription proclaiming that Jesus was Israel's King—as in fact He is. He is the "King of kings, and Lord of lords" (Rev. 19:16), and "at the name of Jesus every knee will bow, of those who are in heaven and on earth and under the earth, and ...every tongue will confess that Jesus Christ is Lord, to the glory of God the Father" (Phil. 2:10–11).

The Expression of Selfless Love

But standing by the cross of Jesus were His mother, and His mother's sister, Mary the wife of Clopas, and Mary Magdalene. When Jesus then saw His mother, and the disciple whom He loved standing nearby, He said to His mother, "Woman, behold, your son!" Then He said to the disciple, "Behold, your mother!" From that hour the disciple took her into his own household. (19:25b–27)

The adversative conjunction **but** introduces a sharp contrast between the callous indifference of the soldiers (v. 25a), who were gambling for Christ's clothes (and, by implication, the sneering hatred of the rulers [Luke 23:35] and the mocking contempt of those passing by [Matt. 27:39–40]), and the compassionate love of a small group of loyal followers. They were **standing by** (*para*; "beside," or, "alongside") **the cross of Jesus,** close enough for Him to speak to them. (Later, either driven away by the soldiers, or unable to bear any longer the sight of Christ's suffering at such close range, they retreated some distance away to where a larger group of Christ's followers was standing [Luke 23:49].) Their love for Jesus overcame their fear (cf. 1 John 4:18), and they came to Him.

The number of women in the group is disputed, but there were most likely four (cf. D. A. Carson, *The Gospel According to John,* The Pillar New Testament Commentary [Grand Rapids: Eerdmans, 1991], 615–16; William Hendriksen, *New Testament Commentary: The Gospel of John* [Grand Rapids, Baker, 1954], 2:431–32). Jesus' **mother,** Mary, was there. This was the time that Simeon had warned her long ago would come, when the sword would pierce her soul as she watched her Son suffer (Luke 2:35). Of the three lists of women (cf. Matt. 27:55–56; Mark 15:40–41), John's is the only one that mentions the presence of Jesus' mother. Her omission by Matthew and Mark is in keeping with her low-key role in the New Testament—and in striking contrast to the significant role assigned to her in Roman Catholic theology. As I wrote in an earlier volume in this series,

> Mary was a woman of singular virtue, or she would never have been chosen to be the mother of the Lord Jesus Christ. For that role she deserves respect and honor (cf. Luke 1:42). But she was a sinner who exalted God *her* Savior. She referred to herself as a humble bondslave to God, who needed mercy (cf. Luke 1:46–50). To offer prayers to her and elevate her to a role as co-redemptrix with Christ is to go beyond the bounds of Scripture and her own confession. The silence of the epistles, which form the doctrinal core of the New Testament, about Mary is especially significant. If she played the important role in salvation assigned her by the Roman Catholic Church, or if she were to receive prayers as an intercessor between believers and Christ, surely the New Testament would have spelled that out. Nor do such Roman Catholic teachings as her virgin birth and bodily assumption into heaven find any biblical support; they are fabrications. (*Acts 1–12,* The MacArthur New Testament Commentary [Chicago: Moody, 1994], 29. Italics in original.)

A comparison of Matthew 27:56 and Mark 15:40 suggests that Jesus' **mother's sister** was Salome, the mother of the sons of Zebedee (i.e., James and John). She appears elsewhere in the New Testament by name only in Mark 16:1 as one of the women who bought spices to anoint the body of Jesus. If she was the mother of James and John, she also appears in Matthew 20:20–21, where she asked Jesus to grant special places of honor to her sons in the kingdom.

Little is known of **Mary the wife of Clopas.** She was the "other Mary" who kept a vigil at Jesus' tomb with Mary Magdalene (Matt. 27:61) and was one of the women who went to the tomb on the morning of the resurrection (Matt. 28:1). She was also one of the women who tried unsuccessfully to persuade the apostles that Christ had risen (Luke 24:10). She was the mother of the apostle James the son of Alphaeus (Clopas is a variant of Alphaeus), who is also called James the Less (Mark 15:40).

Mary Magdalene figures prominently in the accounts of Christ's resurrection (20:1–18; Matt. 27:61; 28:1; Luke 24:10). Her name suggests that she was from the village of Magdala, located on the west shore of the Sea of Galilee between Capernaum and Tiberias. Luke 8:2 describes her as one "from whom seven demons had gone out" through the ministry of Jesus. There is no reason to identify her (as some do) with the prostitute of Luke 7:37–50.

The only man among the group gathered at the foot of the cross was John himself, the disciple whom Jesus loved (cf. 13:23; 20:2; 21:7, 20 and introduction: "The Authorship of John's Gospel," in *John 1–11*, The MacArthur New Testament Commentary [Chicago: Moody, 2006]). His presence led to an important relationship established by the Lord. **When Jesus then saw His mother, and the disciple whom He loved standing nearby, He said to His mother, "Woman, behold, your son!" Then He said to the disciple, "Behold, your mother!"** Even as He was dying, bearing man's sin and God's wrath, Jesus selflessly cared for those whom He loved (cf. 13:1, 34; 15:9, 13). Evidently His earthly father, Joseph, was already dead. The Lord could not commit Mary into the care of His half brothers, the children of Mary and Joseph, since they were not yet believers (7:5). They did not become believers in Jesus until after His resurrection (Acts 1:14; cf. 1 Cor. 15:7, though the James referenced in that verse may be the apostle James). Therefore He entrusted her to John; he became as a **son** to her in Jesus' place, and **from that hour** he **took her into his own household.** This may seem a very mundane thing to be concerned about in the hour of His greatest sacrifice, but the beauty of the Savior's love and compassion for His widowed mother, in the midst of His own excruciating pain, reflects His love for His own (cf. John 13:1).

THE MANIFESTATION OF
SUPERNATURAL KNOWLEDGE AND CONTROL

After this, Jesus, knowing that all things had already been accomplished, to fulfill the Scripture, said, "I am thirsty." A jar full of sour wine was standing there; so they put a sponge full of the sour wine upon a branch of hyssop and brought it up to His mouth. Therefore when Jesus had received the sour wine, He said, "It is finished!" And He bowed His head and gave up His spirit. (19:28–30)

After tenderly establishing His mother's care, **Jesus, knowing that all things had already been accomplished, to fulfill the Scripture, said, "I am thirsty."** In His omniscience, Jesus knew there was only one remaining prophecy to be fulfilled. In Psalm 69:21 David wrote, "They also gave me gall for my food and for my thirst they gave me vinegar (the Septuagint uses the same Greek word translated **sour wine** in v. 29) to drink." Jesus knew that by saying **"I am thirsty"** He would prompt the soldiers to give Him a drink. They, of course, did not consciously do so to fulfill prophecy, still less to show compassion. Their goal was to increase the Lord's torment by prolonging His life.

From a **jar full of sour wine** that **was standing** nearby, one of the bystanders (probably one of the soldiers; or at least someone acting with their approval) **put a sponge full of the sour wine upon a branch of hyssop** (cf. Ex. 12:22) **and brought it up to His mouth.** This was the cheap, sour wine that the soldiers commonly consumed. It was not the same beverage that the Lord had earlier refused (Matt. 27:34). That beverage, which contained gall, was intended to help deaden His pain so He would not struggle as much while being nailed to His cross. Jesus had refused it, because He wanted to drink the cup of the Father's wrath against sin in the fullest way His senses could experience it.

Having **received the sour wine,** Jesus **said, "It is finished!"** (Gk. *tetelestai*). Actually, the Lord shouted those words with a loud cry (Matt. 27:50; Mark 15:37). It was a shout of triumph; the proclamation of a victor. The work of redemption that the Father had given Him was accomplished: sin was atoned for (Heb. 9:12; 10:12;), and Satan was defeated and rendered powerless (Heb. 2:14; cf. 1 Peter 1:18–20; 1 John 3:8). Every requirement of God's righteous law had been satisfied; God's holy wrath against sin had been appeased (Rom. 3:25; Heb. 2:17; 1 John 2:2; 4:10); every prophecy had been fulfilled. Christ's completion of the work of redemption means that nothing needs to be nor can be added to it. Salvation is not a joint effort of God and man, but is entirely a work of God's grace, appropriated solely by faith (Eph. 2:8–9).

His mission accomplished, the time had come for Christ to surrender His life. Therefore, after "crying out with a loud voice ... 'Father, into Your hands I commit My spirit" (Luke 23:46), **He bowed His head and gave up His spirit.** Jesus voluntarily chose to surrender His life by a conscious act of His own sovereign will. "No one has taken it away from Me," He declared, "but I lay it down on My own initiative. I have authority to lay it down, and I have authority to take it up again. This commandment I received from My Father" (10:18). That He still had the strength to shout loudly shows that He was not physically at the point of death. That He died sooner than was normal for someone who had been crucified (Mark 15:43–45) also shows that He gave up His life of His own will.

No human words, no matter how eloquent, can adequately express the meaning of Christ's death. But the words of the familiar hymn "At Calvary" express the gratitude every believer feels:

> Years I spent in vanity and pride,
> Caring not my Lord was crucified,
> Knowing not it was for me He died
> On Calvary.

> Mercy there was great, and grace was free;
> Pardon there was multiplied to me;
> There my burdened soul found liberty,
> At Calvary.

> By God's Word at last my sin I learned,
> Then I trembled at the law I'd spurned,
> Till my guilty soul imploring turned
> To Calvary.

> Now I've giv'n to Jesus ev'rything;
> Now I gladly own Him as my King;
> Now my raptured soul can only sing
> Of Calvary.

> O, the love that drew salvation's plan!
> O, the grace that brought it down to man!
> O, the mighty gulf that God did span
> At Calvary!

The Death-Conquering Savior
(John 19:31–20:10)

32

Then the Jews, because it was the day of preparation, so that the bodies would not remain on the cross on the Sabbath (for that Sabbath was a high day), asked Pilate that their legs might be broken, and that they might be taken away. So the soldiers came, and broke the legs of the first man and of the other who was crucified with Him; but coming to Jesus, when they saw that He was already dead, they did not break His legs. But one of the soldiers pierced His side with a spear, and immediately blood and water came out. And he who has seen has testified, and his testimony is true; and he knows that he is telling the truth, so that you also may believe. For these things came to pass to fulfill the Scripture, "Not a bone of Him shall be broken." And again another Scripture says, "They shall look on Him whom they pierced." After these things Joseph of Arimathea, being a disciple of Jesus, but a secret one for fear of the Jews, asked Pilate that he might take away the body of Jesus; and Pilate granted permission. So he came and took away His body. Nicodemus, who had first come to Him by night, also came, bringing a mixture of myrrh and aloes, about a hundred pounds weight. So they took the body of Jesus and bound it in linen wrappings with the spices, as is the burial

custom of the Jews. Now in the place where He was crucified there was a garden, and in the garden a new tomb in which no one had yet been laid. Therefore because of the Jewish day of preparation, since the tomb was nearby, they laid Jesus there. Now on the first day of the week Mary Magdalene came early to the tomb, while it was still dark, and saw the stone already taken away from the tomb. So she ran and came to Simon Peter and to the other disciple whom Jesus loved, and said to them, "They have taken away the Lord out of the tomb, and we do not know where they have laid Him." So Peter and the other disciple went forth, and they were going to the tomb. The two were running together; and the other disciple ran ahead faster than Peter and came to the tomb first; and stooping and looking in, he saw the linen wrappings lying there; but he did not go in. And so Simon Peter also came, following him, and entered the tomb; and he saw the linen wrappings lying there, and the face-cloth which had been on His head, not lying with the linen wrappings, but rolled up in a place by itself. So the other disciple who had first come to the tomb then also entered, and he saw and believed. For as yet they did not understand the Scripture, that He must rise again from the dead. So the disciples went away again to their own homes. (19:31–20:10)

One indisputable certainty of life is that it will someday end."Man, who is born of woman," Job lamented,"is short-lived and full of turmoil. Like a flower he comes forth and withers.He also flees like a shadow and does not remain" (Job 14:1–2).As the wise woman from Tekoa phrased it to King David,"We shall surely die and are like water spilled on the ground which cannot be gathered up again" (2 Sam. 14:14)."What man can live and not see death?" asked the psalmist rhetorically (Ps. 89:48). Just as there is a time to be born,so also there is a time to die (Eccl.3:2).In Psalm 90 Moses noted the brevity of man's life span:"As for the days of our life, they contain seventy years, or if due to strength, eighty years, yet their pride is but labor and sorrow; for soon it is gone and we fly away" (v. 10). Isaiah (Isa. 40:6–8), James (James 1:10), and Peter (1 Peter 1:24–25) used the grass that so quickly withers to illustrate the ephemeral nature of human life.James reminded boastful men that they "are just a vapor that appears for a little while and then vanishes away" (James 4:14).

Death casts its long shadow (cf. Ps. 23:4) over every aspect of man's existence. It ends his dreams, mocks his hopes, and fills him with dread. People have sought desperately, but unsuccessfully, over the centuries to evade death.One of the most recent high-tech attempts to cheat death is cryonics. According to the Alcor Life Extension Foundation of

Scottsdale, Arizona, one of its leading practitioners, cryonics is "a speculative life support technology that seeks to preserve human life in a state that will be viable and treatable by future medicine" (www.alcor.org; accessed 3 October 2007). The procedure involves using extreme cold to preserve the body (or sometimes just the head and brain). Since the first person was cryopreserved in 1967, more than one hundred people have undergone the procedure (including baseball Hall of Famer Ted Williams), and more than a thousand others have made arrangements to do so after they die (www.alcor.org/AboutCryonics/index.html; accessed 3 October 2007).

But no one can permanently cheat death; it will always win in the end. Solomon wrote that "No man has authority ... over the day of death" (Eccl. 8:8), while Hebrews 9:27 says that "it is appointed for men to die once and after this comes judgment." The universality of death stems from the universality of sin. "By a man came death," Paul wrote, because "in Adam all die" (1 Cor. 15:21–22). It was through Adam that "sin entered into the world, and death through sin, and so death spread to all men, because all sinned" (Rom. 5:12; cf. Ezek. 18:4, 20; Rom. 6:23).

The Bible pictures death as an enemy (1 Cor. 15:26), and as such it is greatly feared; Job 18:14 pictures death metaphorically as the "king of terrors." "My heart is in anguish within me," David cried out, "and the terrors of death have fallen upon me" (Ps. 55:4). The author of Hebrews wrote of "those who through fear of death were subject to slavery all their lives" (Heb. 2:15). That fear prompts people to seek relief in materialism (Luke 12:16–20), hedonism (Isa. 22:13; 1 Cor. 15:32), and false religion (Gen. 3:4).

But the good news of the gospel is that Jesus Christ has conquered death. In John 8:51 He declared, "Truly, truly, I say to you, if anyone keeps My word he will never see death." He comforted Martha, grieving over the loss of her brother Lazarus, with the promise, "I am the resurrection and the life; he who believes in Me will live even if he dies, and everyone who lives and believes in Me will never die" (11:25–26). He described Himself as "the bread which comes down out of heaven, so that one may eat of it and not die" (6:50), and affirmed, "I am the living bread that came down out of heaven; if anyone eats of this bread, he will live forever" (v. 51). Jesus promised the disciples, "Because I live, you will live also" (14:19). Paul reminded Timothy that "our Savior Christ Jesus ... abolished death and brought life and immortality to light through the gospel" (2 Tim. 1:10). The writer of Hebrews insisted that it is only through faith in Jesus Christ that people can be freed from the fear of death: "Therefore, since the children share in flesh and blood, He Himself likewise also partook of the same, so that through death He might render powerless him who had the power of death, that is, the devil, and might free those who through fear of death were subject to slavery all their lives" (Heb. 2:14–15). Because Christ has delivered them from death, believers can say triumphantly with Paul, "O death, where is your victory? O death, where is your sting?" The sting of death is sin, and the power of sin is the law; but thanks be to God, who gives us the victory through our Lord Jesus Christ" (1 Cor. 15:55–57). By dying, the Lord Jesus Christ destroyed death. He has removed its sting, conquered its terror, and turned it into a friend that ushers those who love Him into His presence.

Throughout His life, Jesus performed countless miracles that manifested His divine power (21:25). He healed the sick, cast out demons, and raised the dead. But nothing more clearly reveals the greatness of His power than His own resurrection. Flowing out of this simple narrative are three manifestations of Christ's power over death, each of which also fulfill specific prophecies. His power was revealed in His dying, His burial, and His resurrection.

CHRIST'S POWER OVER DEATH WAS MANIFESTED IN HIS DYING

Then the Jews, because it was the day of preparation, so that the bodies would not remain on the cross on the Sabbath (for that Sabbath was a high day), asked Pilate that their legs might be broken, and that they might be taken away. So the soldiers came, and broke the legs of the first man and of the other who was crucified with Him; but coming to Jesus, when they saw that He was already dead, they did not break His legs. But one of the soldiers pierced His side with a spear, and immediately blood and water came out. And he who has seen has testified, and his testimony is true; and he knows that he is telling the truth, so that you also may believe. For these things came to pass to fulfill the Scripture, "Not a bone of Him shall be broken." And again another Scripture says, "They shall look on Him whom they pierced." (19:31–37)

One of the most unsettling aspects of death is the element of surprise. Death frequently comes suddenly and unexpectedly, leaving words unsaid, plans unfinished, dreams unrealized, and hopes unfulfilled.

That was not the case with Jesus, however. Death could not surprise Him, for He controlled it. In 10:17–18 He declared, "I lay down My life so that I may take it again. No one has taken it away from Me, but I lay it down on My own initiative. I have authority to lay it down, and I have authority to take it up again. This commandment I received from My Father." The previous section of John's gospel closed with Christ voluntary giving up His life as He had said He would. Having accomplished the work of redemption, Jesus cried out, "It is finished!" and, after doing so, "He bowed His head and gave up His spirit" (19:30). Death had tried unsuccessfully to take His life on many occasions (e.g., 5:16–18; 7:1; 8:37, 40, 59; 10:31; 11:53; Matt. 2:16; Luke 4:28–30), but He would not die until the precise moment called for in God's predetermined plan. His was not the death of a victim; it was the death of a victor.

As noted in the previous chapter of this volume, Jesus died much sooner than was normal for victims of crucifixion. He was crucified at the third hour, or 9:00 A.M. (Mark 15:25) and died at the ninth hour, or 3:00 P.M. (v. 34). Thus Jesus was on the cross for only about six hours. Most people who were crucified lingered for two or three days; both the robbers crucified alongside Jesus, for example, were still alive after He died (19:32). Thus when Joseph of Arimathea asked Pilate for the body of Jesus, the governor "wondered if He was dead by this time, and summoning the centurion [the commander of the execution squad], he questioned him as to whether He was already dead" (Mark 15:44). It was only after "ascertaining this from the centurion, [that] he granted the body to Joseph" (v. 45). The reason the Lord died so soon is that He gave up His life to death when He willed to do so.

In an act of blatant, nauseating hypocrisy, **the Jews, because it was the day of preparation, so that the bodies would not remain on the cross on the Sabbath (for that Sabbath was a high day), asked Pilate that their legs might be broken, and that they might be taken away.** It was getting late in the afternoon on **the day of preparation** (for the Sabbath; i.e., Friday). They were concerned **that the bodies** of Jesus and the two robbers **not remain on the cross on the Sabbath,** which began at sundown. The Romans usually left the bodies of crucified individuals to rot, or be eaten by scavenging birds or animals. That particular **Sabbath was a high day** (because it was the Sabbath of Passover week), heightening the Jewish leaders' concern, which evidently stemmed from Deuteronomy 21:22–23. To leave the bodies exposed on the crosses would, in their minds, defile the land. Nothing more clearly illustrates the extreme hypocrisy to which their pernicious legalism had driven them. They were zealous to observe the minutiae of the law while at the same time killing the One who both authored and fulfilled it; they were scrupulously concerned that the land not be defiled, but were unconcerned about their own defilement from murdering the Son of God.

Breaking the legs of crucified persons (a procedure known as *crurifragium*) was done when there was a reason to hasten a crucified person's death. It involved smashing the victim's legs with an iron mallet. That gruesome procedure hastened death, partly from the shock and additional blood loss, but more important by bringing on asphyxiation. The victims could no longer use their legs to help raise themselves up to breathe, so when the strength in their arms gave out, they suffocated.

After Pilate granted the Jews' request, **the soldiers came, and broke the legs of the first man and of the other who was crucified with Him; but coming to Jesus, when they saw that He was already dead, they did not break His legs. But** just to make certain He was dead, **one of the soldiers pierced His side with a spear, and immediately blood and water came out.** The soldiers were experts at determining death; it was part of their job. They had nothing to gain by lying about Jesus' death. Their testimony, and that of their commander (Mark 15:44–45), is irrefutable proof that Jesus was in fact dead. He did not, as some skeptics who deny the resurrection maintain, merely go into a coma and then revive in the coolness of the tomb. (See the discussion of false theories of the resurrection in chapter 33 of this volume.)

By giving up His life when He did, our Lord assured that the soldiers fulfilled prophecy. According to Exodus 12:46 and Numbers 9:12, no bone of the Passover lamb was to be broken. Jesus was the perfect fulfillment of the Passover lamb, and as such could not have any of His bones broken. Beyond that picture is the explicit prophecy of Psalm 34:20, "He keeps all his bones, not one of them is broken," to which John referred when he wrote, **For these things came to pass to fulfill the Scripture, "Not a bone of Him shall be broken."**

His dying early also led to His being pierced to be sure He was dead. That unusual act of piercing Jesus' side was essential to fulfill prophecy; as **again another Scripture says, "They shall look on Him whom they pierced."** The apostle quoted Zechariah 12:10, where God declared,

> I will pour out on the house of David and on the inhabitants of Jerusalem, the Spirit of grace and of supplication, so that they will look on Me whom they have pierced; and they will mourn for Him, as one mourns for an only son, and they will weep bitterly over Him like the bitter weeping over a firstborn.

That God said "they will look on Me whom they have pierced" affirms that Jesus was God incarnate. The ultimate fulfillment of this prophecy will be at Christ's second coming, when the repentant remnant of Israel will mourn over rejecting and killing their King (cf. Rev. 1:7).

The physiological explanation of the **blood and water** has been much discussed. It may be that the Lord's heart literally burst from the tremendous mental agony and sorrow associated with His work of bearing sin and the Father's forsaking of Him. In any case, John's eyewitness account as one **who has seen** and **testified, and** whose **testimony is true; and** who **knows that he is telling the truth,** emphasizes that Jesus was unquestionably dead. John's account is not hearsay, fable, or legend, but rather a sober historical record of actual events. His purpose in relating Jesus' precise fulfillment of prophecy in His death was **so that** his readers **also may believe** that "Jesus is the Christ, the Son of God; and that believing [they] may have life in His name" (20:31). Christ clearly controlled His own death to fulfill Scripture.

CHRIST'S POWER OVER DEATH
WAS MANIFESTED IN HIS BURIAL

After these things Joseph of Arimathea, being a disciple of Jesus, but a secret one for fear of the Jews, asked Pilate that he might take away the body of Jesus; and Pilate granted permission. So he came and took away His body. Nicodemus, who had first come to Him by night, also came, bringing a mixture of myrrh and aloes, about a hundred pounds weight. So they took the body of Jesus and bound it in linen wrappings with the spices, as is the burial custom of the Jews. Now in the place where He was crucified there was a garden, and in the garden a new tomb in which no one had yet been laid. Therefore because of the Jewish day of preparation, since the tomb was nearby, they laid Jesus there. (19:38–42)

Jesus not only exhibited His divine power over death by controlling the details of His dying, but even more remarkably, He also controlled the circumstances of His burial after He was dead. As was the case with His dying, by doing so Jesus both revealed His deity, and fulfilled biblical prophecy. In Isaiah 53:9 the prophet wrote that though Messiah's "grave was assigned with wicked men, yet He was with a rich man in His death." The Romans normally refused to allow those executed for sedition to be buried, leaving them to the vultures and scavengers as the ultimate indignity. The Jews did not refuse burial to anyone, but buried criminals at a separate location outside of Jerusalem.

But even if He escaped being buried with common criminals, how was Jesus to be buried with a rich man? He did not come from a wealthy family, nor could any of the apostles be considered rich men. The answer is that Jesus, "having been put to death in the flesh, but made alive in the spirit" (1 Peter 3:18), moved upon the heart of a rich man, **Joseph,** from **Arimathea** (the location of Arimathea is unknown; some identify it with Ramathaim-zophim, the birthplace of Samuel [1 Sam. 1:1]).

Joseph appears in all four Gospels but only in the accounts of Jesus' burial. He was rich (Matt. 27:57), a prominent member of the Sanhedrin (Mark 15:43), who had not agreed with its decision to condemn Jesus (Luke 23:51). Joseph was a good and righteous man (Luke 23:50), who was waiting for the kingdom of God (Mark 15:43). He was a disciple of Jesus (Matt. 27:57), although **a secret one for fear of the Jews.** The apostle John usually took a dim view of secret disciples (cf. 12:42–43). However he presented Joseph in a positive light in view of his courageous action in asking **Pilate that he might take away the body of Jesus.** Joseph had exhibited sinful, cowardly fear of losing his prestige, power, and position while the Lord was alive. But now he exposed himself to even greater danger than he had tried to avoid by approaching Pilate (who by now had had his fill of the Jewish leaders) and asking for the body of a man who had been executed as a rival king to the emperor. From beyond the grave, however, the Lord moved in Joseph's heart to expedite His burial. After first making sure Jesus was really dead (Mark 15:44–45), **Pilate granted permission** for Joseph to take His body.

Having received the governor's approval, Joseph immediately **came and took away** Christ's **body** and hurriedly began preparing it for burial. In this Joseph was assisted by **Nicodemus,** another member of the Sanhedrin **who,** as John's footnote indicates, **had first come to** Christ **by night** (3:1–21). Though they kept their allegiance to Him secret while Jesus was alive, Joseph and Nicodemus courageously braved the wrath of the rest of the Sanhedrin to bury His body. Nicodemus brought a **mixture of myrrh and aloes, about a hundred pounds weight** (about sixty-five pounds by modern standards). That amount of spices would have been used to anoint the body of a king, or a wealthy, prominent person. **Myrrh** was a fragrant, gummy resin, which in powdered form was often mixed with **aloes,** an aromatic powder made from sandalwood. Joseph and Nicodemus **took the body of Jesus and bound it in linen wrappings with the spices, as is the burial custom of the Jews.** Unlike the Egyptians, the Jews did not embalm their dead; they used fragrant spices to stifle the smell of putrefaction for as long as possible. The spices were probably sprinkled along the entire length of the strips of cloth that were wrapped around the Lord's body. More spices were then packed around and under His body once it was placed in the tomb. It should be noted that neither Joseph or Nicodemus or the women (Luke 23:55–24:1) were expecting Jesus to rise from the dead. If they had believed His repeated predictions that He would do so (2:19; Matt. 16:21; 17:23; 20:19; Luke 24:6–7), they would not have bothered to prepare His body so thoroughly for burial.

Only John relates that **in the place where He was crucified there was a garden, and in the garden a new tomb in which no**

one had yet been laid. Matthew reveals that the tomb was Joseph's own tomb (Matt. 27:60). With the Sabbath—when all work would have to cease—nearly upon them, the nearness of the tomb was providential. **Therefore because . . . the Jewish day of preparation** (Friday) was almost over, and **since the tomb was nearby, they laid Jesus there.** As was commonly done, Joseph's tomb had been carved out of rock, and was sealed by rolling a large stone in front of the entrance (Matt. 27:60).

Joseph and Nicodemus were motivated by the need to finish their work before the Sabbath began. But there was a more significant reason that the Lord needed to be buried before sundown. In Matthew 12:40 Jesus had predicted, "For just as Jonah was three days and three nights in the belly of the sea monster, so will the Son of Man be three days and three nights in the heart of the earth." The Jews counted any part of a day as constituting a day (cf. 1 Kings 12:5 with v. 12; Est. 4:16 with 5:1). Jesus needed to be buried while it was still Friday, so He could be in the tomb for three days (part of Friday afternoon, Saturday, and part of Sunday morning). In His burial, as well as His death, Jesus orchestrated all the details to accomplish God's already revealed purpose.

CHRIST'S POWER OVER DEATH
WAS MANIFESTED IN HIS RESURRECTION

Now on the first day of the week Mary Magdalene came early to the tomb, while it was still dark, and saw the stone already taken away from the tomb. So she ran and came to Simon Peter and to the other disciple whom Jesus loved, and said to them, "They have taken away the Lord out of the tomb, and we do not know where they have laid Him." So Peter and the other disciple went forth, and they were going to the tomb. The two were running together; and the other disciple ran ahead faster than Peter and came to the tomb first; and stooping and looking in, he saw the linen wrappings lying there; but he did not go in. And so Simon Peter also came, following him, and entered the tomb; and he saw the linen wrappings lying there, and the face-cloth which had been on His head, not lying with the linen wrappings, but rolled up in a place by itself. So the other disciple who had first come to the tomb then also entered, and he saw and believed. For as yet they did not understand the Scripture, that He must rise again from the dead. So the disciples went away again to their own homes. (20:1–10)

The ultimate demonstration of Christ's power over death, and hence proof of His deity, was His resurrection. It, too, was the fulfillment of Old Testament prophecy. Speaking prophetically of the Messiah, David wrote, "You will not abandon my soul to Sheol; neither will You allow Your Holy One to undergo decay" (Ps. 16:10; cf. Acts 2:25–28; 13:35).

The first day of the week, Sunday, would forever after be the day believers set aside to commemorate their Lord's marvelous resurrection (Acts 20:7; 1 Cor. 16:2). It eventually became known as the Lord's Day (Rev. 1:10), and on that first Lord's Day morning, **Mary Magdalene came early to the tomb.** The Synoptic Gospels record various women who came to the tomb that morning (Matt. 28:1; Mark 16:1; Luke 24:1, 10). John mentions only Mary, and says that she came **while it was still dark,** in contrast to the others who arrived after sunrise (Mark 16:2). The women evidently set out together, but Mary went on ahead of the others and arrived at the tomb first. Finding **the stone already taken away from the tomb,** she feared the worst. Undoubtedly assuming that grave robbers had broken into the tomb and stolen the Lord's body, she **ran and came to Simon Peter and to the other disciple whom Jesus loved, and said to them, "They have taken away the Lord out of the tomb, and we do not know where they have laid Him."** Thus Mary, running to find Peter and John, was not present at the tomb when the angels appeared to the others and announced Christ's resurrection (Matt. 28:5–7; Mark 16:5–7; Luke 24:4–7). She then returned alone to the tomb, saw the angels, and met the risen Lord (see the exposition of 20:11–18 in chapter 33 of this volume).

Though they were initially skeptical of Mary's and the other women's reports of the empty tomb (Luke 24:11), eventually **Peter and the other disciple** (John, who characteristically did not name himself) **went . . . to the tomb.** The two started out **running together,** but **the other disciple ran ahead faster than Peter and came to the tomb first.** John halted outside, **and stooping and looking in, he saw the linen wrappings lying there; but he did not go in.** Fear, either of the unknown, or that something terrible had happened to the Lord's body, as Mary feared, prevented him from entering. **Simon Peter,** however, had no such fears. Impetuous as always, he **came, following** John, **and** promptly **entered the tomb.**

What he saw was startling. Jesus' body was nowhere to be seen, but **the linen wrappings** in which He had been buried were **lying there.** Unlike Lazarus, who needed help getting out of his grave clothes after his resurrection (11:44), Jesus' glorified resurrection body simply passed through the linen wrappings, as it would soon pass through a wall to enter a locked room (20:19, 26). Even **the face-cloth which had been on His head,** was **not lying with the linen wrappings, but**

rolled up in a place by itself. This seemingly minor detail shows that
the tomb was left in a neat, orderly condition. In contrast, grave robbers
would hardly have taken time to roll up the facecloth, and in their haste
they would have scattered the grave clothes all over the tomb. More likely
still, they would not have removed them at all, since it would have been
easier to transport the body if it were still wrapped. Nor would thieves
likely have left the wrappings, containing expensive spices, behind. The
presence of the grave clothes also shows that the story the Jewish leaders concocted, that the disciples stole Christ's body (Matt. 28:11–15), is
false. If they had stolen the body, why would the disciples dishonor it by
tearing off the grave clothes and spices that covered it?

John **then also entered** the tomb, **and he saw and believed**
that Jesus had indeed risen. The empty tomb, the undisturbed grave
clothes, and the neatly rolled up facecloth were enough for John—even
though he and Peter **did not understand the Scripture, that He must
rise again from the dead** (cf. Ps. 16:10). Whether Peter also believed at
this time is not clear, though Luke 24:12 may suggest that he did not (the
phrase "marveling at what had happened" [NASB] could also be translated,
"wondering what had happened"). Whether in belief or bewilderment,
the disciples went away again to their own homes.

The stage was set for the appearances of the resurrected Lord,
which would erase all doubt whether resurrection had happened. It is to
the first of those appearances, to Mary Magdalene, that John's narrative
now turns.

The Resurrected Christ
(John 20:11–31)

33

But Mary was standing outside the tomb weeping; and so, as she wept, she stooped and looked into the tomb; and she saw two angels in white sitting, one at the head and one at the feet, where the body of Jesus had been lying. And they said to her, "Woman, why are you weeping?" She said to them, "Because they have taken away my Lord, and I do not know where they have laid Him." When she had said this, she turned around and saw Jesus standing there, and did not know that it was Jesus. Jesus said to her, "Woman, why are you weeping? Whom are you seeking?" Supposing Him to be the gardener, she said to Him, "Sir, if you have carried Him away, tell me where you have laid Him, and I will take Him away." Jesus said to her, "Mary!" She turned and said to Him in Hebrew, "Rabboni!" (which means, Teacher). Jesus said to her, "Stop clinging to Me, for I have not yet ascended to the Father; but go to My brethren and say to them, 'I ascend to My Father and your Father, and My God and your God.'" Mary Magdalene came, announcing to the disciples, "I have seen the Lord," and that He had said these things to her. So when it was evening on that day, the first day of the week, and when the doors were shut where the disciples were, for fear of the Jews,

Jesus came and stood in their midst and said to them, "Peace be with you." And when He had said this, He showed them both His hands and His side. The disciples then rejoiced when they saw the Lord. So Jesus said to them again, "Peace be with you; as the Father has sent Me, I also send you." And when He had said this, He breathed on them and said to them, "Receive the Holy Spirit. If you forgive the sins of any, their sins have been forgiven them; if you retain the sins of any, they have been retained." But Thomas, one of the twelve, called Didymus, was not with them when Jesus came. So the other disciples were saying to him, "We have seen the Lord!" But he said to them, "Unless I see in His hands the imprint of the nails, and put my finger into the place of the nails, and put my hand into His side, I will not believe." After eight days His disciples were again inside, and Thomas with them. Jesus came, the doors having been shut, and stood in their midst and said, "Peace be with you." Then He said to Thomas, "Reach here with your finger, and see My hands; and reach here your hand and put it into My side; and do not be unbelieving, but believing." Thomas answered and said to Him, "My Lord and my God!" Jesus said to him, "Because you have seen Me, have you believed? Blessed are they who did not see, and yet believed." Therefore many other signs Jesus also performed in the presence of the disciples, which are not written in this book; but these have been written so that you may believe that Jesus is the Christ, the Son of God; and that believing you may have life in His name. (20:11–31)

The resurrection of the Lord Jesus Christ was the divine affirmation of His atonement accomplished at the cross. When God raised Jesus from the dead, He declared that He was propitiated by Jesus' sacrifice, and had accepted it as payment in full for the sins of His people, completely satisfying the demands of His holy justice. Jesus was, Paul wrote, "delivered over because of our transgressions, and was raised because of our justification" (Rom. 4:25). The resurrection also demonstrated that where sin is atoned for, death is conquered and eternal life is given.

It is impossible to believe in the Jesus of the Bible without believing that He rose bodily from the dead. To reject His resurrection is to invent another Jesus, a pseudo-Christ of unbelieving imagination (2 Cor. 11:4). It is to call God a liar by refusing to believe His testimony concerning Jesus, "who was declared the Son of God with power by the resurrection from the dead" (Rom. 1:4). Those who reject the resurrection of the Lord Jesus Christ remain outside the sphere of salvation, for as Paul wrote in Romans 10:9, it is only "if you confess with your mouth Jesus as

Lord, and believe in your heart that God raised Him from the dead, [that] you will be saved."

Jesus Himself offered His resurrection as convincing, irrefutable proof that His claims to deity were true. Confronted by

> some of the scribes and Pharisees [who] said to Him, "Teacher, we want to see a sign from You." [Jesus] answered and said to them, "An evil and adulterous generation craves for a sign; and yet no sign will be given to it but the sign of Jonah the prophet; for just as Jonah was three days and three nights in the belly of the sea monster, so will the Son of Man be three days and three nights in the heart of the earth." (Matt. 12:38–40)

On another occasion

> The Jews . . . said to Him, "What sign do You show us as your authority for doing these things? [His cleansing of the temple]" Jesus answered them, "Destroy this temple, and in three days I will raise it up." The Jews then said, "It took forty-six years to build this temple, and will You raise it up in three days?" But He was speaking of the temple of His body. So when He was raised from the dead, His disciples remembered that He said this; and they believed the Scripture and the word which Jesus had spoken. (John 2:18–22)

Therefore to deny Christ's resurrection is to make Him a liar.

Further, since the resurrection is essential to the Christian gospel and salvation, denying that Christ rose from the dead renders any professed belief in Him meaningless and absurd. To the Corinthians, being seduced by the damning lies of resurrection-denying false teachers, Paul wrote,

> If Christ has not been raised, then our preaching is vain, your faith also is vain....For if the dead are not raised, not even Christ has been raised; and if Christ has not been raised, your faith is worthless; you are still in your sins. Then those also who have fallen asleep in Christ have perished. If we have hoped in Christ in this life only, we are of all men most to be pitied. (1 Cor. 15:14, 16–19)

To deny the resurrection is also to fly in the face of the overwhelming historical evidence that affirms it. The indisputable facts are that Jesus died, was buried, and three days later His tomb was found empty because He was alive. The only plausible interpretation of the historical record is that Jesus rose from the dead, as the Bible claims. Yet throughout history there have been skeptics, representing "doctrines of demons" (1 Tim. 4:1), who have denied the resurrection. The issue is not lack of evidence, but stubborn unbelief driven by the love of sin. People are unwilling to accept the inescapable consequence of the resurrection; namely, that

Christ is God, the God of Scripture, and they are accountable for every violation of His law and in need of His grace. Thus sinful men, in an irrational
effort to evade their guilt and accountability to the one true God, have concocted various theories in a futile attempt to explain away the reality of the
resurrection.

A favorite of eighteenth- and nineteenth-century rationalists, the
swoon theory argues that Jesus did not really die on the cross. Instead,
He went into a semicoma due to shock and loss of blood. In that condition He appeared to be dead, and so was taken down from the cross and
buried while still alive. Later, the spices and the coolness of the tomb
revived Him. Jesus then left the tomb, met the disciples, and they mistakenly assumed He had risen from the dead.

This theory faces insurmountable difficulties. In the first place
the Roman soldiers who crucified Jesus were experienced executioners,
who knew when a person was dead. They were satisfied that Jesus had
died, because they did not break His legs (John 19:33). Their commander reported to Pilate that Jesus was dead (Mark 15:44–45). Obviously,
the centurion would have made certain of that fact before making his
report to the governor. Further, the spear thrust into Jesus' side that
brought forth blood and water showed clearly that He was dead (see the
discussion of 19:34 in the previous chapter of this volume).

The swoon theory also fails to explain how Jesus, weakened by
the brutal scourging he received and the punishing effects of being crucified, could have survived for three days without food, water, and medical care. Nor does it explain how a man in such a weakened state could
have freed himself from the grave clothes in which his body was
wrapped (something Lazarus was unable to do; John 11:44), moved the
heavy stone that sealed the tomb, overpowered the Roman guard
detachment, and walked several miles to Emmaus on nail-pierced feet.
Most important of all, the swoon theory cannot explain how such a half-
dead individual, desperately in need of triage, could have persuaded the
disciples that He was the risen Lord, the conqueror of death and the
grave. This theory also blasphemes Jesus by making Him into a deceiver
and a fraud, which is to reject the testimony of the Father and Scripture
that He lived a sinless life (Luke 1:35; 3:22; John 8:46; 14:30; 15:10; 2 Cor.
5:21; Heb. 4:15; 7:26; 1 Peter 2:22).

No less far-fetched is the hallucination theory. Its proponents
argue that Jesus' followers, overwhelmed by grief and sorrow, wanted so
desperately for Him to be resurrected that they had hallucinations of
seeing Him alive. Hallucinations are private, individual experiences.
Jesus, however, appeared to various individuals and groups on at least
ten different occasions, including more than five hundred people at
once (1 Cor. 15:6). Nor were the disciples likely candidates for such hallu-

cinations, since they were not expecting Jesus to rise from the dead (John 20:9) and actually scoffed at the initial reports that He had (Luke 24:11). This theory also fails to explain why on at least three occasions the people allegedly having hallucinations of Jesus did not recognize Him (Luke 24:13–31; John 20:15; 21:4). Nor can it explain how a hallucination could eat a piece of fish (Luke 24:42–43), point out a school of fish (John 21:6), or cook a meal (John 21:9–13). And while it purports to account for Christ's resurrection appearances, it fails to account for the empty tomb and the missing body.

Another academic liberal, Kirsopp Lake, argued that the women mistakenly went to the wrong tomb (even though two of them had watched Jesus being buried; Mark 15:47). Finding it empty, they erroneously assumed that Jesus had risen from the dead. But that means that Peter and John must have also gone to the wrong tomb. And surely Joseph of Arimathea and Nicodemus, who buried Jesus, knew which tomb they had put His body in. Obviously the Jewish leaders also knew which tomb was the right one, since they had sealed it and posted a Roman guard outside of it. Why did someone not simply go to the right tomb and produce Jesus' body?

Still other pseudoscholars argue that the tomb was empty because Jesus was never buried in it. Instead, they posit, His body was taken down from the cross and thrown into a common criminal grave. This theory fails to explain why the Gospels say that Jesus was buried in Joseph of Arimathea's tomb, and why history records no other burial story. Nor could the disciples have invented the story that a member of the Sanhedrin had buried Jesus, if in fact he had not; Joseph would have promptly debunked it. And when the disciples began proclaiming that Jesus had risen from the dead, why did whoever had disposed of His body not simply retrieve it?

The oldest denial of Christ's resurrection was invented by the Jewish authorities. As Matthew 28:11–15 records, they claimed that the disciples stole Jesus' body from the tomb. It should be noted first of all that their claim is a tacit admission that the tomb was empty, and that they did not know where the body was. William Lane Craig writes,

> The point is that the Jews did not respond to the preaching of the resurrection by pointing to the tomb of Jesus or exhibiting his corpse, but entangled themselves in a hopeless series of absurdities trying to explain away his empty tomb. The fact that the enemies of Christianity felt obliged to explain away the empty tomb by the theft hypothesis shows not only that the tomb was known (confirmation of the burial story), but that it was empty. . . . The fact that the Jewish polemic never denied that Jesus' tomb was empty, but only tried to explain it away is compelling evidence that the tomb was in fact empty. ("The Historicity

of the Empty Tomb of Jesus," http://www.leaderu.com/offices/billcraig/docs/tomb2.html; accessed 11 October 2007)

Despite its antiquity, this theory fares no better than the other attempts to explain away the resurrection. In the first place, since the disciples were not expecting Christ to rise from the dead (John 20:9; cf. Luke 24:9–11), why would they have faked His resurrection? Further, they had fled when Jesus was arrested (Matt. 26:56); their leader, Peter, had denied Him, and they had gone into hiding out of fear of the Jewish authorities (John 20:19). To have taken on a Roman guard detachment and committed the serious crime of robbing a tomb would have required far more courage than this demoralized, doubt-filled, fearful group possessed. It is hard to see how the disciples, if they stole Jesus' body and fabricated the story of His resurrection, benefitted from it. To assume they would have willingly endured persecution and suffered martyrdom (as most of them did) for what they knew to be a lie is ridiculous.

If the disciples did not steal the body, then perhaps, some argue, the Romans, Jews, or unknown grave robbers did. But the Romans would have had no conceivable motive for taking Christ's body; Pilate would hardly have risked antagonizing the Jews by doing so. Nor would the Jews have taken the body; the last thing they wanted was to fuel speculation that Jesus had risen from the dead (cf. Matt. 27:62–66). But if either the Romans or the Jews had the body, why did they not produce it when the disciples boldly proclaimed the resurrection in the streets of Jerusalem a few weeks later? As noted in the previous chapter of this volume, grave robbers would not have unwrapped the body, left the valuable spices behind, or taken the time to neatly arrange the wrappings before they left. Nor would they have attempted to break into a tomb guarded by Roman soldiers.

The appearances Christ made after He rose from the dead provide the most convincing proof of the resurrection. Scripture records at least ten distinct appearances of Christ between the resurrection and the ascension: to Mary Magdalene (John 20:11–18), to other women who had been at the tomb (Matt. 28:8–10), to two disciples on the road to Emmaus (Luke 24:13–32), to Peter (Luke 24:34), to ten of the eleven remaining apostles, Thomas being absent (Luke 24:36–43; John 20:19–25), to all eleven apostles, with Thomas present (John 20:26–31), to seven of the apostles on the shore of the Sea of Galilee (John 21:1–25), to more than five hundred disciples, probably on a mountain in Galilee (1 Cor. 15:7), to James (1 Cor. 15:7), and to the apostles when He ascended to heaven (Acts 1:3–11). In addition, the risen Christ later appeared to Saul of Tarsus on the road to Damascus (Acts 9:1–9), and several subsequent occasions (Acts 18:9; 22:17–18; 23:11).

It is significant to note that all of the Lord's postresurrection appearances were to believers (except Paul, who was not yet a believer when He appeared to him the first time). His normal method of reaching the lost is not through performing spectacular miracles, such as personally appearing to them, but through the witness of His church in the power of His Spirit (Matt. 28:19–20; Acts 1:8). Nor would such miracles convince unbelievers anyway. "But though He had performed so many signs before them," John noted, "yet they were not believing in Him" (John 12:37). Even a resurrection appearance would not convince hardened unbelievers, since those who "do not listen to Moses and the Prophets,…will not be persuaded even if someone rises from the dead" (Luke 16:31).

Out of all of Christ's postresurrection appearances, John selected three that give special insights into the person of Jesus Christ: to Mary Magdalene, to the ten apostles (without Thomas), and to all eleven apostles (specifically to Thomas).

CHRIST'S APPEARANCE TO MARY MAGDALENE

But Mary was standing outside the tomb weeping; and so, as she wept, she stooped and looked into the tomb; and she saw two angels in white sitting, one at the head and one at the feet, where the body of Jesus had been lying. And they said to her, "Woman, why are you weeping?" She said to them, "Because they have taken away my Lord, and I do not know where they have laid Him." When she had said this, she turned around and saw Jesus standing there, and did not know that it was Jesus. Jesus said to her, "Woman, why are you weeping? Whom are you seeking?" Supposing Him to be the gardener, she said to Him, "Sir, if you have carried Him away, tell me where you have laid Him, and I will take Him away." Jesus said to her, "Mary!" She turned and said to Him in Hebrew, "Rabboni!" (which means, Teacher). Jesus said to her, "Stop clinging to Me, for I have not yet ascended to the Father; but go to My brethren and say to them, 'I ascend to My Father and your Father, and My God and your God.'" Mary Magdalene came, announcing to the disciples, "I have seen the Lord," and that He had said these things to her. (20:11–18)

The Lord's appearance to Mary, the woman from the village of Magdala on the western shore of the Sea of Galilee near Tiberias, symbolizes His special love and faithfulness to all believers, no matter how seemingly insignificant they might be. Mary was not a prominent figure in the gospel accounts; before the crucifixion she appeared only as a name in the list of women who traveled with Jesus and the apostles (Luke 8:2). Yet the Lord chose to appear first to her, a woman, as He had first declared His messiahship to the woman at the well (John 4:28–29).

After Peter and John left (20:10), **Mary** returned and **was standing outside the tomb.** As noted in the discussion of 20:1 in the previous chapter of this volume, Mary apparently had arrived at the tomb before the other women. Seeing that the stone had been removed, she feared that grave robbers had broken in and stolen Jesus' body. She immediately ran and reported the news to Peter and John. Driven by an overwhelming sense of grief and loss, Mary then returned to the tomb. But by the time she did so, the two apostles had come and gone. She did not cross paths with them or the other women on her way back to the tomb, and so did not know about the undisturbed grave clothes or the angels' message.

Disconsolate, Mary stood there **weeping** uncontrollably. Her love for the Lord was greater than her faith in His promise to rise again. Despite her weak faith, however, Jesus would not leave her in sorrow (cf. 16:20–22). At last, while **she** still **wept, she stooped and looked into the tomb.** Like the other women (Luke 24:1–7), **she saw two angels in white sitting, one at the head and one at the feet, where the body of Jesus had been lying.** She could not recognize them as angels, since they had assumed human form (Mark 16:5; Luke 24:4). Their question to her, **"Woman, why are you weeping?"** was a gentle rebuke. The time for mourning was over; the sorrow of death was forever shattered by the joyous reality of the resurrection.

Plaintively, she addressed them, unaware of who they were and **said to them, "Because they have taken away my Lord, and I do not know where they have laid Him."** Mary's despair stemmed from not knowing where the Lord's body was. She believed He was still dead, and she had come back now that the Sabbath was over (Matt. 28:1; Mark 16:1) to finish burial preparations for His body. But as she was about to discover, that task was not necessary.

How Mary suddenly became aware of Jesus' presence is not stated. Perhaps, as some have suggested, the angels gestured toward Him. In any case, **she turned around and saw Jesus standing there.** But her perplexity continued, since she **did not know that it was Jesus.** Jesus' resurrection body was more glorious than before and certainly did not match her vivid memories of Him, especially the battered, bruised, bloody corpse she had seen on the cross. There have been several suggestions for her failure to recognize the Lord. She was sure that He was dead, so the last thing she expected was to see Him alive. Further, her eyes may have been blurred from tears. Moreover she, like the others, was prevented from recognizing Him until He chose to reveal Himself to her (cf. 21:4; Luke 24:16).

Repeating the question asked by the angels, **Jesus said to her, "Woman, why are you weeping?** then added, **"Whom are you seeking?"** Reflecting her continued confusion, she, assuming **Him to be the gardener, said to Him, "Sir, if you have carried Him away, tell me where you have laid Him, and I will take Him away."** In her single-minded devotion, Mary simply wanted to ensure that Jesus' body had a proper burial—even if it meant moving His body by herself.

With a single word, Jesus opened Mary's eyes. He merely spoke her name (cf. 10:3–4, 27), **"Mary!"** and in a flash all of her doubt, confusion, and sorrow vanished. Recognizing Jesus in that moment, **she turned and said to Him in Hebrew, "Rabboni!" (which means, Teacher). Rabboni** is a strengthened form of "Rabbi," and was used as a title to express great honor and supreme reverence (cf. Mark 10:51). Overcome with a profound mix of joy and relief, Mary fell at His feet. Like the other women had done (Matt. 28:9), she clung to Jesus, prompting Him to say to her, **Stop clinging to Me, for I have not yet ascended to the Father.** Having found Him again beyond her wildest hopes, she did not want to lose Him. Her physical grasp symbolized her desire to secure His presence permanently. But He would be physically present for only a brief time, forty days (Acts 1:3), after which He would ascend to the Father. How much knowledge she had of what Jesus had promised in the upper room is not known. But perhaps she had been told by the apostles that He said He was going to the Father to send the Holy Spirit (14:16–18; 16:7), so He said nothing about that, only that He could not stay, but must ascend.

The Lord then sent Mary to the apostles to tell them of His impending ascension: **Go to My brethren and say to them, "I ascend to My Father and your Father, and My God and your God."** For the first time the disciples, who had been referred to as slaves or friends (15:15), are called Christ's **brethren.** It was through His work of redemption on the cross that this new relationship with Him was made possible. It is "in Him we have redemption through His blood, the forgiveness of our trespasses, according to the riches of His grace" (Eph. 1:7). God adopts as His sons (Rom. 8:14–15; Eph. 1:5) those who believe savingly in Jesus Christ (Gal. 3:26). As a result, Jesus "is not ashamed to call them brethren" (Heb. 2:11), and has become "the firstborn among many brethren" (Rom. 8:29). Reflecting this new relationship, the Lord's message to the disciples referred to **My Father and your Father, and My God and your God.**

Excitedly, **Mary Magdalene came, announcing to the disciples, "I have seen the Lord," and that He had said these things to**

her. Predictably, they responded with the same dubiousness with which they had greeted the testimony of the other women who had been at the tomb. Luke reports that they considered the report as "nonsense" and they "would not believe them" (24:11).

CHRIST'S APPEARANCE TO TEN OF THE DISCIPLES

So when it was evening on that day, the first day of the week, and when the doors were shut where the disciples were, for fear of the Jews, Jesus came and stood in their midst and said to them, "Peace be with you." And when He had said this, He showed them both His hands and His side. The disciples then rejoiced when they saw the Lord. So Jesus said to them again, "Peace be with you; as the Father has sent Me, I also send you." And when He had said this, He breathed on them and said to them, "Receive the Holy Spirit. If you forgive the sins of any, their sins have been forgiven them; if you retain the sins of any, they have been retained." (20:19–23)

The scene now shifts to the **evening on that** very resurrection Sunday (for a discussion of the significance of **the first day of the week,** see the exposition of 20:1 in the previous chapter of this volume). The **disciples** (minus Thomas) had gathered together in an unspecified location (possibly the upper room in Jerusalem, scene of the Last Supper) and the **doors were shut** (the Gk. verb can also mean "locked"). The disciples were in hiding **for fear of the Jews,** expecting any minute that the temple police would arrive to end this whole movement by arresting them. The authorities had executed their Master, and not unreasonably they feared they would be next.

Suddenly, something happened that was far more startling than the arrival of the temple police: **Jesus came and stood in their midst.** The locked doors were no deterrent to Him; His glorified resurrection body simply passed through the walls. The words He spoke **to them, "Peace be with you"** (cf. 14:27), were intended to calm and reassure the terrified disciples, who thought they were seeing a ghost (Luke 24:37; cf. Matt. 14:26). They also complemented His words on the cross, "It is finished!" (John 19:30), since it was His work on the cross that brought about peace between God and His people (Rom. 5:1; Eph. 2:14–18). To reassure them that it was really Him, Jesus **showed them both His hands and His side.** Luke records that He said to them, "See My hands and My feet, that it is I Myself; touch Me and see, for a spirit does not have flesh and bones as you see that I have" (Luke 24:39). Recognizing Him at last, **the disciples then rejoiced when they saw the Lord**—but not before He offered a conclusive proof that He was not a spirit by eating a piece of broiled fish (Luke 24:41–43).

With the disciples at last convinced that He had risen from the dead, the Lord proceeded to give them instructions and promise them empowerment. In a preview of the Great Commission He would give them later in Galilee (Matt. 28:19–20), Jesus charged the disciples, **"as the Father has sent Me, I also send you"** (cf. 17:18). Having formally *commissioned* the disciples, Christ ceremonially *empowered* them as a pledge of the power they were actually to receive on Pentecost forty days later (Acts 2:1–4). Signifying that coming reality, **He breathed on them, and said to them, "Receive the Holy Spirit."** This was a purely symbolic and prophetic act, reminiscent of the vivid object lessons frequently employed by Old Testament prophets to illustrate their messages (cf. Jer. 13:1–9; 19:1–11; Ezek. 4:1–4). In other words, Christ did not through this puff of breath actually and literally impart the Spirit in His fullness to them; rather, He declared in a visible figure what would happen to them at Pentecost.

Ten of the original Twelve were present. Judas was already dead by his own treacherous hand (Matt. 27:5). Thomas was the only other member of the original Twelve not present here. These disciples, of course, were already regenerate men (John 15:3). So the fact that they still were waiting to **receive the Holy Spirit** indicates that the Spirit's relationship to individual believers in the new covenant era is profoundly different from His Old Testament ministry. Under the new covenant, every believer is permanently indwelt (1 Cor. 6:19), empowered (Acts 1:8), and gifted (1 Cor. 12:4–11) by the Holy Spirit. Under the old covenant, the Holy Spirit's ministry to individual saints was not so universally personal and prominent. Jesus' actions here indicated the outpouring of the Holy Spirit that was about to occur, completing the transition between the two covenants.

The Gospels are clear that heretofore "the Spirit was not yet given" (cf. John 7:39)—meaning that the new era had not yet been inaugurated. It is likewise clear that the Holy Spirit's new covenant work did not actually commence until Pentecost. All of Scripture affirms the chronology. Jesus Himself expressly said the Spirit would not be given until after His ascension (John 16:17). But "when He ascended on high ... He gave gifts to men" (Eph. 4:8; cf. Ps. 68:18). The Spirit was "poured out upon us from on high" (Isa. 32:15). In fact, on the very day of His ascension, Jesus told the apostles to *wait* for the Spirit to come upon them (Acts 1:8). When they finally did **receive the Holy Spirit,** the result was an immediate, public, and dramatic outpouring of miraculous power (Acts 2:33).

When Jesus **breathed on them** at this point, however, it was a powerful illustration, rich with meaning—because the Holy Spirit is pictured in Ezekiel 37:9–14 as God's breath. So the gesture was an emphatic affirmation of Christ's deity, making His own breath emblematic of the breath of God. It was also reminiscent of the way God first "breathed into [Adam's] nostrils the breath of life" (Gen. 2:7)—thus picturing the impartation of new life through regeneration (the second birth), which under the new covenant is always accompanied by the impartation of the Spirit (Ezek. 36:26-27). The simple act of breathing on the disciples was thus a meaningful emblem on multiple levels. Since then, every Christian has received the Holy Spirit at the moment of salvation (Rom. 8:9).

As part of their witness to Him, the disciples would have His authority delegated to them. **"If you forgive the sins of any, their sins have been forgiven them,"** Jesus told them, but **"if you retain the sins of any, they have been retained."** This verse has been misinterpreted by Roman Catholics to mean that the Roman Catholic Church has had the apostles' authority to forgive sins passed down to it. But Scripture teaches that God alone can forgive sins (Mark 2:7; cf. Dan. 9:9). Nor does the New Testament record any instances of the apostles (or anyone else) absolving people of their sins. Further, this promise was not made to the apostles alone, since others were also present (Luke 24:33). What Christ was actually saying is that any Christian can declare that those who genuinely repent and believe the gospel will have their sins forgiven by God. On the other hand, they can warn that those who reject Jesus Christ will die in their sins (8:24; Heb. 10:26–27).

This was not new information to the disciples, since the Lord had spoken very similar words long before in Caesarea Philippi: "I will give you the keys of the kingdom of heaven; and whatever you bind on earth shall have been bound in heaven, and whatever you loose on earth shall have been loosed in heaven" (Matt. 16:19).

Here Jesus spoke of the delegated authority of believers. He told Peter, the Twelve, and by extension all believers, that they had the authority to declare who is bound in sin and who is loosed from sin. He said believers have the "keys of the kingdom," the realm of salvation, because they have the gospel truth that saves (Rom. 1:16; 1 Cor. 1:18–25). Christians can declare that a sinner is forgiven or unforgiven based on how that sinner responds to the gospel of salvation.

The church's authority to tell someone that he is forgiven or that he is still in sin comes directly from the Word of God. In Matthew 18:15–20, the Lord taught His disciples (and by extension all believers) that if a professing believer refuses to turn from his or her sin, even after being privately confronted (vv. 15–16) and publicly rebuked (v. 17), then the church is commanded to treat that individual as an unbeliever. Those within the church have both the authority and the obligation to call the sinning brother back to repentance (vv. 18–20), and to let him know that because of his blatant disregard for the Word of God, he has subsequently forfeited fellowship with the people of God. The reality is that he may not be a child of God at all (John 8:42; 14:15; 2 Cor. 13:5; 1 John 2:3–6).

Believers have the authority to do this because God has given them His Word as the supreme standard by which to judge. Their authority does not come from anything within them; it is not founded on their own personal righteousness, spiritual giftedness, or ecclesiastical position. Instead it comes from the authoritative Word of God.

That which the Scriptures affirm, Christians can dogmatically and unhesitatingly affirm; that which the Scriptures denounce, Christians can authoritatively and unapologetically denounce. Believers do not decide what is right or wrong, but they are to declare with boldness that which God has clearly revealed in His Word. Because the Scriptures present sin as an affront to God, His people must be faithful to confront it. Insofar as their judgment corresponds to the Scriptures, they can be certain that it harmonizes with God's judgment in heaven.

When people reject the saving message of the gospel, denying the person and work of Jesus Christ, the church has divine authority, based on the revealed Word of God, to tell them that they will perish in hell unless they repent (Luke 13:1–5; cf. John 3:18; 1 Cor. 16:22). Conversely, when people profess faith in Christ as their Savior and Lord, the church can affirm that profession, if it is genuine, with equal confidence—based on passages like Romans 10:9, "If you confess with your mouth Jesus as Lord, and believe in your heart that God raised Him from the dead, you will be saved."

The church's authority comes from the Scriptures. Because Christ is the head of the church (Eph. 1:22; 5:23), the Word of Christ (Col. 3:16) is the supreme authority within the church. When believers act and speak in accord with His Word, they can do so knowing that He stands in agreement with them.

CHRIST'S APPEARANCE TO THOMAS

But Thomas, one of the twelve, called Didymus, was not with them when Jesus came. So the other disciples were saying to him, "We have seen the Lord!" But he said to them, "Unless I see in His hands the imprint of the nails, and put my finger into the place of the nails, and put my hand into His side, I will not believe." After eight days His disciples were again inside, and Thomas with them. Jesus came, the doors having been shut, and stood in their midst and said, "Peace be with you." Then He said to Thomas,

"Reach here with your finger, and see My hands; and reach here your hand and put it into My side; and do not be unbelieving, but believing." Thomas answered and said to Him, "My Lord and my God!" Jesus said to him, "Because you have seen Me, have you believed? Blessed are they who did not see, and yet believed." Therefore many other signs Jesus also performed in the presence of the disciples, which are not written in this book; but these have been written so that you may believe that Jesus is the Christ, the Son of God; and that believing you may have life in His name. (20:24–31)

Not all of the apostles had been present at Jesus' first appearance. **Thomas, one of the twelve, called Didymus, was not with them when Jesus came. Thomas** was nicknamed **Didymus,** ("Twin") for the obvious reason that he had a twin (who does not appear in Scripture). The Synoptic Gospels mention him only in the lists of the twelve apostles; the details of his character come from John's gospel.

Thomas was the eternal pessimist. Like Eeyore in the Winnie the Pooh stories, he was a melancholy person, with an uncanny knack for finding the dark cloud in every silver lining. Thomas first appears in John's gospel in connection with the story of the raising of Lazarus. Aghast that Jesus planned to return to the vicinity of Jerusalem, where the Jews had recently tried to kill Him (11:8), Thomas exclaimed fatalistically, "Let us also go, so that we may die with Him" (v. 16). But Thomas's pessimism should not be allowed to obscure his courage; though he thought the situation was hopeless, he nonetheless was willing to lay his life on the line for the Lord. His love for Jesus was so strong that he would have preferred to die with Him rather than to be separated from Him.

Thomas next appears in the upper room. Jesus had just announced His imminent departure (14:2–3), and reminded the disciples that they knew where He was going. Heartbroken that Jesus was leaving, Thomas promptly contradicted Him, saying despondently, "Lord, we do not know where You are going, how do we know the way?" (14:5), suggesting such devotion that he seemed to think it would be better to die with his Lord than to try to find Him later. Such was his love for Christ.

It is too bad that Thomas missed the Lord's appearance. Why was he not there? Was it due to his being negative, pessimistic, even melancholy? Was he off somewhere feeling sorry for himself because his worst fear had come true?

Thomas may have felt alone, betrayed, forsaken. His hopes may have been crushed. The One he had loved so greatly was gone and his heart was irreparably torn. He may not have been in a socializing mood.

Maybe being alone seemed best. He could not be in a crowd, even with his friends.

But when Thomas returned from wherever he had been, **the other disciples were** exuberantly and eagerly **saying to him, "We have seen the Lord!"** But he would have none of it. Thomas was certain he would never see Jesus again. He refused to get his hopes up, only to have them dashed once more, so he announced skeptically, **"Unless I see in His hands the imprint of the nails, and put my finger into the place of the nails, and put my hand into His side, I will not believe."** It was that remark that earned him the nickname "Doubting Thomas." But the track record of the other ten apostles was no better; they too had scoffed at the initial reports of the resurrection (Mark 16:10–13; Luke 24:9–11) and failed to believe the Scriptures that predicted it (20:9; Luke 24:25–26). What made Thomas different was not that his doubt was greater, but that his sorrow was greater.

Thomas would soon be taken up on his skeptical offer. **After eight days** the **disciples were again inside,** but this time **Thomas** was **with them.** Once again, the doors had been shut, and once again that proved to be no deterrent to the risen Lord. As He had done eight days earlier, **Jesus came** in **and stood in their midst.** He immediately singled out Thomas. Ever the sympathetic High Priest (Heb. 4:15), Jesus gently, lovingly, compassionately **said to** him, **"Reach here with your finger, and see My hands; and reach here your hand and put it into My side; and do not be unbelieving, but believing."** The Lord met Thomas at the point of his weakness and doubt, without rebuke because He knew Thomas's error was connected to his profound love. In patient compassion, He gave Thomas the empirical proof he had demanded.

That was enough for the doubter; his melancholy skepticism dissolved forever in light of the irrefutable evidence in the person confronting him. Overwhelmed, he made perhaps the greatest confession of any of the apostles, rivaled only by Peter's confession of Jesus as the Messiah (Matt. 16:16), exclaiming, **"My Lord and my God!"** Significantly, Jesus did not correct him, but accepted Thomas's affirmation of His deity. Indeed, He praised Thomas for his faith, saying **to him, "Because you have seen Me, have you believed?"** But looking ahead to the time when the tangible, physical evidence Thomas had witnessed would no longer be available, the Lord pronounced those **"blessed . . . who did not see, and yet believed"** (cf. 2 Cor. 5:7; 1 Peter 1:8–9). They, who will never see physical evidence of Christ's rising, will have a greater measure of the Holy Spirit to empower faith in the resurrection. This is the second beatitude in this gospel (cf. 13:17). **Blessed** does not just convey a condition of happiness, but also declares the recipient to be accepted by God.

It must be noted that our Lord's words do not indicate anything defective about the faith of Thomas.

> Thomas's faith is not depreciated ..."but for the fact that Thomas and the other apostles saw the incarnate Christ there would have been no Christian faith at all. Cf. 1:18, 50f.; 2:11; 4:45; 6:2; 9:37; 14:7, 9; 19:35" (Barrett, p. 573)....later believers come to faith through the word of the earlier believers (17:20). Blessed, then, are those who cannot share Thomas' experience of sight, but who, in part because they read of Thomas' experience, come to share Thomas' faith. (D. A. Carson, *The Gospel According to John*, The Pillar New Testament Commentary (Grand Rapids: Eerdmans, 1991), 660)

Thomas's confession and Christ's response are a fitting lead in to John's summary statement of his goal and purpose in writing his gospel: **Therefore many other signs Jesus also performed in the presence of the disciples, which are not written in this book** (cf. 12:37; 21:25). Those who have not and will not see the Lord risen will depend on this gospel penned by John (as well as the other three) to provide the word concerning Christ by which the Spirit can give them regeneration and faith (Rom. 10:17).

And there are many more miraculous **signs** that Jesus did beyond the miracles recorded in chapters 2–12 (and the other Gospels), including the greatest sign—His resurrection—but they are not necessary because what has been written is sufficient. This statement establishes that this gospel of John is about the miraculous signs pointing to Jesus as Christ and Lord—for the purpose John explicitly expresses in the next statement.

But these have been written so that you may believe that Jesus is the Christ, the Son of God; and that believing you may have life in His name. As has been said, to expand this verse one need only to go back through the whole gospel. This is the summary statement. To believe that Jesus Christ is God incarnate (1:1, 14), the Lamb of God who takes away the sin of the world (1:29), and the resurrection and the life (11:25) is to believe that truth that when accepted provides forgiveness of sin and eternal life (3:16). John's purpose is clearly evangelistic. Again, Carson aptly unifies the thought:

> John's purpose is not academic. He writes in order that men and women may believe certain propositional truth, the truth that the Christ, the Son of God, is Jesus, the Jesus whose portrait is drawn in this Gospel. But such faith is not an end in itself. It is directed toward the goal of personal, eschatological salvation: *that by believing you may have life in his name.* That is still the purpose of this book today, and at the heart of the Christian mission (v. 21). (*John*, 663. Italics in original.)

Epilogue—Part 1: Self-effort or Spiritual Power? (John 21:1–14)

34

After these things Jesus manifested Himself again to the disciples at the Sea of Tiberias, and He manifested Himself in this way. Simon Peter, and Thomas called Didymus, and Nathanael of Cana in Galilee, and the sons of Zebedee, and two others of His disciples were together. Simon Peter said to them, "I am going fishing." They said to him, "We will also come with you." They went out and got into the boat; and that night they caught nothing. But when the day was now breaking, Jesus stood on the beach; yet the disciples did not know that it was Jesus. So Jesus said to them, "Children, you do not have any fish, do you?" They answered Him, "No." And He said to them, "Cast the net on the right-hand side of the boat and you will find a catch." So they cast, and then they were not able to haul it in because of the great number of fish. Therefore that disciple whom Jesus loved said to Peter, "It is the Lord." So when Simon Peter heard that it was the Lord, he put his outer garment on (for he was stripped for work), and threw himself into the sea. But the other disciples came in the little boat, for they were not far from the land, but about one hundred yards away, dragging the net full of fish. So when they got out on the land, they saw a charcoal fire already laid and fish

placed on it, and bread. Jesus said to them, "Bring some of the fish which you have now caught." Simon Peter went up and drew the net to land, full of large fish, a hundred and fifty-three; and although there were so many, the net was not torn. Jesus said to them, "Come and have breakfast." None of the disciples ventured to question Him, "Who are You?" knowing that it was the Lord. Jesus came and took the bread and gave it to them, and the fish likewise. This is now the third time that Jesus was manifested to the disciples, after He was raised from the dead. (21:1–14)

The main section of John's gospel ended at the close of chapter 20 with the apostle's summary statement of his purpose in writing. His goal was that his readers "may believe that Jesus is the Christ, the Son of God; and that believing [they] may have life in His name" (v. 31). Chapter 21 is an epilogue that, along with the prologue (1:1–18), bookends the main part of the gospel.

Some argue that John did not write this appendix, but insist that it was added later by one of his close associates. However there is no evidence that John's gospel ever circulated without chapter 21; all extant manuscripts include it. Nor is the epilogue superfluous; it serves as a fitting conclusion to this inspired gospel by answering a number of questions raised in readers' minds.

First, it answers the question of who would care for the disciples after Jesus returned to the Father and was no longer physically present.

Second, it brings closure to the story of Peter. He had denied Christ on the night of His arrest and was nowhere to be found at the crucifixion scene. Even after seeing the empty tomb, he was uncertain about what had really happened. The epilogue reveals that Peter's denial and doubt were not the end of his story by relating his reconciliation with Jesus and the recommissioning by Him.

Third, it addresses a false rumor that the apostle John would not die before the Lord's return.

Fourth, it explains why John did not include the "many other signs Jesus also performed" (20:30) in his gospel.

Fifth, it addresses the issue of the disciples' future now that they would be without their Master. Would He still protect them from the world?

Sixth, it reinforces the truth that the beloved disciple was none other than John himself.

Finally, "The presence of an epilogue seems required by the opening prologue in order to preserve balance and symmetry of structure. . . . Hence both prologue and epilogue frame the Gospel in such a way that they form an integral part of the theological and literary fabric of the entire narrative" (Andreas J. Köstenberger, *John,* Baker Exegetical Commentary on the New Testament [Grand Rapids: Baker, 2004], 583–84).

The first fourteen verses of chapter 21 answer the first question, which was uppermost in the minds of the disciples. For the first time in more than three years, they faced having to fend for themselves, since Jesus had provided for all their needs while He was with them. The Lord made it clear that He would continue to do so. This time He demonstrated His commitment to meet their needs through a living illustration. But before the disciples learned the lesson that Christ would continue to provide for them, they first had to be brought face-to-face with their own inadequacy. As a result, the passage illustrates two contrasting dependencies from which they could choose. The disciples could depend on their former trades and pick up on life as they had left it before Jesus called them, or they could continue in gospel ministry dependant on His power and provision. These two options face those who belong to Christ: are we on our own, or do we follow Christ? The answer is given here.

HUMAN WEAKNESS AND FAILURE

After these things Jesus manifested Himself again to the disciples at the Sea of Tiberias, and He manifested Himself in this way. Simon Peter, and Thomas called Didymus, and Nathanael of Cana in Galilee, and the sons of Zebedee, and two others of His disciples were together. Simon Peter said to them, "I am going fishing." They said to him, "We will also come with you." They went out and got into the boat; and that night they caught nothing. But when the day was now breaking, Jesus stood on the beach; yet the disciples did not know that it was Jesus. So Jesus said to them, "Children, you do not have any fish, do you?" They answered Him, "No." (21:1–5)

The phrase **after these things** refers to an unspecified time after the events recorded in chapter 20. The disciples had left Jerusalem and made their way north to Galilee, as Jesus had commanded them (Matt. 28:10, 16; Mark 14:28; 16:7). Apparently, all eleven did not travel together in one group, since this incident involved only seven of them. The twice-repeated statement that **Jesus manifested Himself . . . to the disciples** emphasizes the truth that after His resurrection He was not recognizable unless He revealed Himself (cf. 20:14). What was true of physically recognizing Jesus is also true spiritually. No one, apart from the leading of the Holy Spirit, can call Jesus Lord (1 Cor. 12:3), because "a natural man does not accept the things of the Spirit of God, for they are foolishness to him;

and he cannot understand them, because they are spiritually appraised"
(1 Cor. 2:14). Since "there is none who seeks for God" (Rom. 3:11), it was
necessary for "the Son of Man [to] come to seek and to save that which
was lost" (Luke 19:10). Apart from such seeking, the gospel remains foolishness (1 Cor. 1:18, 30–31).

The Sea of Tiberias is better known as the Sea of Galilee. The
Bible also refers to it as the Sea of Chinnereth (Num. 34:11; Josh. 13:27),
the Sea of Chinneroth (Josh. 12:3), and the Lake of Gennesaret (Luke
5:1). By the time John wrote his gospel, it had become commonly known
as the **Sea of Tiberias.** That name came from the city of Tiberias on its
western shore, which had been founded by Herod Antipas and named in
honor of Emperor Tiberius (cf. Luke 3:1).

The seven apostles involved in this incident were **Simon Peter**
(here, as always, listed first, indicating his general leadership of the apostles) **and Thomas called Didymus, and Nathanael of Cana in
Galilee, and the sons of Zebedee,** along with **two others of His disciples** (most likely Andrew and Philip, who had close ties to Peter and
the sons of Zebedee [cf. 1:40, 44], and who always appear elsewhere in
connection with the apostles named in this passage).

The first hint that all was not quite right was the disciples' location. They were no longer at the mountain where Jesus had specifically
commanded them to wait for Him (Matt. 28:16), but had gone down to
the lake. **Simon Peter** evidently grew impatient waiting for the Lord to
appear and impulsively **said to** the other six, **"I am going fishing."**
Peter was an impulsive man of action, not given to standing idly by for
very long. He was not suggesting that they do some recreational fishing
to pass the time, but rather was declaring that he was returning to his former livelihood. Three lines of evidence support that conclusion. In 16:32
Jesus had predicted that the disciples would abandon Him: "Behold, an
hour is coming, and has already come, for you to be scattered, each to his
own home." The word "home" was added by the translators; the Greek text
reads simply, "his own," which encompasses one's home, property, possessions, and affairs (cf. 1 Thess. 4:11 where the same Greek phrase is translated "your own business"). Christ's prediction thus implies more than
that the disciples would return to their own houses. Second, the use of
the definite article with the noun translated **boat** suggests a specific
boat, probably one belonging to one of the disciples (or even Peter himself). Finally, the Lord's challenge to Peter in verse 15, "Simon, son of
John, do you love Me more than these?" is best interpreted when "these" is
seen as a reference to the boats, nets, and other paraphernalia associated
with his fishing business. The Lord was calling Peter to turn his back on
his former livelihood and be totally committed to serving Him. (See the
discussion of v. 15 in chapter 35 of this volume.)

Dutifully following Peter's regressive lead, the rest of the disciples **said to him, "We will also come with you."** Certainly feeling inadequate to carry on any spiritual ministry on behalf of the kingdom of God, they were sure fishing was something they could do successfully. The seven **went out and got into the boat** and began fishing. As experienced fishermen, they knew that the nighttime was best for catching fish on the Sea of Galilee (cf. Luke 5:5), but **that night they caught nothing.** The disciples' unsuccessful experience at something they knew how to do well was a lesson from the Lord about their inability to go back to their former lives. There is nothing wrong with fishing; it was a respectable profession. But it was not what the Lord had called them to do. They were chosen to be fishers of men (Matt. 4:19), and having "left their nets and followed Him" (v. 20; cf. Luke 9:23), there was no going back.

After a useless night of fishing, **when the day was now breaking,** the disciples headed back to shore, where **Jesus stood on the beach** waiting for them. As noted above, no one could recognize the Lord after His resurrection unless He revealed Himself to them. Thus, **the disciples did not know that it was Jesus.**

In a mild rebuke highlighting the failure of their fishing expedition, **Jesus said to them, "Children, you do not have any fish, do you?"** Acknowledging that their attempt to return to provide for their own needs had failed, **they answered Him, "No."** They had failed to reckon sufficiently with Jesus' plan for their lives and His ability to supernaturally hinder their efforts. It is as if He said, "Do anything else and I will see that you fail!"

The disciples' failure through that long night established their inability to give themselves successfully to any other enterprise than serving their Lord. Not only had they dramatically been brought face-to-face with their own inability and divine sovereignty, but they were also next shown a miraculous creative act, demonstrating that Jesus would continue to provide their needs.

DIVINE POWER AND SUCCESS

And He said to them, "Cast the net on the right-hand side of the boat and you will find a catch." So they cast, and then they were not able to haul it in because of the great number of fish. Therefore that disciple whom Jesus loved said to Peter, "It is the Lord." So when Simon Peter heard that it was the Lord, he put his outer garment on (for he was stripped for work), and threw himself into the sea. But the other disciples came in the little boat, for

they were not far from the land, but about one hundred yards away, dragging the net full of fish. So when they got out on the land, they saw a charcoal fire already laid and fish placed on it, and bread. Jesus said to them, "Bring some of the fish which you have now caught." Simon Peter went up and drew the net to land, full of large fish, a hundred and fifty-three; and although there were so many, the net was not torn. Jesus said to them, "Come and have breakfast." None of the disciples ventured to question Him, "Who are You?" knowing that it was the Lord. Jesus came and took the bread and gave it to them, and the fish likewise. This is now the third time that Jesus was manifested to the disciples, after He was raised from the dead. (21:6–14)

The Lord began the second lesson by calling out **to them, "Cast the net on the right-hand side of the boat and you will find a catch."** The disciples were no doubt exhausted and frustrated after their failed fishing expedition, and did not know at first who was speaking. They must have been tempted to tell this bold stranger to mind his own business. After all, they were experienced fishermen; who was he to tell them what to do? And did he think the fish knew the difference between one side of the boat and the other?

But there was something authoritative in the voice that allowed for no argument or hesitance, so they obeyed His command. To their astonishment, **they cast** their net, **and then they were not able to haul it in because of the great number of fish.** Just as He had rerouted all the fish away from their boat all through the night, Jesus now redirected a massive school to the right side of it. As a result, the net was so full that all seven of them could not haul it in.

The parallel between this incident, which led to the disciples' (especially Peter's) recommissioning, and their original call to be Jesus' disciples is stunning:

Now it happened that while the crowd was pressing around Him and listening to the word of God, He was standing by the lake of Gennesaret; and He saw two boats lying at the edge of the lake; but the fishermen had gotten out of them and were washing their nets. And He got into one of the boats, which was Simon's, and asked him to put out a little way from the land. And He sat down and began teaching the people from the boat. When He had finished speaking, He said to Simon,"Put out into the deep water and let down your nets for a catch." Simon answered and said,"Master, we worked hard all night and caught nothing, but I will do as You say and let down the nets."When they had done this, they enclosed a great quantity of fish, and their nets began to break; so they signaled to their partners in the other boat for them to come and help them. And they came and filled both of the boats, so that they began to sink. (Luke 5:1–7)

The **disciple whom Jesus loved** (John; cf. the discussion of 21:20 in chapter 35 of this volume) immediately recognized who the stranger was and **said to Peter, "It is the Lord."** Only He had such supernatural knowledge and power. Impulsive as ever, **when Simon Peter heard that it was the Lord, he put his outer garment on (for he was stripped for work,** probably wearing only a loincloth in the warm spring season), **and threw himself into the sea.** So intense was his desire to be with Jesus that Peter could not wait for the boat to reach the shore. Characteristically, John was quicker to perceive; Peter was quicker to act.

Meanwhile **the other disciples,** lacking Peter's impulsiveness, **came** struggling toward the shore **in the little boat, for they were not far from the land, but about one hundred yards away.** Since they were unable to haul it in, they were **dragging the net full of fish** behind them.

When they all arrived at the shore and **got out on the land, they saw a charcoal fire already laid and fish placed on it, and bread.** Showing His compassionate care for the tired, hungry disciples, Jesus had prepared breakfast for them, perhaps miraculously creating the fish as He had done before (6:11–13). He had said to them earlier, "I am among you as the one who serves" (Luke 22:27), and He had washed their feet as an example of humble service (John 13:1–15). Now the risen Lord showed that He would still serve the disciples who were faithful to Him by meeting their needs—which they had been unable in disobedience to meet themselves. Here was a practical illustration of the words of Jesus in the upper room:

> Whatever you ask in My name, that will I do, so that the Father may be glorified in the Son. If you ask Me anything in My name, I will do it. (John 14:13–14)

> If you abide in Me, and My words abide in you, ask whatever you wish, and it will be done for you. My Father is glorified by this, that you bear much fruit, and so prove to be My disciples. Just as the Father has loved Me, I have also loved you; abide in My love. If you keep My commandments, you will abide in My love; just as I have kept My Father's commandments and abide in His love. These things I have spoken to you so that My joy may be in you, and that your joy may be made full. (John 15:7–11)

> You did not choose Me but I chose you, and appointed you that you would go and bear fruit, and that your fruit would remain, so that

whatever you ask of the Father in My name He may give to you. (John 15:16; cf. Phil. 4:19)

When the disciples had all made it ashore, **Jesus said to them, "Bring some of the fish which you have now caught."** The fish and bread He had already prepared would serve to get the meal underway while they cooked some of the fish caught in the disciples' net. In response, **Simon Peter went up and drew the net to land.** That he was able to haul the net **full of large fish** onto the shore by himself shows that he was a man of considerable physical strength. Many fanciful explanations have been offered for the alleged hidden significance of the number of fish in the net, **a hundred and fifty-three.** The simple, obvious explanation, however, is that this was the actual number of fish they had caught. Here is another indication that John was an eyewitness of the events he recorded (1 John 1:1–3; cf. *John 1–11,* The MacArthur New Testament Commentary [Chicago: Moody, 2006], 5–6). To the question of why the fish were counted, D. A. Carson replies,

> It is unsurprising that someone counted them, either as part of dividing them up amongst the fishermen in preparation for sale, or because one of the men was so dumbfounded by the size of the catch that he said something like this:"Can you believe it? I wonder how many there are?" (*John*, 672)

Surprisingly, **although there were so many, the net was not torn.** This again is the type of detail that an eyewitness would note, especially a fisherman like John. That the Lord provided far more fish than they could eat at one meal is further evidence of His provision for them. The disciples could have preserved and eaten the fish over the next several days, or sold them and lived off the proceeds.

The Lord's invitation **to them, "Come and have breakfast,"** was a call to full fellowship. Feeling guilty for their disobedience in trying to return to their former trade and awed by the supernatural presence of their resurrected Master, however, they were surely uneasy, hesitant, and uncertain. But **none of the disciples ventured to question Him, "Who are You?"** They suppressed their question, **knowing that it** could only be **the Lord.**

Evidently the disciples were too overwhelmed to accept Jesus' invitation and start eating. Acting as a gracious host, **Jesus came and took the bread and gave it to them, and the fish likewise,** thus beginning the meal. John gave no details of what happened during the meal; he picked up the narrative afterward in verse 15 with the story of Jesus' restoring of Peter. The apostle concluded this account by noting that **this is now the third time that Jesus was manifested to the dis-**

ciples, after He was raised from the dead; that is, the third time recorded in John's gospel (cf. 20:19–23, 26–29).

Just as their disobedience had resulted in failure, the disciples' obedience brought overwhelming success. The miraculous catch of fish and the meal He provided for them demonstrated to the disciples that Jesus could and would still meet their needs. This story also reminds all believers that obedience always brings blessing (cf. Gen. 22:18; Ex. 19:5; Lev. 26:3–12; Deut. 28:1–14; Pss. 19:11; 119:1–2; Isa. 1:19; Jer. 7:23; John 13:17; James 1:25; Rev. 22:7). The point at the historical moment this event happened and the primary sense of the event was to overcome the disciples' fear of failure and weakness that was causing them to drift back into their old ways. What our Lord did here settled forever in the minds of the apostles that they were called to serve the Lord Jesus Christ for the rest of their lives.

The Lord, as always, uses weak and sinful people to advance His kingdom because there are no other kinds of people (cf. Isa. 6:5–8; 1 Cor. 1:26–31; 2 Cor. 12:7–10; 1 Tim. 1:12–15).

Epilogue—Part 2: How to Be a Committed Christian (John 21:15–25)

35

So when they had finished breakfast, Jesus said to Simon Peter, "Simon, son of John, do you love Me more than these?" He said to Him, "Yes, Lord; You know that I love You." He said to him, "Tend My lambs." He said to him again a second time, "Simon, son of John, do you love Me?" He said to Him, "Yes, Lord; You know that I love You." He said to him, "Shepherd My sheep." He said to him the third time, "Simon, son of John, do you love Me?" Peter was grieved because He said to him the third time, "Do you love Me?" And he said to Him, "Lord, You know all things; You know that I love You." Jesus said to him, "Tend My sheep. Truly, truly, I say to you, when you were younger, you used to gird yourself and walk wherever you wished; but when you grow old, you will stretch out your hands and someone else will gird you, and bring you where you do not wish to go." Now this He said, signifying by what kind of death he would glorify God. And when He had spoken this, He said to him, "Follow Me!" Peter, turning around, saw the disciple whom Jesus loved following them; the one who also had leaned back on His bosom at the supper and said, "Lord, who is the one who betrays You?" So Peter seeing him said to Jesus, "Lord, and what about this man?" Jesus said to

him, "If I want him to remain until I come, what is that to you? You follow Me!" Therefore this saying went out among the brethren that that disciple would not die; yet Jesus did not say to him that he would not die, but only, "If I want him to remain until I come, what is that to you?" This is the disciple who is testifying to these things and wrote these things, and we know that his testimony is true. And there are also many other things which Jesus did, which if they were written in detail, I suppose that even the world itself would not contain the books that would be written. (21:15–25)

The true gospel call to follow Jesus Christ is a call to self-denial. It is not a man-centered call to self-fulfillment; there is no "Christianity lite." The gospel calls sinners to submit fully to Jesus Christ, to find their lives by losing them, to gain their lives by abandoning them, to live life to the fullest by emptying themselves. Our Lord's message, frankly, was not user friendly; it was not so much comforting as threatening. He did not make salvation easy, but hard; Christ's preaching, while motivated by love and compassion, filled with grace and mercy, and offering forgiveness, peace, and joy now and forever, was still demanding in the extreme. Jesus was never guilty of making things easy for sinners, and thereby contributing to a false confidence, a false assurance of salvation. "No one," He declared, "after putting his hand to the plow and looking back, is fit for the kingdom of God" (Luke 9:62). He warned that those who would follow Him must be willing to die to themselves, and He stressed the importance of counting the cost of commitment to Him:

> If anyone comes to Me, and does not hate his own father and mother and wife and children and brothers and sisters, yes, and even his own life, he cannot be My disciple. Whoever does not carry his own cross and come after Me cannot be My disciple. For which one of you, when he wants to build a tower, does not first sit down and calculate the cost to see if he has enough to complete it? Otherwise, when he has laid a foundation and is not able to finish, all who observe it begin to ridicule him, saying, "This man began to build and was not able to finish." Or what king, when he sets out to meet another king in battle, will not first sit down and consider whether he is strong enough with ten thousand men to encounter the one coming against him with twenty thousand? Or else, while the other is still far away, he sends a delegation and asks for terms of peace. So then, none of you can be My disciple who does not give up all his own possessions. (Luke 14:26–33)

In Matthew 7:13–14 the Lord exhorted, "Enter through the narrow gate; for the gate is wide and the way is broad that leads to destruction, and there are many who enter through it. For the gate is small and the way is narrow that leads to life, and there are few who find it." Jesus does not offer sinners a superficial makeover to satisfy their desire for self-improvement; He calls them to submit to a complete takeover of their lives for His glory—with eternal benefits.

As noted in the previous chapter of this volume, chapter 21 forms an appendix or epilogue to John's gospel, bringing closure to it by resolving some questions left unanswered at the end of chapter 20. The first fourteen verses dealt with the disciples' question of whether Jesus would still provide for them now that He was ascending to the Father. He would still meet their needs, as He illustrated with the incident of the fish, and by providing them breakfast. That settles a huge concern—divine care. The remainder of the chapter focuses mainly on another concern— Jesus' restoration of Peter, the leader of the apostles so critical to the gospel ministry after Christ's ascension and the sending of the Holy Spirit. He was God's choice to be the most significant voice for the gospel to the Jews in the beginning days of the church. As such, he is the main figure in the opening chapters of Acts (2–12), and the other apostles needed to continue to follow his leadership. In the process of tying things up with Peter, believers can see an example of the essential means to being a committed Christian: by loving Christ more than everything else, by being willing to sacrifice everything for Christ, and by following Christ.

COMMITTED CHRISTIANS LOVE
CHRIST MORE THAN ANYTHING ELSE

So when they had finished breakfast, Jesus said to Simon Peter, "Simon, son of John, do you love Me more than these?" He said to Him, "Yes, Lord; You know that I love You." He said to him, "Tend My lambs." He said to him again a second time, "Simon, son of John, do you love Me?" He said to Him, "Yes, Lord; You know that I love You." He said to him, "Shepherd My sheep." He said to him the third time, "Simon, son of John, do you love Me?" Peter was grieved because He said to him the third time, "Do you love Me?" And he said to Him, "Lord, You know all things; You know that I love You." Jesus said to him, "Tend My sheep." (21:15–17)

The primary mark of the redeemed has always been love for God. The Shema, the great Old Testament confession of faith, declares,

"You shall love the Lord your God with all your heart and with all your soul and with all your might" (Deut. 6:5). Later in Deuteronomy Moses exhorted Israel to manifest that love by obeying God's commandments (10:12–13; 11:1). When Daniel poured out his heart in prayer for his people, he addressed God as "the great and awesome God, who keeps His covenant and lovingkindness for those who love Him and keep His commandments" (Dan. 9:4). After the exile Nehemiah echoed Daniel's prayer: "I beseech You, O Lord God of heaven, the great and awesome God, who preserves the covenant and lovingkindness for those who love Him and keep His commandments" (Neh. 1:5). The theme of loving God was also on the heart of David, who wrote, "I love You, O Lord, my strength" (Ps. 18:1).

The New Testament also teaches that love is the mark of a true believer. When asked to name the greatest commandment of the law, Jesus replied, "You shall love the Lord your God with all your heart, and with all your soul, and with all your mind" (Matt. 22:37). In 1 Corinthians 8:3 Paul wrote, "If anyone loves God, he is known by Him." On the other hand the apostle warned, "If anyone does not love the Lord, he is to be accursed" (1 Cor. 16:22). Only those who love God receive eternal life (James 1:12) and inherit the kingdom (James 2:5). Peter wrote in his first epistle, "Though you have not seen Him [Christ], you love Him" (1 Peter 1:8). Love is also the driving, compelling force that motivates Christian service (2 Cor. 5:14).

Peter learned the hard way what it means to love Jesus Christ. He had vociferously declared his unfailing devotion to Him more than once. At the Last Supper, "Simon Peter said to [Jesus], 'Lord, where are You going?' Jesus answered, 'Where I go, you cannot follow Me now; but you will follow later.' Peter said to Him, 'Lord, why can I not follow You right now? I will lay down my life for You'" (John 13:36–37). A short while later he boldly proclaimed, "Even though all may fall away because of You, I will never fall away" (Matt. 26:33). Yet when the chips were down, Peter's self-confessed love failed and he openly denied three times that he even knew Jesus. His vaunted courage proved to be nothing but empty talk when facing a threatening situation.

Peter's failure highlights the biblical truth that obedience is the essential evidence of genuine love. In John 14:15 Jesus put it plainly: "If you love Me, you will keep My commandments." In verse 21 He added, "He who has My commandments and keeps them is the one who loves Me" (cf. 15:10). In 1 John 5:3 John echoed the Lord's teaching: "For this is the love of God, that we keep His commandments; and His commandments are not burdensome," while in his second epistle he added, "And this is love, that we walk according to His commandments. This is the commandment, just as you have heard from the beginning, that you should walk in it" (2 John 6).

Jesus knew that if Peter was to play the crucial role in the early church that He had chosen him for, he would need to be restored. Peter needed to understand that although he had forsaken Christ, Christ had not forsaken him (cf. Rom. 8:31–39). The Lord had evidently already appeared to Peter privately (Luke 24:34; cf. 1 Cor. 15:5), but Scripture does not record any details of that meeting. Whatever may have happened in Peter's personal encounter with the risen Lord, since his denials were public knowledge, he needed to be publicly restored. The other disciples needed to hear Peter's reaffirmation of his love for Christ and Christ's recommissioning of him, so they would be willing to loyally support his leadership.

As soon as they **had finished breakfast** (cf. 21:12–13), Jesus initiated the restoration by confronting Peter. That He addressed him as **"Simon, son of John"** suggests that what followed was a rebuke. Jesus had given Simon the nickname "Peter" (John 1:42), but sometimes referred to him as "Simon" when Peter did something that needed rebuke or correction (e.g., Matt. 17:25; Mark 14:37; Luke 22:31). It was as if our Lord called him by his former name when he was acting like his former self. The Lord's pointed question, **"Do you love Me more than these** (i.e., the boat, nets, and other fishing paraphernalia)?" went right to the heart of the issue. As noted in the previous chapter of this volume, Peter, impatient at Jesus' delay in meeting the disciples and beleaguered by his own failures, had impulsively decided to return to being a fisherman (21:3). That he was sure he could do well—or so he had thought. But Jesus confronted Peter and called him to follow Him and be the fisher of men he was first called to be (Matt. 4:19). "No servant can serve [be a slave to] two masters," He had previously told them, "for either he will hate the one and love the other, or else he will be devoted to one and despise the other. You cannot serve God and wealth" (Luke 16:13). Jesus challenged Peter to permanently abandon his former life and be exclusively devoted to following Him, based on his love.

Peter replied **to Him, "Yes, Lord; You know that I love You."** There is an interesting wordplay in the Greek text. The word Jesus used for **love** is *agapaō*, the highest love of the will, love that implies total commitment (cf. 1 Cor. 13:4–8). Peter, painfully aware of his disobedience and failure, felt too guilty to claim that type of love. The brash pronouncements were a thing of the past; broken and humbled and fully aware that his action precluded him from a believable claim to the highest love, Peter answered by using the word *phileō*, a less lofty term that signifies affection. He also appealed to Jesus' omniscience, reminding Him, **"You know that I love You."**

Accepting Peter's humble acknowledgement that his love was less than he had claimed and Christ deserved, Jesus still recommissioned him, graciously saying to him, **"Tend My lambs."** **Tend** translates a form of the verb *boskō*, a term used of herdsmen pasturing and feeding their livestock. The present tense of the verb denotes continuous action. In keeping with the metaphor He introduced in 10:7–16 (cf. Pss. 95:7; 100:3; Ezek. 34:31), Jesus described believers as His **lambs,** emphasizing not only their immaturity, vulnerability, and need, but also that they are His (cf. Matt. 18:5–10). It is the same responsibility given to every pastor, as Paul pointed out in Acts 20:28 and as Peter himself exhorted in 1 Peter 5:2. Paul instructed the young pastor Timothy that the means to doing this was to "preach the word; be ready in season and out of season; reprove, rebuke, exhort, with great patience and instruction" (2 Tim. 4:2).

Continuing to reinforce His point on the supremacy of love as the motive to faithfulness, Jesus **said to** Peter **again a second time, "Simon, son of John, do you love Me?"** Once again He used the verb *agapaō*, and once again Peter was unwilling to use that word; in his reply, **"Yes, Lord; You know that I love You,"** Peter again used the verb *phileō*. The Lord then charged him, **"Shepherd My sheep."** Jesus chose a different term than the one translated "tend" in verse 15. This word, a form of the verb *poimainō*, is likely a synonym for the previous verb, both of which are suitable to express the full scope of responsibility that pastoral oversight entails (cf. Acts 20:28; 1 Peter 5:2).

But Jesus still was not through with Peter, so **He said to him the third time, "Simon, son of John, do you love Me?" Peter was grieved because He said to him the third time, "Do you love Me?"** The reason for Peter's grief was a change in the Lord's vocabulary. Unlike His two previous questions, this third time Jesus used Peter's word for love, *phileō*. He called into question even the less than total devotion Peter thought he was safe in claiming. The implication that his life did not support even that level of love broke Peter's heart. All he could do was appeal even more strongly to Jesus' omniscience, saying **to Him, "Lord, You know all things** (cf. 2:24–25; 16:30)**; You know that I love You."** For the third time Jesus accepted the apostle's recognized failure and imperfection (cf. Isa. 6:1–8) and graciously charged Peter to care for His flock, saying **to him, "Tend My sheep."** Peter's restoration was thus complete. As Andreas Köstenberger notes,

> Perhaps at long last Peter has learned that he cannot follow Jesus in his own strength and has realized the hollowness of affirming his own loyalty in a way that relies more on his own power of will than on Jesus' enablement. . . . Likewise, we should soundly distrust self-serving pledges of loyalty today that betray self-reliance rather than a humble awareness of one's own limitations in acting on one's best intentions

[cf. 2 Cor. 12:9–10]. (*John*, Baker Exegetical Commentary on the New Testament [Grand Rapids: Baker, 2004], 598)

Peter remained obedient to the Lord's commission for the rest of his life. His ministry from that point forward involved not only proclaiming the gospel (Acts 2:14–40; 3:12–26), but also feeding the flock the Lord had entrusted to him (cf. Acts 2:42). Nearing the end of his ministry many years later, Peter wrote,

> Therefore, I exhort the elders among you, as your fellow elder and witness of the sufferings of Christ, and a partaker also of the glory that is to be revealed, shepherd the flock of God among you, exercising oversight not under compulsion, but voluntarily, according to the will of God; and not for sordid gain, but with eagerness; nor yet as lording it over those allotted to your charge, but proving to be examples to the flock. (1 Peter 5:1–3)

COMMITTED CHRISTIANS ARE
WILLING TO SACRIFICE EVERYTHING FOR CHRIST

"Truly, truly, I say to you, when you were younger, you used to gird yourself and walk wherever you wished; but when you grow old, you will stretch out your hands and someone else will gird you, and bring you where you do not wish to go." Now this He said, signifying by what kind of death he would glorify God. (21:18–19a)

Jesus' prophecy of Peter's martyrdom underscores the truth that commitment to Him may require paying the ultimate price. "He who does not take his cross and follow after Me is not worthy of Me," Jesus had told the disciples when He commissioned them. Then He warned, "He who has found his life will lose it, and he who has lost his life for My sake will find it" (Matt. 10:38–39; cf. 16:24–26; Rom. 14:8; Phil. 1:21).

As it does throughout John's gospel, the solemn phrase **truly, truly** introduces a significant truth (1:51; 3:3, 5, 11; 5:19, 24, 25; 6:26, 32, 47, 53; 8:34, 51, 58; 10:1, 7; 12:24; 13:16, 20, 21, 38; 14:12; 16:20, 23). **When** he was **younger,** Peter **used to gird** himself **and walk wherever** he **wished;** in other words, he was in control of his actions. **"But,"** Jesus told him, **"when you grow old, you will stretch out your hands and someone else will gird you, and bring you where you do not wish to go."** There would come a time, Jesus warned, when others would seize Peter, bind him, and lead him away to be executed. Peter's death, as the phrase **stretch out your hands** implies, would be by crucifixion.

John's footnote, **Now this He said, signifying by what kind of death he would glorify God,** makes that clear.

Peter spent the last three decades of his life serving the Lord and anticipating his martyrdom. Yet he faced that prospect with confidence, comforted by the knowledge that he would not deny the Lord again, but instead would glorify Him in his death (cf. 1 Peter 4:14–16). According to tradition, Peter was crucified, but requested to be crucified upside down, because he felt unworthy to be crucified like his Lord (Eusebius, *Ecclesiastical History* III.1).

COMMITTED CHRISTIANS FOCUS ON FOLLOWING CHRIST'S LEADING

And when He had spoken this, He said to him, "Follow Me!" Peter, turning around, saw the disciple whom Jesus loved following them; the one who also had leaned back on His bosom at the supper and said, "Lord, who is the one who betrays You?" So Peter seeing him said to Jesus, "Lord, and what about this man?" Jesus said to him, "If I want him to remain until I come, what is that to you? You follow Me!" Therefore this saying went out among the brethren that that disciple would not die; yet Jesus did not say to him that he would not die, but only, "If I want him to remain until I come, what is that to you?" This is the disciple who is testifying to these things and wrote these things, and we know that his testimony is true. And there are also many other things which Jesus did, which if they were written in detail, I suppose that even the world itself would not contain the books that would be written. (21:19*b*–25)

Following Jesus Christ is the sine qua non of the Christian life. In John 12:26 Jesus put it simply: "If anyone serves Me, he must follow Me." It is the mark of His sheep that they follow Him (John 10:27; cf. 8:12), no matter what the cost (Matt. 16:24; 19:27; Luke 5:11, 27–28; 9:23–25; 18:28). To follow Jesus means not only to be willing to sacrifice everything in submission to His will, but also to obey His commands (Matt. 7:21; Luke 6:46) and to imitate Him (1 Thess. 1:6; 1 John 2:6; cf. 1 Cor. 11:1).

After Jesus **had spoken** His prophecy of Peter's death, **He said to him, "Follow Me!"** Evidently they had stood up and were walking (possibly along the shore of the lake) when **Peter, turning around, saw the disciple whom Jesus loved following them; the one who also had leaned back on His bosom at the supper and said, "Lord, who is the one who betrays You?"** Throughout his gospel, John never names himself, preferring to refer to himself in other ways. That he further identified that person as **the one who also had leaned back on His bosom at the supper and said, "Lord, who is the one who betrays You?** leaves no question that the beloved disciple and the one who leaned on Jesus was John (cf. John 13:23). Obviously, as that reference indicates, he was one of the inner circle of Jesus' followers. Yet he cannot have been Peter, since the two are distinguished in this text and others. Nor can he have been James, who was martyred too early (Acts 12:2) to have written the gospel of John. By process of elimination, the beloved disciple had to have been the apostle John (see the discussion of the beloved disciple's identity in *John 1–11*, The MacArthur New Testament Commentary [Chicago: Moody, 2006], 6–7).

Evidently Christ's prediction of Peter's martyrdom prompted concern about what would happen to his intimate friend, John. Therefore he asked **Jesus, "Lord, and what about this man?"** Jesus' abrupt and censuring reply, **"If I want him to remain until I come, what is that to you?"** was not an answer, but it was a rebuke that made it clear to Peter that what was to happen to John was none of his business. If John lived until the second coming, it had no bearing on his responsibility. Reiterating His command from verse 19, Jesus said emphatically, **"You follow Me!"** Peter's attention was not to be on anyone else, but on his own devotion and duty to Jesus Christ. All believers will do well to embrace this truth that the Lord has a unique plan for each of His followers.

John finished the inspired gospel by answering a few final questions that bring closure to his account. The Lord's hypothetical response to Peter caused a rumor to go **out among the brethren that that disciple would not die.** John was quick to debunk that rumor, lest his death cause some to believe the Lord made a false prediction: **Yet Jesus did not say to him that he would not die, but only, "If I want him to remain until I come, what is that to you?"**

John reminded his readers that he **is the disciple who is testifying to these things and wrote these things, and we** (either the apostles, or more likely an editorial device referring only to John) **know that his testimony is true.** John was an eyewitness to the events recorded in his gospel, and **his testimony** concerning them **is true** (cf. *MNTC John 1–11*, 5–6). But while what he wrote was true, it was by no means exhaustive. **There are,** the apostle noted, **also many other things which Jesus did, which if they were written in detail, I suppose that even the world itself would not contain the books that would be written.** Under the inspiration of the Holy Spirit, John had selectively chosen his material in keeping with his stated purpose of presenting Jesus Christ as the Messiah and Son of God (20:30–31). His statement that Jesus did more works than the world's books could hold is evidence that even in the four Gospels there is given only a very limited and selective record of events. This makes the point stronger regarding how great Israel's unbelief and subsequent culpability truly was, since she denied her Messiah in the face of such a massive display of divine power. In light of the vast evidence of His deity, Israel's rejection of the Lord Jesus renders her subject to the severest judgment. This was especially true of the leaders, to whom the Lord said,

> Therefore, behold, I am sending you prophets and wise men and scribes; some of them you will kill and crucify, and some of them you will scourge in your synagogues, and persecute from city to city, so that upon you may fall the guilt of all the righteous blood shed on earth, from the blood of righteous Abel to the blood of Zechariah, the son of Berechiah, whom you murdered between the temple and the altar. Truly I say to you, all these things will come upon this generation. (Matt. 23:34–36; cf. Luke 11:49–52)

This was symbolized in the destruction of Jerusalem in A.D. 70:

> When He approached Jerusalem, He saw the city and wept over it, saying, "If you had known in this day, even you, the things which make for peace! But now they have been hidden from your eyes. For the days will come upon you when your enemies will throw up a barricade against you, and surround you and hem you in on every side, and they will level you to the ground and your children within you, and they will not leave in you one stone upon another, because you did not recognize the time of your visitation." (Luke 19:41–44)

Jesus had challenged Peter to love Him above all else. Faced with the prospect of sacrificing everything for Christ, from here on Peter did not back down. He learned the lesson that following Jesus was to be the singularly supreme objective of his love. Peter and his fellow apostles, empowered by the Holy Spirit, turned the world upside down through their fearless witness to Jesus Christ (cf. Acts 17:6) and in almost every case died as martyrs for the love of Christ and the truth of the gospel.

Bibliography

Barclay, William. *The Gospel of John.* Volume 1. Louisville: Westminster John Knox, 2001.

_____. *The Gospel of John.* Volume 2. Louisville: Westminster John Knox, 2001.

Borchert, Gerald L. *John 1–11.* The New American Commentary. Nashville: Broadman & Holman, 2002.

Bruce, F. F. *The Gospel of John.* Grand Rapids: Eerdmans, 1983.

Calvin, John. *John.* The Crossway Classic Commentaries. Edited by Alister McGrath and J. I. Packer. Wheaton: Crossway, 1994.

Carson, D. A. *The Gospel According to John.* The Pillar New Testament Commentary. Grand Rapids: Eerdmans, 1991.

Carson, D. A. Douglas J. Moo, and Leon Morris. *An Introduction to the New Testament.* Grand Rapids: Zondervan, 1992.

Guthrie, Donald. *New Testament Introduction.* Revised edition. Downers Grove, Ill.: InterVarsity, 1990.

Heading, John. *What the Bible Teaches: John.* Kilmarnock, Scotland: John Ritchie, 1988.

Hendriksen, William. *The Gospel According to John.* Volume 1. Grand Rapids: Baker, 1953.

_____.*The Gospel According to John.* Volume 2. Grand Rapids: Baker, 1954.

Hiebert, D. Edmond. *An Introduction to the Gospels and Acts.* Chicago: Moody, 1975.

Kent, Homer A. *Light in the Darkness: Studies in the Gospel of John.* Grand Rapids: Baker, 1974.

Köstenberger, Andreas J. *John.* Baker Exegetical Commentary on the New Testament. Grand Rapids: Baker, 2004.

Kruse, Colin. *The Gospel According to John.* The Tyndale New Testament Commentaries. Grand Rapids: Eerdmans, 2003.

Lenski, R. C. H. *The Interpretation of St. John's Gospel.* repr.. Peabody, Mass.: Hendrickson, 1998.

MacArthur, John. "The Gospel According to John." In *The MacArthur Bible Commentary.* Nashville: Thomas Nelson, 2005.

_____.*Twelve Ordinary Men.* Nashville: W Publishing Group, 2002.

Michaels, J. Ramsey. *John.* New International Biblical Commentary. Peabody, Mass.: Hendrickson, 1989.

Morris, Leon. *The Gospel According to John.* The New International Commentary on the New Testament. Grand Rapids: Eerdmans, 1979, 1995.

Tasker, R. V. G. *The Gospel According to St. John.* The Tyndale New Testament Commentaries. Grand Rapids: Eerdmans, 1975.

Tenney, Merrill C. "The Gospel of John." In Frank E. Gaebelein, ed. *The Expositor's Bible Commentary.* Volume 9. Grand Rapids: Zondervan, 1981.

Towns, Elmer. *The Gospel of John.* Twenty-first Century Biblical Commentary Series. Chattanooga: AMG, 2002.

Wallace, Daniel B. "The Gospel of John: Introduction, Argument, Outline." Biblical Studies Press, www.bible.org, 1999.

Westcott, B. F. *The Gospel According to St. John.* Reprint, Grand Rapids: Eerdmans, 1978.

Indexes

Index of Greek Words and Phrases

phulassō, 278
pisteuō, 99, 159
pneuma, 114
poimainō, 402
prōi, 325

skandalizō, 190

tarassō, 38, 98
telos, 63
tēreō, 263, 278
tetelestai, 356
tithēmi, 163

Index of Scripture

Apocryphal Works

Ancient Texts

Ancient Texts

Index of Subjects

Titles in the
MacArthur New Testament Commentary Series

MOODY
PUBLISHERS

THE NAME YOU CAN TRUST.

1-800-678-6928 www.MoodyPublishers.org